CIVIL LITIGATION

Kevin Browne LLB, Solicitor

Margaret J Catlow BA (Law), Solicitor

Published by

College of Law Publishing

Braboeuf Manor, Portsmouth Road, St Catherines, Guildford GU3 1HA

British Library Cataloguing-in-Publication Data

A catalogue record for this book is available from the British Library.

ISBN: 978 1 905391 97 4

Typeset by Style Photosetting Ltd, Mayfield, East Sussex

Printed in Great Britain by Ashford Colour Press Ltd, Gosport, Hampshire

347

Preface

This book has been written as a tool for learning about civil procedure in England and Wales. In it we examine the practical issues which arise from the start of a case until its ultimate conclusion, whether that is by settlement, court judgment or otherwise.

We have divided up the civil process into five stages. But it is important to remember that each stage cannot be learnt in isolation from the others. We urge anyone using this book to make frequent reference to the overview of the five stages at **1.3** and the flow diagram at **Appendix C(1)**. These will serve as a reminder of the various steps and how one part fits into the whole process.

In this edition we have taken the opportunity not only to carry out the usual annual updating of the text but to make some significant changes. In particular, we have included a new **Appendix B** of templates of how to draft key documents (Letter before Claim under Practice Direction on Pre-action Conduct, Letter of Claim under Professional Negligence Pre-action Protocol, Particulars of Claim, Case Summary for use at a Multi-track Case Management Conference, Witness Statement, Hearsay Notice, Part 36 Offer Letter, Case Summary for use at a Fast Track Trial and Case Summary for use at a Multi-track Trial ('Skeleton Argument')). We have also revised and expanded the case study at **Appendix D**, which now includes a request for further information and a witness statement. The case study concerns Mr and Mrs Simpson. They own a large house locally and had agreed to let out part of it to Mr Templar. Apparently, when he arrived to take up his tenancy, he lost control of his car when driving up their driveway and crashed into their recently completed extension. You will first encounter the case study at the end of **Chapter 2**.

In addition, we have included details of a solicitor's core (professional) duties; funding notice requirements; a guide to drafting statements of truth; new examples on deemed service and calculating time limits; changes to Part 35 on experts; and a guide to contesting an assessment of costs.

Cases included in this edition include *Crosbie v Munroe* (2003) (contentious proceedings); *Interdigital Technology Corp v Nokia Corp* (2008) (Part 18); *Earles v Barclays Bank Plc* (2009) (standard disclosure); *Pearce v Ove Arup Partnership* (2001) and *Meadow v General Medical Council* (2006) (experts); *AF v BG* (2009) (Part 36); *Shah v Ul-Haq* (2009) and *Widlake v BAA Ltd* (2009) (conduct and costs).

In the interest of brevity, the masculine pronoun has been used throughout to include the feminine.

KEVIN BROWNE AND MARGARET J CATLOW
The College of Law
London

Contents

Table of Cases

Table of Statutes

Table of Statutory Instruments and Codes of Practice

Table of Abbreviations

ADR	alternative dispute resolution
CCA	County Courts Act 1984
CCR	County Court Rules 1981
CEDR	Centre for Dispute Resolution
CFA	conditional fee agreement
CFA Regulations 2000	Conditional Fee Agreements Regulations 2000
CLS	Community Legal Service
CLSF	Community Legal Service Fund
CPR	Civil Procedure Rules 1998
ECHR	European Convention for the Protection of Human Rights and Fundamental Freedoms
ECtHR	European Court of Human Rights
HCEO	High Court Enforcement Officer
LA	Limitation Act 1980
LSC	Legal Services Commission
PD	Practice Direction
RCJ	Royal Courts of Justice
RSC	Rules of the Supreme Court 1965
SCA	Senior Courts Act 1981

Chapter 1

Introduction to Civil Litigation

1.1 The Woolf reforms

The nature of civil litigation in England and Wales changed fundamentally on 26 April 1999, when the Civil Procedure Rules 1998 (CPR 1998) (SI 1998/3132) came into force. These Rules are the courts' attempt to implement the 'Woolf Reforms', as set out in Lord Woolf's report, *Access to Justice*, which was published in 1996. The philosophy behind this report was that the litigation system at the time was too expensive, too slow and incomprehensible to many litigants. Even the simplest case could take years to get to trial, with the costs often exceeding the amount in dispute. Furthermore, because the system was almost entirely adversarial, it did not necessarily operate in the interests of justice as a whole.

1.1.1 The overriding objective

Lord Woolf hoped that his proposed reforms, now enshrined in the CPR 1998, would lead to a civil justice system that was just in the results it delivered, fair in the way it treated litigants, and easily understood by users of that legal system. It was hoped that the new system would also provide appropriate procedures at a reasonable cost which could be completed within a reasonable time-scale. In particular, he thought it necessary to transfer the control of litigation from the parties to the court. The court would then determine how each case should progress by making appropriate directions, setting strict timetables and ensuring that the parties complied with them, backed up by a system of sanctions which the court could impose itself without the need for an application by any party. The overriding objective of the reforms is set out in r 1.1 of CPR 1998:

(1) These Rules are a new procedural code with the overriding objective of enabling the court to deal with cases justly.

(2) Dealing with a case justly includes, so far as is practicable—

    (a) ensuring that the parties are on an equal footing;

    (b) saving expense;

    (c) dealing with the case in ways which are proportionate—

        (i) to the amount of money involved;

        (ii) to the importance of the case;

        (iii) to the complexity of the issues; and

        (iv) to the financial position of each party;

    (d) ensuring that it is dealt with expeditiously and fairly; and

    (e) allotting to it an appropriate share of the court's resources, while taking into account the need to allot resources to other cases.

In *Maltez v Lewis* (1999) *The Times*, 4 May, the claimant's application was for a court order that the defendants should be prevented from instructing leading or senior counsel (barrister) for a copyright dispute between the parties as the claimant had only been in a position to instruct a junior counsel of seven years' experience. The court held that it was the fundamental right of citizens to be represented by counsel or solicitors of their own choice. The court did not have a power to require a party to change their solicitors, but the court was able to ensure compliance with the overriding objective. For example, if one party had instructed a big firm of expensive solicitors and the other party could only afford to instruct a small firm then the court could and should ensure that a level playing field was achieved. That might occur on disclosure (see **Chapter 11**) by allowing the smaller firm more time, or in the preparation of trial bundles (see **Chapter 14**) the court could direct that the larger firm prepared them. The court had a duty to ensure a fair trial and was used to dealing with one side being more expertly represented than the other. The court could ensure compliance with the overriding objective where the representatives could be said to be unequal. The court has power to prevent a party being unfairly required to pay excessive costs because the other party has instructed unreasonably expensive advisers (see generally **Chapter 14**).

In addition, note that in his *Final Report*, Lord Woolf suggested that:

> Where one of the parties is unable to afford a particular procedure, the court, if it decides that that procedure is to be followed, should be entitled to make its order conditional upon the other side meeting the difference in costs of the weaker party, whatever the outcome.

The overriding objective must be borne in mind at all times when conducting civil litigation, both by the court, because r 1.2 states:

> The court must seek to give effect to the overriding objective when it—
>
> (a)   exercises any power given to it by the Rules; or
>
> (b)   interprets any rule.

and by the parties and their legal advisers, because r 1.3 states:

> The parties are required to help the court to further the overriding objective.

1.1.2 Parties' duty to further overriding objective

In a sense, all the other rules in the CPR 1998 are designed to try to achieve the overriding objective. It is important to note that solicitors and their clients have a positive duty, pursuant to r 1.3, to help the court to further the overriding objective. As the Commercial Court Guide (para A1.6) states, 'The Court expects a high level of co-operation and realism from the legal representatives of the parties. This applies to dealings (including correspondence) between legal representatives as well as dealings with the Court'.

In the case of *Hannigan v Hannigan* [2000] 2 FCR 650, the Court of Appeal was faced with a claim that should have been started under Part 8 using Form N208, but in fact was commenced on a pre-CPR form with the same number. The defendants sought to strike out the claim. The claimant conceded eight failings, namely:

(a)   the claim was issued on the wrong form;

(b)   the statement of case was not verified by a statement of truth;

(c)   there was a failure to include the Royal Coat of Arms;

(d)   the first defendant was incorrectly named;

(e)   Mrs Hannigan's witness statement was signed in the name of her firm rather than by her personally;

(f)   her witness statement did not have the requisite legend in the top right-hand corner;

(g)   her witness statement failed to have marginal notes or a 3.5cm margin; and

(h)   the exhibit to her witness statement failed to have the requisite legend in the top right-hand corner, or a front page setting out a list of the documents and the dates of all the exhibits. It also failed to have the documents paginated.

The district judge said that the proceedings were 'fundamentally flawed' and the circuit judge held that 'there is too much wrong with these proceedings to exercise a discretion in the appellants' favour'. In the Court of Appeal, Brooke LJ said:

> [32] ... It has not been suggested that the claimant's solicitors did not set out all the information required of a claimant using the Part 8 procedure (see CPR 8.2) or that the written evidence on which she intended to rely was not filed with the form which was used as a claim form or served on the defendant with that document (see CPR 8.5(1) and (2)). The problem was the technical one that her solicitors did not use CPR practice form N208 (the Part 8 claim form) to start the claim contrary to para 3.1 of the first Practice Direction supplementing CPR Part 7, and that they also made the other technical mistakes.

> [33] I am in no doubt that the manner in which the judge exercised his discretion was seriously flawed, because he wholly failed to take into account the fact that in these proceedings, sealed by the county court within the relevant limitation period, the defendants were given all the information they required in order to be able to understand what order Mrs Hannigan was seeking from the court and why she was seeking it.

> ...

> [36] ... The interests of the administration of justice would have been much better served if the defendants' solicitors had simply pointed out all the mistakes that had been made in these very early days of the new rules and Mrs Hannigan's solicitor had corrected them all quickly and agreed to indemnify both parties for all the expense unnecessarily caused by his incompetence. CPR 1.3 provides that the parties are required to help the court to further the overriding objective, and the overriding objective is not furthered by arid squabbles about technicalities such as have disfigured this litigation and eaten into the quite slender resources available to the parties.

1.1.3 Judicial case management

Before the introduction of the CPR 1998, the speed at which cases progressed was largely determined by the parties' solicitors. Under the CPR 1998, the court has a duty to manage cases and will therefore determine the pace of the litigation. Rule 1.4 states:

(1) The court must further the overriding objective by actively managing cases.

(2) Active case management includes—

    (a) encouraging the parties to co-operate with each other in the conduct of the proceedings;

    (b) identifying the issues at an early stage;

    (c) deciding promptly which issues need full investigation and trial and accordingly disposing summarily of the others;

    (d) deciding the order in which issues are to be resolved;

    (e) encouraging the parties to use an alternative dispute resolution procedure if the court considers that appropriate and facilitating the use of such procedure;

    (f) helping the parties to settle the whole or part of the case;

    (g) fixing timetables or otherwise controlling the progress of the case;

    (h) considering whether the likely benefits of taking a particular step justify the cost of taking it;

    (i) dealing with as many aspects of the case as it can on the same occasion;

    (j) dealing with the case without the parties needing to attend at court;

    (k) making use of technology; and

    (l) giving directions to ensure that the trial of a case proceeds quickly and efficiently.

Case management by the court is considered in further detail in **Chapter 9**.

1.2 The Rules

1.2.1 Scope

The CPR 1998 apply to all proceedings in the county courts, High Court and the Civil Division of the Court of Appeal, except:

(a)   insolvency proceedings;

(b)   family proceedings;

(c)   adoption proceedings;

(d)   proceedings within the meaning of Pt VII of the Mental Health Act 1983;

(e)   non-contentious probate proceedings;

(f)   proceedings where the High Court acts as a Prize Court (eg, Admiralty proceedings).

Therefore, the CPR 1998 apply to virtually all types of civil litigation proceedings in England and Wales.

1.2.2   Practice Directions

In order to understand and interpret the Rules correctly, it is necessary also to look at the Practice Directions which supplement the Rules.

In some cases, the Practice Direction (PD) for a particular Rule is more expansive than the Rule itself. In a sense, the Practice Direction puts flesh on the bare bones of the Rule.

Reference is made to the Rules and Practice Directions throughout this book. Sometimes a Rule or Practice Direction has been quoted in full; at other times it is paraphrased. When conducting civil litigation, it is essential always to check the wording of any relevant Rule or Practice Direction as there are frequent amendments. The 'official' version of the CPR 1998 is contained in a three-volume looseleaf folder – the 'Blue Book'. Because it is a looseleaf service, it can be kept up to date as the Rules and Practice Directions are amended or added to. The Rules can also be accessed on the Internet, via the website of the Ministry of Justice (www.justice.gov.uk). The Court Service website (www.courtservice.gov.uk) provides access to court forms, leaflets and details of current court fees (amongst other things). See further **1.5**.

1.2.3   'Old' rules

When the CPR 1998 were drafted to replace the old High Court and county court rules, there was insufficient time to draft new Rules for every aspect of the civil litigation process. For that reason, some of the 'old' Rules have been retained and are contained in two Schedules to the CPR 1998. Schedule 1 contains the Rules of the Supreme Court 1965 (RSC 1965). Unless otherwise stated, these apply only to proceedings in the High Court. Schedule 2 contains the old County Court Rules 1981 (CCR 1981). Again, unless otherwise stated, these apply only to proceedings in the county court.

1.3   An overview of a civil claim

Appendix C(1) sets out a flowchart showing the structure of a case that proceeds from the pre-action steps right through to a trial and the matters that may arise thereafter. We shall call these the five stages of litigation.

1.3.1   Stage 1: pre-commencement of proceedings

1.3.1.1   Client's objectives

With a new client it is vital to identify the client's objectives. Ask yourself: what is the client really seeking to achieve, legally or otherwise? Does he want compensation, an apology or his 'day in court'? Are all the suggested heads of damage recoverable? Is it too late to claim a remedy, eg rejection of goods? In a commercial case, is a dispute damaging the client's business, and is maintaining a business relationship with the other side important?

1.3.1.2   Prospective parties

It is vital to ensure you consider who will constitute all the potential parties to any negotiations and court proceedings. Issues of professional conduct may arise (eg, a conflict of interest (see **2.3**)). Moreover, the general rule is that 'all persons to be sued should be sued at the same time and in the same action': see *Morris v Wentworth-Stanley* [1999] QB 1004. Once all potential defendants have been identified and located, consideration must be given as to whether each is worth pursuing (see **2.6**).

1.3.1.3 Evidence

At the end of the first interview summarise the steps you and the client will take and the reasons for these. The key task for a solicitor is to set about collecting relevant evidence. Never delay taking a statement, known as a proof of evidence, from the client and potential witnesses. Memories fade and evidence has a nasty habit of vanishing. So, if a person has a story to tell or documents that might help, get that information quickly.

1.3.1.4 Costs

Of course, the client will need to know from the outset how his legal costs are to be calculated and paid for. As to the important topic of funding, see **2.4**.

1.3.1.5 Limitation and jurisdiction

You also need to address the questions of limitation and jurisdiction. You must work out when the limitation period expires and ensure that a careful diary note is kept of this. If, for example, a client is involved in a commercial dispute, you should check to see if the contract provides for any litigation to be conducted in England and Wales or elsewhere (see further **2.8**).

1.3.1.6 Dispute resolution

A client should not just launch into litigation. That is the last resort. A solicitor must always consider with the client what form of dispute resolution would be appropriate. The advantages and disadvantages of viable options should be discussed, and the client's expectations will have to be carefully managed. Therefore, a solicitor must ensure that the client receives a full and frank assessment of the merits of his case. The client will need to weigh up many factors, such as the costs involved, the time and resources that the client will have to commit to the matter, and the effect any particular dispute resolution process may have on the client's business.

1.3.1.7 Pre-action protocols

Pre-action protocols govern the steps parties should take before commencing a court case. The parties should establish what issues are in dispute, share information that is available to each of them concerning those issues and endeavour to resolve those matters. Failure to follow a protocol step or its spirit, without good reason, will usually incur a sanction for that party if litigation is commenced (eg, a successful claimant might be penalised by the award of less or no interest and/or costs).

A number of protocols have been approved by the Ministry of Justice, and these set out how parties should behave pre-action in particular types of cases, such as professional negligence claims (see **3.7**). Where no approved pre-action protocol applies, there is a Practice Direction on Pre-action Conduct that the parties should follow (also see **3.7**). The main pre-action considerations for parties under either an approved protocol or the Practice Direction are set out at **1.3.1.8** to **1.3.1.10** below.

1.3.1.8 Alternative Dispute Resolution (ADR)

Parties and their legal representatives are encouraged to enter into discussions and/or negotiations prior to starting proceedings. Whilst the Practice Direction and approved protocols do not usually specify how or when this should be done, the parties must give serious consideration to using any suitable form of available ADR (see **Chapter 4**). If proceedings are commenced, the parties must remember that by r 1.4(2)(e), active case management by the court will include encouraging them to use an ADR procedure if the court considers that appropriate. See, for example, **9.5.1.1** and **14.3.4.1** (as to costs).

1.3.1.9   The standard letter before claim

Immediately after collecting sufficient evidence to substantiate a realistic claim, and before addressing issues of quantum in detail, the potential claimant should send to the proposed defendant a letter detailing the claim. Where the claim is one to which an approved protocol applies, such as professional negligence, the information to be included in the letter before claim will be specified in the protocol (see further **3.7** and **Appendix A(19)**). Where no approved protocol applies, see **Appendix A(18), Practice Direction – Pre-action Conduct**. Enough information must be given so that the prospective defendant can commence investigations and at least put a broad valuation on the claim. The prospective claimant should set out any proposals he has for ADR.

1.3.1.10   The letter of response

The approved protocols and the Practice Direction on Pre-action Conduct give guidance on the matters to be dealt with in the letter of response. (See **3.8** and **Appendices A(18)** and **(19)**.) The prospective defendant should acknowledge safe receipt of the letter of claim and, after investigating the matter, should state whether or not liability is admitted. Reasons should be given if liability is denied. Where primary liability is admitted but contributory negligence is alleged, details of that should be provided. Note that the potential claimant should also respond to any such allegation before issuing proceedings. The question of ADR should also be addressed.

1.3.2   Stage 2: commencement of the claim

Before starting a court case, the client should be fully aware of what will be involved. That is more than the chances of success and the pros and cons of litigation. The client should have a good idea of what will happen next, as well as how long that might take and the likely cost. In particular, the client should appreciate that the court will impose a strict timetable of steps that must be taken. Not only must the client keep relevant documentation safe, it must be clear to the client what documents, if any, that are harmful to his case will have to be shown to the other side (see **Chapter 11**). In addition, the client should be told that he might have to attend court, not only for the trial but for hearings before that. The client must be informed that if he wants to stop the litigation at any time (see **13.6**), he will have to pay the opponent's costs, unless a more favourable settlement can be negotiated. At all times, the client's expectations must be carefully managed.

Proceedings are commenced by lodging at a county court or High Court a completed claim form. A specimen can be seen at **7.2.1.6**. To activate the claim, this must be served on the defendant. Full details of the claim, called particulars, must also be served on the defendant. If the defendant wishes to contest the claim, he must file at the court and serve on the claimant a defence. This triggers in the county court the allocation of the case to a particular 'track'. A claim of up to £5,000 will usually be allocated to the small claims track. Typically, these claims concern consumer disputes and the court does not expect parties to be legally represented.

Claims exceeding £5,000 and up to £25,000 are usually allocated to the fast track. Whilst parties will usually have legal representation on this track, the court will tightly control costs, as well as the type and amount of evidence each party can rely on. In particular, the expectation is that a single joint expert should be used by the parties where expert evidence is necessary, and the trial must be conducted within one day (effectively five hours). Claims exceeding £25,000 are usually allocated to the multi-track. As a claim cannot be started in the High Court unless it exceeds £25,000, all claims in that court are dealt with on the multi-track.

1.3.3   Stage 3: interim matters

Once on a track, the court carefully manages a case. Directions will be given to the parties as to the steps that must be taken to prepare for trial. A strict timetable will be imposed as to when each step must be taken. On the small claims track and fast track the expectation is that these directions can be given without any court hearing. In multi-track cases of any complexity it is usual for the parties to meet with a judge at a so-called case management conference in order clearly to define the issues in dispute and determine what steps need to be taken and when, in order to prepare for trial. The most common case management directions are for:

(a)   standard disclosure (ie, the parties list the documents in their possession that they intend to rely on, or which are adverse to their case, or support an opponent's case (see **Chapter 11**)); and

(b)   the exchange of evidence before trial that the parties intend to rely on (eg, experts' reports and statements, known as 'witness statements', of non-expert witnesses (see **Chapter 12**)).

Whatever the track, the parties will be working towards either a known trial date, or at least a period of time in the future when the trial will occur.

As to case management generally, see **Chapter 9**.

In addition to case management directions, parties may during this stage apply to the court for any specific orders that might be required (eg, to force an opponent who has neglected to take a required step in accordance with the timetable to do so on pain of having his case thrown out by the court). See further **Chapter 10**.

1.3.4   Stage 4: trial

A trial on the small claims track is informal and conducted at the discretion of the judge. The formal rules of evidence apply on the fast track and multi-track. At the end of a fast track trial, the judge will usually have resolved all issues (ie, liability, quantum (if relevant) and costs). As to costs, the judge will decide if any party should pay the other's costs and, if so, how much. This is known as a summary assessment of costs. The parties must provide each other and the court with a detailed breakdown of costs for this purpose. On the multi-track, the trial judge will decide who should pay costs. The general rule is the loser pays the winner's costs. If the parties cannot subsequently agree on the amount of those costs, they are determined post trial by a different judge, known as a costs judge, via a process called detailed assessment. See generally **1.3.5** and **14.3**.

1.3.5   Stage 5: post-trial

On all tracks a party may decide to appeal all or part of the trial judge's decision. As stated at **1.3.4** above, in a multi-track case, a detailed assessment of costs as awarded by the trial judge will take place if the parties cannot agree on the amount.

A party awarded damages and/or costs will expect to be paid by the date set by the court. What if that does not happen? The party will have to apply to the court to enforce the judgment. Most commonly, this involves instructing court officials to attend the debtor's premises and to take his belongings to be sold at public auction. The proceeds are then paid to the party. It is therefore vital, as indicated at **1.3.1** above, to ensure that at stage 1 steps are taken to check that any potential defendant is actually worth suing.

1.4 Case analysis

1.4.1 Causes of action

A cause of action is the legal basis of a claim. Examples include breach of contract, negligence, negligent misstatement, nuisance and trespass. To determine whether a client has a cause of action and his prospects of success, it is vital at the outset that a solicitor analyses all the known facts, whether given orally by the client and any witnesses, or contained in documentation. Lawyers call this evidence, and it is important to appreciate that the term is not limited to court proceedings.

1.4.2 Example: breach of contract

Take a claim for breach of contract as an example. The first thing to do is to assess the evidence that is available that will establish that there was a contract. Common law requires there to be an agreement with a promise, consideration, and intention to create legal relations. The last, certainly in any business context, will not be an issue. In practical terms, the solicitor will need to consider how and when the contract in dispute was formed, and whether it was written or oral. If it was written, then a copy should be obtained. If it was oral, the solicitor needs details of when and where it was made, who actually entered into the contract for each party, and the express terms agreed.

If the dispute concerns what express terms were agreed in a contract, the solicitor needs to assess the available evidence. If it is a written agreement, then the document will help; however, there may still be questions over the interpretation of those terms. In the case of an oral contract, this can be particularly tricky, as often the only evidence appears to come from the parties who made the contract. If they have different recollections of what was agreed, then the case can turn on their credibility. In such circumstances, it is important to look for other evidence, for example, someone else present when the contract was discussed or notes of the meeting made by the client. In addition, where a contract is entered into in the course of business, there may also be implied terms. These apply to both written and oral contracts.

When the solicitor is satisfied that the existence of a contract can be established (or is not likely to be in dispute) and its terms, the solicitor will then need to consider how the client will prove that there was a breach which has resulted in recoverable losses. What does the client say the opponent did (or failed to do) which amounts to a breach of the contract? This is a question of fact, and the solicitor must assess the evidence the client has to prove the claim. Likewise, each item of loss claimed will have to be similarly investigated. Finally, an assessment needs to be made of the overall strengths and weaknesses of the claim, and consideration given to what further evidence needs to be obtained.

Often, solicitors record their analysis in a grid chart. An example follows.

Client: Factory Goods (Mythshire) Limited ('FG')			
Opponent: Cool Systems (Mythshire) Limited ('CS')			
Cause of action: Breach of oral contract made on 27 November 2009 for CS to supply and install an air conditioning system at FG's factory.			
Implied term relied on: The air conditioning system would be of satisfactory quality – s 4(2) of the Supply of Goods and Services Act 1982.			
Elements to establish	**Facts to establish**	**Evidence available**	**Evidence to obtain**
Contract	CS, by its employee, Mr Wise, agreed on 27 November 2009, with Ms Riley, FG's employee, to supply FG with a new air conditioning system.	CS's estimate, invoice and receipted account. Proof of evidence of Ms Riley.	If necessary, proof of evidence from Mrs Clark who was present with Ms Riley on 27 November 2009.
Implied term	CS supplied the air conditioning system (goods) to FG and installed it (services) at FG's factory as part of CS's business.	N/a – not likely to be disputed.	N/a – not likely to be disputed.
Breach	The air conditioning system does not adequately cool the factory premises.	Complaints by FG's staff about the hot temperatures since installation. Daily record of factory temperatures kept by Mrs Vaux, FG's employee responsible for health and safety.	A report from an expert confirming FG's allegation.
Causing loss	(1) Cost of upgrading system supplied or replacement of that system with a suitable system. (2) Loss of profit – time factory had to close due to excessively hot working conditions. (3) Client tried to mitigate loss – hired portable air conditioning units but these were insufficient.	(1) None. (2) Records of Mr Frame, FG's head of human resources, recording time factory closed. (3) Receipted invoices for portable units.	(1) A report from an expert. (2) FG's profit and loss accounts, production records, etc. (3) Expert needs to consider this point.

As a case develops, you should continually review which issues remain in dispute and how those are to be proved.

There are three key case analysis points: viability, liability, and quantum. **Chapters 2 and 3** will discuss the steps you will need to take in order to complete your case analysis.

1.5 Useful websites

The starting point for any exploration of the Web in this area should probably be the Ministry of Justice website that hosts the Civil Procedure Rules (www.justice.gov.uk/civil/procrules_fin/index.htm). Court forms and guides are on HM Court Service site (www.hmcourts-service.gov.uk). For ease of reference copies of commonly used court forms can be found in **Appendix A**. However, these forms are often subject to change and you should check on the website for the most recent version. In addition, from the website you can use the related websites page to find other useful links, eg Community Legal Service (www.justask.org.uk/index.jsp), European Court of Justice (www.europa.eu.int/cj/en/index.htm), etc. Of course, these websites will then give you other links, and you will soon find an incredibly diverse range of sites dealing with a whole range of legal matters.

Chapter 2

Considerations at the First Interview Including Funding the Claim

2.1 Introduction

In **Chapter 1** we looked at the five stages of a civil claim (see **1.3**). Stage 1 – pre-commencement – is one of the key stages. You will be gathering evidence and establishing the facts in order to advise on viability. If any evidence or facts are overlooked, incorrect decisions could be made – at worst this could result in the case being lost or costs being wasted.

In **Chapters 2** and **3** we discuss each step you will have to consider at Stage 1; not all will be necessary in every case, but you should always run through the checklist at **3.13** every time you open a new file.

In this chapter we consider the first interview and the issues you will need to discuss with the client before proceeding to the detailed fact- and evidence-gathering phase which is outlined in **Chapter 3**.

2.2 Purpose of the first interview

The first interview between the solicitor and client is very important from both parties' points of view. The client will be anxious that the solicitor appreciates his problem, and will want to be assured that there is a satisfactory solution to it. The client is likely to be concerned about the potential amount of legal costs and will want some idea of the timescale involved. At the same time, the solicitor needs to be able to extract relevant information from the client in order to give preliminary advice on such issues as liability and quantum.

A solicitor will need to bear in mind now, and at all times, his professional obligations. These start with r 2.02(1) of the Solicitors' Code of Conduct. The solicitor must:

(a) identify clearly the client's objectives in relation to the work to be done for the client;

(b) give the client a clear explanation of the issues involved and the options available to the client;

(c) agree with the client the next steps to be taken; and

(d) keep the client informed of progress …

In addition, r 2.03(1) requires the solicitor to give the client the best information possible about the likely overall cost of the matter. The solicitor must:

(a) advise the client of the basis and terms of [the firm's] charges;

(c) advise the client of likely payments … to others [eg court fees, barristers' fees, experts' fees];

(d)   discuss with the client how the client will pay ...; and

(f)   advise the client of their potential liability for another party's costs.

There is no comprehensive list of those matters which need to be dealt with at first interview because each case is different. However, the matters set out below should always be considered.

2.3 Professional conduct

A detailed consideration of this area is contained in *Legal Foundations*, **Part II, Professional Conduct**.

The solicitor acting in civil proceedings must, in particular, have regard to the following rules of professional conduct.

2.3.1 Duty of confidentiality

By r 4 of the Solicitors' Code of Conduct, a solicitor is under a duty to maintain the confidentiality of his client's affairs unless the client's prior authority is obtained to disclose particular information, or exceptionally the solicitor is required or permitted by law to do so. It is important to note that the duty of confidentiality continues after the end of the retainer.

If a solicitor holds confidential information in relation to a client or former client (A), he must not risk breaching confidentiality by acting, or continuing to act, for another client (B) on a matter where that information might reasonably be expected to be material and client B has an interest adverse to client A. Ideally, therefore, before the first interview you should check that you do not have confidential information in respect of client A which you would be under a duty to disclose to the proposed new client B.

2.3.2 Conflict of interest

By r 3 of the Solicitors' Code of Conduct, a solicitor cannot act for two or more clients where this would cause a conflict of interests. A conflict of interests exists if the solicitor owes separate duties to act in the best interests of two or more clients in relation to the same or related matters, and those duties conflict or there is a significant risk that those duties may conflict.

> **Examples**
>
> 1.   A firm of solicitors already acts for a client in negotiating with publishers for the publication of the client's novel. The firm is now asked to act for a new client who alleges that the novel is plagiarised and breaches his copyright. As that is a related matter, there is a conflict of interest and the firm cannot act for the new client. (This example is taken from note 2 to r 3.)
>
> 2.   A solicitor is instructed to act by two partners in a firm which has been sued for damages for fraudulent misrepresentation. However, the allegation is that only one of the partners made the fraudulent misrepresentation. The potential conflict arises because there is a significant risk that the 'innocent' partner may have a claim against the 'guilty' partner for the same matter, namely if the fraudulent misrepresentation is established.

2.3.3 Money laundering

Solicitors are subject to the money laundering legislation, and it is extremely important to ensure that adequate procedures are in place to check a new client's identity – see Legal Foundations for further information.

2.3.4 Who is my client and am I authorised to act?

A solicitor warrants his authority to take any positive step in court proceedings, eg to issue a claim form or serve a defence on behalf of the client (see further **5.4.6**). So a solicitor must always be able to answer the questions posed above.

Example

Assume you attend a new client called Mrs Freeman. She wants to claim under a contract she entered into with Megawindows (Mythshire) Limited.

First, we need to ask: in what capacity are we acting for Mrs Freeman? Is she an individual who entered into the contract on her own behalf? Was she acting as an agent for her principal? Is she a trustee acting on behalf of a trust? Is she, say, one of a hundred partners in a firm, and did she contract on behalf of the partnership such that the partnership is our client? Is she a director in a limited company, and did she contract on behalf of that company such that the company is our client?

Secondly, if we are not acting for her as an individual in her own right, we need to consider whether she is the correct person to give us instructions on behalf of her principal, the trust, the partnership or limited company. Note that a solicitor may be ordered to pay personally the costs that are incurred where any steps are taken without authority, even if he does not know that he lacks authority. For example, where the client gives instructions on behalf of a non-existent company, or is a person not properly authorised to give instructions on behalf of a company.

As r 2.01(1)(c) of the Solicitors' Code of Code makes clear, if a solicitor receives instructions from someone other than the client, or by only one client on behalf of others in a joint matter, the solicitor must not proceed without checking that all clients agree with the instructions given.

2.3.5 Solicitor's duty as an officer of the court

As well as owing duties to the client, the solicitor also has an overriding duty not to mislead the court (see r 11.01 of the Solicitors' Code of Conduct). The duty to the court means that the solicitor must disclose all relevant legal authorities to the court, such as statutory provisions or case law, even if these are not favourable to his case. The advocate is also under a duty to help the court achieve the overriding objective.

Under r 1.3 of the CPR 1998, the parties, and therefore their solicitors, are required to assist the court in advancing the overriding objective. This creates a potential risk of conflict between the solicitor's duty to the court under CPR 1998, r 1.3 and his duty to act in the best interests of his client pursuant to r 1.04 of the Solicitors' Code of Conduct (see **2.3.6**). However, as note 3 to r 1 of that Code provides, if two duties come into conflict, the determining factor must be the public interest, and especially the public interest in the administration of justice under the CPR.

2.3.6 Solicitor's core duties

Rule 1 of the Solicitors' Code of Conduct sets out certain core duties of a solicitor which are said in note 2 to perform the following functions:

(a)   They define the values which should shape your professional character and be displayed in your professional behaviour.

(b)   They form an overarching framework within which the more detailed and context-specific rules in the rest of the Code can be understood, thus illuminating the nature of those obligations and helping you to comply.

(c)   The core duties can help you to navigate your way through those situations not covered in the detailed rules, as no code can foresee or address every ethical dilemma which may arise in legal practice.

(d)   The core duties are fundamental rules. A breach may result in the imposition of sanctions.

So what are these core duties and how might they affect a civil litigation practitioner? Table 2.1 below flags up some possible examples.

Table 2.1   Solicitor's core duties

Rule	Examples of potential problem areas
1.01 Justice and the rule of law You must uphold the rule of law and the proper administration of justice.	Client asks you to act illegally or not within the spirit of the CPR. A court order or provision of the CPR conflicts with your duty to act in the client's best interest.
1.02 Integrity You must act with integrity.	You use your position to take unfair advantage of a client, an opponent or a third party. You use your position unfairly to advance your client's case.
1.03 Independence You must not allow your independence to be compromised.	Any arrangement for a third party to fund your client's civil claim which imposes constraints on how you conduct the case that are beyond the legitimate interests of the funder.
1.04 Best interests of clients You must act in the best interests of each client.	A court order or provision of the CPR conflicts with this duty. Also see **2.3.2**.
1.05 Standard of service You must provide a good standard of service to your clients.	If you cannot exercise competence, skill and diligence.
1.06 Public confidence You must not behave in a way that is likely to diminish the trust the public places in you or the legal profession.	If you breach any of the other core duties.

Professional conduct checks to make before the first interview

1.   Confidentiality and conflict of interest

    Check name of client and opponent against existing and past clients.

2.   Money laundering

    Check identity of client.

2.4   Funding

It is very important on taking instructions to discuss costs with the client. The solicitor should give his client the best information he can about the likely cost of the matter. This includes advising the client on the different types of funding available.

As note 36 to r 2 of the Solicitors' Code of Conduct recognises, it is often impossible to tell at the outset of a case, particularly one involving prospective litigation, what the overall cost will be. Rule 2.03(1) allows for this and requires the solicitor to provide the client with as much information as possible at the start and to keep the client regularly updated. Unless a fixed fee is agreed, where the client is paying privately the solicitor should explain the potential steps in the litigation and the potential costs, and agree a ceiling figure or review dates. The client should be told how the solicitor's fee will be calculated, eg who is going to do the work and the hourly charging rate of that person. Often a payment on account will be required immediately, with interim bills delivered as the case progresses. The client should be advised of any foreseeable disbursements, such as court fees and barristers' fees.

The consequences for a litigation solicitor who does not follow the r 2 requirement regularly to give the client the best information then available about costs, can be seen in the case of *Reynolds v Stone Rowe Brewer* [2008] EWHC 497. There, a firm of solicitors was held to be bound by its original estimate of costs given to the client, because the firm failed to warn her that costs were increasing and that, as ultimately happened, the estimate would have to be revised upwards. See also *Mastercigars Direct Ltd v Withers LLP* [2009] EWHC 651.

The solicitor should also consider whether the client's liability for costs may be covered by existing legal expenses insurance cover (see **2.4.5**), and whether the likely outcome of the matter justifies the expense involved by conducting a costs–benefit analysis (see **3.12**).

In addition, the solicitor should advise the client of the risk that the client may be ordered to pay the opponent's costs if the case is lost.

2.4.1 Solicitor and client costs and costs between the parties

In litigation cases, the solicitor should explain to the client the distinction between solicitor and client costs (ie, the sum the client must pay to his own solicitor) and costs that may be awarded between the parties in litigation.

If the client loses the case, he will have to pay his own solicitor's costs and normally, in addition, his opponent's costs. Rule 44.3(2)(a) of the CPR 1998 provides that as a general rule the unsuccessful party in litigation will be ordered to pay the costs of the successful party. The opponent's costs are not necessarily all the costs incurred by the opponent. The court will assess what costs the client must pay towards the opponent's costs (unless there is agreement on this amount between the parties). The client will have to pay to his opponent only such costs as are ordered by the court or agreed between the parties.

If the client wins the case, he will still have to pay his own solicitor's costs. Indeed, if he is paying privately, he will usually already have paid these costs. He will normally receive his costs from his opponent. Again, this will be an agreed amount or a sum assessed by the court. If the costs recovered are, as is usual, less than the costs paid, the client will have to bear the loss.

A client should always be warned that even if he wins the case, he may not recover any costs if, for example, the opponent goes bankrupt or disappears.

2.4.2 Conditional fee agreements

A conditional fee agreement (CFA) is defined by s 58(2)(a) of the Court and Legal Services Act 1990 as 'an agreement with a person providing advocacy or litigation services which provides for his fees and expenses, or any part of them, to be payable only in specified circumstances'. Those circumstances are whether or not the client succeeds with a claim or, alternatively, successfully defends a claim.

A CFA is an agreement under which the solicitor receives no payment, or less than normal payment, if the case is lost, but receives normal, or higher than normal, payment if the client is successful. Many think of CFAs as 'no win, no fee' agreements. However, whilst a CFA may amount to 'no win, no fee', it can equally be 'no win, lesser fee', or 'win and pay usual fees' or 'win and pay increased usual fees'. The important point to grasp is that any fee payable is based on the solicitor's usual hourly charging rates, and a fee payable on success is a percentage increase in those usual hourly charging rates up to a maximum of 100%. The fee is not based on the solicitor receiving any proportion of money recovered by the client (as to such a contingency, see **2.4.4**).

A CFA is enforceable only if it meets the requirements of ss 58 and 58A of the Courts and Legal Services Act 1990. These provide that a CFA:

(a)   may be entered into in relation to any civil litigation matter, except family proceedings;

(b)   must be in writing; and

(c)   must state the percentage by which the amount of the fee which would be payable if it were not a CFA is to be increased (the success fee).

Where it is agreed that the solicitor should receive higher than normal payment if the case is won, the success fee cannot exceed 100% of the solicitor's normal charges. This limit is set by the CFA Order 2000 (SI 2000/823), reg 4.

Example

A solicitor normally charges £200 an hour. A 10% success fee would mean an additional £20 per hour. A 50% success fee would mean an additional £100 per hour. The maximum 100% success fee would mean an additional £200 per hour.

Normal charge per hour	Success fee as percentage of normal charges	Amount of success fee	Total hourly charge to client if client wins
£200	10%	£20	£220
£200	50%	£100	£300
£200	100%	£200	£400

When advising a client about costs, r 2.03(2) of the Solicitors' Code of Conduct provides that in respect of a CFA, the solicitor must explain the circumstances in which the client may be liable for his own legal costs (and when the solicitor would seek payment) and his right to an assessment of those costs. In addition, the core duty (r 1.3) to act in the best interests of the client means that a solicitor should always check to see if the client has the benefit of suitable before-the-event legal expenses insurance cover (see **2.4.5** and the case of *Sarwar v Alam*). If such exists then there is no need for the client to enter into a CFA. Likewise, a solicitor must always be careful to ensure that any settlement achieved for a client under a CFA is in the client's best interests and not made with a view to obtaining the solicitor's fee.

Normally, a CFA will cover all work done by the solicitors' firm for the client over the five stages, apart from an appeal. This will include any charges incurred in enforcing a judgment (see **Chapter 15**). The CFA is usually worded so the solicitors' firm has a right to take enforcement action in the client's name. An appeal will normally require its own risk assessment and so typically has its own CFA.

2.4.2.1   Drafting the CFA

It is of course essential that the CFA is drafted carefully. Consider, for example, the importance of a clear definition of the term 'win'. Does the client win if he succeeds on all aspects of his claim, or is it enough that he recovers some damages (even if they represent only a small percentage of his claim)? The Law Society provides assistance in the form of a model CFA for personal injury cases, which can be adapted for other types of work. Precedents are also available in practitioner works.

2.4.3   The success fee

If the client wins the case and his opponent is ordered to pay his costs, these may include the success fee. The opponent will, however, be required to pay the success fee only to the extent that it is reasonable (see further **14.3.8.2**). Where part (or all) of the success fee is disallowed, the solicitor is not entitled to recover the remainder from his client unless the court orders otherwise. It is vital that the factors taken into account are carefully recorded so that, if necessary, the solicitor can justify the level at which the success fee was set.

Whenever he enters into a CFA, the solicitor takes a financial risk. The solicitor who regularly acts on this basis will stay in business only if the success fees he recovers on his 'wins' outweigh the fees sacrificed on his 'losses'. It is therefore essential that before entering into a CFA or agreeing the level of the success fee with a client, the solicitor performs a thorough risk assessment. Relevant factors would include:

(a)   the chances of the client succeeding on liability;

(b)   the likely amount of the damages;

(c)   the length of time it will take for the case to reach trial;

(d)   the number of hours the solicitor is likely to have to spend on the case.

The solicitor may need to spend some time gathering evidence and information about the client's case before he can perform a full risk assessment. For example, it may be appropriate to obtain an expert opinion and/or interview witnesses (see **Chapter 3**). It is, of course, essential to discuss with the client what work will have to be performed before a decision can be reached about whether the solicitor is prepared to enter into a CFA, and how that work is to be funded.

A solicitor should never arbitrarily set the level of a success fee. A proper risk assessment should always be carried out. But what if the client suggests a success fee well in excess of what the solicitor might set? Should the solicitor just accept that? The answer is no, and as you might expect it is to be found in the Solicitors' Code of Conduct. By r 1.02, a solicitor must act with integrity; and pursuant to r 1.04, he must act fairly by not taking advantage of a client (see also r 10.01). Rule 2.03 must be followed as to client care and the giving of information about costs.

2.4.3.1   Funding disbursements and liability for the other side's costs

If a client with a CFA loses the case, he will not usually have to pay his own solicitor's fees but will nevertheless be liable for his opponent's costs. In addition, the client will, during the course of the litigation, have to fund disbursements such as the fees of a barrister and expert witnesses, as well as items such as travelling expenses. Many CFA-funded clients are not in a position to pay these disbursements and/or may be concerned by the fact that they will not know until the end of the litigation whether they are liable to their opponent for costs and, if so, for how much.

In such circumstances, the client may benefit from purchasing after-the-event insurance (AEI), which provides cover for the other side's costs and his own disbursements in the event of losing the case. The premium payable depends on the strength of the client's case and the level of cover required. It may be possible to arrange a 'staged' premium, whereby additional instalments are paid if the case continues beyond certain defined stages. For example, in *Rogers v Merthyr Tydfil CBC* [2006] EWCA Civ 1134, the claimant had the benefit of AEI cover with a three-stage premium: namely, £450 was payable when the policy was taken out, a further £900 when proceedings were issued, and a final £3,510.60 just before the trial.

If the client wins, the premium, like the success fee, is recoverable from his opponent to the extent that it is reasonable. Rule 2.03(1)(g) of the Solicitors' Code of Conduct requires the solicitor to discuss with his client whether insurance is appropriate before the CFA is entered into. There are several sources available to solicitors either online or through journals, which can help them find an insurance policy at a competitive premium.

Of course, obtaining AEI insurance to cover the client's disbursements in the event that he loses, does not solve the problem of how those disbursements are to be paid for during the course of the litigation. There are various solutions – for example, some banks offer loans to fund disbursements. As far as counsel's fees are concerned, counsel may be willing to enter into a CFA with the client. However, such an arrangement cannot be entered into with an expert witness. This is to avoid any possibility that the expert's evidence, which should be impartial, will be influenced if he is instructed on a 'no win, no fee' basis.

If necessary, many AEI insurers will arrange a loan to the client or his solicitors to fund both the disbursements and the cost of the AEI premium. The loan may even be on terms that it is not repayable in the event that the client loses. If he wins, the interest on the loan is not recoverable from his opponent. It is usually deducted from the damages recovered.

2.4.3.2   Notifying the other side of a CFA or AEI cover

If the client enters into a CFA before proceedings have been issued, or if he has obtained AEI cover, he must inform other potential parties to the dispute that he has done so. This is because para 9.3 of the Practice Direction on Pre-action Conduct (see **3.7**) provides that:

> Where a party enters into a funding arrangement within the meaning of rule 43.2(1)(k), that party must inform the other parties about this arrangement as soon as possible and in any event either within 7 days of entering into the funding arrangement concerned or, where a claimant enters into a funding arrangement before sending a letter before claim, in the letter before claim.

Note that a CFA and AEI cover fall within the definition of a funding arrangement under r 43.2(1)(k).

The information is usually included in a letter. However, some solicitors adapt Form N251 (see below). What information must be given? This is prescribed by para 19.4 of the Practice Direction on Costs as follows:

> (2)   Where the funding arrangement is a conditional fee agreement, the party must state the date of the agreement and identify the claim or claims to which it relates (including Part 20 claims if any. [See **Chapter 8**]
>
> (3)   Where the funding arrangement is an insurance policy, the party must–
>
>   (a)   state the name and address of the insurer, the policy number and the date of the policy and identify the claim or claims to which it relates (including Part 20 claims if any);
>
>   (b)   state the level of cover provided by the insurance; and
>
>   (c)   state whether the insurance premiums are staged and, if so, the points at which an increased premium is payable. [See **2.4.3.1**]

The amount of the CFA success fee and/or the AEI premium should not be included. These details are not required and remain confidential (until a party seeks to recover one or both at the conclusion of a case: see **14.3.8**). It would clearly not be in the best interests of a party to disclose his risk assessment at this stage, and would also be a breach of client confidentiality if done without the consent of the client.

Once proceedings are issued, the client must file with the court and serve on all parties a Notice of Funding in Form N251 (a copy appears in **Appendix A(4)**).

Where the client is a claimant and the CFA or insurance cover was entered into before the issue of proceedings, Form N251 must be filed when the claim form is issued. Where the client is a defendant and the CFA or insurance cover is entered into before the defendant files any documents with the court, Form N251 must be filed with the first such document. Otherwise, where the CFA or insurance cover is entered into later, Form N251 must be filed within seven days of the date of the CFA or insurance cover being taken out. See generally para 19.2 of the Practice Direction on Costs.

If, during the course of the proceedings, there is any change to the relevant information concerning a CFA or AEI cover, a notice of the change must be filed and served on all parties within seven days.

2.4.3.3 Failing to notify the other side of a CFA or AEI cover

What if a party fails to give notice of a CFA and/or AEI cover entered into pre-action? Rule 44.3B imposes the following sanction:

> (1) Unless the court orders otherwise, a party may not recover as an additional liability–
>
>   ...
>
>   (c) any additional liability for any period during which that party failed to provide information about a funding arrangement in accordance with a rule, practice direction or court order;
>
>   ...
>
>   (e) any insurance premium where that party has failed to provide information about the insurance policy in question by the time required by a rule, practice direction or court order.

Note that a CFA and AEI cover fall within the definition of additional liability under r 44.3B.

So what is the sanction? For a CFA, the success fee cannot be recovered on any costs incurred during the period the party failed to give the prescribed information. In respect of AEI cover, the premium is not recoverable if the prescribed information was not given on time. We also take the view that the sanction applies if the information given is inaccurate or incomplete, since in those circumstances the party will have failed to provide the information in accordance with the Practice Direction on Pre-action Conduct and/or the CPR.

A party will have to apply to the court to be given any relief from this sanction (see **9.4.2**).

Example

Pre-action on 25 January 2010 the claimant enters into a CFA with his solicitors that provides for a 30% success fee. On 11 February 2010 the claimant takes out an AEI policy. The letter before claim is sent on 19 March 2010, but no reference is made to the CFA and AEI until the claimant's solicitors issue proceedings and serve a Form N251 on the defendant's solicitors on 25 August 2010. At trial the claimant succeeds and the defendant is ordered to pay the claimant's costs. By r 44.3(B)(1)(c) the claimant will be unable to recover any of the 30% success fee on his costs incurred between 19 March 2010 and 25 August 2010 unless he successfully applies to the court. Also, by r 44.3(B)(1)(e) the claimant will be unable to recover any of the AEI premium unless he successfully applies to the court.

2.4.4 Contingency fees

A contingency fee is any sum, normally calculated as a percentage of money recovered by the client, which is payable only in the event that the client succeeds in a claim, eg if the client wins, he pays his solicitor 30% of the money recovered. The most popular uses of a contingency fee in practice are for bulk debt recovery work where the client does not want to take any court proceedings and for some tribunal claims (see below).

Rule 2.04 of the Solicitors' Code of Conduct prohibits all contingency fees in contentious proceedings except CFAs (see **2.4.2**). In particular, it should be noted that it is not lawful to enter into an agreement with the client whereby, if the case is won during Stages 2, 3 or 4 of civil litigation, the solicitor is paid as a fee a percentage of the money recovered.

What constitute 'contentious proceedings'? These are defined by s 87 of the Solicitors Act 1974 as 'business done, in or for the purpose of proceedings *begun* before a court or before an arbitrator' (emphasis added). So it is possible to agree a contingency fee for all the usual pre-action work (eg, investigation of issues, the initial letters of claim and response, negotiations, etc). Whilst court and arbitration proceedings are contentious, what about proceedings before a tribunal? You should note that only proceedings before the Lands Tribunal and the Employment Appeal Tribunal are treated as contentious. Claims made to the Motor Insurers Bureau (provided proceedings are not issued) (see **2.9.6**), the Criminal Injuries Compensation Authority (see **2.9.7**) and as part of an ADR procedure (see **Chapter 4**) are non-contentious.

If the matter is settled without a claim form being issued, a contingency fee is lawful and payable, provided the contingency has been met. However, it is unlawful, and so unenforceable, once proceedings have begun.

If a contingency fee is agreed but the claim is not settled during Stage 1, what is the effect of a claim form being issued? Are the client's pre-action costs treated as non-contentious and so potentially recoverable under the contingency fee agreement, or do all the costs become contentious? Unfortunately the position is unclear. In *Crosbie* v *Munroe* [2003] EWCA Civ 350, Brooke LJ suggested that the dealings between parties which lead up to the disposal of a claim should be treated as contentious proceedings even if the dispute is settled without the need to issue a claim form. In light of this, a client may be offered a contingency fee agreement, but with a CFA taking its place in respect of Stage 1 work and future work where a claim form is issued.

Like a CFA (see **2.4.2.1**), it is vital that the contingency is clearly defined in the agreement. For example, a contingency fee agreement to represent a client in an Employment Tribunal claim might state: 'Win means that your claim is decided in your favour whether by a tribunal or an agreement to pay you damages.'

To be valid, a contingency fee must be recorded in a non-contentious business agreement (as defined by s 57 of the Solicitors Act 1974; see further *Legal Foundations*).

2.4.5   Insurance

Regardless of whether the client is going to enter a CFA, the solicitor should always check to see if the client has the benefit of an existing legal expenses insurance policy (often called before-the-event insurance, or 'BEI') which might fund the litigation. Such insurance is commonly purchased as part of household or motor insurance policies.

In the case of *Sarwar v Alam* [2001] EWCA Civ 1401, [2002] 1 WLR 125, the Court of Appeal laid down the following guidance:

> In our judgment, proper modern practice dictates that a solicitor should normally invite a client to bring to the first interview any relevant motor insurance policy, any household insurance policy and any stand alone before-the-event insurance policy belonging to the client and/or any spouse or partner living in the same household as the client.

Rule 2.03(1)(g) of the Solicitors' Code of Conduct requires a solicitor to discuss with the client (at the first interview and, as appropriate, thereafter) whether the client's liability for another party's costs is covered by existing insurance (BEI), or whether specially purchased insurance should now be obtained (AEI).

Where BEI cover is not available, the client may wish to consider purchasing AEI even if he does not fund the litigation by way of a CFA. As discussed at **2.4.1**, one of the disadvantages of litigation is that if the case is lost, the loser will generally have to pay the winner's costs, and this liability cannot be quantified until the end of the proceedings. By purchasing AEI, the litigant removes this uncertainty (provided the cover bought is sufficient). Moreover, if he wins the case, he is likely to be able to recover the premium paid from the other side. Given these advantages, a solicitor who fails to discuss the possibility of such insurance with a client at the outset of litigation may well be negligent and in breach of professional conduct.

If a firm of solicitors advises a client on and/or arranges AEI cover for a client, the firm must either be regulated by the Financial Service Authority (FSA), or be registered with the FSA's Exempt Professional Firm's register to engage in insurance mediation work (this also includes other types of insurance policies, such as defective title indemnity insurance).

A firm on the FSA's Exempt Professional Firm's register should note the following when advising or arranging AEI cover for a client:

(a) By the Solicitor's Financial Services (Scope) Rules 2001, rule 4(c), it must account to the client for any pecuniary reward or other advantage which the firm receives from a third party.

(b) By the Solicitors' Financial Services (Conduct of Business) Rules 2001, where a firm recommends a contract of insurance to a client, the firm must inform the client whether or not it has given advice on the basis of a fair and proper analysis of the insurance market. If not, the firm must:

(i) advise the client whether the firm is contractually obliged to conduct insurance activities only with one or more insurer;

(ii) advise the client that he can request details of the insurer with which the firm conducts business; and

(iii) provide the client with such details on request.

2.4.6 Trade unions and professional organisations

If a client is a member of a trade union or professional organisation, it may be possible to arrange for his union or organisation to be responsible for payment of his solicitor's costs.

2.4.7 Public funding

In limited circumstances, clients may receive public funding (previously called legal aid) for civil litigation, and the solicitor should always consider whether this might be available. Most civil litigation matters within the scope of this book will not, however, benefit from public funding and what follows is, therefore, no more than a broad outline.

Public funding for both civil and criminal matters is administered by the Legal Services Commission (the LSC). The civil litigation scheme is ran by the Community Legal Service (the CLS), which operates the Community Legal Service Fund (the CLSF).

The effect of these arrangements has been to reduce substantially the scope of public funding in litigation. Community Legal Service funding will not usually be available for cases that could be financed by a CFA. With very limited exceptions, claims in negligence for personal injury, death or damage to property (including intellectual property) are excluded. Neither is funding available for matters arising out of the carrying on of a business, including claims brought or defended by sole traders.

In addition to these restrictions, public funding is only open to clients whose income and capital falls within financial eligibility limits. These limits vary, depending on whether the client is seeking full representation in proceedings or merely wants assistance from a solicitor to investigate a proposed claim.

Furthermore, where the client is financially eligible and the claim is of a type covered by the CLSF, public funding will be offered only if a merits test is also satisfied. This involves considering the client's prospects of success and applying cost–benefit criteria (ie, weighing the likely cost of the proceedings against their benefit to the client). Put simply, a client who has a strong claim that will not be expensive to pursue, but which would result in substantial damages, has a much better chance of securing funding than one whose prospects of winning are marginal or who wishes to pursue a claim which would involve costs that are disproportionate to its likely benefits.

Where a party is in receipt of public funding, he may be required to make a contribution from his disposable capital or his income towards the costs. Where a contribution is required from income, this is payable on a monthly basis for as long as the case is funded by the LSC. Any change in the client's circumstances must be notified to the LSC as it may affect the amount of the contribution or the client's entitlement to funding.

In *David Truex, Solicitor (a firm) v Kitchin* [2007] EWCA Civ 618, the Court of Appeal held that a solicitor must from the outset of a case consider whether a client might be eligible for legal aid. Why? First, it is quite wrong to incur substantial expenditure chargeable privately to the client if public funding is available. Secondly, a client will find it more difficult to change firms of solicitors if work has been done and a relationship built up before advice is given that a different firm could become involved. In this case, the Court observed that if the financial position of the defendant had been considered properly, and considered in the context of whether she might be eligible for public funding, the result would have been advice to go to a different firm offering legal aid at a very early stage. As a result, the claimant solicitors' firm was negligent and was denied its fees.

2.4.7.1 The statutory charge

Where a publicly-funded client recovers money as a result of the proceedings, he may have to repay some or all of his legal costs to the LSC out of the money recovered. This is known as the statutory charge, and it will apply only to the extent that the client does not succeed in recovering his costs from his opponent.

The same principle applies where the dispute involves property rather than money. Any property that is retained or transferred to the client is subject to the statutory charge.

The solicitor must ensure that the client has understood the statutory charge prior to accepting an offer of public funding.

2.5   Case analysis

As was indicated at **1.4**, there are three key case analysis points – viability, liability, and quantum – which we would summarise in the following series of questions that need to be answered pre-action.

2.5.1   Liability

What is the cause of action? Is there more than one? If so, analyse each independently and identify the relevant law. Establish the legal elements which must be proved for the claim to succeed. Your objective will be to identify evidence already available or that can be obtained in respect of each of these elements. Does it support the case, or is it adverse? How strong is it?

2.5.2   Limitation

2.5.2.1 Solicitor's role

From the outset, a solicitor must ascertain when the limitation period began and when it will expire. The matter must be reviewed continually in the light of any new facts. Careful diary notes must be kept to remind the solicitor that time is marching on and the expiration of the limitation period draws closer. Proceedings must be issued before the limitation period expires, otherwise the solicitor is likely to face a negligence claim.

Whilst it is always best practice to ensure that proceedings are started well before the limitation period expires, unfortunately some claim forms are sent, or delivered, to the court very close to the expiry date. In *St Helens Metropolitan BC v Barnes* [2006] EWCA Civ 1372, the Court of Appeal had to determine if proceedings had been 'brought' within the limitation period. The claimant's solicitors had delivered the claim form to the county court on the day prior to the expiry of the limitation period, and requested that the claim should be issued.

However, the claim form was not issued by the court staff until four days later. The Court held that the matter was resolved in favour of the claimant by PD 7, para 5.1, which provides that:

> Proceedings are started when the court issues a claim form at the request of the claimant (see rule 7.2) but where the claim form as issued was received in the court office on a date earlier than the date on which it was issued by the court, the claim is 'brought' for the purposes of the Limitation Act 1980 and any other relevant statute on that earlier date.

The Limitation Act 1980 (LA 1980) (as amended) prescribes fixed periods of time for issuing various types of proceedings. This is important to a client because if this period of time elapses without proceedings being issued, the case becomes 'statute-barred'. The claimant can still commence his claim, but the defendant will have an impregnable defence. If the defendant wishes to rely on this, it must be stated specifically in his defence (see **Chapter 7**).

2.5.2.2   Claims founded on contract or tort (LA 1980, ss 2 and 5)

The basic rule is that the claimant has six years from the date when the cause of action accrued to commence his proceedings.

In contract, the cause of action accrues as soon as the breach of contract occurs. This will be a question of fact, and you will need to check to see if case law has established when the cause accrues. For example, with an anticipatory breach of contract, the cause of action accrues when the intention not to perform the contract is made clear, and not at the later date when performance was due to occur (*Hochester v de la Tour* (1853) 2 E & B 678).

In tort, the cause of action accrues when the tort is committed. In the tort of negligence, as damage is an essential element, the cause of action accrues only when some damage occurs. This may be at a date considerably later than that when the breach of duty itself occurred. Like contract claims, it may be necessary to research any relevant case law. For example, in a negligent misstatement claim, the cause of action will accrue on the date the claimant sustains damage as a result of reliance on the advice (*Forster v Outred & Co* [1982] 2 All ER 753).

This basic rule is modified in the case of certain specific types of claim. As to personal injury cases, see *Personal Injury and Clinical Negligence Litigation*.

2.5.2.3   Latent damage

In a non-personal injury claim based on negligence, where the damage is latent at the date when the cause of action accrued, s 14A of the LA 1980 provides that the limitation period expires either:

(a)   six years from the date on which the cause of action accrued; or

(b)   three years from the date of knowledge of certain material facts about the damage, if this period expires after the period mentioned in (a).

In theory, these rules could mean that a defendant is indefinitely open to the risk of proceedings being issued in latent damage cases. In order to avoid this, there is a long-stop limitation period of 15 years from the date of the alleged breach of duty (LA 1980, s 14B). This long-stop can bar a cause of action at a date earlier than the claimant's knowledge; indeed, it can even bar a cause of action before it has accrued.

2.5.2.4   Persons under disability

A person under a disability is either a child (ie, someone who has not yet attained the age of 18), or a protected party (ie, a person of unsound mind within the meaning of the Mental Capacity Act 2005 and who is incapable of managing and administering his property and affairs).

Where the claimant is a person under a disability when a right of action accrues, the limitation period does not begin to run until the claimant ceases to be under that disability. See generally **5.4.1**.

2.5.2.5 Contractual limitation

In a contract case it is very important to check whether a contractual limitation period is specified in the contract. This is because any such provision is usually shorter than the statutory limitation periods referred to above, and the claim should therefore be commenced within the contractually specified period.

2.5.2.6 Summary

Type of claim	Statutory limitation period
Contract (excluding personal injury)	6 years (LA 1980, s 5)
Tort (excluding personal injury and latent damage)	6 years (LA 1980, s 2)
Latent damage	6 years or 3 years from date of knowledge (LA 1980, s 14A)

2.5.3 Remedies

There are a number of alternative remedies which a claimant can pursue against the defendant, assuming liability can be established. The most common remedy sought is damages. It is important to establish at an early stage what the client's objective is. If the client has unrealistic expectations or requires a remedy which the court has no power to award, you should identify and discuss this at the earliest possible stage.

2.5.3.1 Damages

The rules as to quantum of damages in civil cases depend on the type of claim being pursued. As to claiming interest on damages, see **2.7** below.

2.5.3.2 Contract

A claim for damages arises when one party to the contract has failed to perform an obligation under the contract. The purpose of damages in such a situation is to place the injured party in the position he would have been in if the contract had been performed properly.

For example, damages can be recovered either for the repair of defective goods, or for repayment of the purchase price. In addition, there may be a claim for general damages in respect of physical discomfort and/or inconvenience. However, damages for injured feelings or mental distress are not generally recoverable. There is an exception where the subject matter of the contract was to provide enjoyment, peace of mind or freedom from distress, eg a contract for a holiday. In such cases, damages for mental distress and loss of enjoyment are recoverable.

The test for the recovery of damages for breach of contract is that they must not be too remote from the breach. In other words, did the loss flow naturally from the breach, or was the loss within the reasonable contemplation of the parties at the time the contract was made as being the probable result of the breach?

2.5.3.3 Tort

A claim for damages in tort arises where injury, loss or damage is caused to the claimant or the claimant's property. The aim of damages is, so far as possible, to place the claimant in the position he would have been in if the damage had not occurred. Damages are therefore compensatory in nature and, as a result, the claimant can seek compensation for any direct loss and consequential loss, provided the rules on remoteness are not broken. The rules on remoteness require that in order to be recoverable the loss must be a reasonably foreseeable consequence of the tort.

2.5.3.4   Reduction in damages – duty to mitigate

Any potential claim for damages for either breach of contract or tort may be reduced if it can be shown that the claimant has failed to mitigate his loss. In *Frost v Knight* (1872) LR 7 Ex 111 the court observed that this duty means looking at what the claimant 'has done, or has had the means of doing, and, as a prudent man, ought in reason to have done, whereby his loss has been, or would have been, diminished'. So a claimant cannot recover by way of damages 'any greater sum than that which he reasonably needs to expend for the purpose of making good the loss' (*Darbishire v Warran* [1963] 1 WLR 1067).

The duty arises only on the breach of contract or commission of the tort. If a defendant alleges that the claimant has failed to take all reasonable steps to mitigate his loss, he should raise that in pre-action correspondence (see **Chapter 3**) and state it in his defence (see **7.3**). The burden of proof will be on the defendant at any trial. If, however, the claimant wishes to contest the issue properly, he should produce appropriate evidence: see *Bulkhaul Ltd v Rhodia Organique Fine Ltd* [2008] EWCA Civ 1452.

2.5.3.5   Debt

A debt action is a particular type of contract claim. Instead of claiming damages for breach of contract, the claimant is claiming a sum which the defendant promised to pay under the contract.

For example, in a sale of goods case, if the buyer wrongfully rejects the goods (and the seller accepts this as repudiation of the contract), the seller has a claim for damages for breach of contract. However, if the buyer takes delivery but then fails to pay then the action is for debt. The significance is that in the latter case the claimant has no duty to mitigate his loss.

2.5.4   Quantum

When you have determined the amount the client is claiming (quantum), you will need to think about the evidence you have to prove the loss. As with liability, the claimant must prove each item and what evidence is currently available or may be obtainable. Are any figures or estimates available? Do any issues of remoteness or mitigation of loss arise? Do you need to take any steps to preserve evidence? If you have evidence which cannot be preserved (eg perishable goods), make sure you carry out any necessary tests/expert examination before it is too late; and where possible, offer your opponents facilities for inspection so that they can carry out their own tests.

2.6   Viability and burden of proof

2.6.1   Viability

If your case analysis indicates that there is a legal basis for the claim and evidence to support the claim, there are a number of other issues affecting the overall viability of pursuing a claim against a potential defendant which need to be considered with the client at the earliest possible stage.

Viability involves a number of issues of which the claimant needs to be aware, including:

- Who is the prospective defendant?
- Is there more than one possible defendant?
- Where is the defendant?
- Is the defendant solvent?
- Where are his assets?
- What are those assets worth?
- Will the defendant be able to pay any judgment?

- What can the client afford to pay?
- Does the client have any suitable BEI?
- Is the case suitable for a CFA and/or AEI cover?
- Does the client qualify for public funding?
- How much time and resources will the client have to commit to investigate and deal with the case?
- Does a cost–benefit analysis suggest the desirability of a quicker and cheaper solution than litigation can offer?

2.6.1.1   Identify all potential defendants and their status

As we saw at **1.3** above, the general rule is that all persons to be sued should be sued at the same time and in the same claim. Your case analysis must identify against whom each cause of action lies. Very often there is only one potential defendant, but, for example, where an employee or agent commits a tort when acting in the course of his employment, it is usual to sue both the employee or agent and the employer. This is because the latter is vicariously liable for the former. Likewise, a consumer may, in certain circumstances, have a cause of action against both the retailer and the manufacturer of a defective product.

Not only must you identify the prospective defendants, you must also ensure they are sued in their correct capacity. Broadly, you should consider if the potential defendant is an individual, a partnership or a limited company. Sometimes it is not as obvious as it seems.

Example

Assume your client entered into a contract negotiated with a Mr Jones. We need to ask in what capacity Mr Jones acted. Did he act as an individual on his own behalf? Was he acting as an agent for someone else and, if so, did our client know that? Is he one of, say, 10 partners in a firm called Jones & Co, and did he contract on behalf of the partnership? Is he a director in a limited company called Jones Ltd, and did he contract on behalf of that company? Just exactly with whom did the client contract? Will he end up negotiating with, and potentially litigating against, Mr Jones, Mr Jones's principal, Jones & Co (a firm) or Jones Ltd? See further **5.4**.

2.6.1.2   Defendant's solvency

There is little point in suing a defendant who is on the verge of either bankruptcy or liquidation. Enforcement of any judgment obtained would be impossible. If there is doubt as to the liquidity of the prospective defendant then further enquiries should be made. For example, if the proposed defendant is a company, a company search should be carried out. For an individual, a bankruptcy search should be done. In any case an inquiry agent could be instructed, although the costs of doing this must be considered. It may also be possible to use various Internet search engines to see if there is any relevant information about the proposed defendant.

2.6.1.3   Defendant's whereabouts

Clearly, the defendant needs to be traceable and his whereabouts known in order to communicate the claim and, if necessary, serve proceedings. Again, an inquiry agent may be able to help.

2.6.1.4   The claim itself

This involves balancing the merits of the claim itself against the overall cost of pursuing it and the prospects of a successful outcome. The client may believe he has a good claim but will be concerned as to the costs of litigation. Finance has been discussed above (see **2.4**), but the client must be advised at this stage on the law, and any possible defences to the claim should be anticipated. The client must be told of the overriding objective and the requirement in r 1.3 that parties must help the court further the overriding objective.

2.6.1.5 Alternative remedies

The solicitor should consider whether there are any alternative remedies available to the client for resolving the problem, and advise the client accordingly. For example, the client may wish to use one of the forms of alternative dispute resolution (see **Chapter 4**).

2.6.2 Burden of proof

There are two questions of proof which need to be considered.

2.6.2.1 Legal burden

The party asserting a fact must prove it unless it is admitted by his opponent. For example, a claimant who alleges negligence must prove all the elements of the tort (ie, a duty existed between the parties, the defendant breached that duty, and the claimant sustained damage as a result). Similarly, a claimant alleging breach of contract must prove that a contract existed between the parties, the defendant broke the relevant express and/or implied terms of the contract, and the claimant suffered loss as a result.

What about a defendant? Whilst he does not have to prove his defence, any allegation of failure to mitigate loss (see **2.5.3.4**) or contributory negligence will have to be proved. Note that as to contributory negligence, the defendant must also prove that the claimant's failure was a contributory cause of the defendant's damage: see *Lewis v Denye* [1939] 1 KB 540.

2.6.2.2 Balance of probabilities

In civil cases, the claimant is required to prove a fact on a balance of probabilities. This simply requires the judge to be persuaded that the claimant's version of events is more likely to be true than the defendant's. Your case analysis should enable you to take a preliminary view on whether you are able to discharge the burden of proof and succeed on liability and quantum.

2.7 Interest

2.7.1 Specified and unspecified claims for money

The CPR 1998 provide no definition of a claim for a specified or unspecified sum of money. The N1A Notes for a claimant on completing the claim form (see copy at **Appendix A(1)**) refer to a claim for a *fixed amount of money* as being a specified amount. On that basis a specified claim is in the nature of a debt (ie, a fixed amount of money due and payable under and by virtue of a contract). The amount will be known already (from, say, an invoice), or it should be capable of being determined by mere mathematics (from, say, a contractual formula). Examples might include the price of goods sold, commission said to be due under express contractual terms or consideration said to have failed totally.

If the court will have to conduct an investigation to decide on the amount of money payable, the claim is best seen as being for an unspecified amount, even if the claimant puts some figures forward for the amount claimed. For example, in a damages claim for breach of contract the claimant might have had to repair or replace goods. Whilst a figure might be placed on the cost of such, it will be for the trial judge to determine if it is reasonable. Thus, damages claims should usually be regarded as unspecified.

What if a claim is a mixture of specified and unspecified amounts? For example, the recovery of consideration paid that has failed totally (a specified amount), plus damages for breach of contract (unspecified amounts). In these circumstances the entire claim is treated as an unspecified claim.

2.7.2   Entitlement to interest

Pre-action, a prospective claimant can demand interest on a claim only if entitled to it under any contractual provision (including any provision implied by the Late Payments of Commercial Debts (Interest) Act 1998: see further below).

Where the remedy sought by the claimant is either damages or the repayment of a debt, the court may award interest on the sum outstanding. The rules vary according to the type of claim. A claimant seeking interest must specifically claim interest in the particulars of claim.

2.7.2.1   Breach of contract including debt claims

In contract cases, there are three alternative claims to interest:

(a)   The contract itself may specify a rate of interest payable on any outstanding sum. This will be the rate which was negotiated between the parties. The court will usually apply this rate.

(b)   It may be possible to claim interest under the Late Payment of Commercial Debts (Interest) Act 1998 (see below).

(c)   In all other cases, the court has a discretion to award interest either under s 35A of the Senior Courts Act 1981 (SCA 1981) in respect of High Court cases, or under s 69 of the County Courts Act 1984 (CCA 1984) in respect of county court cases. The current rate of interest payable under either statute is 8% pa in non-commercial cases and, generally, 1% pa over base rate in commercial cases.

Since a debt claim is for a specified amount of money, interest must be claimed precisely, giving as a lump sum the amount of interest which has accrued from breach of contract up to the date of issue of the proceedings and a daily rate thereafter. In a debt claim, where s 35A of the SCA 1981 or s 69 of the CCA 1984 applies, the convention is to claim interest from and including the day after the last day payment was due. In a damages claim, the request for interest is not set out in detail as the claim is for an unspecified amount of money.

Example: specified claim

You act for Mr Tibbs, a local builder. He is in dispute with one of his customers, Mrs Little. He entered into a written contract to convert her basement into a bedroom last year. He finished the work on 8 July 2009 but, despite reminders, Mrs Little has not paid him the contract price of £13,000. The written contract between Mr Tibbs and Mrs Little provides that interest is payable on late payment. This is due at the rate of 20% per annum from and including the day of completion of the works. If a claim form is issued on 28 August 2009, how much interest should be claimed?

Mr Tibbs is entitled to interest on £13,000 for 52 days (namely, 24 days in July and 28 days in August). For each day, he is entitled to interest of £7.12 (that is £13,000 × 20% ÷ 365; the answer of £7.1232876 is rounded down in the circumstances). So, on the claim form he should claim £370.24 by way of interest.

What if the contract did not provide for interest payable on late payment. Mr Tibbs would then claim interest in county court (non-commercial) proceedings at 8% pa under s 69 of the CCA 1984. That would give him a daily rate of interest of £2.85 (£13,000 x 8% ÷ 365; the answer of £2.849315 is rounded up in the circumstances).

Late Payment of Commercial Debts (Interest) Act 1998

This Act gives a statutory right to interest on commercial debts which are paid late if the contract itself does not provide for interest in the event of late payment. The term 'commercial debt' includes debts arising from the supply of goods and services. As the Act is only concerned with commercial debt, it does not apply to unspecified claims or a specified amount owed by a consumer.

Interest under the Act can be claimed at a rate of 8% pa above the Bank of England's reference rate on the date the debt became due for payment. The reference rate is the base rate applicable on 31 December and 30 June each year, and will apply for the following six months. For example, if the base rate is 4.5% pa on 30 June, this is the reference rate for the period 1 July to 31 December, and so interest of 12.5% pa in total can be claimed under the Act. The interest accrues from the expiry of any period of credit under the contract. If the contract does not provide for any such period, interest can be claimed from 30 days after the latest of:

(a)   delivery of the bill;

(b)   delivery of the goods;

(c)   performance of the service.

In addition to the debt and interest, the Act also provides for payment of a fixed sum of between £40 and £100 compensation for late payment, the amount varying according to the size of the debt.

An example appears in the claim form at **7.2.1.6**.

2.7.2.2   Tort

The court has a general discretion to award interest on damages in any negligence claim. This power is derived from SCA 1981, s 35A in respect of High Court claims, and from CCA 1984, s 69 in respect of county court claims. Generally speaking, if interest has been claimed properly, the court will normally exercise its discretion to award interest for such period as it considers appropriate.

2.7.2.3   From what date is interest payable and for how much?

In a contract or tort claim for damages, from what date is the court likely to start an award of interest? In theory interest can be awarded from when the cause of action first arose (see **2.5.2.2**). However, in practice, the award is normally made from when the loss is sustained (if this is later). Consider the facts in the case of *Kaines (UK) Ltd v Osterreichische* [1993] 2 Lloyd's Rep 1. There, in June 1987 the defendants repudiated a contract to sell the claimants oil for lifting in September 1987 and payment in October 1987. As a result the claimants contracted to buy the same quantity of oil at a higher price from another supplier but on exactly the same terms (lifting in September 1987 and payment in October 1987). In August 1987 the claimants issued proceedings. The Court of Appeal held that it was only in October 1987, when the claimants had paid the higher price, that the claimants had sustained any loss. Therefore, interest did not start to run on the damages until October 1987. So the key is to work out carefully the date of loss.

Example

In a negligent surveyor's case, liability is established and quantum assessed by the court as the diminution in value of the property, ie the difference between what the claimant actually paid and the value of the property in its true condition. Assume the diminution in value is assessed at 10%. When is loss sustained by the claimant?

There are two dates to consider. First, when the claimant paid the deposit on exchange of contracts, because he paid 10% too much and so was then out of pocket by that amount. (If a deposit of £25,000 was paid, the damages would be £2,500 plus interest from exchange.) Secondly, when the claimant paid the balance of the purchase price on completion, because again he had paid 10% too much and so was out of pocket. (If the balance paid was £225,000, the damages would be £22,500 plus interest from completion.) On both dates that money could have been in the claimant's bank earning interest. See *Watts v Morrow* [1991] 1 WLR 1421.

In a contract or tort claim for damages, how much interest is the court likely to award? Such an award is compensatory in nature. In *Kuwait Airways Corporation v Kuwait Insurance Company SAK* [2001] LTL, 16 June, Langley J stated that 'In principle interest is to be awarded to compensate the claimant for being kept out of the money from the date when it has been established that it was due to him'. In *Tate & Lyle Food and Distribution Ltd v Greater London Council* [1982] 1 WLR 149, Forbes J said:

> One looks, therefore, not at the profit which the defendant wrongly made out of the money he withheld – this would indeed involve a scrutiny of the defendant's financial position – but at the cost to the [claimant] of being deprived of the money which he should have had. I feel satisfied that in commercial cases the interest is intended to reflect the rate at which the [claimant] would have had to borrow money to supply the place of that which was withheld.

What is a commercial case? Generally, this is where all the parties are businesses and the claim is based on the transaction of trade and commerce, such as a business document or contract, the export or import of goods, banking and financial services, and the purchase and sale of commodities. Typically, non-commercial cases involve one party acting as a consumer, for example a prospective domestic house-buyer engaging the services of a surveyor.

In non-commercial cases, the courts award interest at their discretion under s 35A of the SCA 1981 or s 69 of the CCA 1984 at 8% pa. Traditionally, in commercial cases, the award of interest has been at 1% pa above base rate. However, in *Jaura v Ahmed* [2002] EWCA Civ 210, the Court of Appeal held that it is permissible for a judge to depart from this conventional rate if it is necessary to reflect the higher rate at which the claimant had to borrow, eg if the claimant was a small businessman who could only borrow from a bank at 3% pa over base rate.

As a general rule, unless a contractual term provides for it, an award of simple interest is made rather than an award of compound interest. In exceptional cases, such as a claim for restitution, compound interest may be awarded if that will achieve full justice for the claimant: see *Sempra Metals Ltd v Inland Revenue Commissioners* [2007] UKHL 34.

2.7.2.4 Key questions to be addressed

The flowchart at **Appendix C(4)** highlights the following key questions that you need to address:

(a) *Pre-action* (to be demanded in the letter before claim): is the claim based on a written contract that provides for the payment of interest? Is the claim for the payment of a commercial debt?

(b) *During proceedings* (to be demanded in the particulars of claim): is the claim based on a written contract that provides for the payment of interest? Is the claim for the payment of a commercial debt? Is the claim (contract and/or tort based) proceeding in the High Court or a county court?

Remember that a defendant might also be in a position to make a claim in contract and/or tort that includes interest. So pre-action he might demand such in a letter of response (see **3.8.5**) and during proceedings in a counterclaim (see **8.2.1**).

2.8 Foreign element and choice of forum

If a solicitor is instructed by a client who is based abroad, or is instructed to take proceedings against a party based abroad, one of the first things which must be considered is the question of jurisdiction – in which country's courts can proceedings be commenced?

Different rules apply depending on whether the foreign country involved is in the EU or outside it.

2.8.1 EU and Lugano Convention Member States

The question of jurisdiction as between Member States of the EU (apart from Denmark) is governed by Council Regulation 44/2001 ('the Regulation'). Norway, Switzerland, Iceland and Denmark are governed by a similar provision called the Lugano Convention. These are incorporated into English law by virtue of the Civil Jurisdiction and Judgments Act 1982. The 1982 Act also regulates jurisdiction as between the various parts of the UK (given that Scotland and Northern Ireland are separate jurisdictions).

2.8.1.1 The basic rule (Article 2)

The basic rule under the Regulation is that the defendant must be sued in his local courts. For an individual, that means the place where he is domiciled. For a company, it means its statutory seat, central administration or principal place of business (Article 60). The statutory seat of a UK company is its registered office address.

So, the basic rule states that if you want to sue someone domiciled in France, you must do so in the French courts.

2.8.1.2 Co-defendants and third parties (Article 6)

If a defendant is domiciled in an EU country, he can be sued there; and then other parties can be joined into the claim even though they are domiciled elsewhere in the EU.

2.8.1.3 Contract cases (Article 5(1))

The Regulation confers jurisdiction in contract cases on the courts of the State where the contract was to be performed. This is an alternative to suing the defendant where he is domiciled. In a sale of goods case, unless the parties have agreed otherwise, the place of performance of the obligation in question is deemed to be the State where, under the contract, the goods were delivered or should have been delivered. In the case of the provision of services, unless the parties have agreed otherwise, the place of performance of the obligation in question is deemed to be the State where, under the contract, the services were provided or should have been provided.

Many contracts contain jurisdiction clauses stating that, for example, the contract is governed by the law of England and Wales, and that any dispute must be resolved in the courts of England and Wales. In such a case, unless both parties agree to waive the jurisdiction clause, proceedings must take place in England and Wales, irrespective of the defendant's domicile or where the obligation in question under the contract was to be performed (Article 23).

2.8.1.4 Tort cases (Article 5(3))

The Regulation confers jurisdiction in tort cases on the courts of the State where the tort was committed, or the State where the harm caused by the tort occurred. Again, this is an alternative to suing a defendant where he is domiciled. So, if an Italian driver causes a road traffic accident in England, he can be sued in England or in Italy.

2.8.1.5 Exclusive jurisdiction (Article 22)

In some cases, such as disputes over land, the Regulation confers jurisdiction on the courts of one State and proceedings must be taken there.

2.8.1.6 Submission to the jurisdiction (Article 24)

If a defendant is sued in England and believes that the English courts do not have jurisdiction, he should simply acknowledge service of the claim and apply under Part 11 of the CPR 1998 for an order declaring that the court does not have jurisdiction. If he takes any further steps in the proceedings (eg, by filing a defence), he will be taken to have submitted to the jurisdiction of the English courts. The application must be made within 14 days of filing the acknowledgement of service.

Appendix C(5) sets out a flowchart dealing with the order in which the matters set out at **2.8.1.1** to **2.8.1.6** should be applied in determining jurisdiction.

2.8.2 The rest of the world

2.8.2.1 Defendant served in this country

The English courts can hear any proceedings if the claim form was served on the defendant whilst he was present in England and Wales (no matter how briefly). The defendant could then, however, object to the proceedings continuing in England on the ground that the English courts are not the most appropriate ones for resolving the dispute.

So, if an Englishman has an accident in New York caused by the negligence of a local New Yorker, and then is able to serve the defendant with a claim form whilst he is in England on holiday, the defendant could object to the proceedings continuing in England on the basis that New York state was a more convenient forum.

2.8.2.2 Applying for permission to serve out of the jurisdiction

If, on the other hand, the defendant cannot be served with the proceedings in England and Wales, the permission of the court needs to be obtained to serve him outside the jurisdiction (see **5.5.7**).

2.9 Alternatives to litigation

There are several alternatives to court proceedings which may produce the remedy the client wants, possibly at less cost. These alternative procedures should always be considered at first interview and reviewed regularly. See the Solicitors' Code of Conduct, r 2.02, guidance note 14.

2.9.1 Arbitration

Arbitration is an adjudication operating outside the normal court process, by which a third party reaches a decision which is binding on the parties in dispute. Many business contracts contain an arbitration clause requiring the parties to refer their disputes to arbitration rather than litigation. In the absence of such a clause, the parties in dispute may agree to arbitration once the dispute has arisen, and may choose their own arbitrator with the relevant expertise. Arbitration itself is largely governed by statute, namely the Arbitration Act 1996 (provided the agreement to arbitrate is in writing).

The main advantages of the parties agreeing to arbitration instead of litigation are that:

(a)   arbitration may be quicker than litigation;

(b)   the procedures are less formal and occur in private;

(c)   the solutions reached are often more practical than those a court has power to order; and

(d)   at the same time those decisions are binding on the parties.

The winning party to an arbitration can apply to the High Court for permission to enforce the arbitration award as if it were a court judgment (Arbitration Act 1996, s 66).

On the other hand, the main disadvantages of using arbitration are that certain remedies, such as injunctions, are not available and, depending on the procedures adopted, the dispute may not receive the depth of investigation it would have done in the courts. Further, it is not always necessarily cheaper than litigation.

2.9.2   Alternative dispute resolution

Alternative dispute resolution (ADR) is a means of resolving disputes by using an independent third party to help the parties to reach a solution. The third party may suggest a solution to the parties but cannot impose one. The decision to use ADR is voluntary; the parties choose the process and either of them can withdraw at any time before a settlement is reached. If either party does not like the proposed solution, he does not have to accept it.

There are various types of ADR, such as mediation, expert appraisal or expert determination.

Under the CPR 1998, the courts actively encourage parties to use some form of ADR. This is considered in more detail in **Chapter 4**.

Can a court order that parties must use an ADR method? No, held the Court of Appeal in *Halsey v Milton Keynes General NHS Trust* [2004] EWCA Civ 576, [2004] 4 All ER 920. As Dyson LJ stated:

It is one thing to encourage the parties to agree to mediation, even to encourage them in the strongest terms. It is another to order them to do so. It seems to us that to oblige truly unwilling parties to refer their disputes to mediation would be to impose an unacceptable obstruction on their right of access to the court.

However, as to the costs consequences of unreasonably refusing to use ADR, see **14.3.4.1**.

2.9.3   Trade schemes

Some professional bodies and trade associations operate schemes under which a potential claimant may be able to pursue a remedy outside the courts. This is often cheaper and quicker than court proceedings.

2.9.4   Negotiating settlements

A solicitor should always consider with the client whether it is possible to negotiate a settlement with the opponent. Negotiations should be commenced as soon as possible and a genuine attempt made to limit the areas of dispute between the parties. Once all reasonable attempts to settle have been exhausted, there may well be no alternative but to issue proceedings. However, the matter must always be kept under review. Paragraph 6.1(2) of the Practice Direction on Pre-Action Conduct (see **Chapter 3**) states that parties should make appropriate attempts to resolve the matter without issuing proceedings. Failure to do so may result in one or more of the parties being punished financially during litigation.

Negotiations are considered in more detail in **Chapter 13**.

2.9.5   Insurance

Many defendants to civil claims are insured. Drivers of motor vehicles are required by law to possess insurance which covers them for at least the minimum insurance (basically third party) under the Road Traffic Act 1988. Most professional bodies require their practising members to be insured against negligence claims by clients.

The existence of insurers does not in any way affect the conduct of the proceedings, and the insurers are not a party to the claim as there is no cause of action against them. However, the majority of insurance policies require the insured to notify the insurers of any potential claim in order that they can consider taking over the claim on behalf of the insured. Where an insurance company is involved, the company, or its solicitors, will usually deal with any negotiations or subsequent court proceedings.

In certain circumstances, a judgment against an insured defendant can be enforced against the insurers. Notice of the proceedings must be served on the insurers either before or within seven days of commencing proceedings to invoke these provisions.

2.9.6   Motor Insurers Bureau

The Motor Insurers Bureau (MIB) operates two schemes which allow the victims of either uninsured or untraced drivers to recover compensation for certain losses sustained. The MIB is a scheme set up by the insurance companies and is also financed by them.

2.9.7   Criminal Injuries Compensation Authority

The Criminal Injuries Compensation Authority (CICA) is a body set up by the Government to provide the victims of criminal acts with *ex gratia* compensation for any personal injuries sustained as a result of those acts.

2.9.8   Criminal compensation order

The criminal courts have powers to order compensation in respect of any personal injury, loss or damage resulting from a criminal offence when imposing sentence at the conclusion of criminal proceedings.

Case Study: First Interview Considerations for Mr and Mrs Simpson

Professional Conduct

When Mr and Mrs Simpson made the appointment for the first interview with their solicitor, basic information, such as their full names, address, telephone number and Mr Templar's details, would have been taken. This would enable checks to be carried out to ascertain whether the solicitors' firm was acting or had acted in the past for Mr Templar. Obviously, if the firm already had instructions from Mr Templar to act for him in this matter, there would be a conflict of interest and the firm could not act for Mr and Mrs Simpson. But what if the firm had acted for Mr Templar in the past? Might the firm risk breaching the duty of confidentiality still owed to him? The answer might not be straightforward, as the confidential information held in respect of Mr Templar would have to be evaluated. If that information might reasonably be expected to be material to Mr and Mrs Simpson, such as Mr Templar's financial position or his attitude towards settling litigation then, given that the parties have opposing interests, the firm could not act for Mr and Mrs Simpson.

In our case study the checks reveal no problems. Moreover, Mr and Mrs Simpson provide satisfactory evidence of their identities so that the firm can complete its money laundering checks.

Funding

The solicitor must act in the best interests of Mr and Mrs Simpson, and that includes identifying the most cost-effective ways of achieving their objectives. They should be asked if they have any existing legal expenses insurance cover, and any policies should be checked. Enquiries should be made of any trade or professional organisations which might provide them with funding. Whether or not the firm acts under CFAs or provides AEI, these options should be discussed. Eligibility for and availability of public funding should also be examined.

For the purposes of the case study, assume that Mr and Mrs Simpson decide to instruct their solicitors privately. The solicitors provide them with full details in accordance with r 2 of the Solicitors' Code of Conduct.

Case Analysis

See Appendix D(1). At this stage the facts as outlined by Mr and Mrs Simpson point to negligent driving by Mr Templar that has caused them loss. But will Mr Templar admit that? What evidence of quantum do they have? As the case progresses we shall be revisit the facts and evidence to see how the analysis develops.

Note that in order to keep this case study a straightforward claim against one defendant, the potential liability of the claimants' builders, if they did leave glass on the driveway, is ignored.

We have set out below a few key factors addressed in this chapter that form part of the analysis.

Limitation

The claim is in the tort of negligence and the limitation period will start from the date when the damage occurred. Here that is the date of the accident, namely 2 August 2010. As there is no claim for personal injuries, Mr and Mrs Simpson will have six years (ie until 1 August 2016) to start proceedings.

Viability

In this case we know the identity of the potential defendant, Mr Geoffrey Templar, and Mr and Mrs Simpson have contact details for him. These should be checked. If ultimately he cannot be located then he cannot be sent correspondence or later served with court documents.

Can he pay damages and costs if these become payable? As the damage occurred whilst he was driving his car, he can claim under his car insurance policy (assuming he is insured). This should be checked and his insurer's details obtained so that it can be notified of the claim.

Jurisdiction

As both parties are resident within England and Wales and the incident happened here, there are no jurisdiction issues in this case.

Alternatives to Litigation

The solicitor should consider with Mr and Mrs Simpson now and as the case develops whether any ADR method might be appropriate. Obviously, whether any method is viable will first depend upon Mr Templar also wishing to use it. See further **Chapters 3** and **4**.

Chapter 3

Early Action

As we saw at **1.4** and **2.5**, case analysis is the key to representing a client effectively. So when you take the initial statement, otherwise known as a proof of evidence, from the client (or indeed any other witness), you should make a careful note of the main points and ask questions to obtain further information in order to develop that analysis. The key to obtaining a full and accurate set of instructions from the client is to probe but not prompt. Bear in mind that the statement should be in the client's own words. Let the client tell his story, and try to ensure that he develops this chronologically. Some clients will fail to do this, and you should make a note of any gaps and fill these in by questioning. If any part is ambiguous, get it clarified. You must end up with a clear picture of what the client's case is all about. You can then advise as to its strengths and weaknesses, and consider what further evidence needs to be obtained. You will not be in a position to negotiate effectively with the other side, or present your client's case in an ADR process or to a court, if you do not understand that case properly.

After the first interview with a potential claimant (or defendant), there are a number of practical preliminary steps the solicitor can take to advance the client's claim (or defence). The main requirements are to confirm the client's instructions and your advice in writing, and to obtain relevant evidence. The solicitor will also have to bear in mind at all times the pre-action protocols under the CPR 1998. Where no specific approved protocol applies to the claim, the solicitor must still comply with the 'spirit' of the protocols and the Practice Direction on Pre-action Conduct which provides general guidance on the conduct of the case at this stage: see further **3.7** below.

3.1 Writing to the client

You should set out your advice to the client in writing as soon as possible after the interview. By now you should have identified the cause of action, undertaken any necessary legal research and assessed the available evidence. If a proof of evidence has been taken from the client, this should be sent to the client for approval and signature. If there are any 'gaps' in the case – factual issues in respect of which there is no evidence or weak evidence – you must explain this to the client and outline the options.

The solicitor should, of course, comply with all the requirements of r 2 of the Solicitors' Code of Conduct. For example, the initial letter of advice to the client should, in accordance with r 2.02(1):

(a) identify clearly the client's objectives in relation to the work to be done for the client;

(b)   give the client a clear explanation of the issues involved and the options available to the client; and

(c)   list the steps that are to be taken next.

In addition, r 2.03(1) requires the solicitor to give the client the best information possible about the likely overall cost of the matter. This should include:

(a)   advising the client of the basis and terms of the firm's charges;

(b)   advising the client of likely payments to third parties (eg court fees, barristers' fees, experts' fees);

(c)   setting out how the client has agreed to pay; and

(d)   advising the client of his potential liability for another party's costs.

Further, by r 2.03(6), a solicitor must have discussed with the client whether the potential outcomes of any legal case would justify the expense or risk involved, including, if relevant, the risk of having to pay an opponent's costs. It is best practice to record this advice in writing in the initial letter of advice and subsequently as the case develops.

Lastly, the letter should explain the next steps which are to be taken by the solicitor and remind the client of any matters which he has agreed to undertake.

3.2   Interviewing witnesses

3.2.1   Proof of evidence

The solicitor should arrange to take a proof of evidence from any witnesses as soon as possible, while matters are still fresh in their minds. There is no 'property' in a witness, and the solicitor may request an interview with anyone who may have information about the case. However, there is nothing that can be done if a witness absolutely refuses to give a statement. A witness may do this, for example, because he does not wish to say anything against his employer, or simply because he does not wish to get involved.

3.2.2   Professional conduct

It is permissible for a solicitor to interview and take a proof of evidence (statement) from a prospective witness where that witness has already been interviewed by another party. However, there is a risk that the solicitor will be exposed to the allegation that he has improperly tampered with evidence. This can be overcome by offering to conduct the interview in the presence of a representative of the other party. See note 13(f) to r 11 of the Solicitors' Code of Conduct.

Is there any objection to a client, through his solicitors, paying reasonable expenses to a witness and reasonable compensation for loss of time attending court? The answer is no – see the Solicitors' Code of Conduct, r 11, guidance note 30.

3.2.3   The reluctant witness

At the eventual trial of the case, a person can be compelled to attend as a witness, but the solicitor will be reluctant to advise his client to call someone as a witness if he has not obtained a full statement from him beforehand, because, of course, he will have no guarantee that the witness is going to say anything relevant or favourable in the witness-box. Therefore, it is most important to persuade potential witnesses to give a statement if at all possible. If the witness refuses, the solicitor could use a witness summary (see **12.5**).

3.2.4   Taking a proof of evidence

The solicitor will normally write to the witnesses initially and arrange a convenient time for an interview to take place. This may be at the solicitor's office, or the solicitor may have to go out to the witness's home or place of work.

Start an interview by taking down the basics, ie the witness's full name, address, date of birth, telephone contact numbers, e-mail address, etc. If you are not interviewing the client, make a note of any relationship the witness has with the client, eg relative or employee.

Obtaining facts from a witness can be a difficult task. Let the witness tell his own story by using open questions. This should give you a fair idea of what the witness can say. Then fill in any gaps in the detail by using closed questions. Clarify points that are unclear and ensure that you have the entire story. Pose probing questions but do not prompt a witness. Do not put words in the witness's mouth. Moreover, remember that it is the witness's words that you want to record and have in the proof of evidence, not your own version. Make suitable notes, or record the interview with the witness's consent.

Make sure that you obtain any relevant documents. You may have to think laterally about what relevant documents a witness can provide. Probe, as the witness may not volunteer a document (eg, ask if there was any written contract; pre-contract and/or post-contract correspondence; letters of complaint; in-house reports and memos; faxes; e-mails; documents held on a computer or laptop; documents in storage, etc).

Think of an interview as a 'picture painting' task. Ask yourself during the interview: do you understand what is being portrayed; can you picture in your mind what the witness is describing? It is best to take down the details in chronological order. Is the story clear? If it is not comprehensible to you then how are you going to communicate it effectively to the other side, or to an arbitrator or an ADR representative, or ultimately to a judge at trial? A site visit may also help, where appropriate. You can then observe the scene of any incident and will not have to imagine it. Equally, photographs and/or site plans may assist in some cases.

So that you can adapt a proof of evidence later for any court proceedings, it is best set out in numbered paragraphs. Each paragraph should deal with only one topic.

'Picture painting' and the credibility of a witness are intrinsically linked. If a witness has already made a written statement, perhaps to the factory manager after an accident, make sure that you look out for any inconsistencies when you now interview that person. For example, in his statement to the manager the witness said that the injured person had 'put his hand on top of the machine'. Now, perhaps months later, the witness tells you that the injured person's hand was 'inside the machine'. If you fail to sort out this inconsistency, no doubt your opponent will use it to discredit the witness at trial.

Pursue any other lines of enquiry opened up by the interview. So if a witness tells you, 'I was advised by Mr Quinn who inspected my vehicle immediately after the incident that ...', do not rely on this witness repeating what Mr Quinn said. You should take a proof of evidence from Mr Quinn.

When interviewing witnesses, the solicitor should be wary of people who try too hard to be helpful, and he should try to ensure that the witness's story will stand up to cross-examination. It is better that any weakness in the case is identified at this stage rather than later on when a great deal of time and money has been spent on the case. The proof of evidence should be as comprehensive as possible, including background information which may not be directly relevant to the claim but which may assist in understanding the case. A formal statement (known as a witness statement) containing only the evidence which the witness will give at the hearing will be prepared at a later stage, and this later statement is the one which will be served on the other parties before the hearing (see **12.2**). At this stage, therefore, there is no need to worry unduly if the statement contains matters which will not be admissible in evidence at the trial, although, before proceedings are commenced, the solicitor must ensure that he has, or will have, enough admissible evidence to prove his client's case at trial.

At the end of an interview, summarise for the witness what you have grasped as the key parts of his story to ensure that there are no fundamental misunderstandings. Get the proof of evidence typed up while the interview is fresh in your mind. Further, send it out to the witness for correction and approval as quickly as possible.

Practical points to consider when taking a proof of evidence

1.   How are you going to record the interview?

2.   Start with the basics: full name, address, contact details.

3.   Try to get the witness to tell the story in chronological order.

4.   Use open questions to let the witness tell the story in his own words.

5.   Use closed questions to fill any gaps in the facts.

6.   Do not put words in the witness's mouth.

7.   Collect any relevant documents from the witness.

8.   At the end, summarise for the witness what you understand him to have said.

3.3   Preserving documents

The solicitor should ask the client to bring all relevant documents to him as soon as possible. A solicitor is under an obligation, both as a matter of professional conduct and under the CPR 1998, to ensure that the client understands the rules relating to disclosure of documents (see **Chapter 11**). A client who has little or no experience of the civil litigation process may be unaware, for example, that he is under an obligation during the course of the proceedings to disclose documents to the other side, even if those documents harm his case. Furthermore, if the solicitor reads the documents at an early stage, this should ensure that there is nothing to take him by surprise later on in the proceedings which may throw a different light on the case. In a case involving a contractual dispute, it is obviously imperative that the solicitor should see the contract as soon as possible to be able to advise the client properly. For example, the contract may include a provision imposing a limitation period for claims arising under the contract which may be considerably shorter than the statutory limitation period (see **2.5.2.5**).

The client should also be made aware that the term 'documents' includes any method of recording information, such as video tapes and computer disks, and is not merely limited to written documents. It is advisable to explain his disclosure obligations to the client from the outset and to confirm this in writing. In this initial letter you should explain that the duty extends to documents that the client may previously have had in his physical possession, even if they have now been, say, lost, destroyed or given to someone else.

It is also important to identify important documents in the possession of the opponent and to decide whether it is necessary to take any steps to ensure they are preserved.

3.4   Obtaining expert evidence

3.4.1   Instructing an expert

There are numerous instances when a solicitor may need to obtain expert evidence to advance a client's claim. For example, consulting engineers are regularly requested to report on accidents at the workplace and on road traffic accidents. Similarly, if expert evidence is required on building work, it is likely that the solicitors' firm already has contacts with suitable architects and surveyors. If counsel is involved at an early stage, he may be able to recommend suitable experts for the case. Alternatively, a suitable expert may be found through The Law Society (which maintains a register of experts), or from the Academy of Expert Witnesses or other similar organisations.

Specialist expertise is the vital quality required of an expert witness, but it is not the only quality. The ability to present a convincing report which can be easily understood, and to perform well as a witness, particularly under cross-examination, is equally important. There is no fixed test to qualify as an expert witness – anyone who has special expertise in an area can be considered as an expert. Expertise does not depend on qualifications alone, although frequently the expert will be highly qualified in his field. Expertise may have been acquired through years of practical experience. For example, an experienced carpenter with no formal qualifications could nevertheless be an expert on the proper seasoning of wood, and so assist in deciding whether, say, an oak dining table was of satisfactory quality.

The usual method of instructing an expert is by letter, the content of which will vary depending on what is required of the expert.

It will be necessary to provide an expert with all the relevant documents and statements from witnesses. It may also be necessary to arrange for an inspection of any relevant machinery or site. The solicitor may need to take urgent steps to ensure that material to be inspected is preserved, or, where this is not possible, to obtain the best alternative evidence, such as photographs or a video.

Where the client is to pay the expert's fees (eg, if they are not covered by insurance or public funding), the solicitor should obtain an estimate of the likely fees and then clear this with the client. In such cases, the solicitor will prefer to obtain money on account to cover the expert's fees. Where this is not done, the solicitor takes a risk, since he is responsible to the expert for payment of his charges.

Can an expert be instructed on a conditional or contingency fee basis? The answer is no – see para 7.6 of the Protocol for the Instruction of Experts to give Evidence in Civil Claims (**Appendix A(20)**).

It is not only when acting for the prospective claimant that the solicitor will be obtaining expert evidence. The potential defendant is also entitled to have expert evidence available. Proper facilities for inspection and observation should be granted for this.

It should be noted that the use of expert evidence during proceedings requires permission from the court (see **3.4.4**). Therefore the client should be told that whilst the report is necessary to evaluate the strength of the claim, the fee paid to the expert may not be recoverable from the opponent even if the client is successful in litigation.

3.4.2 Experts' reports

When the expert's report is received, the solicitor should check it carefully. Mistakes can be made, even by an expert. The solicitor should send a copy to the client, so that he may also check it and inform the solicitor of any errors.

Whoever the expert is, never be afraid to return to him for clarification of the report. If the solicitor does not understand it, there is a good chance that no one else will, and that will defeat the object of obtaining the report.

3.4.3 Opinion

A significant advantage which the expert has over the ordinary witness (see **12.8**) is that the expert can give opinion evidence. For example, a surveyor may form the view that an earlier surveyor had been negligent in not observing certain defects in the structure of a building.

This is a matter of opinion, but nevertheless the expert is permitted to state it. Section 3(1) of the Civil Evidence Act 1972 provides that:

> ... where a person is called as a witness in any civil proceedings, his opinion on any relevant matter on which he is qualified to give expert evidence shall be admissible in evidence.

Case Study

Would an expert help in this case? Mr and Mrs Simpson allege that Mr Templar was negligent, as he was driving too fast and so lost control of his vehicle. But they are assuming that. Are there other explanations? Tyre tracks on the drive, etc may be useful evidence, and so photographs should be taken to preserve that evidence. Consideration should be given to appointing an accident reconstruction expert, who can examine the scene and give his opinion as to the speed at which and path along which Mr Templar's car travelled, and what caused him to crash into Mr and Mrs Simpson's house.

3.4.4 Restrictions on the use of expert evidence

The CPR 1998 have introduced very significant restrictions on the use of expert evidence. Although a party to proceedings is free to obtain as much expert evidence as he wishes, the extent to which such evidence may be used in court is strictly controlled. By r 35.1 of the CPR 1998, expert evidence is restricted to that which is reasonably required to resolve the proceedings. The court can therefore limit the number of expert witnesses who can give evidence, or order that a single joint expert be appointed, or restrict expert evidence to a written report rather than oral evidence in court. A solicitor advising a client on whether to obtain expert evidence should always bear in mind that the costs of doing so will usually be recoverable from the opponent (assuming the case is won) only if the court gives permission for the expert evidence to be used.

As a general rule, if the area of expertise is settled, such that any two or more experts are likely to give the same opinion, a single joint expert is appropriate. Where a range of views is likely then normally it serves the overriding objective for the court to allow each party to have its own expert so that the court has such a range of views.

The use of expert evidence in proceedings is considered further in **Chapter 12**.

3.5 Site visits

Site visits may be needed for the purpose of taking photographs or making plans. Plans and photographs are unlikely to be disputed if they are accurate; but in the event of a dispute, the person who prepared the plan or took the photographs may have to give evidence, so they should be prepared by someone other than the solicitor who will be acting as an advocate at the hearing. If a formal plan is required (eg, in a boundary dispute) then this should normally be prepared by a surveyor. In some cases, a visit to the site of the incident, such as in a factory accident case, may be useful. On other occasions, it might help to visit the client's place of business to gain a better understanding of the nature of that business.

If the inspection will be expensive, the solicitor should obtain prior authorisation from the client.

3.6 Instructing counsel

3.6.1 Use of counsel

It is not necessary to instruct a barrister (also known as counsel) in every case. As a highly-trained lawyer, the solicitor should have confidence in his own knowledge and ability. The solicitor will be capable of forming an assessment of both the chance of success and the level of damages. Too frequent use of counsel may result in the costs being disallowed on an assessment of costs at the end of a case. Assessment of costs is discussed in more detail in **Chapter 14**.

Nevertheless, judicious use of counsel is sensible. If the issues are difficult, it is wise to instruct counsel to advise on liability.

Similarly, counsel's opinion on quantum may be needed at an early stage if the case is not straightforward. For example, if it appears that some element of the client's claim might arguably be too remote, it might be appropriate to check with counsel. Even in these cases, however, the solicitor should have formulated his own view and counsel should be assisting with this. The solicitor should not be abrogating responsibility.

3.6.2 Method

Instructing counsel requires the preparation of a formal document (called 'Instructions to counsel'). It will bear the heading of the claim (or proposed claim) and should contain a list of the enclosures being forwarded to counsel. The enclosures will obviously vary with the case but will typically include copies of the client's statement, any other proofs of evidence, any existing statements of case, any experts' reports, and any relevant correspondence. It is not necessary to send counsel the whole file; some judgement should be exercised in deciding which papers counsel needs to have available.

The body of the instructions to counsel will identify the client and set out briefly both sides of the case. Counsel can refer to the enclosures for detail, but the instructions should contain sufficient information to enable the barrister to identify the major issues. The solicitor should indicate his own view of the case and draw counsel's attention to those areas on which particular advice is required.

The instructions will end with a formal request to counsel to carry out the required task.

The instructions must carry a back sheet endorsed with the title of the claim, what the instructions are (eg, 'Instructions to counsel to advise on quantum'), counsel's name and chambers, and the solicitor's firm's name, address and reference.

Sometimes, counsel may not be able to proceed without a conference (the name given to a meeting with counsel) with the solicitor and the client. This could occur, for example, because the facts of the case are too detailed and complicated to be able to cover all the aspects in the instructions. Alternatively, it may be that counsel's advice will, to some extent, depend on his assessment of the client as a potential witness, and this will have to be done face to face.

If a conference is needed, counsel is still instructed in the usual way, but arrangements are then made with counsel's clerk for the solicitor and the client to visit counsel in chambers (the name given to a barrister's office) to discuss the case. Counsel will not normally expect to provide a written opinion after the conference, so the solicitor must take comprehensive notes at the conference. If a written opinion is required, this should be made clear in the instructions, but the costs of both will not be recoverable from the other side unless the court thinks it was reasonable to seek a written opinion.

Traditionally, instructions to counsel are prepared using the third person ('Counsel is instructed to …', and 'Instructing Solicitors seek Counsel's advice on …'). Many firms now adopt a more modern approach, setting out the instructions as if writing a letter. Each firm can decide which approach it prefers. Nevertheless, the instructions should still be in a formal document, accompanied by a covering letter to counsel's clerk.

3.6.3 Professional conduct

How far can a solicitor rely on counsel's advice? In *Locke v Camberwell Health Authority* [1991] 2 Med LR 249, the Court of Appeal set out the following principles:

(a)   In general a solicitor is entitled to rely upon the advice of counsel properly instructed.

(b)   For a solicitor, without special experience in a particular field, to rely on counsel's advice is to make normal and proper use of the Bar.

(c)   However, the solicitor must not do so blindly but must exercise his independent judgement. If he thinks that counsel's advice is obviously or glaringly wrong, he is under a duty to reject it.

3.7 Pre-action protocols

Pre-action protocols are an important aspect of the CPR 1998. There are approved protocols for personal injury, clinical disputes, construction and engineering, judicial review, defamation, disease and illness, possession claims based on rent arrears, possession claims of residential property based on mortgage arrears, housing disrepair and professional negligence claims. The details of these protocols, save the last, are outside the scope of this book. It is vital to check to see whether any approved protocol applies to a client's case. Note, however, that there is also a Practice Direction on Pre-action Conduct which contains general guidance that should be followed in all cases (unless an approved protocol otherwise applies).

A copy of the Practice Direction on Pre-action Conduct is set out at **Appendix A(18)**, and a copy of the Professional Negligence Protocol may be found at **Appendix A(19).**

The aims of the Practice Direction and approved pre-action protocols are:

(a)   to initiate and increase pre-action contact between the parties;

(b)   to encourage better and earlier exchange of information;

(c)   to encourage better pre-action investigation by both sides;

(d)   to put the parties in a position where they may be able to settle cases fairly and early without litigation;

(e)   to enable proceedings to run to the court's timetable and efficiently, if litigation does become necessary.

The Practice Direction and protocols deal with matters such as notification to the defendant of a possible claim as soon as possible, the form of the letter before claim, disclosure of documents and the instruction of experts, where relevant. Annex A to the Practice Direction on Pre-action Conduct sets out guidance on steps to be taken where no approved protocol applies: see **3.8.**

Compliance with the Practice Direction or a relevant protocol should help the parties involved make an informed decision on the merits of the case and lead to a greater number of settlements without the need for court proceedings. In particular, the parties must give serious consideration to ADR. For example, para 8.1 of the Practice Direction on Pre-action Conduct states that the parties should consider whether some form of ADR procedure would be more suitable than litigation and, if so, endeavour to agree which form to adopt. If proceedings occur, both the claimant and defendant may be required by the court to provide evidence that alternative means of resolving the dispute were considered. The courts take the view that litigation should be a last resort, and that claims should not be issued prematurely when a settlement is still actively being explored. Parties are warned that if this provision is not followed then the court must have regard to such conduct when determining costs (see **14.3.4.1**).

Paragraph 4.2 of the Practice Direction on Pre-action Conduct states that the court will expect the parties to have complied with both the Practice Direction and the substance of any approved protocol that applies to their dispute. Where non-compliance has led to proceedings that might otherwise not have been commenced, or has led to unnecessary costs being incurred, the court may impose sanctions. These can include an order:

(a) that the party at fault pay some or all of his opponent's costs (perhaps on the penalty, indemnity basis – see **14.3.3**);

(b) depriving a claimant who is at fault of some or all of the interest he may subsequently be awarded on any damages he recovers; or

(c) requiring a defendant who is at fault to pay interest on some or all of any damages that are subsequently awarded to the claimant at a rate of up to 10% pa above base rate.

In exercising these powers, the court should aim to place the innocent party in no worse a position than he would have been in had the Practice Direction or approved protocol been complied with (see *Straker v Tudor Rose (a firm)* [2007] EWCA Civ 368). As to sanctions, see **9.3**.

On the other side of the coin, if proceedings occur, the party awarded his costs should usually be able to recover his pre-action costs (see **14.3.2**), including those costs reasonably incurred in complying with the Practice Direction or approved pre-action protocol (see *Callery v Gray* [2001] EWCA Civ 1246).

In *Cundall Johnson and Partners LLP v Whipps Cross University Hospital NHS Trust* [2007] EWHC 2178, the court held that the claimant's failure to comply with the Pre-action Protocol for Construction and Engineering meant that the proceedings should be stayed in order to facilitate such compliance. Why? Because there was a real possibility of settlement if the parties went through the Protocol processes. It was therefore in their best interests. It might well save both parties from incurring unnecessary litigation costs and lead to an earlier resolution of the dispute between the parties. Also, it was unfair on the defendant to proceed immediately with litigation as it had not yet received a proper summary of the claim.

Paragraph 6.1 of the Practice Direction on Pre-action Conduct makes it clear that in all cases the courts expect the parties to act reasonably in exchanging information and documents, and in trying to avoid the need for proceedings. As para 8.1 states, 'Starting proceedings should usually be a step of last resort, and proceedings should not normally be started when a settlement is still actively being explored.'

3.8 Pre-action correspondence

3.8.1 The letter before claim

When the solicitor is satisfied that the client has a valid claim, he should advise the client and obtain instructions to send a letter to the prospective defendant setting out full details of the claim. This is called a 'letter before claim'. If the claim is of a type which is governed by a pre-action approved protocol, the letter should contain all the information required by the protocol.

Note that in the case of professional negligence, a preliminary notice of claim should be sent first.

Also note that where a business is claiming a debt from an individual, Annex B to the Practice Direction on Pre-action Conduct will apply.

3.8.2 Professional conduct

The letter is normally addressed to the potential defendant in person, but if the solicitor is already aware that the defendant has solicitors acting for him, it should be addressed to the solicitors, as it is a breach of the Solicitors' Code of Conduct (r 10.04) to write directly to a defendant in those circumstances. If the potential defendant is likely to be insured in respect of the claim, the solicitor should ask that the letter is passed on to the insurers and will usually enclose a copy for that purpose.

3.8.3 The letter before claim under the Practice Direction

3.8.3.1 Content

Annex A to the Practice Direction on Pre-action Conduct provides at para 2.1 that the claimant's letter before claim should give concise details about the matter. This should enable the defendant to understand and investigate the issues without needing to request further information. The letter should include:

(1) the claimant's full name and address;

(2) the basis on which the claim is made (ie why the claimant says the defendant is liable);

(3) a clear summary of the facts on which the claim is based;

(4) what the claimant wants from the defendant;

(5) if financial loss is claimed, an explanation of how the amount has been calculated; and

(6) details of any funding arrangement within the meaning of rule 43.2(1)(k) of the CPR [such as a CFA or an AEI (see **2.4.3.2**)] that has been entered into by the claimant.

By para 2.2 the letter should also:

(1) list the essential documents on which the claimant intends to rely;

(2) set out the form of ADR (if any) that the claimant considers the most suitable and invite the defendant to agree to this;

(3) state the date by which the claimant considers it reasonable for a full response to be provided by the defendant; and

(4) identify and ask for copies of any relevant documents not in the claimant's possession and which the claimant wishes to see.

As to para 2.2(3) above, given that the Practice Direction indicates at para 3.1 of Annex A that the defendant should acknowledge the letter before claim within 14 days if a full response cannot be given in the time stated by the claimant, it will usually make sense for the claimant to demand an acknowledgement within 14 days and a full response within a later specified time. The claimant should take into account any need the defendant might have to take advice. As para 3.6 suggests that the defendant should be given at least 14 days to take advice, a claimant might normally give a deadline of 28 days for a full response in most cases.

By para 2.3 of Annex A, unless the defendant is known to be legally represented, the letter should also:

(1) refer the defendant to the Practice Direction and in particular draw attention to paragraph 4 concerning the court's powers to impose sanctions for failure to comply with the Practice Direction; and

(2) inform the defendant that ignoring the letter before claim may lead to the claimant starting proceedings and may increase the defendant's liability for costs.

In our opinion it should also warn the defendant about any claim for interest. Indeed, if interest is now claimed under a contractual provision, the details should have been set out already.

3.8.3.2 Templates

Note that **Appendices B(1) and B(2)** are templates to assist you draft the letter before claim under the Practice Direction on Pre-action Conduct and the letter of claim under the Professional Negligence Pre-action Protocol.

3.8.3.3 Flow diagrams

Note that **Appendices C(2) and C(3)** are flow diagrams that set out the main steps to be taken under the Practice Direction on Pre-action Conduct and the Professional Negligence Pre-action Protocol.

Case Study: The Letter Before Claim

Assume that Mr and Mrs Simpson obtained a report from an accident reconstruction expert who states that the most likely cause of the accident was Mr Templar's speeding. The letter before claim is set out at **Appendix D(2)**. Let us consider how it was drafted.

1. As Mr Templar has not instructed solicitors, the letter is sent to him. Formal notification has been given to his insurers and a copy of that letter is enclosed for his reference.

2. The letter has a heading which is sufficient to enable Mr Templar to identify the claim being made against him. The full names and address of Mr and Mrs Simpson are then given, and Mr Templar can immediately see the purpose of the letter.

3. Under a suitable heading the relevant background facts are briefly stated. You do not have to set out the evidence relied on here. In most cases the events leading up to the dispute will be largely undisputed.

4. The legal basis of the claim is dealt with next. In a contractual dispute you would identify the express and/or implied terms of the contract alleged to have been broken. In a negligence claim, as here, the duty breached by the defendant should be stated.

5. Having explained why the defendant is liable, full details of 'how' must be given; in other words, the factual basis of the claim. For a solicitor who has conducted a thorough case analysis, this will be a matter of translating the factual issues from the grid chart. As a general rule it is best practice to summarise the facts on liability rather than attaching any expert's report at this stage. The question of expert evidence will usually be addressed by the parties later, following the defendant's response.

6. Quantum must then be dealt with clearly and in as much detail as possible. Give an explanation of how the losses claimed flow from the breaches alleged. Where convenient, list each head of damage claimed separately, and give an estimate for any loss claimed where an actual figure is unavailable. As to documents relied on, it is usual to include those that support the amounts claimed, such as receipts, estimates, etc.

7. The letter gives calendar dates for acknowledging and giving a full response, so Mr Templar can be in no doubt. Failing that, Mr Templar is warned of legal proceedings and their potential financial consequences for him.

8. As no approved protocol applies here, a copy of the Practice Direction is enclosed and Mr Templar's attention is drawn to para 4.

9. As Mr and Mrs Simpson are not aware that Mr Templar has any grounds to dispute their claim, it is rather premature in the circumstances to propose any ADR mechanism. Once any full written response is received, with any ADR proposal from Mr Templar, this can be reviewed.

10. As Mr and Mrs Simpson are paying their solicitors privately and have not taken out any AEI cover, no notice of any CFA or AEI has been required.

11. Note how well described sub-headings make this letter clear and easy to read. These also help to ensure that the topics listed in the Practice Direction are covered.

3.8.4 The letter of acknowledgement under the Practice Direction

Annex A to the Practice Direction on Pre-action Conduct provides at para 3 that if the defendant is unable to provide a full written response within 14 days of receipt of the letter before claim, the defendant should, instead, provide a written acknowledgement within 14 days. That acknowledgement should state whether an insurer is or may be involved and the date by which the defendant (or insurer) will provide a full written response, and it may request any further information needed by the defendant to provide a full response.

If a defendant is unable to provide a full response within 14 days of receipt of the letter before claim because he intends to seek advice, the written acknowledgement should so state and include details of from whom the defendant is seeking advice and when the defendant expects to have received that advice and be in a position to provide a full response.

3.8.5 The letter of response under the Practice Direction

Annex A to the Practice Direction on Pre-action Conduct provides at para 4.1 that the defendant's full written response should:

(1)   accept the claim in whole or in part; or

(2)   state that the claim is not accepted.

By para 4.2, unless the defendant accepts the whole of the claim, the response should:

(1)   give reasons why the claim is not accepted, identifying which facts and which parts of the claim (if any) are accepted and which are disputed, and the basis of that dispute;

(2)   state whether the defendant intends to make a counterclaim against the claimant (and, if so, provide information equivalent to a claimant's letter before claim);

(3)   state whether the defendant alleges that the claimant was wholly or partly to blame for the problem that led to the dispute and, if so, summarise the facts relied on;

(4)   state whether the defendant agrees to the claimant's proposals for ADR and if not, state why not and suggest an alternative form of ADR (or state why none is considered appropriate);

(5)   list the essential documents on which the defendant intends to rely;

(6)   enclose copies of documents requested by the claimant, or explain why they will not be provided; and

(7)   identify and ask for copies of any further relevant documents, not in the defendant's possession and which the defendant wishes to see.

Paragraph 4.3 provides that if the defendant (or insurer) does not provide a full response within the period stated in the claimant's letter before claim (or any longer period stated in the defendant's letter of acknowledgement), and a claim is subsequently started, the court is likely to consider that the claimant has complied with the Practice Direction.

Case Study: The Letter of Response

Assume that Mr Templar has instructed solicitors and obtained his own report from an accident reconstruction expert, who states that the most likely cause of the accident was shards of glass on the driveway which caused Mr Templar to lose control of his car. The letter of response is set out at **Appendix D(3)**. Let us briefly consider how it was drafted:

1.   Mr Templar's solicitors acknowledged receipt of the letter before claim within 14 days and agreed a new deadline for a full response.

2.   Under suitable headings the relevant details are given. First, why the claim is denied. Then details of the counterclaim. As an alternative to totally denying the claim, Mr Templar also makes an allegation of contributory negligence against Mr and Mrs Simpson.

3.   The quantum of the counterclaim is then detailed and documents in support of each item are enclosed.

4.   Given that each side has differing expert evidence on liability, Mr Templar suggests that ADR on that issue is inappropriate. He leaves open the question of whether ADR might be suitable to determine the quantum of the claim and/or counterclaim. As the case develops the parties should review the suitability of ADR for any issues that remain in dispute.

3.8.6 Claimant's reply under the Practice Direction

Annex A to the Practice Direction on Pre-action Conduct provides at para 5 that the claimant should provide the documents requested by the defendant within as short a period of time as is practicable, or explain in writing why the documents will not be provided.

If the defendant has made a counterclaim, the claimant should provide information equivalent to the defendant's full response (see **3.8.5**).

3.8.7 Taking stock

After their initial exchange of correspondence, the parties should have a genuine opportunity to resolve the matter without needing to start proceedings. At the very least, it should be possible to establish what issues remain outstanding so as to narrow the scope of any subsequent court proceedings, and therefore limit potential costs.

As para 6.2 of Annex A states, 'If having completed the procedure the matter has not been resolved then the parties should undertake a further review of their respective positions to see if proceedings can still be avoided.'

3.8.8 Instructing experts

Annex C to the Practice Direction on Pre-action Conduct gives guidance on how the parties might approach the question of expert evidence, but first see **3.4** above.

Paragraph 3 reminds the parties that many matters can and should be resolved without the need for advice or evidence from an expert. If an expert is needed, the parties should consider how best to minimise the expense, for example by agreeing to instruct either a single joint expert (ie engaged and paid for jointly by the parties, whether instructed jointly or separately) or an agreed expert (ie the parties agree the identity of the expert but only one party instructs the expert and pays the expert's costs). As to a single joint expert, see **12.13.8**.

Paragraphs 4 to 6 of Annex C lay down the following procedure:

4.   If the parties do not agree that the nomination of a single joint expert is appropriate, then the party seeking the expert evidence (the first party) should give the other party (the second party) a list of one or more experts in the relevant field of expertise whom the first party would like to instruct.

5.   Within 14 days of receipt of the list of experts, the second party may indicate in writing an objection to one or more of the experts listed. If there remains on the list one or more experts who are acceptable, then the first party should instruct an expert from the list.

6.   If the second party objects to all the listed experts, the first party may then instruct an expert of the first party's own choice. Both parties should bear in mind that if proceedings are started the court will consider whether a party has acted reasonably when instructing (or rejecting) an expert.

Note that the appointment of an agreed expert under para 5 does not mean that the second party will necessarily get to see the expert's report. This is because the report belongs as a matter of law to the first party as he instructed the expert. If, having read the report, the first party does not want to rely on it, usually because some of its contents do not support his case, he does not have to give a copy to the second party. This is because the report attracts what is known as legal professional privilege from inspection (see **11.11.1**).

Where the parties go ahead and instruct their own expert or experts pre-action, it will be for the court to determine later if any party can rely on any particular expert's evidence and how expert evidence should be given at a trial (see further **12.13**).

3.9 Pre-action disclosure

In a relatively small number of cases it may be necessary for a prospective claimant to see documents held by a potential defendant who is unwilling to show them voluntarily.

An application for disclosure of documents prior to the start of proceedings is permitted under s 33 of the SCA 1981, or s 52 of the CCA 1984. The application must be supported by evidence, and the procedure is dealt with in r 31.16(3) of the CPR 1998. The court may make an order for disclosure only where:

(a)   the respondent is likely to be a party to subsequent proceedings;

(b)   the applicant is also likely to be a party to the proceedings;

(c)   if proceedings had started, the respondent's duty by way of standard disclosure set out in rule 31.6, would extend to the documents or classes of documents of which the applicant seeks disclosure; and

(d)   disclosure before proceedings have started is desirable in order to—

(i)   dispose fairly of the anticipated proceedings;

(ii)   assist the dispute to be resolved without proceedings; or

(iii)   save costs.

An order under this rule must specify the documents or class of documents which the respondent must disclose, and require him, when making such disclosure, to specify any of those documents which he no longer has, or which he claims the right or duty to withhold from inspection. The order may also specify the time and place for disclosure and inspection to take place.

The most common examples of pre-action disclosure where the claimant is deciding whether or not to make a claim are to be found in personal injury litigation, for example where the other side holds the records of an accident. However, pre-action disclosure may also be ordered in significant commercial cases to try to resolve a dispute without proceedings or to save costs: see, for example, *Burrells Wharf Freeholders Ltd v Galliard Homes Ltd* [1999] 2 EGLR 81.

Disclosure and inspection of documents are dealt with fully in **Chapter 11**.

3.10 Settlement

3.10.1 'Without prejudice' negotiations

A solicitor may soon find that he is in a position to commence negotiations with his opposite number, or with the opponent directly (provided he is not represented) or with an insurance company (eg, in a professional negligence case). The opportunity to negotiate will continue throughout the pre-action stage, the proceedings, and even during the trial itself.

Any negotiations which take place as a part of a genuine attempt to settle a claim are impliedly 'without prejudice'. However, it is preferable to mark any correspondence accordingly, or to clarify at the start of a meeting/telephone negotiation that this is the basis on which you are proceeding. If 'without prejudice' negotiations take place, neither party may rely upon anything said or written in the course of the negotiations for the purpose of proving liability and/or quantum at trial.

> **Example**
>
> A is suing B for damages of £150,000. A's solicitor writes to B's solicitor on a without prejudice basis, saying A will accept £120,000 if that sum is paid within 28 days. B does not accept that proposal.
>
> Neither A nor B can refer to this letter at trial, and A can still try to obtain judgment for the full amount of the claim. Note that if A had marked the letter 'without prejudice save as to costs' then A could unilaterally show the letter to the judge when the judge was deciding the question of costs.

This rule exists to encourage litigants to reach a settlement, if possible. It means that all negotiations which are genuinely aimed at a settlement are excluded from being given in evidence. The rule applies whether the negotiations are oral or in writing, and thus applies to an attendance note of a without prejudice conversation as well as to correspondence. As Oliver LJ stated in *Cutts v Head* [1984] Ch 290:

> That the rule rests, at least in part, upon public policy is clear from many authorities, and the convenient starting point of the inquiry is the nature of the underlying policy. It is that parties should be encouraged so far as possible to settle their disputes without resort to litigation and should not be discouraged by the knowledge that anything that is said in the course of such negotiations (and that includes, of course, as much the failure to reply to an offer as an actual reply) may be used to their prejudice in the course of the proceedings. They should, as it was expressed by Clauson J in *Scott Paper Co v Drayton Paper Works Ltd* (1927) 44 RPC 151, 156, be encouraged fully and frankly to put their cards on the table ... The public policy justification, in truth, essentially rests on the desirability of preventing statements or offers made in the course of negotiations for settlement being brought before the court of trial as admissions on the question of liability ... The rule applies to exclude all negotiations genuinely aimed at settlement whether oral or in writing from being given in evidence.

Although as a matter of good practice the words 'without prejudice' should appear on this type of correspondence, the presence or absence of the words is not conclusive. What is important is that the letter is a genuine attempt to settle the case. If there is a dispute as to whether or not a communication is protected in this way, the court can examine the document (obviously in advance of the trial by someone other than the trial judge) to see whether or not its purpose was to settle the dispute. If it was, it cannot be used or referred to in evidence; if not then, even if it carries the words 'without prejudice', it can.

Once a settlement is concluded, any 'without prejudice' correspondence can be produced in court to show the terms agreed between the parties. This might be necessary if, for example, a dispute arose as to enforcement of an agreed settlement.

As noted in the example above, if a party wishes to reserve the right to draw the trial judge's attention to a without prejudice offer to settle a case on the question of costs then he should mark the offer 'without prejudice save as to costs' (see *Cutts v Head* [1984] Ch 290 and also **3.10.2** below).

Details about the solicitor's authority to negotiate are to be found at **13.1**.

3.10.2 Pre-action offers under Part 36

As we have seen, before litigation starts the parties are encouraged to negotiate and settle the claim. It is open to the parties to make 'without prejudice' offers to settle (see **3.10.1**). Part 36 of CPR 1998 formally recognises this and gives 'teeth' to such offers which are made 'without prejudice save as to costs' (ie, once a trial judge has dealt with the issues of liability and quantum, he can be addressed on Part 36 offers when dealing with the question of costs). Any party can offer to settle a monetary claim for a specified sum, or on express terms for any non-monetary claim. So if litigation occurs and the claimant fails to obtain a judgment more advantageous than a defendant's Part 36 offer, the claimant will usually suffer severe financial penalties (see **13.4.5**). Likewise, if a claimant makes a Part 36 offer and the judgment against the defendant is at least as advantageous to the claimant as the proposals contained in his Part 36 offer, the defendant will usually suffer severe financial penalties (see **13.4.6**).

3.11   Researching the law

Researching the law will often not be necessary. The solicitor will be familiar with the relevant law in the areas in which he practises. Nevertheless, from time to time, unfamiliar points arise which need to be researched.

On a point of law, reference should be made to the recognised practitioner works in the relevant subject; but as textbooks rapidly become out of date, it is essential to check a current authority.

If the point to be researched is procedural then the solicitor needs to refer to the CPR 1998 and Practice Directions themselves, together with any relevant case law on their interpretation and any recognised practitioners' works. For this purpose, it can be useful to look at one of the hard-copy versions of the CPR 1998 which are annotated and contain references to relevant cases and statutory instruments where appropriate.

3.12   Cost–benefit analysis

As we have seen, litigation is the last resort. By r 2.03(6) of the Solicitors' Code of Conduct, a solicitor has a duty to discuss with the client whether the potential outcomes of any legal case will justify the expense or risk involved, including, if relevant, the risk of having to pay an opponent's costs. So, a form of cost–benefit analysis needs to be done at the beginning of a case, and this must be reviewed regularly.

The client will have already incurred legal costs at Stage 1. These will include the costs of investigating the case (whether a potential claim or a defence to such), taking the steps required by the appropriate pre-action protocol and possibly attempting some form of ADR. These costs may include barristers' and experts' fees. Hundreds or thousands of pounds may already have been spent. Once court proceedings start, legal costs will escalate. Have a quick look at the estimate of costs at **Appendix A(12)**. If you just skim-read the description of work done, you can see that court fees will have to be paid, court documents prepared and further time will be spent by the solicitor with the client and witnesses, etc. Also, quickly do the same with the bill of costs at **Appendix A(16)**.

You should now appreciate that a client runs up a solicitor's bill rather like a taxi fare – in other words, the longer a case goes on, the bigger the legal bill. This analogy is rather apt, as the professionals involved in a typical case – solicitors, barristers and experts – will all charge by the hour. Statistics from the Supreme Court Costs Office show that in recent years the average costs recovered by a successful party in a High Court case exceeded £52,000 in the Queen's Bench Division and £107,000 in the Chancery Division; whilst in the county court the figure was £32,000. This gives you a very rough idea of the potential costs that may be incurred.

3.13   Summary of pre-action steps

(1)   Check any professional conduct points:
- conflict of interests
- confidentiality
- identity of client for money laundering regulation purposes.

(2)   Identify the client's objectives:
- what does the client want?
- what might realistically be achieved?

(3) Identify and locate, if necessary, all potential parties.

(4) Check the financial viability of the defendant:

– will the defendant be able to pay any judgment and costs?

– what assets are available?

(5) Check jurisdiction:

– any relevant contractual clause?

– are one or more parties outside the jurisdiction?

(6) Ascertain the limitation period:

– any relevant contractual clause?

(7) Discuss and agree funding with the client:

– explain all options

– send rule 2 letter.

(8) Collect and preserve evidence:

– is pre-action disclosure required?

– is a preservation of evidence order required?

– what witnesses can proofs of evidence be taken from?

– is an expert's report needed?

– are photographs or a site visit needed?

(9) Carry out any necessary legal research.

(10) Do a case analysis:

– have you identified all potential causes of action?

– for each element, have you identified all the factual issues?

– what is the likelihood of success?

– what further evidence is needed?

(11) Write letter of advice to client summarising analysis and advising on options.

(12) Explore possible methods of ADR.

(13) Comply with any approved pre-action protocol requirements or the Practice Direction.

(14) Keep the client informed.

(15) Should the client make a Part 36 offer?

Chapter 4

Alternative Dispute Resolution

This chapter develops further the concept that it may be possible to use less confrontational modes of dispute resolution to reach a quick, cheap and commercially realistic solution. It explains:

(a)   how alternative dispute resolution differs from arbitration and litigation;

(b)   the advantages and disadvantages of alternative dispute resolution;

(c)   the various types of methods available to resolve disputes; and

(d)   the organisations which may be able to help if the parties do choose to use some method of dispute resolution instead of arbitration or litigation.

4.1   The nature of ADR

Alternative dispute resolution (ADR) is a means of resolving disputes by using an independent third party, who may help the parties to reach their own solution but who cannot impose a solution. It is voluntary and without prejudice. The parties choose the process, and either of them can withdraw at any time before a solution is agreed. If either party does not like the proposed solution, he does not have to accept it.

4.1.1   How ADR differs from other forms of dispute resolution

Litigation is not voluntary (save in the sense that the claimant chooses to issue a claim in the first place). Once the case is started, usually neither party can withdraw without paying the opponent's costs (see **13.6**). If the parties are unable to negotiate a settlement, the court will impose its own solution. The winner will enforce that solution.

Arbitration is voluntary in the sense that the parties voluntarily entered into an arbitration agreement. When a relevant dispute arises, however, one party can force the other to arbitrate against his will because of the original contractual agreement to do so, provided it is enforceable. The arbitrator will impose a solution which the winner can enforce. Of course, parties can always voluntarily take a dispute to arbitration. Strictly speaking, arbitration is a form of ADR. We have already dealt with it at **2.9.1** and shall not consider it further in any detail in this chapter.

Negotiation is both voluntary and non-binding, but it is not the same as ADR. In a negotiation there is no independent third party. The negotiators are identified with their respective 'sides' and each may see the case only from their side's point of view. In ADR, there is a third party who is totally independent and who can see both sides' points of view.

4.1.2   The independent third party

The independence of the third party is an essential feature of ADR, as is the fact that he cannot impose a solution. As the parties know that he is independent and cannot do anything to harm them, they are more likely to trust him and be open with him. They are less likely to be aggressive towards each other in his presence. They will not want to be seen by him as an obstacle towards a settlement and are likely to be more accommodating in his presence. He may therefore be able to defuse the dispute and make settlement more likely. A further advantage is that the independent third party not only will be trained to act as a neutral, but also should have any necessary industry knowledge required to understand the dispute.

The third party can help the parties to settle their dispute in another way. A commercially-minded neutral may come up with ideas which the parties might not have thought of and which solve the problem without either side losing face.

4.2 Advantages of ADR

The CPR 1998 specifically recognise the advantages of ADR. Rule 1.4(2)(e) provides that the court may further the overriding objective of dealing with cases justly by

> encouraging the parties to use an alternative dispute resolution procedure if the court considers that appropriate and facilitating the use of such procedure.

In *Practice Statement (Alternative Dispute Resolution) (No 2)* [1996] 1 WLR 1024, Waller J said:

> ... the settlement of actions by means of ADR (i) significantly helps to save litigants the ever mounting cost of bringing their actions to trial; (ii) saves them the delay of litigation in reaching finality in their disputes; (iii) enables them to achieve settlement of their disputes while preserving their existing commercial relationships and market reputation; (iv) provides them with a wider range of settlement solutions than those offered by litigation; and (v) is likely to make a substantial contribution to the more efficient use of judicial resources ...

Arbitration and ADR procedures are confidential. However, court proceedings are usually conducted in open court. The media can attend and are able to report on most proceedings. As a general rule, anyone can obtain a copy of a statement of case, order or judgment that is on a court file (see CPR 1998, r 5.4C(1)).

Some of these points are amplified below.

4.2.1 Cheapness and speed

Apart from the fact that an independent third party may find it easier to lead the parties to a settlement, ADR has many other attractions. It can be significantly cheaper than both arbitration and litigation. This is because it is quicker. A skilled neutral can, in most cases which are suitable for ADR, help the parties to resolve their dispute in a relatively short period of time.

The parties do, of course, have to pay the third party for his services. They will usually instruct lawyers to help them on the day, and they will have to pay those lawyers. If ADR works, however, there will be a significant reduction in the amount of time the lawyers spend in preparing and presenting the case. This will save costs. Even more importantly, the client saves on the indirect costs involved in its employees and executives having to spend time reading court documents, consulting lawyers and attending court.

However, clients should not be given the impression that ADR comes at bargain basement prices. Any lawyer representing the client will want to be fully prepared, and that will take time (including the client's time in dealing with the lawyer's enquiries) and will cost money.

4.2.2 Flexibility

Speed and cheapness are the principal attractions of ADR, but it is also very flexible. The parties can choose one of several forms of ADR. They can choose the procedure to be followed in conjunction with their chosen neutral. They do not have to comply with any statutes or rules of court. There is not even any case law limiting what the parties or the neutral can do.

4.2.3   Preserving a business relationship

Arbitration and ADR share the virtue of privacy. Alternative dispute resolution is also ideal for cases where the parties to the dispute are going to have to continue to deal with each other. The fact that they have chosen a non-confrontational method of solving their problem makes it much easier for them to continue their relationship, since the solution is theirs and has not been imposed upon them.

4.2.4   Commercial reality

A third party unconnected with the dispute may be able to assist the parties to arrive at realistic and workable terms of settlement.

4.3   Disadvantages of ADR

4.3.1   It does not bind the parties to the procedure

As a general principle, no one can be forced to resolve a dispute by any form of ADR against their wishes. If one party suggests ADR, the other parties do not have to agree; and even if the parties have started to resolve a dispute by ADR, most ADR agreements allow any party to withdraw at any stage before a solution has been agreed. It will then be necessary to resort to litigation or, if there is an arbitration agreement, to arbitration.

The court can stay litigation which has been commenced in breach of an agreed method of resolving disputes. This is the case even if that method is not technically an arbitration agreement under the Arbitration Act 1996. Indeed, the courts have increasingly stayed proceedings for ADR to take place, whether or not pursuant to a contractual agreement. For example, in *Cable & Wireless v IBM UK Ltd* [2002] BLR 89, the parties were directed to pursue a previously agreed ADR method. The court held that there were strong case management grounds for allowing the reference to ADR to proceed. Any delay was not such that it would be unfair to impose the ADR procedure.

4.3.2   The awards are not so easily enforceable

There is no equivalent of s 66 of the Arbitration Act 1996 (see **2.9.1**) enabling ADR awards to be enforced as if they were court judgments. However, if the parties do agree to terms suggested as a result of ADR, they have entered into a contract. If one of the parties does not carry out that contract, he can be sued for breach of contract, and the claimant would usually expect to obtain summary judgment (see **10.5.2**) under Part 24 of the CPR 1998 without any difficulty.

It is standard practice in many forms of ADR to provide that no agreement will be binding upon the parties unless it is put in writing and signed by the parties.

A party who has commenced court proceedings but then resolved the dispute by ADR, can record the agreement reached in a consent order, which can be enforced by the usual methods.

4.3.3   The facts may not be fully disclosed

The speed of ADR has an associated disadvantage. Because there is no equivalent of disclosure, there is a risk that the parties may resolve the dispute without knowing all the facts. This may lead to the wrong decision. Many businessmen, however, take the view that a quick decision, even if it is not completely accurate, is better than wasting time and money on a protracted dispute in order to get a more correct decision. They often feel that litigation is a lottery anyway.

4.3.4   ADR is not appropriate for all cases

Alternative dispute resolution is not appropriate in the following cases:

(a)   where the client needs an injunction (though afterwards ADR may become appropriate);

(b)   where there is no dispute. If the case is a simple debt collection matter, the creditor should issue a claim form followed by a summary judgment application (see **10.5.2**), or consider insolvency proceedings (see **15.5.6**);

(c)   where the client needs a ruling on a point of law.

4.4   Types of ADR

4.4.1   Mediation and conciliation

Mediation and conciliation are usually interchangeable terms. For ease of reference, the term 'mediation' will be used to cover both processes in this chapter.

In a typical mediation, the third party who has been selected as mediator will have received written statements from both parties. Following that, the mediator will discuss the case with the parties. They will tell him what they think about each party's case on a without prejudice basis. The mediator will not pass on to the other party information which is confidential, unless he is given permission to do so.

These discussions help the mediator to identify the real areas of disagreement and the points which are most important to the respective parties. He can then move the parties towards constructive solutions to the problem.

The method of mediation described above assumes that the mediator and the parties will meet in the same building. This enables things to be dealt with quickly because, if necessary, the parties can meet face to face to iron out their differences. There are, however, other forms of mediation. The parties do not have to meet. The matter can be dealt with by correspondence and telephone conversations.

It is vital that the parties are represented at the mediation by people who have authority to instruct their lawyers to reach agreement.

4.4.2   'Med-arb'

Under this form of ADR, the parties agree to submit their dispute to mediation and that, if this does not work, they will refer the matter to arbitration. They may, if they wish, use the person who has been acting as their mediator as their arbitrator. This will save costs, because the arbitrator will already know the facts of the case. There is a risk, however, that during the mediation, he will have become privy to confidential information belonging to one of the parties. This would compromise his position as arbitrator, so any agreement for 'med-arb' should give either party the right to object to the mediator becoming the arbitrator.

4.4.3   'Mini-trial' or 'structured settlement procedure'

Under this procedure, the parties appoint a neutral who will sit as chairman of a tribunal composed of himself and a senior representative of each of the parties. These representatives may not be immediately connected with the dispute and should have authority to reach such compromise as they see fit. They will then hear and/or read the cases of the two parties (sometimes with an expert), after which they will negotiate with each other with the help of the independent arbiter.

4.4.4   Expert appraisal

The parties can refer all or part of their dispute to an expert in the disputed field for his opinion. His opinion is not binding on the parties but could influence their approach to subsequent negotiations. It will be for the parties to choose the appropriate procedure, which could even involve a short trial before the expert makes his recommendation.

4.4.5   Judicial appraisal

The Centre for Dispute Resolution (CEDR) has a scheme whereby former judges and senior counsel are available to give a quick preliminary view on the legal position, having heard representations from both parties. It is a matter for agreement between the parties as to whether this opinion is to be binding on them or not.

4.4.6   Expert determination

Expert determination is a halfway house between arbitration and ADR. As in arbitration, the parties select an expert to decide the case for them. They agree to accept his decision, and if one fails to do so, the other can sue for breach of contract. The expert's decision cannot, however, be enforced as a court order, and he does not have the powers of an arbitrator under the Arbitration Act 1996. Also, unlike an arbitrator, he can be sued in negligence by a party who thinks his decision was wrong.

4.4.7   Final offer arbitration

The parties can instruct their chosen neutral that they will both make an offer of the terms on which they will settle, and that he must choose one of those two offers and no other solution. Neither party can afford to make an unrealistic offer, because that will mean that the neutral will choose the opponent's offer. Thus, at least in theory, the offers are likely to be realistic.

4.4.8   Early neutral evaluation

As its name suggests, this method allows the parties to instruct their chosen neutral to make a preliminary assessment of the facts at an early stage in the dispute. Normally the parties submit written case summaries and supporting documents. The evaluator then makes a recommendation. This very often helps the parties to negotiate a settlement (or move to another ADR method), avoiding the expense of litigation.

4.4.9   Ombudsman and similar schemes

The number of ombudsmen schemes has grown over the years as the Government, as well as various public and private sector organisations, has sought to resolve complaints without litigation. Thus you can find schemes covering such diverse matters as financial services, pensions, police, telecommunications, local government, housing, estate agents, legal services, and the like. Full details can be found at the Ombudsman Schemes in the UK website www.bioa.org.uk/index.html.

Some service and goods providers also offer similar schemes. Probably the best known is the travel industry ABTA arbitration scheme.

4.5   Organisations providing ADR

Anyone can provide help in resolving disputes, but the job is not as easy as it sounds. It should be done by someone who has been trained. The two main organisations that have pioneered ADR in commercial matters in this country are the CEDR and ADR Group.

The CEDR is an independent, non profit-making organisation promoting ADR, which runs training courses and maintains a panel of neutrals.

The ADR Group is a private company which undertakes mediation and training, and which has established a network of mediators in firms of solicitors throughout the country.

Two other organisations which are very active in the field of ADR, although their principal *raison d'être* arose from other functions, are the Chartered Institute of Arbitrators and the Academy of Experts.

Lastly, there is Mediation UK, whose general services include all forms of mediation.

Many professional bodies, like the Royal Institution of Chartered Surveyors (RICS), provide ADR services for disputes involving their members.

The judges of the commercial list in the High Court may be prepared to offer their services to help litigants to resolve their disputes without going to trial.

4.6   Using ADR

Parties to a dispute can always reach an ad hoc agreement, when the dispute arises, to use any form of ADR they see fit to solve their problems. It is more proactive, however, to agree in the original contract that, if any dispute does arise between the parties, they will resolve it by some specified form of ADR.

Such contracts may not be effective (see **4.3.1**), because a party cannot be forced to reach a consensual solution, but they do give the parties an opportunity to resolve their disputes peaceably. There is a very strong case for recommending that existing contracts which include an arbitration agreement should be amended, so that the agreement provides for mediation before the parties go to formal arbitration (which they would do only if mediation failed).

4.6.1   Disclosure obligations

An agreement to use ADR should include clauses dealing with some of the potential pitfalls associated with ADR. The parties should decide whether to have a clause requiring full disclosure. The drawback of such a clause is that the more information the parties have to provide to each other, the longer the proceedings may take and the more expensive they will be. Its advantage is that it would be possible to set aside any settlement reached, as a result of ADR, on discovering that one of the parties had concealed vital information. To prevent vexatious applications to set aside any settlement, it might be wise to stipulate in the disclosure clause that a settlement can be challenged only for fundamental non-disclosure of matters which would significantly have affected the result of the ADR process.

4.6.2   Confidentiality

A confidentiality clause in the agreement will encourage full disclosure. The mediator is always under a duty of confidentiality, but the parties will be more likely to disclose information to each other if they know that the other party has agreed not to divulge the information to anyone else. However, if the parties are commercial rivals, who need to keep their methods secret from each other, disclosure and confidentiality clauses are pointless.

4.6.3   Other matters

An ADR agreement should explain how the mediator or other arbiter will be appointed and specify the procedure he should follow. It should also specify that the representatives who attend any ADR process must have full authority to settle the dispute there and then.

4.7   Choosing ADR

A solicitor should discuss with the client the possible uses of ADR whenever a dispute arises in a commercial matter. If the client is willing (or has already agreed) to use ADR, it should be used unless it is obviously inappropriate, for example because an injunction is required, or the other party cannot be trusted to comply with an award or to cooperate in the process. There is no point, however, in proceeding with ADR if it looks like failing. In such cases, at the first sign of non-cooperation or lack of trust (eg, where the opponent will not help in the selection of the neutral), litigation or arbitration should be used. This does not mean abandoning ADR altogether – it may be appropriate to continue with ADR in conjunction with litigation, using the latter as a spur to cooperation with the former.

Not surprisingly, given r 1.4(2)(e) (see **4.2**), parties who do choose to litigate may well receive judicial encouragement (and sometimes a degree of pressure) at the case management conference (see **9.6.3.2**) and other hearings to attempt ADR.

Chapter 5

Commencing Proceedings

5.1 Choice of court

Although the CPR 1998 apply to both the High Court and the county courts, in some cases a client will have a choice as to the court in which to start proceedings. The general rule is that county courts have unlimited jurisdiction to hear all tort and contract cases. This is because PD 7, para 2.1 provides that proceedings may not be started in the High Court unless the value of the claim is more than £25,000. So, if the value of the case is £25,000 or less, it must be started in a county court. If the value of the case exceeds £25,000 then it can, if the client so wishes, be started in the High Court. In some cases, the High Court has exclusive jurisdiction, but those types of cases are beyond the scope of this book.

Where a claimant has the choice of issuing in the High Court or county court then, by PD 7, para 2.4, a claim should be started in the High Court if by reason of:

(1)   the financial value of the claim and the amount in dispute, and/or

(2)   the complexity of the facts, legal issues, remedies or procedures involved, and/or

(3)   the importance of the outcome of the claim to the public in general,

the claimant believes that the claim ought to be dealt with by a High Court judge.

A claim should therefore be commenced in the High Court only if that is where the case should be tried. Unless the case is complex or important to the general public (not just the parties themselves), it is unlikely to be tried in the Central Office of the Royal Courts of Justice if the claim is less than £50,000 (see PD 29, para 2.2). As a rough rule of thumb, therefore, particularly in London, you should issue in the county court for claims below £50,000.

There are approximately 200 county courts situated throughout England and Wales, and in most cases the claimant can issue proceedings in any court he chooses. Similarly, if the claimant is issuing proceedings in the High Court, he has the choice of issuing in any of the District Registries of the High Court, which are usually situated in the same building as the county court, or the Central Office of the High Court in London. Most claimants will choose to start proceedings in the court closest to their home or business.

The High Court has three divisions, namely:

(a)   the Queen's Bench Division, which includes the Admiralty Court and the Commercial Court;

(b)   the Chancery Division, which includes the Companies Court and the Patents Court; and

(c)   the Family Division.

If the claimant is claiming damages for breach of contract or tort, the claim should be commenced in the Queen's Bench Division. The Queen's Bench Division produces a *Guide to Litigation*, which is particularly aimed at those litigating in the Central Office.

The Commercial Court, which is part of the Queen's Bench Division, sits in London, and there are separate mercantile lists in Birmingham, Bristol, Cardiff, Chester, Leeds, Liverpool, Manchester and Newcastle for cases relating to commercial transactions. The Commercial Court produces a *Commercial Court Guide*, which gives guidance on the day-to-day practice in that court. Also see CPR 1998, Part 58.

The Chancery Division of the High Court deals with such matters as trusts, contentious probate business, partnership claims, disputes about land, and landlord and tenant disputes. A claim should be commenced in the Chancery Division if the claimant is claiming an equitable remedy such as specific performance, or if it is an intellectual property claim, such as copyright or passing-off. As with Queen's Bench proceedings, a Chancery claim can be commenced either in the Central Office in London or in a District Registry. Chancery matters can also be commenced in a county court.

The Family Division deals with High Court family matters which are outside the scope of this book.

Part 30 of the CPR 1998 deals with the powers of the High Court and county court to transfer matters from one court to another.

There are also provisions for automatic transfer to the defendant's home court in certain circumstances (see **9.5**), and provisions for transfer from Central Office to a county court if the claim is worth less than £50,000 (see above).

Case Study: Choice of Court

Negotiations between the parties' solicitors fail. Experts disagree over liability. Whilst some items of quantum are agreed, subject to liability, Mr Templar's expert does not agree that Mr and Mrs Simpson's extension needs demolishing and rebuilding. He is of the opinion that it can be repaired.

Court proceedings could be started by either party. Where would these be started, and why? We know from the receipts and estimates that Mr and Mrs Simpson's claim is in the region of £185,000. Likewise, Mr Templar's documents reveal a claim of around £70,000. In either case the figures are well in excess of the minimum amount of £25,000 required to commence a claim in the High Court (PD 7, para 2.1), but are the criteria in PD 7, para 2.4 satisfied? The case is not factually complicated, but there appear to be some complex expert issues. The case has no general importance to the public. Arguably the value of either claim is sufficient to satisfy para 2.4(1) and justify issuing the proceedings in the High Court. There is no good reason why the case should be tried in the Central Office and so proceedings should be started in the local District Registry where this will be more convenient for the parties and solicitors.

5.2   Court personnel

The great bulk of both county court and High Court work is dealt with by district judges and, for matters proceeding in the Central Office in London, masters. These deal with the majority of interim applications (see **Chapter 10**) and also have jurisdiction to hear trials where the amount involved does not exceed £25,000. Trials for amounts in excess of that figure are heard by circuit judges in a county court and by High Court judges in the High Court. Under Part 3 of the CPR 1998, the judges have extensive case management powers (see **Chapter 9**).

5.3 Issuing proceedings

A party who wishes to start proceedings must complete a claim form in the prescribed way (PD 7, para 3.1), which should either be handed in or sent to the court office. Proceedings are commenced when the court 'issues' the claim form by sealing it with the court seal (although for limitation purposes, the relevant date is the date when the court receives the claim form: see **2.5.2**). A copy of a claim form appears at **Appendix A(1)**.

5.3.1 Completing the claim form

In addition to the points set out here, the Court Service provides detailed guidance notes on the completion of the claim form which appear at **Appendix A(1)**.

5.3.1.1 Claimant and defendant details

The person who makes the claim is described as the claimant, and the person against whom the claim is made is the defendant.

Practice Direction 16, para 2 provides as follows:

2.2   The claim form must include an address at which the claimant resides or carries on business. This paragraph applies even though the claimant's address for service is the business address of his solicitor.

2.3   Where the defendant is an individual, the claimant should (if he is able to do so) include in the claim form an address at which the defendant resides or carries on business. This paragraph applies even though the defendant's solicitors have agreed to accept service on the defendant's behalf.

2.4   Any address which is provided for the purpose of these provisions must include a postcode, unless the court orders otherwise. Postcode information may be obtained from www.royalmail.com or the Royal Mail Address Management Guide.

2.5   If the claim form does not show a full address, including postcode, at which the claimant(s) and defendant(s) reside or carry on business, the claim form will be issued but will be retained by the court and will not be served until the claimant has supplied a full address, including postcode, or the court has dispensed with the requirement to do so. The court will notify the claimant.

2.6   The claim form must be headed with the title of the proceedings, including the full name of each party. The full name means, in each case where it is known:

(a)   in the case of an individual, his full unabbreviated name and title by which he is known;

(b)   in the case of an individual carrying on business in a name other than his own name, the full unabbreviated name of the individual, together with the title by which he is known, and the full trading name (for example, John Smith 'trading as' or 'T/as' 'JS Autos');

(c)   in the case of a partnership (other than a limited liability partnership (LLP))—

(i)   where partners are being sued in the name of the partnership, the full name by which the partnership is known, together with the words '(A Firm)'; or

(ii)   where partners are being sued as individuals, the full unabbreviated name of each partner and the title by which he is known;

(d)   in the case of a company or limited liability partnership registered in England and Wales, the full registered name, including suffix (plc, limited, LLP, etc), if any;

(e)   in the case of any other company or corporation, the full name by which it is known, including suffix where appropriate.

It is important to note the effect of para 2.5 above. Whilst the court will issue a claim form that lacks service address details, it will not be served until the claimant has supplied a full address, including postcode, or the court has dispensed with the requirement to do so. If the claimant cannot supply full service address details, an application to dispense with such should be made when filing the claim form.

Where one of the parties is not an individual over the age of 18, or is not suing or being sued in his personal capacity, special considerations may apply (see **5.4**). The Court Service guidance notes (see **5.3.1**) set out how these should be reflected in the claim form.

5.3.1.2   Brief details of claim

The claim form must contain a concise statement of the nature of the claim and specify the remedy that the claimant is seeking (see r 16.2(1) and the notes on completing the claim form).

5.3.1.3   The amount claimed/value

Rule 16.2(1)(cc) requires that where the claimant's only claim is for a specified sum, the claim form must contain a statement of the interest accrued on that sum (see also **2.7** and **7.2.1.5**).

Rule 16.3(2) requires that if the claim is for money, the claim form must either state the amount claimed or, if the claim is for an unspecified amount of money, whether or not the claimant expects to recover:

(a)   not more than £5,000; or

(b)   more than £5,000 but not more than £25,000; or

(c)   more than £25,000; or

(d)   that the claimant cannot say how much he expects to recover.

This information assists the county court in allocating the claim to the multi-track, fast track or small claims track, as appropriate. Allocation of cases in the county court is dealt with in detail in **Chapter 9**.

5.3.1.4   High Court cases

Practice Direction 7, para 3.6 provides that if a claim for an unspecified sum of money is started in the High Court, the claim form must:

(a)   state that the claimant expects to recover more than £25,000; or

(b)   state that some enactment provides that the claim may only be commenced in the High Court and specify that enactment; or

(c)   state that the claim is to be in one of the specialist High Court lists (see CPR 1998, Part 49) and specify that list.

The Notes for Claimant on completing the claim form (see **Appendix A(1)**) suggest a form of words such as 'I wish my claim to issue in the High Court because', followed by one of the above grounds (eg, 'I expect to recover more than £25,000'). Arguably, the Notes are aimed at litigants in person, and most solicitors, when relying on the value exceeding £25,000 as giving the High Court jurisdiction, will simply put, 'The Claimant expects to recover more than £25,000'.

5.3.1.5   The court fee

The claimant is obliged to pay a fee on issue of the claim form, based on the value of the claim. The amount of the fee should be stated on the front of the form. Details of court fees are contained in the Guide to Supreme Court Fees and the Guide to County Court Fees (which are available on the Court Service website www.courtservice.gov.uk).

5.3.1.6   Solicitor's costs

If the claim is for a specified amount of money, and was issued by a solicitor, the form should also include a figure for solicitor's costs. These are fixed costs payable by the defendant, in addition to the court fee, should he admit the claim. Fixed costs are dealt with in Part 45 of the CPR 1998.

5.3.1.7 Issues under the Human Rights Act 1998

The claimant is obliged to state whether the claim does or will include any issues under the Human Rights Act 1998.

5.3.1.8 The particulars of claim

The details of the claimant's claim, known as the particulars of claim, must be set out either in the claim form itself, or in a separate document that is served either with the claim form or within 14 days of service of the claim form. Care is needed in the drafting of the particulars of claim, and this issue is considered in **Chapter 7**.

5.3.2 The statement of truth

The CPR 1998 require that various documents, including the claim form, are verified by a statement of truth (see CPR 1998, Part 22). If the particulars of claim are served separately, they must also be so verified and the statement of truth in the claim form should be amended to read, 'the facts stated in this claim form are true'.

Who can sign the statement of truth? Practice Direction 22, para 3.1 gives this answer:

> In a statement of case, a response or an application notice, the statement of truth must be signed by:
> (1)   the party or his litigation friend [see **5.4.1**], or
> (2)   the legal representative of the party or litigation friend.

So how should you draft a statement of truth in a statement of case? Practice Direction 22, para 2.1 states as follows:

> [I believe] [The (*claimant or as may be*) believes] that the facts stated in this [*name document being verified*] are true.

5.3.2.1 Signed by the client

An individual signing as a party or on behalf of a party, eg a partner or company director, should express his own personal belief and sign, 'I believe . . .'

Who can sign on behalf of a partnership? Practice Direction 22, para 3.6 states:

> Where the document is to be verified on behalf of a partnership, those who may sign the statement of truth are:
> (1)   any of the partners, or
> (2)   a person having the control or management of the partnership business.

Who can sign on behalf of a company? Practice Direction 22, para 3.4 requires that it must be signed by a person holding a senior position in the company, and para 3.5 states that such a person may be a director, the treasurer, secretary, chief executive, manager or other officer of the company.

You should note that some practitioners draft a statement of truth for a company officer to sign as, 'The [claimant or defendant etc] believes', rather than as 'I believe'. There is nothing in the CPR indicating that either version is right or wrong. Whatever way it is drafted, the individual signing on behalf of the company is assuming personal responsibility. If he does not have an honest belief in the truth of the contents of the document, he could be prosecuted for contempt of court.

Where an individual signs on behalf of a party, it is best practice and follows the model set out on various court forms to state that the person has authority to do so, ie by adding 'I am duly authorised by the [party] to sign this statement'.

5.3.2.2   Signed by a solicitor

Where a solicitor signs on behalf of the client, he should sign 'The [party] believes . . .'.

Practice Direction 22, para 3.7 clarifies that the statement refers to the client's belief and not the solicitor's. In addition the solicitor must state the capacity in which he signs and the name of his firm, where appropriate. However, by PD 22, para 3.10, note that the solicitor must sign in his own name and not that of his firm.

Example

The Claimant believes that the facts stated in these particulars of claim are true. I am duly authorised by the Claimant to sign this statement.

Signed: *Lawrence Hodges*

Lawrence Hodges, assistant solicitor with Singleton Trumper & Co, solicitors acting for the Claimant in these proceedings.

Where a legal representative signs a statement of truth, para 3.8 of PD 22 states that this will be taken as his statement:

(a)   that the client on whose behalf he has signed had authorised him to do so;

(b)   that before signing he had explained to the client that in signing the statement of truth he would be confirming the client's belief that the facts stated in the document were true; and

(c)   that before signing he had informed the client of the possible consequences to the client if it should subsequently appear that the client did not have an honest belief in the truth of those facts.

The consequences referred to in para 3.8(3) above are that proceedings for contempt of court may be brought against the client: see r 32.14.

5.3.2.3   What if the statement is omitted?

By PD 22, para 4, if a statement of case (which includes a claim form) is not verified by a statement of truth, it remains effective unless the court strikes it out, which the court may do on its own initiative or on the application of another party. If the statement of case is not struck out, the claimant will not, however, be allowed to rely on its contents as evidence (for example, on an interim application: see **Chapter 10**).

5.3.3   Compliance with a pre-action protocol or Practice Direction

Paragraph 9.7 of the Practice Direction on Pre-action Conduct (see **Chapter 3**) requires the claimant to state in the claim form (or the particulars of claim: see **Chapter 7**) whether he has complied with Sections III and IV of the Practice Direction or any approved protocol that applies.

Case Study: Completing the Claim Form

Let us briefly consider how the claim form would be completed in the case study.

1.   Mr and Mrs Simpson start proceedings. Their solicitors have decided to issue the claim in the nearest District Registry of the High Court (see **5.1** above). The heading will therefore be as follows:

In the High Court of Justice
Queen's Bench Division
Weyford District Registry

The court will assign a claim number when the claim form is issued. This information must be included on the claim form and all subsequent statements of case (PD 7, para 4.2).

2. The Parties need to be described accurately. Here there are two claimants, both of whom are individuals. Practice Direction 16, para 2.6(a) requires that their full names and title should be given as follows:

Mr William Ulysses Simpson (1)

Mrs Rupinder Simpson (2)

In addition their full address, including a postcode, should be stated (PD 16, paras 2.2 and 2.4).

The same information is required for the defendant. His name and full address will also appear in the box in the bottom left-hand corner of the claim form.

3. Brief details of claim and remedy sought.

This might read: 'The Claimants claim damages arising out of the Defendant's negligent driving on 2 August 2010.'

4. Value.

This information will help the court when managing the case. As the claim is for damages (an unspecified claim) exceeding £25,000, it should state: 'The Claimants expect to recover more than £25,000.'

5. The court fee payable on issue is based on the value of the claim – full details are on the court service website. There is no need for a figure to be inserted in the 'Solicitor's costs' box as this is an unspecified claim and any costs awarded will be assessed by the court.

6. Whilst particulars of claim could be inserted on the form, these will be prepared separately. If they are to be served with the claim form the words 'to follow' should be deleted.

7. A statement of truth will be required as the claim form is a statement of case and r 22.1(1)(a) requires that all statements of case should be verified by a statement of truth.

8. Either here or in the particulars of claim, the claimants should state whether or not they have complied with Sections III and IV of the Practice Direction on Pre-action Conduct.

9. An address for service within the jurisdiction must be given. As solicitors act for Mr and Mrs Simpson and are instructed to accept service of court documents on their behalf, the name, address and reference details of the firm should be given.

5.4 Parties to the proceedings

If the claimant and defendant are both individuals of full age, suing or being sued in their personal capacity, there are no special considerations. As much of the full, unabbreviated name of the individual party should be stated as possible (including first, middle and last names, and the title by which the party is known, eg Mr Thomas Patrick Clark, Dr Laurie J Brown, Professor Mary Banister, etc). In other cases, there may be special considerations because of the nature of the party concerned, for example in cases where the claimant or defendant is a child, a protected party, a sole trader, a partnership or a limited company. These special rules are considered below.

5.4.1 Children and protected parties

A child is a person aged under 18, and a protected party is a person who is incapable of managing and administering his own affairs (including court proceedings) because of a mental disorder, as defined by the Mental Capacity Act 2005. Part 21 of the CPR 1998 contains special provisions relating to these types of litigant.

5.4.1.1   The requirement for a 'litigation friend'

The Rules require a protected party to have a litigation friend to conduct proceedings, whether as claimant or defendant, on his behalf. A child must also have a litigation friend to conduct proceedings on his behalf, unless the court orders otherwise. In the case of protected parties, the litigation friend will usually be a person authorised under the 2005 Act to conduct legal proceedings in the name of a protected party; and in the case of a child, the litigation friend will normally be a parent or guardian.

If a solicitor is unsure whether or not his client falls within the definition of a protected party, the solicitor may seek an order of the court directing that the Official Solicitor consider the evidence, appoint a medical expert and appear at the hearing: see *Lindsay v Wood* [2006] EWHC 2895.

In relation to proceedings against a child or protected party, a person may not, without permission of the court, make an application against a child or protected party before proceedings have started, or take any step in proceedings except:

(a)   issuing and serving a claim form; or

(b)   applying for the appointment of a litigation friend under r 21.6.

5.4.1.2   Steps to be taken by a litigation friend

A person authorised under the 2005 Act to act as a litigation friend on behalf of a protected party must file an official copy of the document which is his authority to act. Otherwise, a litigation friend acting on behalf of a protected party or child must file a certificate of suitability. If acting on behalf of a claimant, this must be done when making the claim; and if acting on behalf of a defendant, it must be done when first taking a step in the proceedings. The certificate of suitability must state that the proposed litigation friend:

(a)   consents to act;

(b)   believes the party to be a child or protected party (with reasons and medical evidence);

(c)   can fairly and competently conduct proceedings on behalf of the party;

(d)   has no adverse interest;

(e)   if acting as a litigation friend for a claimant, undertakes to pay any costs which the claimant may be ordered to pay in the proceedings. Note that a counterclaim (see **Chapter 8**) is treated like a claim for the purposes of the costs undertakings.

The litigation friend must serve the certificate of suitability on every person on whom the claim form should be served, and must then file a certificate of service when filing the certificate of suitability.

5.4.1.3   Cessation of appointment of a litigation friend

In relation to a child, the appointment of a litigation friend ceases when the child becomes 18. The appointment of a litigation friend for a protected party does not cease when the party ceases to be a protected party. It continues until the appointment is ended by a court order sought by the former protected party, the litigation friend, or any party.

5.4.1.4   Settlement of cases brought by or against a child or protected party

Special provisions apply where a case involving a child or protected party is settled. Such a settlement is not valid unless it has been approved by the court. Before the court approves a settlement, it will need to know:

(a)   whether and to what extent the defendant admits liability;

(b)   the age and occupation (if any) of the child or protected party;

(c)   that the litigation friend approves of the proposed settlement.

The application to the court must, in most cases, be supported by a legal opinion on the merits of the settlement and the instructions on which it was based. Although the application will be heard in private, the formal approval of the settlement will usually be given publicly in open court – see *Beathem v Carlisle Hospitals NHS Trust* (1999) *The Times*, 20 May.

If a claim by or against a child or protected party is settled before proceedings are begun, and proceedings are issued solely to obtain the court's approval of the settlement, the claim must include a request to the court for approval of the settlement and must be made under Part 8 of the CPR 1998 (see **8.4**).

If money is recovered by or on behalf of or for the benefit of a child or protected party, the money should be dealt with in accordance with the directions of the court. The court will usually direct that the money be paid into the High Court for investment. In relation to a child, the money will be paid out when the child becomes 18.

5.4.2 Partnerships

5.4.2.1 Where a partnership is the claimant

Partnerships must normally sue in the name of the firm, rather than by naming individual partners. Pursuant to PD 7, para 5A.3, it is usually easier and more convenient to use the name under which the partnership carried on business at the time the cause of action accrued, eg 'ABC & Co (a firm)'.

5.4.2.2 Where a partnership is the defendant

Partnerships must normally be sued in the name of the firm rather than in the names of the individual partners. Practice Direction 7, para 5A.3 provides that where a partnership has a name, unless it is inappropriate to do so, claims must be brought against the name under which that partnership carried on business at the time the cause of action accrued. In practice, it is usually simpler and more efficient to sue a partnership in the name of the firm, especially as service on the firm can be effected by serving any one of the partners, or by serving the firm at its principal place of business (see **5.5**).

5.4.3 Sole traders

5.4.3.1 Where a sole trader is the claimant

It is generally accepted practice that sole traders should sue in their own name and not in any trading or business name. However, there is no objection to adding any trading name, eg 'Mary Clarke trading as Clarke's Designs'.

5.4.3.2 Where a sole trader is the defendant

By PD 7, para 5C.2, sole traders carrying on business within the jurisdiction and under a name other than their own can be sued in that name. If the trader is sued under his trade name, he will be referred to in the heading to the claim as, for example, 'Anthony Tucker T/A Marble Designs'. Note that T/A is an acceptable abbreviation of 'trading as'. If the claimant does not know the name of the sole trader, he may sue naming the defendant under his business name, eg 'Welcome Homes (a trading name)'.

5.4.4 Limited companies

5.4.4.1 Where a limited company is the claimant

A company can sue under its corporate name.

5.4.4.2 Where a limited company is the defendant

A company can be sued under its corporate name.

Before commencing proceedings against a company, the claimant should carry out a company search to confirm the corporate status and continued existence of the proposed defendant company, to confirm the correct name of the company and to ascertain the registered address of the company if it is intended to serve the company at its registered office.

5.4.5 Addition and substitution of parties

On occasions, it will be necessary for another party to be added to a claim or for one party to be replaced by another. For example, A may take proceedings against B for damages for negligence, and subsequently may discover that C was also negligent. A may then want to add C to the proceedings as a second defendant. Or A may sue B (an individual) for a debt, but then discovers that his contract was not with B trading on his own account but with a company controlled by B. A will want to substitute the company for B as defendant.

As stated in r 19.4(2) of the CPR 1998, an application for permission to remove, add or substitute a party may be made by:

(a)   an existing party; or

(b)   a person who wishes to become a party.

The application may be made without notice and must be supported by evidence.

Nobody may be added or substituted as a claimant unless he has given his consent in writing and that consent has been filed with the court.

Rule 19.2 states:

>   (2)   The court may order a person to be added as a new party if—
>
>   (a)   it is desirable to add the new party so that the court can resolve all the matters in dispute in the proceedings; or
>
>   (b)   there is an issue involving the new party and an existing party which is connected to the matters in dispute in the proceedings, and it is desirable to add the new party so that the court can resolve that issue.
>
>   (3)   The court may order any person to cease to be a party if it is not desirable for that person to be a party to the proceedings.
>
>   (4)   The court may order a new party to be substituted for an existing one if—
>
>   (a)   the existing party's interest or liability has passed to the new party; and
>
>   (b)   it is desirable to substitute the new party so that the court can resolve the matters in dispute in the proceedings.

Special provisions apply where parties are to be added or substituted after the end of the relevant limitation period. Rule 19.5 states:

>   (2)   The court may add or substitute a party only if—
>
>   (a)   the relevant limitation period was current when the proceedings were started; and
>
>   (b)   the addition or substitution is necessary.
>
>   (3)   The addition or substitution of a party is necessary only if the court is satisfied that—
>
>   (a)   the new party is to be substituted for a party who was named in the claim form in mistake for the new party;
>
>   (b)   the claim cannot properly be carried on by or against the original party unless the new party is added or substituted as claimant or defendant; or
>
>   (c)   the original party has died or had a bankruptcy order made against him and his interest or liability has passed to the new party.

Part 19 also contains provisions enabling the Crown to be joined as a party to proceedings in which the court may wish to make a declaration of incompatibility in accordance with s 4 of the Human Rights Act 1998.

5.4.6 Professional conduct

A solicitor warrants his authority to take any positive step in court proceedings, for example to issue a claim form or serve a defence on behalf of the client. If a solicitor conducts proceedings without that authority, he will usually be personally liable for the costs incurred: see, for example, *Warner v Masefield* [2008] EWHC 1129.

Note in particular that r 2.01(1)(c) of the Solicitors' Code of Code provides that if a solicitor receives instructions from someone other than the client, or by only one client on behalf of others in a joint matter, the solicitor must not proceed without checking that all clients agree with the instructions given.

5.5 Service of the claim form

Once a claim form has been issued by the court, it must be served on the other parties if the claimant is to pursue the claim.

The rules governing service of court documents are set out in Part 6 of the CPR 1998.

5.5.1 How to serve a claim form

The following methods of service are permitted under r 6.3:

(a) personal service;

(b) first-class post, document exchange or other service which provides for delivery on the next business day;

(c) leaving the claim form at a specified place;

(d) fax or other means of electronic communication; or

(e) any other method authorised by the court.

5.5.1.1 Personal service

Rule 6.5(3)(a) provides that a claim form is served personally on an individual by leaving it with that individual. So personal service is carried out by handing the claim form to the individual party whilst he is in the jurisdiction (ie England or Wales). If he will not take the claim form, it can be dropped at his feet.

What if the defendant is a partnership? According to r 6.5(3)(c), a document is served personally on a partnership (where partners are being sued in the name of their firm: see **5.4.2.2**) by leaving it either with a partner, or with a person who, at the time of service, has the control or management of the partnership business at its principal place of business. A notice in Form N218 must also be served (see **Appendix A(6)**). Note that the principal place of business of a partnership is its main office, not a branch office.

If you wish to serve a partner, PD 7, para 5B.2 allows you to obtain from the partnership a written statement of the names and last-known places of residence of all the persons who were partners in the partnership at the time when the cause of action accrued.

By r 6.5(3)(b) and PD 6, para 6.2, a document is served personally on a registered company (or other corporation) by leaving it with a person who holds a senior position within the company (or corporation), such as a director, the treasurer, secretary or chief executive.

5.5.1.2 First-class post or alternative 'next working day' delivery

First-class post, or an alternative service which provides for delivery on the next working day, is permitted, but note that the Rules do not allow for service by second-class post or any other postal method, such as recorded delivery, unless the alternative method provides for delivery on the next working day. See **5.5.3** for the address to be used where this method of service is adopted.

5.5.1.3 Leaving the claim form at a specified place

Here the claim form is delivered by hand. See **5.5.3** below for the address to be used for this method of service.

5.5.1.4 Through a document exchange (DX)

If a party has given a DX box number as its address for service then that can be used to serve the claim form (PD 6, para 2.1). Alternatively, where a party or his solicitor's headed notepaper includes a DX box number, that may be used unless the party or his solicitors have indicated in writing that they are unwilling to be served by DX. If a solicitors' firm has a DX number but does not want to accept service by that method, it normally includes next to the DX number something like 'not for the purposes of service'.

5.5.1.5 By fax

To serve a claim form by fax transmission, the party to be served or his solicitors must have indicated in writing a willingness to accept service by fax and also stated the fax number to which the claim form should be sent (PD 6, para 4). A fax number on the party's headed notepaper is not sufficient for this purpose. However, the fax number on a party's solicitors' headed notepaper is treated as agreement to service by this method on behalf of their client, unless the solicitors indicate otherwise in writing. If a solicitors' firm has a fax number and does not want to accept service by that method, it normally includes next to the fax number something like 'not for the purposes of service'.

5.5.1.6 By other electronic means such as e-mail

A party to be served by e-mail or similar electronic method must have expressly indicated in writing the e-mail address or electronic identification to which it should be sent (PD 6, para 4). An e-mail address on a party's headed notepaper is not enough. If the party has instructed solicitors to accept service on its behalf, an e-mail address on the solicitors' notepaper is not enough unless it states that the e-mail address may be used for service purposes.

Note that in addition, PD 6, para 4.2 requires the party who wishes to serve the claim form by e-mail or other electronic means (but not fax) to clarify with the intended recipient whether there are any limitations to the recipient's agreement to accept service by such means, including the format in which documents are to be sent and the maximum size of attachments that may be received.

5.5.1.7 Service on limited companies

Where the party to be served is a limited company, s 1139(1) of the Companies Act 2006 provides an alternative method of service in addition to the CPR (see *Murphy v Staples UK Limited* [2003] 3 All ER 129). The Act provides that documents may be left at or posted to the registered office of the company. Whilst second-class post can be used when serving under s 1139(1), it is not recommended.

5.5.2 Who should be served?

5.5.2.1 General rule: any solicitor authorised to accept service

Rule 6.7 provides that if a defendant has given in writing the business address of a solicitor within the jurisdiction as an address at which the defendant may be served with the claim form, or a solicitor acting for the defendant has notified the claimant in writing that the solicitor is instructed by the defendant to accept service of the claim form on behalf of the defendant at a business address within the jurisdiction, the claim form must be served at the business address of that solicitor.

If parties' solicitors have been in correspondence before litigation starts, it is usual for the claimant's solicitors to ask the defendant's solicitors if they are 'authorised to accept service of proceedings'. Rather uniquely, in *Smith v Probyn* (2000) *The Times*, 29 March, the parties' solicitors had corresponded prior to a claim form being issued but the defendant's solicitors were never asked if they were authorised to accept service. Equally, the defendant's solicitors had never intimated in any way that they were instructed to accept service. Just before the deadline to serve the claim form expired, the claimant's solicitors sent it in the DX to the defendant's solicitors. Morland J held that there had been no effective service of the claim form.

5.5.2.2   Other provisions

Where r 6.7 does not apply, the claimant must serve the defendant with the claim form by one of the permitted methods detailed at **5.5.1**, unless any special provision concerning service of the claim form applies: see r 6.11 for any contractually agreed method of service; r 6.12 for service on the agent of an overseas principal; and r 6.15 for service by an alternative method or at an alternative place in accordance with a court order.

5.5.3   Where to serve?

By r 6.9, where no solicitor is authorised to accept service and the defendant has not given any address for service, the claim form must be served on the defendant at the place shown in the following table:

Nature of defendant to be served	Place of service
1. Individual	Usual or last known residence.
2. Individual being sued in the name of a business	Usual or last known residence of the individual; or principal or last known place of business.
3. Individual being sued in the business name of a partnership	Usual or last known residence of the individual; or principal or last known place of business of the partnership.
4. Limited liability partnership	Principal office of the partnership; or any place of business of the partnership within the jurisdiction which has a real connection with the claim.
5. Corporation (other than a company) incorporated in England and Wales	Principal office of the corporation; or any place within the jurisdiction where the corporation carries on its activities and which has a real connection with the claim.
6. Company registered in England and Wales	Principal office of the company; or any place of business of the company within the jurisdiction which has a real connection with the claim.
7. Any other company or corporation	Any place within the jurisdiction where the corporation carries on its activities; or any place of business of the company within the jurisdiction.

What if a claimant has reason to believe that the address of the defendant referred to in entries 1, 2 or 3 in the above table is an address at which the defendant no longer resides or carries on business? Rule 6.9(3) provides that the claimant must take reasonable steps to ascertain the address of the defendant's current residence or place of business ('current address'). If the claimant ascertains the defendant's current address, the claim form must be served at that address; but if he is unable to do so, the claimant must consider whether there is an alternative place where or an alternative method by which service may be effected and make an application to the court accordingly.

5.5.4 When to serve?

By r 7.5(1), a claimant who wishes to serve a claim form in the jurisdiction must complete the step required by the following table in relation to the particular method of service chosen, before 12.00 midnight on the calendar day four months after the date of issue of the claim form.

Method of service	Step required
Personal service	Completing the relevant step required by the rules (see **5.5.1.1**)
First-class post, DX or other service which provides for delivery on the next business day	Posting, leaving with, delivering to or collection by the relevant service provider (see **5.5.1.2** and **5.5.1.4**)
Delivery of the document to or leaving it at the relevant place	Delivering to or leaving the document at the relevant place (see **5.5.1.3** and **5.5.3**)
Fax	Completing the transmission of the fax (see **5.5.1.5**)
Other electronic method	Sending the e-mail or other electronic transmission (see **5.5.1.6**).

5.5.5 When is the claim form deemed to be served?

The potential problem with any method of service, apart from personal service, is that the claimant cannot know precisely when the defendant receives the claim form. A claimant needs to know when service has occurred in order to take the next step in the proceedings. So, if the claim form was served marked 'particulars of claim to follow', the claimant must serve those next (see **5.8**). If particulars of claim have been served then the claimant must allow the defendant the requisite number of days to respond, and can apply for default judgment if the defendant fails to respond (see **6.3** and **6.4**). Rule 6.14 introduces a simple, indisputable presumption that the claim form is deemed to have been served on the second business day after the step set out in **5.5.4** has occurred.

Note that by r 6.2(b) a 'business day' here means any day except Saturday, Sunday, a bank holiday, Good Friday or Christmas Day.

Examples
1.   An individual defendant is personally served with a claim form on a Monday. It is deemed to be served on the Wednesday, provided Tuesday and Wednesday are business days.
2.   A firm of solicitors authorised to accept service is served with the claim form by fax that is transmitted on a Saturday. Sunday will not count. Assume the Monday is a bank holiday and so does not count either. If Tuesday and Wednesday are business days then deemed service of the claim form is on the Wednesday.

5.5.6 Service by the court or the claimant?

The claim form will usually be served by the court, and the court will choose the appropriate method of service, which will normally be by first-class post. The claimant must provide the court with enough copies for the court to serve the claim form on all other parties, together with a copy for the court's file.

Rule 6.4(1) provides that the court will not effect service where:

(a)   a rule or Practice Direction provides that the claimant must serve the claim form; or

(b)   the claimant notifies the court that he wants to serve it; or

(c)   the court orders or directs otherwise.

Note that r 6.18 provides that where the court serves the claim form by post but the claim form is returned to the court, the court will send notification to the claimant that the claim form has been returned. However, the claim form will be deemed to be served unless the address for the defendant on the claim form is not the relevant address for the purpose of the Rules. This is rather an odd provision, but its purpose is to try to bring some certainty and finality to service of the claim form. So, if the address was that of a firm of solicitors authorised to accept service, the service is deemed to have occurred. However, it would obviously make sense to check that the correct address was used, and perhaps to telephone the solicitors for an explanation and agree a new method, such as fax or e-mail. Where service was to an address listed in the table at **5.5.3** the service is again deemed to have occurred. However, we take the view that the claimant should normally treat this as a situation where he has reason to believe that the address of the defendant referred to in entries 1, 2 or 3 in the table is an address at which the defendant no longer resides or carries on business. Therefore, the claimant should take reasonable steps to ascertain the current address of the defendant.

Where the claim form is served by the claimant, under r 6.17(2) he must file a certificate of service within 21 days of service of the particulars of claim (unless all the defendants have filed acknowledgements of service within that period), and may not obtain judgment in default (see **5.6**) unless he has filed the certificate of service. A copy is set out at **Appendix A(5)**.

5.5.7   Service out of the jurisdiction

5.5.7.1   EU countries

No special permission is required to serve a defendant based in Scotland, Northern Ireland or any other EU country, provided the English courts have jurisdiction under Council Regulation 44/2001 (see **Chapter 2**). The claim form must, however, be accompanied by a notice (N510) setting out the grounds on which the claimant is entitled to serve it outside the jurisdiction (r 6.34). The time for responding to the claim form will usually be extended to 21 days.

There are special provisions as to the methods of service that are acceptable where the claim form is to be served outside the jurisdiction (see rr 6.40–6.44).

5.5.7.2   Non-EU countries

The claimant must obtain permission to serve proceedings on a defendant outside the EU, for example an American company (but note that if such a company has an office in England and Wales, it could be served there just as if it were an English company).

The grounds for obtaining permission are set out in PD 6B, para 3.1. Examples of the grounds set out in para 3.1 are where the claim is brought to enforce a contract which is governed by English law, or where the breach of contract occurred in England and Wales. The application must be supported by evidence and is made without notice.

If an order permitting service outside the jurisdiction is made, the time limit for responding to the claim will again be extended. Service is usually effected through the judicial authorities of the State in question or the British Consul.

5.6   Extending time for service of the claim form

What if a claimant is not able to serve the claim form before midnight on the calendar day four months after the date of issue (see **5.5.4**)? The court has a general discretion to extend this period. The application should always be made before the time limit expires. What if it is made after the limit has expired? The court still has a discretion to extend time retrospectively but, as you would expect, the test is much more difficult to meet, as r 7.6(3) provides that the court may extend time for service only if:

(a)   the court has been unable to serve the claim form; or

(b)   the claimant has taken all reasonable steps to serve the claim form but has been unable to do so; and

(c)   in either case, the claimant has acted promptly in making the application.

In *Vinos v Marks & Spencer plc* [2001] 3 All ER 784, the claim form was served nine days after the expiry of the four-month period. The claimant's solicitors had no explanation for this other than that it was an oversight, and their application for an extension was dismissed. The Court of Appeal upheld the decision, holding that the wording of r 7.6(3) was such that an extension could not be granted in these circumstances as neither ground (a) nor (b) applied.

This decision has been followed in other cases. For example, extensions have been refused where the claimant's solicitor was mistaken as to the date on which the claim form was issued or simply overlooked serving it (*Satwinder Kaur v CTP Coil Ltd* [2000] LTL, 10 July; *Hashtroodi v Hancock* [2004] EWCA Civ 652, [2004] 3 All ER 530). Where the claimant's solicitors mistakenly served the defendant when they should have served the claim form on the defendant's solicitors who were nominated to accept service, an extension was also refused (*Nanglegan v Royal Free Hampstead NHS Trust* [2001] EWCA Civ 127, [2001] 3 All ER 793).

Note that r 2.11 provides that 'Unless these Rules or a practice direction provide otherwise or the court orders otherwise, the time specified by a rule or by the court for a person to do any act may be varied by the written agreement of the parties.' So the parties' solicitors can enter into a written agreement to extend the time for service of the claim form. The dangers of this for a claimant were highlighted In *Thomas v Home Office* [2006] EWCA Civ 1355, where the Court of Appeal held that a written agreement to extend the time for service of the claim form does not have to be in a single document but may consist of an exchange of letters or e-mails. An oral agreement that is then confirmed in writing by both sides is also a written agreement. However, an oral agreement between two solicitors that is subsequently recorded in a letter sent by one solicitor to the other, but not answered by the other, does not constitute a written agreement. Further, it is not enough for solicitors each to make an attendance note of an oral agreement, unless those notes are subsequently exchanged.

5.7   Service of documents other than the claim form

5.7.1   How, who and where?

Rules 6.20 to 6.29 contain provisions relating to the service of all other court documents, such as statements of case. These are basically the same as for claim forms in respect of how to serve (see **5.5.1**), who to serve (see **5.5.2**) and where to serve (see **5.5.3**).

5.7.2   Deemed service of other documents

Rather surprisingly, a complex set of rules exist which produce different deemed dates of service for other documents according to the method used. These are as shown in the table below.

Method of service	Deemed date of service
Personal service	If the document is served personally before 4.30pm on a business day, on that day; or in any other case, on the next business day after that day.
First-class post (or other service which provides for delivery on the next business day)	The second day after it was posted, left with, delivered to or collected by the relevant service provider provided that day is a business day; or if not, the next business day after that day.

Method of service	Deemed date of service
Delivering the document to or leaving it at a permitted address	If it is delivered to or left at the permitted address on a business day before 4.30pm, on that day; or in any other case, on the next business day after that day.
Document exchange	The second day after it was left with, delivered to or collected by the relevant service provider provided that day is a business day; or if not, the next business day after that day.
Fax	If the transmission of the fax is completed on a business day before 4.30pm, on that day; or in any other case, on the next business day after the day on which it was transmitted.
Other electronic method	If the e-mail or other electronic transmission is sent on a business day before 4.30pm, on that day; or in any other case, on the next business day after the day on which it was sent.

Note that by r 6.2(b) a 'business day' here means any day except Saturday, Sunday, a bank holiday, Good Friday or Christmas Day.

Examples

1.   A document is personally served at 3.30pm on a Monday. Provided that is a business day, service is deemed to occur that day as it has taken place before 4.30pm. If it was not a business day or had it been personally served after 4.30pm, deemed service would be on the next business day.

2.   A document is posted first class on a Tuesday. The day of deemed service is the Thursday, the second day after it was posted, provided that is a business day. If the second day after posting first class (or its equivalent) is not a working day, the day of deemed service is the next business day.

3.   A document is delivered to a permitted address at 5pm on a Thursday. Even though that is a business day, because it is after 4.30pm that is not the day of deemed service. Assume that the next day is Good Friday and so that does not count. Saturday and Sunday will not count. The following Bank Holiday Monday will not count. So the day of deemed service is the next business day, namely Tuesday.

4.   A document is left in a numbered box at the Document Exchange (DX) on a Friday. The day of deemed service is the second day after it is left, provided that is a business day. The second day will be Sunday. As that is not a business day, it does not count. The day of deemed service is the next day, Monday, provided that is a business day.

5.   A document is sent by fax on a Saturday and the transmission of that fax is completed by 11.25am. Although that occurs before 4.30pm, it is not done on a business day and so does not count as the day of deemed service. Sunday also does not count. So the day of deemed service is Monday, provided that is a business day.

5.8   Service of particulars of claim

What if a claim form is served marked 'particulars of claim to follow'. When must the particulars of claim be served? Practice Direction 7, para 6.1 provides the following answer:

> Where the claimant does not include the particulars of claim in the claim form, they may be served separately:
>
> (1)   either at the same time as the claim form, or
>
> (2)   within 14 days after service of the claim form provided that the service of the particulars of claim is within 4 months after the date of issue of the claim form [see **5.5.4**].

Example

A claim form marked 'particulars of claim to follow' is issued on 1 March 2010. The claim form must be served by 12 midnight on 1 July 2010.

If the claim form is served on, say, 5 April 2010, the claimant must serve the particulars of claim within 14 days, ie by 19 April 2010. However, if it is served later on, say, 28 June 2010, the claimant does not have 14 days after that to serve the particulars of claim, as that must be done by 1 July 2010.

Chapter 6

Responding to Proceedings and Judgment in Default

6.1 Introduction

What is the first step that a defendant must take in civil litigation? It is when served with the particulars of claim that a defendant must respond, otherwise the claimant will be able to 'win by default'. So where the defendant is served with a claim form marked 'particulars of claim to follow', there is nothing for the defendant to do but await service of the particulars of claim. He will in these circumstances receive Form N1C (Notes for Defendants) explaining this. See the copy at **Appendix A(2)**.

When either the court or the claimant serves the particulars of claim on the defendant, the defendant must also be sent Form N9 (the response pack). A copy of this form appears at **Appendix A(3)**. The response pack explains to the defendant how he should respond to the claim and the time limits for doing so. There are three ways in which a defendant may respond, namely:

(a) by filing an acknowledgement of service;

(b) by filing a defence;

(c) by filing an admission.

See further the flowcharts in **Appendix C(6)–(10)**.

Before considering these steps in turn, it is important to be clear about the rules relating to the calculation of the time for doing any act, such as filing an acknowledgement of service and/or a defence. As we shall see at **6.6**, if the defendant does not respond within the appropriate time period, the claimant may enter judgment in default against the defendant. It is therefore essential that a party and his legal adviser are clear about the meaning of the various time periods prescribed in the rules.

6.2 Computation of time

Rule 2.8 sets out how to calculate any period of time for doing an act which is specified in the Rules, a Practice Direction, or by a judgment or order of the court.

If the time for doing an act ends on a day when the court office is closed, the time does not actually expire until the end of the first day on which the court office is next open.

Any order imposing a time limit should, wherever practicable, give a calendar date, ie the day, month, year and deadline time for compliance, for example 'by Monday, 20 December 2010, by 4pm'.

Any period of time expressed as a number of days will be a period of 'clear days', as defined by r 2.8.

Examples

1.   On 5 October, the defendant is served with the particulars of claim.

The defendant has 14 days (not including the day of service of the particulars of claim) within which either to acknowledge service or file a defence.

The deadline for doing so is therefore 19 October.

2.   An application to the court has been fixed for hearing on a Monday.

Generally, the notice of the application must be served on the other party at least three days prior to the hearing.

The notice must be served on the preceding Tuesday (ie, where notice of a hearing is being given, both the day on which notice is served and the day of the hearing are excluded in calculating the clear days.) However, it should be noted that in computing a period of five days or less, any weekend or bank holiday must be ignored.

3.   Month means a calendar month.

So if a claim form for service within the jurisdiction is issued on 5 May, it must be served no later than four months later, namely by 5 September.

6.3   Acknowledgement of service (Part 10)

6.3.1   Time limits

When served with the particulars of claim, the defendant usually has a choice of what to do: he may either simply acknowledge service, or he may file a defence. The defendant may acknowledge service if he is unable to file a defence in time, or if he wishes to contest the court's jurisdiction.

If the defendant fails to respond within a set time, the claimant can usually enter judgment. This is because r 10.2 provides that:

> If–
> (a)   a defendant fails to file an acknowledgment of service within the period specified in rule 10.3; and
> (b)   does not within that period file a defence in accordance with Part 15 [see **6.4**] or serve or file an admission in accordance with Part 14 [see **6.5**],
> the claimant may obtain default judgment if Part 12 allows it [see **6.6**].

The words 'within that period' in (b) indicate that judgment in default of both an acknowledgement of service and a defence is calculated by reference to the following time period prescribed by r 10.3:

> (1)   The general rule is that the period for filing an acknowledgment of service is–
> (a)   where the defendant is served with a claim form which states that particulars of claim are to follow, 14 days after service of the particulars of claim; and
> (b)   in any other case, 14 days after service of the claim form.

These rules may be summarised as follows:

	When default judgment can be entered
Claim form served with particulars of claim	15th day after (deemed) service of the claim form
Particulars of claim served after claim form served	15th day after (deemed) service of the particulars of claim

It can be seen from the above table why the defendant must be careful to calculate correctly the 14 days he has to respond; and equally why a claimant must accurately work out the first available date he can enter default judgment if the defendant fails to respond. This is because the date of deemed service of the claim form (see **5.5.5**) may be different from the date of deemed service of particulars of claim (see **5.7.2**).

6.3.2 Completing the acknowledgement form

The acknowledgement of service form is part of the response pack (Form N9). On the form, the defendant should set out his name in full; and if his name has been incorrectly set out in the claim form, it should be correctly set out on the acknowledgement of service form, followed by the words 'described as' and the incorrect name (eg, 'John Patrick Smith described as Pat Smith'). The defendant's address for service, including full postcode, which must be within England or Wales, must be stated. This will either be the defendant's residence or business address, or, if the acknowledgement of service form is signed by his solicitor, his solicitor's address. The defendant must state on the form whether he intends to defend all of the claim, part of the claim, or wishes to contest jurisdiction. The form must be signed by the defendant or his solicitor. The defendant must file the completed acknowledgement of service form at the court where the claim was issued. The court will then forward a copy to the claimant.

6.3.3 Defendant is a partnership

Practice Direction 10, para 4.4 provides that where a claim is brought against a partnership, service must be acknowledged in the name of the partnership on behalf of all persons who were partners at the time when the cause of action accrued. The acknowledgement of service may be signed by any of those partners, or by any person authorised by any of those partners to sign it.

6.3.4 Defendant is a registered company

What if the defendant is a registered company? Pursuant to PD 10, para 4.2, a person holding a senior position in the company, such as a director, the treasurer, secretary or chief executive, may sign the acknowledgement of service, provided he states the position that he holds.

6.3.5 Defendant disputes jurisdiction

By r 11, if a defendant wishes to dispute the jurisdiction of the court, he must indicate this on the acknowledgement of service. After filing the acknowledgement of service, he must then challenge the jurisdiction by making an application within 14 days or he will be treated as having submitted to the jurisdiction. The application to the court to dispute the court's jurisdiction must be supported by evidence as to why England and Wales is not the proper forum for the case. If the court grants the defendant's application and finds that the claim should not have been brought in England and Wales, service of the claim form will usually be set aside. In effect, that brings the proceedings to an end.

If the court refuses the defendant's application then the original acknowledgement of service ceases to have effect and the defendant must file a further acknowledgement within 14 days or such other period as the court may direct.

6.4 The defence (Part 15)

6.4.1 Time limits

As we have seen, a defendant can respond to proceedings first by acknowledging service (see **6.3**) and then filing a defence, or by just filing his defence. What is the time limit, given the choice? That is laid down by r 15.4, as follows:

(1)   The general rule is that the period for filing a defence is –

    (a)   14 days after service of the particulars of claim; or

    (b)   if the defendant files an acknowledgment of service under Part 10, 28 days after service of the particulars of claim.

Arguably (a) above is inconsistent with the situation addressed at **6.3.1** where the claimant serves the claim form with particulars of claim. In those circumstances, r 10.3 suggests the defendant has 14 days after (deemed) service of the claim form to respond. We take the view that r 15.4 sets out the general position but r 10.3 applies in respect of default judgment. The point is not academic, since the calculation of the day of deemed service of a claim form or particulars of claim (see **5.5.5.** and **5.7.2** respectively) will not always be the same.

However, (b) above is clear, and if the defendant files an acknowledgement of service then he has 28 days after (deemed) service of the particulars of claim within which to file a defence.

Example

Assume a claim form with particulars of claim is deemed to have been served on Wednesday, 2 June 2010 (as to deemed service, see **5.7.2**). By what date must the defendant acknowledge service and indicate an intention to defend or file a defence? He must do so within 14 days of service, not including the day of deemed service. So he must act by Wednesday, 16 June (otherwise the claimant can enter default judgment on Thursday, 17 June: see **6.6**). If he chooses to file an acknowledgement in time, he then has until Wednesday, 30 June to file his defence.

6.4.2   Extending the time limit

The time for filing a defence may be extended by agreement between the parties for a period of up to 28 days. If the parties do reach such an agreement, the defendant must give the court written notice of the agreement (see r 15.5).

Any further extension can only be authorised by the court. The court will usually grant an extension, but if the claimant has complied with the Practice Direction on Pre-action Conduct or an approved pre-action protocol, such extension will probably be for a short period of time and will be granted at the defendant's expense. If, however, the claimant did not so comply, the court is likely to conclude that the defendant should be granted a significant extension of time. If the claimant has unreasonably refused to grant a voluntary extension of time and/or has opposed the defendant's application to the court unreasonably, the court may well order the claimant to pay the defendant's costs of seeking the extension.

6.4.3   Drafting

There are forms which the defendant can use which will have been served as part of the response pack. In the case of a claim for a specified amount, the appropriate form is Form N9B; and in the case of a claim for an unspecified amount or a non-money claim, the appropriate form is Form N9C. In practice, these forms will usually be used by defendants who are acting in person. Where solicitors are acting for a defendant, the defence is usually prepared as a separate document (see **Chapter 7**).

6.4.4   Filing and serving

When the defence is filed, a copy must be served on all other parties. The court will effect service, unless the defendant's solicitor has told the court that he will do so.

6.5   Admissions (Part 14)

If a defendant wishes to admit either the whole or part of the claim, he should complete the appropriate sections of the response pack. The way in which the defendant should complete the forms and the consequences of doing so vary depending on the nature of the claim and whether the admission is in full or only in part. See the flowcharts in **Appendix C(7) and C(8)**.

6.5.1 Admission in full of a claim for a specified amount

If a defendant admits the whole of a claim for a specified amount, he should serve the appropriate form of admission (Form N9A) on the claimant. This should be done within 14 days of service of the particulars of claim. On Form N9A, the defendant has to give certain personal details, together with details of his income and expenditure, and he should also make an offer of payment, which can be an offer to pay either in full by a certain date, or by monthly instalments.

Upon receipt of the form, the claimant may then file a request for judgment. If the claimant accepts the defendant's offer to pay either by a certain date or by monthly instalments, the claimant simply accepts the defendant's offer and files a request for judgment. See the flowchart in **Appendix C(7)**.

If the claimant rejects the defendant's offer to pay by a certain date or to pay by instalments then the court will decide the appropriate order. If the claim is for not more than £50,000, a court officer may decide the rate of payment without any court hearing; alternatively, the rate of payment will be decided by a judge. Where the rate of payment is to be decided by a judge, the proceedings must be automatically transferred to the 'defendant's home court', if the defendant is an individual. So where is the 'defendant's home court'? For a county court claim, it is the county court for the district in which the defendant resides or carries on business. For a High Court claim, it is the District Registry for the district in which the defendant resides or carries on business, or, where there is no such District Registry, the Royal Courts of Justice.

The judge may make the decision without any hearing, but if there is to be a hearing, the parties must be given at least seven days' notice. In deciding the time and rate of payment, the court will take into account:

(a)   the defendant's statement of means;

(b)   the claimant's objections to the defendant's request; and

(c)   any other relevant factors.

6.5.2 Part admission of a claim for a specified amount

If a defendant admits only part of a claim for a specified amount, he must do so by filing Form N9A at the court within 14 days of service of the particulars of claim. The court will then give notice of the admission to the claimant, who must say whether he:

(a)   accepts the offer in full satisfaction of his claim; or

(b)   accepts the offer but not the defendant's proposals for payment; or

(c)   rejects the offer and wishes to proceed with his claim.

The claimant has 14 days in which to file his notice and serve it on the defendant. If he does not do so, the claim will be stayed until he does file his notice.

If the claimant accepts the offer, he will request judgment.

If the defendant has not requested time to pay, the claimant's request can stipulate the time for payment and the court will enter judgment accordingly.

If the defendant has requested time to pay, the procedure in **6.5.1** applies.

If the claimant rejects the offer, the case continues as a defended action.

See the flowchart in **Appendix C(8)**.

6.5.3 Admission of a claim for an unspecified amount (no offer made)

Where the defendant admits liability for a claim for an unspecified amount and makes no offer of payment, he must do so within the usual time for making an admission. The court will serve a copy of the admission on the claimant, who may then apply for judgment.

The court will then enter judgment for the damages to be assessed. The hearing at which the damages are assessed is often called a 'disposal hearing'. Where needed, the court will give directions to the parties as to the steps to be taken to prepare for the disposal hearing, and may also allocate the case to a track if that is appropriate (see **Chapter 9**).

See the flowchart in **Appendix C(7)**.

6.5.4 Admission of a claim for an unspecified amount (offer made)

Where the defendant admits liability for a claim for an unspecified amount and offers a sum of money in satisfaction of the claim, he must do so in the usual time for making an admission.

The court will serve a notice on the claimant requiring him to return the notice stating whether or not he accepts the amount in satisfaction of the claim. If he does not file the notice within 14 days, his claim will be stayed until he does file the notice.

If the claimant does not accept the amount offered, he will enter judgment for damages to be assessed at a disposal hearing.

If the claimant accepts the offer and the defendant has not asked for time to pay, the claimant may enter judgment for the amount offered and will stipulate when payment should be made.

If the defendant has asked for time to pay the usual procedure applies (see **6.5.1**).

6.5.5 Challenging the court's decision

Where the court has decided the time and rate of payment, and the decision was made either:

(a)   by a court officer; or

(b)   by a judge without any hearing,

either party may apply for a re-determination by a judge. Such application must be made within 14 days of service of the determination on the applicant.

The case must be transferred to the defendant's home court if the claim is for a specified amount and the defendant is an individual (unless the case was started in a specialist list) (see **6.5.1**).

If the original decision was made by a court officer, the re-determination will be made by a judge without a hearing unless the application notice requests a hearing.

If the original decision was made by a judge, the re-determination must be at a hearing unless the parties agree otherwise.

6.5.6 Interest

Judgment where the defendant admits liability for the whole amount of a claim for a specified amount will include interest up to the date of judgment if:

(a)   the particulars of claim include the details required by r 16.4 (see **7.2.1**); and

(b)   where interest is claimed under s 35A of the SCA 1981 or s 69 of the CCA 1984 (see **2.7.2.1**), the rate is no higher than the rate of interest payable on judgment debts (currently 8% pa) at the date when the claim form was issued; and

(c)   the claimant's request for judgment includes a calculation of the interest claimed for the period from the date up to which interest was stated to be calculated in the claim form to the date of the request for judgment.

If the above conditions are not satisfied, the judgment will be for an amount of interest to be decided by the court, and the court will give directions as to how this should be achieved. For example, condition (b) will not be met if the claim was for a commercial debt and interest was claimed under the Late Payment of Commercial Debts (Interest) Act 1998 (see **2.7.2.1**).

6.5.7   Varying the rate of payment

By para 6.1 of PD 14, either party may apply to vary the time and rates of payment of a judgment on admissions if there has been a change of circumstances.

6.6   Default judgments (Part 12)

6.6.1   Introduction

Once the proceedings have been served upon the defendant, it may be that the defendant takes no action. The defendant may fail to return the acknowledgement of service or file a defence. In those circumstances, the claimant can obtain judgment in default against the defendant. This means that the claimant obtains judgment without there being a trial of the issues involved in the case. See the flowchart in **Appendix C(10)**.

6.6.1.1   Cases where default judgment is not available

The claimant may not enter a default judgment in the following types of cases:

(a)   a claim for delivery of goods under an agreement regulated by the Consumer Credit Act 1974;

(b)   a Part 8 claim (see **Chapter 8**);

(c)   a mortgage claim;

(d)   a claim for provisional damages;

(e)   a claim in a specialist court.

6.6.2   Procedure

The claimant applies for default judgment by filing a request using the relevant form if he is claiming money (whether or not it is a claim for a specified amount) or goods (if the claim form gives the defendant the option of returning the goods). There are different forms, depending on whether the claim is for a specified or an unspecified amount. (See Forms N205A, N205B, N225 and N227.)

The claimant must satisfy the court that:

(a)   the particulars of claim have been served on the defendant;

(b)   the defendant has not acknowledged service/filed a defence and the relevant time period has expired;

(c)   the defendant has not satisfied the claim;

(d)   the defendant has not admitted liability for the full amount of the claim.

6.6.3   Claims for specified amounts

A request for default judgment for a specified amount may indicate the date for full payment, or the times and rate at which it is to be paid by instalments. If it does not, the court will normally give judgment for immediate payment. Additional fixed costs are payable by the defendant (see CPR 1998, Part 45).

6.6.4 Claims for unspecified amounts

A request for default judgment for a claim for an unspecified amount is a request for the court to decide the amount of the claim and costs. This will involve a full hearing before a trial judge to decide the amount of the claim (again often called a disposal hearing), and it may, therefore, be necessary to allocate the claim to a track and give directions (see **Chapter 9**).

6.6.5 Interest

The default judgment may, in the case of a claim for a specified amount, include interest up to the date of judgment if:

(a)   the particulars of claim include the details required by r 16.4 (see **7.2.1.5**); and

(b)   where interest is claimed under s 35A of the SCA 1981 or s 69 of the CCA 1984 (see **2.7.2.1**), the rate is no higher than the rate of interest payable on judgment debts (currently 8% pa) at the date when the claim form was issued; and

(c)   the claimant's request for judgment includes a calculation of the interest claimed for the period from the date up to which interest was stated to be calculated in the claim form to the date of the request for judgment.

Otherwise the court will decide the amount of interest and will give directions for this.

Example: specified claim

Assume county court debt proceedings were issued on 9 July 2010. Interest is claimed under s 69 of the CCA 1984 at 8% pa from when the debt was due to and including the day of issue. The daily rate of interest is £5.35. If default judgment is entered on 30 July, how much additional interest should be claimed? 21 days have passed since issue, so a further £112.35 (21 x £5.35) should now be claimed when entering default judgment.

6.6.6 Co-defendants

Where there are co-defendants, the claimant may enter a default judgment against one or more of the co-defendants while proceeding with his claim against the other defendants, provided the claim can be dealt with separately. Otherwise, the court will not deal with the default judgment until it deals with the claim against the other defendants.

6.6.7 Setting aside a default judgment

A defendant against whom a default judgment has been entered may apply to have it set aside. Such applications are considered in **Chapter 10**.

6.6.8 Summary

A defendant might respond to a specified claim in any of the following ways:

(a)   admit the full amount and pay it. Alternatively he can ask for time to pay, which, if rejected by the claimant, will be determined by the court; or

(b)   admit part of the claim and offer to pay it. Alternatively, he can ask for time to pay. If the claimant accepts the part admitted in full and final settlement but rejects the proposal as to payment, the court will determine the time for payment. However, if the claimant does not accept the part admitted in full and final settlement, the case will continue as a defended claim.

A defendant might respond to a claim for an unspecified amount of money in any of the following ways:

(a)   admit liability but make no offer of payment. The court will enter judgment for damages to be assessed at a disposal hearing; or

(b)   admit liability and make an offer to pay a sum of money. Additionally he may ask for time to pay that amount. If the claimant accepts the offer but rejects any proposal as to payment, the court will determine the time for payment. However, if the claimant does not accept the offer, he will enter judgment for damages to be assessed at a disposal hearing.

Where a claimant enters default judgment on a specified claim, the judgment will be for a final sum of money as calculated by the claimant and he can immediately proceed to enforcement.

Where a claimant enters default judgment on a claim for an unspecified amount of money, the judgment will be for damages to be assessed by the court at a disposal hearing.

See further the flow diagrams in **Appendix C(6)–(10)**.

Chapter 7
Statements of Case

7.1 Introduction

Statements of case are the formal documents in which the parties concisely set out their respective cases. They are served between the parties (as well as being filed at court) so that each party knows the case he will have to meet at the trial. The statements of case are central to the litigation, since at trial the court will decide only those issues which are raised in the statements of case. They must therefore be drafted carefully and reviewed continually as the case develops. The trial court will not usually allow a party to pursue an issue which, on a fair reading of the statement of case, is not stated: see *Royal Brompton Hospital NHS Trust v Hammond & Others* [2000] LTL, 4 December.

By r 2.3 a 'statement of case':

(a) means a claim form, particulars of claim where these are not included in a claim form, defence, Part 20 claim [see **Chapter 8**] or reply to defence; and

(b) includes any further information given in relation to them voluntarily or by court order under r 18.1 [see **7.7**].

We considered how to draft a claim form at **5.3.1**. In this chapter, at **7.2**, we shall examine in detail the contents of particulars of claim.

The defendant's statement of case is called a defence. Frequently, the only statements of case in a claim will be the claim form, separate particulars of claim and the defence. In some cases, however, a claimant may wish to serve a reply to the defence, and in other cases a defendant may wish to make his own claim against the claimant by way of a counterclaim (see **Chapter 8**).

The rules relating to statements of case are contained in Part 16 of the CPR 1998 and the accompanying Practice Directions. Part 16 does not apply if the claimant has used the Part 8 procedure (see **Chapter 8**).

7.1.1 Setting parameters

In the case of *McPhilemy v Times Newspapers Limited* [1999] 3 All ER 775, Lord Woolf MR said:

> [Statements of case] mark out the parameters of the case that is being advanced by each party [and] identify the issues and the extent of the dispute between the parties ... The need for extensive [statements of case] including particulars should be reduced by the requirement that witness statements are now exchanged. In the majority of proceedings identification of the documents upon which a party relies, together with copies of that party's witness statements, will make the detail of the nature of the case the other side has to meet obvious.

7.1.2   Where they fit into the five stages

When thinking about the five stages of litigation (see **1.3),** it can be seen that statements of case are dealt with at Stage 2. The detailed evidence is dealt with subsequently at Stage 3. So a statement of case should be thought of as putting together only the bare bones of the case. The 'flesh' will be put on by way of detailed evidence later.

For example, the particulars of claim in respect of a breach of contract claim should deal with the essential material facts that will establish the cause of action, namely:

(a)   the status of the parties (eg, defendant's business when relying on sale during course of that business to establish terms implied by the Sale of Goods Act 1979 or the Supply of Goods and Services Act 1982);

(b)   chronological story (eg, request for a sample; relevant pre-contract statements, etc);

(c)   contract, ie date, type (written or oral), parties, subject matter, consideration;

(d)   express terms relied on;

(e)   implied terms relied on;

(f)   chronological story (eg, delivery, payment, etc);

(g)   breach alleged and particularised;

(h)   factual consequences of breach;

(i)   chronological story (eg, rejection or acceptance of repudiation, etc);

(j)   damage and loss alleged and particularised;

(k)   interest (contract; Late Payment of Commercial Debts (Interest) Act 1998; SCA 1981, s 35A, or CCA 1984, s 69 – see **2.7.2).**

It is important to bear in mind that the witness statements served later in the proceedings by the claimant and on which he intends to rely at trial will flesh out the detail as to the formation of the contract, etc. Any technical matters will, of course, be dealt with by expert evidence (see **12.13).**

7.1.3   Referring to law, witnesses and attaching documents

In relation to either the particulars of claim or the defence, by para 13.3 of PD 16, a party may:

(1)   refer in his statement of case to any point of law on which his claim or defence, as the case may be, is based,

(2)   give in his statement of case the name of any witness he proposes to call, and

(3)   attach to or serve with this statement of case a copy of any document which he considers is necessary to his claim or defence, as the case may be (including any expert's report to be filed in accordance with Part 35).

As a general rule there is no need to state any law. Exceptionally the relevant law should be stated if the parties and the court would otherwise 'be left to speculate upon the relevance in law of a purely factual narrative' (*per* Buxton LJ in *Loveridge v Healey* [2004] EWCA Civ 173, (2004) *The Times*, 27 February). It will normally be a defendant, however, who will wish to raise a point of law, eg that the claim discloses no cause of action, such as a promise unsupported by consideration, or a defence under the LA 1980: see **7.3.**

Whilst excessive factual details should not be given in a statement of case, a party can state 'the name of any witness he proposes to call'. So a party can choose to indicate if he has any particular witness in mind who will prove a particular fact. There is little advantage in this unless, perhaps, the details have already been given to the other party pre-action, or it helps to particularise the party's case; for example, in an industrial accident claim, part of the defendant's case may be that the machinery in question was regularly checked, and so he should state by whom and when.

A party can attach to a statement of case any document he considers 'necessary' to his claim or defence. This provision ensures that the court has the fullest possible knowledge of relevant facts from the outset. So, if a party has voluntarily disclosed a document pre-action, or has received a document from the other side that assists his case, and it is admissible, then it may be appropriate to attach a copy. Should an expert's report be attached? Arguably only if the court has already given permission for the party to rely on that expert (which will be most unlikely at this stage). It therefore seems sensible to follow para C1.3(e) of the *Commercial Court Guide*, which states: 'An expert's report should not be attached to the statement of case and should not be filed with the statement of case.'

7.1.4 Formalities

By PD 5, para 2.2, every document prepared by a party for filing or use at the court must:

(1)   unless the nature of the document renders it impracticable, be on A4 paper of durable quality having a margin not less than 3.5cm wide;

(2)   be fully legible and should normally be typed;

(3)   where possible, be bound securely in a manner which would not hamper filing, or otherwise each page should be endorsed with the case number;

(4)   have the pages numbered consecutively;

(5)   be divided into numbered paragraphs;

(6)   have all numbers, including dates, expressed as figures; and

(7)   give in the margin the reference of every document mentioned that has already been filed.

Note that the requirement to express dates in figures and not words under (6) above refers to the day of the month and year only. For example, the correct way to express a date is 17 May 2010 and not 17/05/10.

The following principles (see the *Queen's Bench Guide*, para 5.6.4) should be followed:

(a)   a statement of case must be as brief and concise as possible;

(b)   a statement of case should be set out in separate consecutively numbered paragraphs and sub-paragraphs;

(c)   so far as possible each paragraph or sub-paragraph should contain no more than one allegation;

(d)   the facts and other matters alleged should be set out as far as reasonably possible in chronological order;

(e)   the statement of case should deal with the claim on a point-by-point basis, to allow a point-by-point response;

(f)   where a party is required to give reasons, the allegation should be stated first and then the reasons listed one by one in separate numbered sub-paragraphs;

(g)   a party wishing to advance a positive claim must identify that claim in the statement of case;

(h)   any matter which if not stated might take another party by surprise should be stated;

(i)   where they will assist, headings, abbreviations and definitions should be used and a glossary annexed; contentious headings, abbreviations, paraphrasing and definitions should not be used, and every effort should be made to ensure that they are in a form acceptable to the other parties;

(j)   particulars of primary allegations should be stated as particulars and not as primary allegations;

(k)   schedules or appendices should be used if this would be helpful, for example where lengthy particulars are necessary, and any response should also be stated in a schedule or appendix;

(l)   any lengthy extracts from documents should be placed in a schedule.

Further, as the *Commercial Court Guide* (Appendix 4) stresses, particular care should be taken to set out only those factual allegations which are necessary to support the case. Evidence should not be included.

By PD 5, para 2.1, where a firm of solicitors prepares a statement of case, the document should be signed in the name of the firm.

7.1.5 Professional conduct

Rule 11.01(1) of the Solicitors' Code of Conduct provides that a solicitor must never deceive, or knowingly or recklessly mislead, the court. By r 11.01(3), this includes not drafting a statement of case that contains either:

(a)   any contention which the solicitor does not consider to be properly arguable; or

(b)   any allegation of fraud, unless the solicitor is instructed to do so and he has material which he reasonably believes establishes, on the face of it, a case of fraud.

What if the client has filed a statement of case and subsequently tells his solicitor before the litigation ends that it contains a material error and the effect of that error is to mislead the court? In those circumstances, the solicitor should advise the client to amend the statement of case. If the client refuses to do so, the solicitor should cease to act for the client. In order to keep client confidentiality (see r 4), the solicitor should not inform the court or any other party of the reasons for ceasing to act.

7.2 Contents of the particulars of claim

7.2.1 What must be included?

Rule 16.4(1) states that the particulars of claim must include:

(a)   a concise statement of the facts on which the claimant relies;

(b)   if the claimant is seeking interest, a statement to that effect and the details set out in paragraph (2) (see below).

7.2.1.1 Purpose

The primary function of the particulars of claim is to state concisely the facts upon which the claimant relies. The claimant should state all facts necessary for the purpose of showing that he has a complete cause of action. This might include, for example, a defendant's knowledge of a material fact that demonstrates a particular head of damage claimed is not too remote. This is often relevant where loss of a particular contract and/or profits is claimed.

Practice Direction 16 goes into more detail as to what must be, or may be, included in the particulars of claim. There are particular requirements for certain types of cases, eg recovery of land and hire purchase claims.

7.2.1.2 Claim based on written contract

More generally, where a claim is based upon a written agreement, then by para 7.3 of PD 16:

(1)   a copy of the contract or documents constituting the agreement should be attached to or served with the particulars of claim and the original(s) should be available at the hearing, and

(2)   any general conditions of sale incorporated in the contract should also be attached (but where the contract is, or the documents constituting the agreement are bulky this practice direction is complied with by attaching or serving only the relevant parts of the contract or documents).

Therefore, where the claim arises out of a breach of a written contract, a copy of the relevant contract should be attached to, or served with, the particulars of claim.

7.2.1.3 Claim based on oral contract

By para 7.4 of PD 16:

> Where a claim is based upon an oral agreement, the particulars of claim should set out the contractual words used and state by whom, to whom, when and where they were spoken.

See para 4 of the example at **7.2.1.7** below.

7.2.1.4 Other particular matters

Paragraphs 8.1–8.2 of PD 16 set out further matters which must be specifically set out in the particulars of claim. For example, by para 8.2:

> The claimant must specifically set out the following matters in his particulars of claim where he wishes to rely on them in support of his claim:
> (1)   any allegation of fraud,
> (2)   the fact of any illegality,
> (3)   details of any misrepresentation,
> (4)   details of all breaches of trust,
> (5)   notice or knowledge of a fact,
> (6)   details of unsoundness of mind or undue influence,
> (7)   details of wilful default, and
> (8)   any facts relating to mitigation of loss or damage.

7.2.1.5 Interest

Rule 16.4(2) sets out the details which must be supplied where, as will usually be the case, the claimant is seeking interest. In such cases, the claimant must:

> (a)   state whether he is doing so—
> > (i)   under the terms of a contract;
> > (ii)   under an enactment and if so which; or
> > (iii)   on some other basis and if so what that basis is; and
> (b)   if the claim is for a specified amount of money, state—
> > (i)   the percentage rate at which interest is claimed;
> > (ii)   the date from which it is claimed;
> > (iii)   the date to which it is calculated, which must not be later than the date on which the claim form is issued;
> > (iv)   the total amount of interest claimed to the date of calculation; and
> > (v)   the daily rate at which interest accrues after that date.

A claimant may be entitled to claim interest pursuant to a particular clause in a contract. A claimant would normally seek to do this where the contractual interest rate is higher than the current statutory interest rate, ie usually 8% pa in non-commercial cases or 1% pa above base rate in commercial cases.

Where the contract does not provide for payment of interest, the claimant may nevertheless be entitled to claim a higher rate of interest than the statutory rate if the Late Payment of Commercial Debts (Interest) Act 1998 applies. A claimant who claims for interest under contract or the 1998 Act may well seek statutory interest under s 35A of the SCA 1981 or s 69 of the CCA 1984 in the alternative, just in case the court refuses to award interest under the contract or the 1998 Act.

In all cases a claimant can seek interest pursuant to statute. In the High Court this would be under s 35A of the SCA 1981, and in the county court under s 69 of the CCA 1984.

For further details see **2.7.2** and the flowchart in **Appendix C(4)**.

There now follow two examples of particulars of claim, both concerning a breach of contract claim. In the first example the claim is for a specified amount of money. Interest is claimed under the Late Payment of Commercial Debts (Interest) Act 1998 where a reference rate of 2% pa has been assumed.

7.2.1.6   Example of particulars of claim in a county court debt claim (particulars of claim set out on claim form)

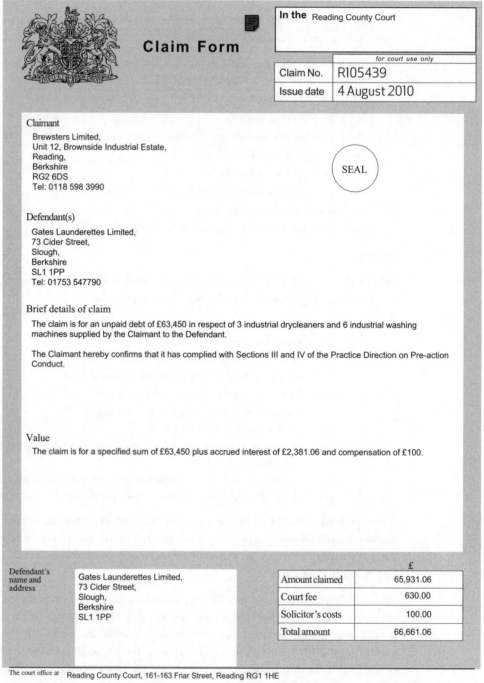

In the	Reading County Court

Claim Form

	for court use only
Claim No.	R105439
Issue date	4 August 2010

SEAL

Claimant

Brewsters Limited,
Unit 12, Brownside Industrial Estate,
Reading,
Berkshire
RG2 6DS
Tel: 0118 598 3990

Defendant(s)

Gates Launderettes Limited,
73 Cider Street,
Slough,
Berkshire
SL1 1PP
Tel: 01753 547790

Brief details of claim

The claim is for an unpaid debt of £63,450 in respect of 3 industrial drycleaners and 6 industrial washing machines supplied by the Claimant to the Defendant.

The Claimant hereby confirms that it has complied with Sections III and IV of the Practice Direction on Pre-action Conduct.

Value

The claim is for a specified sum of £63,450 plus accrued interest of £2,381.06 and compensation of £100.

Defendant's name and address	Gates Launderettes Limited, 73 Cider Street, Slough, Berkshire SL1 1PP		£
		Amount claimed	65,931.06
		Court fee	630.00
		Solicitor's costs	100.00
		Total amount	66,661.06

The court office at   Reading County Court, 161-163 Friar Street, Reading RG1 1HE

is open between 10 am and 4 pm Monday to Friday. When corresponding with the court, please address forms or letters to the Court Manager and quote the claim number.

N1 Claim form (CPR Part 7) (01.02)   *Printed on behalf of The Court Service*

	Claim No.	R105439

Does, or will, your claim include any issues under the Human Rights Act 1998?   ☐ Yes   ☑ No

Particulars of Claim (attached)(to follow)

1. By clause 1 of a written agreement (the 'Agreement') dated 3 March 2010 the Claimant agreed to sell to the Defendant machinery, namely 3 Chloridal dry cleaning machines and 6 Isadal washing machines for an agreed price of £63,450.00. A copy of the Agreement is attached.

2. By clause 4 of the Agreement payment of the agreed price was due within 7 days of delivery.

3. In pursuance of clause 6 of the Agreement the machinery was delivered to the Defendant's premises at 6, Station Road, Reading on 13 March 2010.

4. In breach of the Agreement the Defendant has failed to pay the agreed price or any part thereof.

5. The Claimant claims the sum of £63,450.00.

6. The Claimant claims interest on the sum of £63,450.00 and compensation under The Late Payment of Commercial Debts (Interest) Act 1998.

AND THE CLAIMANT CLAIMS

1. The sum of £63,450.00

2. Interest pursuant to The Late Payment of Commercial Debts (Interest) Act 1998. For the purposes of the Act, both parties acted in the course of business. The statutory interest began to run from and including 21 March 2010 (the 8th day after delivery) at 8% over the reference rate of 2% then in force, totalling 10% per annum. Interest due to the date of issue is £2,381.06 (21 March 2010 to 4 August 2010 inclusive being 137 days) and is continuing until judgment or sooner payment at the daily rate of £17.38.

3. Compensation for late payment pursuant to The Late Payment of Commercial Debts (Interest) Act 1998 in the sum of £100.

DATED: 4 August 2010

Statement of Truth
*(I believe)(The Claimant believes) that the facts stated in these particulars of claim are true.
* I am duly authorised by the claimant to sign this statement

Full name   Brian Charlton

Name of claimant's solicitor's firm   Collaws

signed   *Brian Charlton*   position or office held   Managing Director

*(Claimant)(Litigation friend)(Claimant's solicitor)   (if signing on behalf of firm or company)

*delete as appropriate

Collaws,
14 Ship Street,
Weyford,
Guildshire WE1 8HQ
Ref: BM/ABC/Brewsters
DX 1599 Weyford
Fax: 01904 876554

Claimant's or claimant's solicitor's address to which documents or payments should be sent if different from overleaf including (if appropriate) details of DX, fax or e-mail.

7.2.1.7   Example of particulars of claim in a High Court claim for breach of contract

IN THE HIGH COURT OF JUSTICE   2010 I No 876

QUEEN'S BENCH DIVISION

READING DISTRICT REGISTRY

BETWEEN

INDUSTRIAL MANUFACTURING LIMITED	Claimant
and	
HEATECHS LIMITED	Defendant

PARTICULARS OF CLAIM

1.   At all material times the Defendant carried on business as a manufacturer and supplier of central heating boilers and systems.

2.   By a written contract made on 21 April 2010 between the Claimant and Defendant, the Defendant agreed to sell to the Claimant a central heating gas boiler and integrated water pump described in clause 1 as a Heatechs Powerheat Unit Model 312K ('the Unit') for the sum of £70,000. A copy of the contract is attached.

3.   The Claimant bought the Unit from the Defendant who sold it in the course of its business. It was an implied term of the contract that the Unit should be of satisfactory quality.

4.   Further, during a telephone conversation at about 11.30 am on 20 April 2010, the Claimant by its contracts manager, Ian Jones, expressly or by implication made known to the Defendant (represented by their sales manager, Polly Rees) the particular purpose for which it required the Unit, namely for the purpose of installation in the Claimant's factory 'as part of a heating system required to be in continuous use for 6 days per week'. It was an express and/or implied term of the contract that the Unit to be delivered by the Defendant should be reasonably fit for that particular purpose.

5.   In purported performance of the contract the Defendant delivered the Unit on 23 June 2010 when the Claimant paid the Defendant the agreed sum of £70,000. The Unit was installed by the Claimant on or about 3 July 2010.

6.   In breach of the express and/or implied terms the Unit delivered by the Defendant was not of satisfactory quality and was not reasonably fit for its particular purpose.

PARTICULARS OF BREACH

The impeller retaining nut on the integrated water pump was insufficiently secure because the thread was 0.4cm wide whereas the maximum that it should have been was 0.2cm wide.

7.   As a consequence of the breaches of terms the integrated water pump failed to operate and the boiler in the Unit became or had become drained of water on 3 August 2010 and overheated as a result. When the pump effectively re-engaged cold water flowed into the boiler causing it to explode and rupture on 3 August 2010 and the pipe connections to distort. As a result the boiler house had to be pumped out and repaired and a new boiler installed. During this time the Claimant lost 5 days of production.

8.   By reason of the above the Claimant has suffered loss and damage.

PARTICULARS OF LOSS AND DAMAGE

Cost of new boiler	£72,500
Cost of installation of new boiler	£4,700
Cost of pumping out boiler house and repairing damaged premises	£17,625
Consequential losses as the result of production losses (estimated)	£25,000

9.   In respect of damages awarded the Claimant is entitled to interest pursuant to s 35A of the Senior Courts Act 1981 at such rates and for such period as the Court thinks just.

AND THE CLAIMANT CLAIMS:

(1)   Damages pursuant to paragraph 8 above;

(2)   Interest pursuant to paragraph 9 above.

Dated 8 December 2010.

Singleton Trumper & Co

STATEMENT OF TRUTH

I believe that the facts stated in these Particulars of Claim are true. I am duly authorised by the Claimant to sign this statement.

Signed: *D Smith*
           DAVID SMITH
           Director of Claimant company

The Claimant's Solicitors are Singleton Trumper & Co of Bank Chambers, Streatham, Reading RD62 5PA where they will accept service of proceedings on behalf of the Claimant.

To the Defendant

To the Court Manager.

7.2.2   Particulars of breach and damage

It is necessary to include detailed particulars of some aspects of the claim. For example, particulars of the breach of a contract or tortious duty must always be stated so that the defendant knows exactly the manner in which he is alleged to have been in breach. Similarly, the detail of the claim for damages is often most conveniently set out in 'particulars of loss and damage' where each head of damage is itemised. See paras 6 and 8 in the example at **7.2.1.7**.

7.2.2.1   The summary for relief

The relief or remedy claimed must be specifically stated in the particulars of claim. Traditionally, although not a requirement of the CPR 1998, it is often repeated in summary form towards the end of the particulars of claim, immediately before the date, and will vary depending upon the subject matter of the claim.

In a debt claim, the summary will often include the claim for the amount of the debt, the exact amount of interest claimed up to the date of issue of the proceedings and the daily rate of interest claimed thereafter. In a damages claim, it will include the claim for damages plus interest.

7.2.3   The statement of truth

If the particulars of claim are not part of the claim form itself, they must be verified by a statement of truth (see **5.3.1.9**).

7.2.4   Practical points

Whilst the CPR 1998 provide for the content and format of statements of case, practitioners will adopt their own style within that framework. For example, in the '*Industrial Manufacturing Limited v Heatechs Limited*' particulars of claim at **7.2.1.7**, para 3 states that the sale was in the course of the defendant's business. This is because the claimant wishes to rely upon the terms implied by the Sale of Goods Act 1979, which apply only where the sale was made in the course of the defendant's business. However, many practitioners do not consider it necessary to state this explicitly, as they rely upon the description of the defendant's business in the opening paragraph and the subsequent entry into the contract as satisfying this requirement. When looking at precedents, you will see that this additional paragraph appears in some but not others – neither is wrong, they are merely alternatives.

Another point to consider is the chronology of the material facts in the same example. We refer first (in para 2) to the contract that was made on 21 April 2010 and later (in para 4) to a conversation which took place on 20 April 2010. This is because the conversation became incorporated into the contract as a condition. This is the traditional way of setting out such material. However, an alternative would be to deal with the conversation first, then with the contract and, thirdly, to refer back to the conversation when stating the relevant condition of the contract.

A vital point to remember is that there must be a link or thread between the key parts of the particulars of claim. So, in a breach of contract claim:

(a)   the express and/or implied terms relied on must be the same ones said to have been breached by the defendant;

(b)   the factual consequences of the breach should be the same ones said to constitute the damage and loss.

You can see this in the *Industrial Manufacturing Limited v Heatechs Limited* example at **7.2.1.7**. Namely:

(a)   the terms relied on are set out in paras 3 and 4, whilst exactly the same terms are said to have been broken in para 6;

(b)   the factual consequences of the breach are set out in para 7 (boiler exploded, boiler house pumped out and repaired, new boiler installed and five days of production lost), and these are then quantified and particularised in para 8.

7.2.5 Template

A template to help you draft particulars of claim is set out at **Appendix B(3)**.

Case Study: Drafting the Particulars of Claim

Let us now consider how the particulars of claim were drafted in the case study at **Appendix D(4)**.

In **Chapter 5** we demonstrated how the claim form would have been drafted. The heading of the particulars of claim will be identical, namely:

In the High Court of Justice   [Number]
Queen's Bench Division
Weyford District Registry

BETWEEN

MR WILLIAM ULYSSES SIMPSON (1)
MRS RUPINDER SIMPSON (2)   Claimants

-and-

MR GEOFFREY IAN TEMPLAR   Defendant

Then we should identify the document itself. Traditionally this is done in the centre of the page, and sometimes the title appears in capital letters in tramlines or underlined. However, the rules do not dictate how this is done.

PARTICULARS OF CLAIM

You will recall that in **Chapter 3** the parties set out their respective positions in the pre-action correspondence. Drafting the particulars of claim is like preparing the letter before claim but, as we have seen above, we have to do so according to a totally different set of rules.

Remember that the cause of action here is negligence. So the initial material facts need to establish the duty of care situation, ie:

Paragraph 1 that the Claimants own the property, as defined, and

Paragraph 2 that on the material day and time the defendant drove his car onto that property.

Next in para 3 the allegation of breach of that duty, namely negligence by the defendant, is made, followed by detailed particulars of that negligence. The purpose is to enable the defendant to understand exactly what he is alleged to have done wrong so that he can respond. In this case you will recall from Chapter 3 that the claimants obtained a report from an accident reconstruction expert. From that report their solicitors will be able to identify the allegations which show the defendant fell below the required standard of care and so breached the duty of care that he owed to the claimants.

Note that the particulars of negligence are listed for ease of reference. The defendant will know that the claim against him is that he was driving too fast and lost control of the vehicle. This was apparent from his swerving on and off the driveway – an allegation based on the evidence of Mr Simpson, who was an eye-witness, and the conclusions drawn by the Simpsons' accident reconstruction expert from the tyre marks on the driveway. Note, however, that these sources of the allegation are not stated. Remember, the detailed evidence from witnesses and experts comes next, at Stage 3. Here, at Stage 2, only material facts should be stated, and these include the final particulars of negligence against the defendant of failing to use his brakes properly and manoeuvre the car so as to avoid the collision.

Next, in para 4 it is stated that the defendant's negligence caused loss to the claimants. So that the defendant knows how much is being claimed, figures are stated where these are available, but otherwise estimates are given of each item claimed (otherwise known as the heads of damage).

What do the claimants want on any damages awarded? Interest – so this is stated at para 5. The principles relating to the award of interest on damages were outlined at **7.2.1.5** but the detail can be found at **2.7**. As this is an unspecified claim, the claimants cannot calculate how much interest will be awarded as they have to rely on the court's discretionary power to award interest at such rate and for such period as the court sees fit.

The particulars of claim are dated and signed by the claimants' solicitors in the name of the firm: see PD 5, para 2.1.

A statement of truth is then included. Whilst a party's solicitor may sign the statement of truth, it is preferable, where possible, for the client to sign it. See **5.3.1.9** for a further discussion of the significance of the statement of truth and the options available. Here both claimants sign, but expressing their own personal and individual belief in the contents of the document.

The document ends with the name and address of the claimants' solicitors and confirms that the address is the claimants' address for service. One copy of the particulars of claim will be filed at the court and another served on the defendant.

7.3 The defence

7.3.1 Contents

As we saw in **Chapter 6**, the defendant has a limited amount of time in which to file a defence with the court, depending upon whether or not an acknowledgement of service has been filed.

Rule 16.5 sets out what must be contained in the defence:

(1)   In his defence, the defendant must state—

    (a)   which of the allegations in the particulars of claim he denies;

    (b)   which allegations he is unable to admit or deny, but which he requires the claimant to prove; and

    (c)   which allegations he admits.

(2)   Where the defendant denies an allegation—

    (a)   he must state his reasons for doing so; and

    (b)   if he intends to put forward a different version of events from that given by the claimant, he must state his own version.

(3)   A defendant who—

    (a)   fails to deal with an allegation; but

    (b)   has set out in his defence the nature of his case in relation to the issue to which that allegation is relevant,

shall be taken to require that allegation be proved.

(4)   Where the claim includes a money claim, a defendant shall be taken to require that any allegation relating to the amount of money claimed be proved unless he expressly admits the allegation.

(5)   Subject to paragraphs (3) and (4), a defendant who fails to deal with an allegation shall be taken to admit that allegation.

(6)   If the defendant disputes the claimant's statement of value under rule 16.3 he must—

    (a)   state why he disputes it; and

    (b)   if he is able, give his own statement of the value of the claim.

(7)   If the defendant is defending in a representative capacity, he must state what that capacity is.

(8)   If the defendant has not filed an acknowledgement of service under Part 10, he must give an address for service.

A party is required to verify that the facts stated in the defence are true by way of a statement of truth (see **5.3.1.9**).

7.3.2   Admissions, non-admissions, denials and assertions

The defence must provide a comprehensive response to the particulars of claim, and therefore, in respect of each allegation in the particulars of claim, there should be an admission, a denial or, where the defendant has no knowledge of the matter stated, a requirement that the claimant prove the point, ie a non-admission. Any denial must be explicit and a defendant must state his reasons for denying the allegation in the particulars of claim. If the defendant wishes to put forward a version of events different from that given by the claimant, the defendant must state his own version. A bare denial is not acceptable. Moreover, by the so-called 'rule of implied admissions', a defendant who fails to deal with an allegation is taken to admit it: see r 16.5(5) at **7.3.1** above.

7.3.3   Point-by-point response

In order to ensure that every allegation in the particulars of claim is dealt with and nothing is admitted through omission (see r 16.5(5)), the defence usually answers each paragraph of the claim in turn. If a paragraph contains more than one allegation, each should be answered point by point. This is the approach adopted in the defence to the breach of contract claim between Industrial Manufacturing Limited and Heatechs Limited in the example set out at **7.3.7** below.

7.3.4   Causation and mitigation of loss

Very often, on the issue of causation, the defence will allege that the claimant caused his own loss. If known, the defendant should assert how. Also, it may be appropriate for the defendant to allege that the claimant failed to mitigate his loss. Details of the allegation should be given, for example an explanation of why the head of damage is said to be unreasonably large and an assertion as to what would have been a reasonable amount.

7.3.5 Defence of limitation

By PD 16, para 13.1, a defendant must give details of the expiry of any relevant limitation period that is relied on in his defence.

7.3.6 Address for service

When giving an address for service, the defendant must include a postcode. If the defendant is an individual, he must provide his date of birth in the defence (or acknowledgement of service, admission, defence, reply or other response). See PD 16, paras 10.6 and 10.7.

7.3.7 Example of a defence in a High Court claim for breach of contract

IN THE HIGH COURT OF JUSTICE   2010 I 876
QUEEN'S BENCH DIVISION
READING DISTRICT REGISTRY

BETWEEN

INDUSTRIAL MANUFACTURING LIMITED   Claimant

and

HEATECHS LIMITED   Defendant

DEFENCE

1. The Defendant admits paragraphs 1 to 4 of the Particulars of Claim.

2. The delivery of the Unit referred to in paragraph 5 of the Particulars of Claim was wholly in accordance with the terms of the contract and constituted full and complete performance thereof by the Defendant. Payment of the agreed sum of £70,000 by the Claimant is admitted. No admission is made as to the installation of the Unit by the Claimant as the Defendant has no knowledge of that matter.

3. The Defendant denies it was in breach of contract as alleged in paragraph 6 of the Particulars of Claim, or at all. The Defendant asserts that the Unit supplied was of satisfactory quality and fit for its purpose. In particular, the impeller retaining nut on the water pump was sufficiently secure by means of a 0.4cm thread.

4. The Defendant makes no admission as to the matters stated in paragraph 7 as the Defendant has no knowledge of these matters.

5. As to paragraph 8 it is not admitted that the Claimant has suffered the alleged or any loss and damage as the Defendant has no knowledge of these matters.

6. If, which is not admitted, the Claimant suffered the loss and damage alleged in paragraph 8, it is denied that such occurred as a result of the alleged or any breach of term by the Defendant. Any such loss or damage was caused by the Claimant's installation and/or subsequent use of the Unit.

7. If, which is not admitted, the Claimant suffered the loss and damage alleged in paragraph 8, the Claimant failed to mitigate that loss and damage. In particular, it was unreasonable to stop production for 5 days.

8. In all the circumstances it is denied that the Claimant is entitled to the relief claimed or any relief.

Dated 5 January 2011.

Haughton & Co

STATEMENT OF TRUTH

I believe that the facts stated in this Defence are true. I am duly authorised by the Defendant to sign this statement.

Signed: *D Bennett*

D. BENNETT, Managing Director of the Defendant company

The Defendant's Solicitors are Haughton & Co, 19 High Pavement, Reading RD61 4UZ, where they will accept service of proceedings on behalf of the Defendant.

To the Court Manager and the Claimant.

7.3.8   Some points to note from the example

The consequence of making admissions in the defence is that the claimant does not have to prove the point at trial. Such admissions are most often made in respect of facts which came into existence prior to the alleged breach of contract or negligent act, such as the date, the parties and the terms of the contract. See para 1 of the example in **7.3.7** above.

When answering each paragraph of the claim, the defendant should clearly deny any allegations which are disputed and make clear admissions in respect of the factual issues which are not in dispute, eg para 1 in the above example. Any allegations of loss or damage which are disputed should be 'not admitted' in the defence, such as in para 4 of the example at **7.3.7**. The defendant should also include any additional facts in the defence which make his side of the story clearer (see paras 3, 6 and 7 of the example).

7.3.9   Counterclaim

If a defendant wishes to make his own claim against a claimant, he should do this by way of a counterclaim. The defence and counterclaim will form one document. Counterclaims are considered in more detail in **Chapter 8**.

7.4   Reply to defence

A claimant may wish to file a reply to the defence but is under no obligation to do so. He should do so if he needs to allege facts in answer to the defence which were not included in the particulars of claim. By r 16.7(1), a claimant who does not file a reply to the defence is not taken to admit the matters raised in the defence. There is therefore no corresponding rule of implied admission which we saw when looking at the defence itself (see **7.3.2**). In practice, replies to defences are most common where the defendant has made a counterclaim. Then a claimant must file a defence to the counterclaim to prevent default judgment being entered against him, and will usually incorporate a reply to the defence as well.

7.5   The role of statements of case

7.5.1   Defining the issues

How do the statements of case define the issues between the parties? If the particulars of claim have set out the factual allegations and the defence answered each allegation by way of admission, non-admission or denial, then by comparing the two documents we can identify the issues in dispute (namely, those not admitted and denied). So if we compare these documents in the *Industrial Manufacturing Limited v Heatechs Limited* example at **7.2.1.7** and **7.3.7**, we have the following agreed issues and issues in dispute:

Example 1 – Agreed issues

Particulars of claim	Defence	Issue
Paragraph 1	Paragraph 1	Defendant a manufacturer and supplier of central heating boilers and systems.
Paragraph 2	Paragraph 1	Written contract made on 21 April 2010 for the Unit.
Paragraph 3	Paragraph 1	Implied term that Unit to be of satisfactory quality.
Paragraph 4	Paragraph 1	Express or implied term that Unit to be reasonably fit to heat Claimant's factory continuously six days a week.
Paragraph 5	Paragraph 2	Unit delivered to Claimant on 23 June 2010 when payment of £70,000 made.

Example 2 – Issues in dispute

Particulars of claim	Defence	Issue
Paragraph 5	Paragraph 2	Claimant installed Unit on 3 July 2010.
Paragraph 6	Paragraph 3	Defendant breached contract as impeller retaining nut had insufficient thread.
Paragraph 7	Paragraph 4	On 3 August 2010 boiler overheated and exploded.
Paragraph 8	Paragraph 5	Claimant suffered loss due to Defendant's breach.
Paragraph 8	Paragraph 5	Claimant's loss consists of cost of new boiler and its installation, cost of pumping out and repairing boiler house and loss of profit.
Paragraph 8	Paragraph 6	Claimant caused own loss by way installed and/or subsequently used Unit.
Paragraph 8	Paragraph 7	Claimant failed to mitigate its loss.

Case Study: The Defence

Let us consider how the defendant's solicitors set about drafting the defence at **Appendix D(5)**. Look again at the claimants' particulars of claim at **Appendix D(4)**. What facts is the defendant going to admit, not admit and dispute? For the disputed facts, what is the defendant's own version?

The defendant will admit that at the material time he was the driver of the car and that his vehicle collided with the extension of the claimants' property. The defendant does not strictly know that the Simpsons own the property and he could make a non-admission requiring the claimants to prove it. However, the defendant is prepared to admit it here. He will, of course, dispute that he drove negligently and that he is liable for any loss. At this stage he will not make any admissions about the amount of the claimants' loss as he has no knowledge of that.

So for the purposes of the defence the response to the particulars of claim in the case study will be:

Particulars of Claim	Issue	Response
Paragraph 1	Claimant is owner of Bliss Lodge	Admit – defendant does not dispute this
Paragraph 2	Date and time of accident, details of vehicle	Admit – these facts are agreed
Paragraph 3	Allegation of negligence resulting in collision with extension together with Particulars of Negligence.	Deny negligence and explain why. What about the collision? This is admitted. His car did collide with the extension but he denies it was his fault.

Particulars of Claim	Issue	Response
Paragraph 4	Allegation of loss caused by the negligence of the defendant and particulars of loss.	As above the defendant will admit the collision but will deny that the damage was caused by his negligence. He will make no admissions as to the losses claimed as he has no knowledge of these and will require the claimants to prove the amount of their losses.
Paragraph 5	Interest	There is no need to respond to the claim for interest. Interest can be awarded here only if the claimants are awarded damages, and the defendant will deny that the claimants are entitled to any damages.

In addition, the defendant can allege in the alternative that the claimants were contributory negligent. But does that deal with all the issues the defendant wants the court to decide? Look again at **Appendix D(3)**. From this letter we can see that the defendant has indicated an intention to defend the claim and make a claim of his own. He could start separate proceedings, but this would not be cost-effective and so his best course of action is to make his own claim by way of a counterclaim (**7.3.9** above). In **Chapter 8** we shall consider how to draft that part of the document.

7.6 Amendments to statements of case (Part 17)

In a perfect world, nobody would ever have to amend their statements of case. However, sometimes mistakes are made, and on other occasions fresh information comes to light after the statement of case has been served. Part 17 of CPR 1998 provides the ways in which statements of case can be amended.

7.6.1 Amendments before service

A party may amend his statement of case at any time before it has been served.

7.6.2 Amendments with permission

After a party has served his statement of case, he can amend it only with either:

(a)   the written consent of all of the parties; or

(b)   the permission of the court.

On making an application for permission to amend the statement of case, the applicant should file a copy of the statement of case with the proposed amendments along with the application notice (see **Chapter 10**).

If the court grants permission for the amendment, the applicant must file the amended statement of case and serve the order and the amended statement of case on all other parties.

The statement of case will be endorsed with the words:

> Amended [describe the type of statement of case] by Order of [name of master/district judge] dated [   ].

The amended statement of case need not show the original text unless the court directs otherwise.

7.6.3 Directions following amendment

If the court gives permission to amend the statement of case, it may give directions regarding amendments to any other statement of case and service of the amended statements of case. It is common, for example, for a defendant to be allowed to amend his defence if the court has given the claimant permission to amend his particulars of claim.

7.6.4 Application to amend the statement of case outside the limitation period

If a claim is made after the relevant limitation period has expired, the defendant has an absolute defence (see **2.5.2.1**). So, if the amendment will add or substitute a new claim, the new claim must arise out of the same facts or substantially the same facts as the claim which the applicant has already made in the proceedings.

If the amendment is to correct a mistake as to the name of a party, the mistake must be genuine and one which would not have caused reasonable doubt as to the identity of the party in question.

If the amendment alters the capacity in which a party brings his claim, the new capacity must be one which that party had when the proceedings commenced or has since acquired.

7.6.5 Statements of truth

By r 22.1(2), amendments to the statement of case have to be verified by a statement of truth (see **5.3.2**), unless the court orders otherwise.

7.6.6 Costs

A party applying for an amendment will usually be responsible for the costs of and caused by the amendment being allowed (see **10.3**).

7.6.7 Amendments without permission

Where a party has amended his statement of case without requiring the court's permission (ie, in the case of an amendment by consent or before service), the court may disallow the amendment (r 17.2). A party may apply to the court asking it to exercise its discretion to disallow within 14 days of service of the amended statement of case.

7.7 Requests for further information (Part 18)

7.7.1 The request

A party to the proceedings, or the court itself, may wish another party to give further information about its case. By r 18.1(1), the court may at any time order a party to:

(a)   clarify any matter which is in dispute in the proceedings; or

(b)   give additional information in relation to any such matter,

whether or not the matter is contained or referred to in a statement of case.

If one of the parties requires further information then, before applying to the court for an order, that party should first serve a written request on the other party stating a date for the response, which must allow a reasonable time for the response.

A request should be concise and strictly confined to matters which are reasonably necessary and proportionate to enable the applicant to prepare his own case or to understand the case he has to meet. The most common request is by a defendant seeking further information from a claimant who has failed to give sufficient particulars of breach and/or damage (see **7.2.2**).

Requests must be made as far as possible in a single comprehensive document and not piecemeal.

If the text of the request is brief and the reply is likely to be brief, the request may be made by letter. If so, the letter must state that it contains a request made under Part 18 and must not deal with any other matter. Otherwise, the request should be made in a separate document.

Any request must:

(a)   be headed with the name of the court and the title and number of the claim;

(b)   state in its heading that it is a Part 18 request, identify the applicant and the respondent, and state the date on which it is made;

(c)   set out each request in a separate numbered paragraph;

(d)   identify any document and (if relevant) any paragraph or words in that document to which the request relates;

(e)   state the date for a response.

If the request is not in the form of a letter, the applicant may, if this is convenient, put the request on the left-hand side of the document so that the response may appear on the right-hand side. If so, the applicant should serve two copies of the request on the respondent.

7.7.2   Response to the request

The response must be in writing, dated and signed by the respondent or his solicitor. If the original request was made in a letter, the response can also be in the form of a letter or a formal reply. If in a letter, it should state that it is a response to the request and should not deal with any other matters. The response should set out the same information as the request and then give details of the response itself. The respondent must file at court and serve on all parties a copy of the request and his response.

The response must be verified by a statement of truth (see **5.3.2**).

Example

In *InterDigital Technology Corp v Nokia Corp* [2008] EWHC 504, the parties were already involved in litigation known as UK2 and UK3. The defendant's defence to these proceedings included the following assertion:

> 9.1   This action is not brought for real commercial reasons but for tactical reasons relating to the ongoing litigation between InterDigital and Nokia . . .

The claimant asked for further information about para 9.1 as follows:

> Request
>
> Of paragraph 9.1 of the Defence.
>
> Please specify each and all of the 'tactical reasons' for which it is alleged this action has been brought.

The defendant's answer included the following:

> *Response*
>
> InterDigital's full motives are known only to it. But without limitation to the scope of paragraph 9.1, InterDigital's reasons for commencing this litigation include the tactical reasons listed below:
>
> (1)   in retaliation for and to punish Nokia for bringing the UK2 proceedings;
>
> (2)   to deter Nokia from pursuing UK2 and/or from bringing further proceedings in respect of InterDigital 's claimed essential patents;
>
> (3)   to force a more favourable settlement of UK2, in particular as a result of other matters referred to herein;
>
> (4)   to trap Nokia into adopting inconsistent positions in UK2 and UK3;
>
> (5)   to distract Nokia and in particular its external legal and expert advisers and from UK2 by imposing further burdensome work on them in the run-up to the UK2 trial.

> **Case study: Part 18 request**
>
> A further example of a Part 18 Request is in the case study at **Appendix D(7)**. There you will see that the Defendant has requested further information about certain aspects of the particulars of claim.

7.7.3 Cases where the respondent does not respond to the initial request

If the respondent objects to all or part of the request, or cannot comply with the request, he should inform the applicant, giving reasons and, where relevant, giving a date by which he will be able to comply with the request. He may do so by letter or by formal response. If the respondent considers that a response will involve disproportionate expense, he should explain briefly in his reply why he takes this view.

7.7.4 Applications for court orders

If no response is received or the response is considered to be inadequate, the applicant can apply for an order from the court (see **Chapter 10**). The court will grant an order only if it is satisfied that the request is confined to matters which are reasonably necessary and proportionate to enable the applicant to prepare his case or understand the case he has to meet.

7.8 Summary: how should you approach drafting particulars of claim?

7.8.1 Structure formalities: PD 5

Examples include:

(1) Paragraph 2.1 provides that statements of case drafted by a legal representative as a member or an employee of a firm should be signed in the name of the firm.

(2) Paragraph 2.2 includes that the document should be divided into numbered paragraphs, with all numbers, including dates, expressed as figures.

7.8.2 Content: PD 16

Examples include:

(1) If relying on written contract: PD 16, para 7.3 – a copy of the contract or documents constituting the agreement should be attached to or served with the particulars of claim.

(2) If relying on oral contract: PD 16, para 7.4 – the particulars of claim should set out the contractual words used and state by whom, to whom, when and where they were spoken.

(3) Stating a claim for interest: PD 16, para 3.7 (cross-referring to r 16.4(2)).

(4) Statement of truth: PD 16, para 3.4.

7.8.3 General points

(1) Be as brief and concise as possible. Include only material facts, but ensure all material facts are stated.

(2) State the case on a point-by-point basis in separate, consecutively numbered paragraphs and sub-paragraphs. So far as possible, each paragraph or sub-paragraph should contain no more than one allegation.

(3) Put the facts in chronological order, unless it is inappropriate to do so.

(4) Allege breach of terms and/or duty, or loss and damage, then follow that with particulars listed one by one in separately numbered sub-paragraphs.

(5) Use definitions where appropriate.

(6)   Refer to evidence and law only where it is proportionate and necessary to help particularise the case.

(7)   Attach documents only where it is proportionate and necessary to help particularise the case.

7.9   Summary: how should you approach drafting a defence?

7.9.1   Structure formalities: PD 5

Examples include:

(1)   Paragraph 2.1 provides that statements of case drafted by a legal representative as a member or an employee of a firm should be signed in the name of the firm.

(2)   Paragraph 2.2 includes that the document be divided into numbered paragraphs, with all numbers, including dates, expressed as figures.

7.9.2   Content: Rule 16.5

(1)   In his defence, the defendant must state—

(a)   which of the allegations in the particulars of claim he denies;

(b)   which allegations he is unable to admit or deny, but which he requires the claimant to prove; and

(c)   which allegations he admits.

(2)   Where the defendant denies an allegation—

(a)   he must state his reasons for doing so; and

(b)   if he intends to put forward a version of events different from that given by the claimant, he must state his own version.

(3)   A defendant who—

(a)   fails to deal with an allegation; but

(b)   has set out in his defence the nature of his case in relation to the issue to which that allegation is relevant,

shall be taken to require that allegation be proved.

(4)   Where the claim includes a money claim, a defendant shall be taken to require that any allegation relating to the amount of money claimed be proved unless he expressly admits the allegation.

(5)   Subject to paragraphs (3) and (4), a defendant who fails to deal with an allegation shall be taken to admit that allegation.

(6)   If the defendant disputes the claimant's statement of value under rule 16.3 he must—

(a)   state why he disputes it; and

(b)   if he is able, give his own statement of the value of the claim.

(7)   If the defendant is defending in a representative capacity, he must state what that capacity is.

(8)   If the defendant has not filed an acknowledgement of service under Part 10, he must give an address for service.

Part 22 requires a defence to be verified by a statement of truth.

7.9.3   General points

(1)   Be as brief and concise as possible. Include only material facts, but ensure all material facts are stated in the defence.

(2)   Answer each allegation point-by-point by reference to the numbered paragraphs of the particulars of claim.

(3)   Assert own case by way of defence and any contributory negligence, eg allege breach of duty then follow that with particulars listed one by one in separately numbered sub-paragraphs.

(4)   Use same definitions as in particulars of claim and any additional ones, where appropriate.

(5)   Refer to evidence and law only where it is proportionate and necessary to help particularise the defence.

(6)   Attach documents only where it is proportionate and necessary to help particularise the defence.

Chapter 8
Additional Proceedings and Part 8 Claims

8.1 Introduction

We have so far looked at the rules relating to a claimant bringing a claim against a defendant. Part 20 of the CPR 1998 deals with other types of additional claims which may be brought in the proceedings. The types of additional claims covered by Part 20 are set out in r 20.2:

   (1)   This Part applies to—

      (a)   a counterclaim by a defendant against the claimant or against the claimant and some other person;

      (b)   an additional claim by a defendant against any person (whether or not already a party) for contribution or indemnity or some other remedy; and

      (c)   where an additional claim has been made against a person who is not already a party, any additional claim made by that person against any other person (whether or not already a party).

   (2)   In these Rules—

      (a)   'additional claim' means any claim other than the claim by the claimant against the defendant; and

      (b)   unless the context requires otherwise, references to a claimant or defendant include a party bringing or defending an additional claim.

Frequently, a defendant who has been sued by a claimant wants to make a claim against that person.

Example

A supplies goods to B.

B has paid 50% of the price, but the other 50% is unpaid.

B sues A for damages for breach of contract based on the allegation that the goods were not of satisfactory quality.

A defends the claim (on the basis that the goods were of satisfactory quality) and also counterclaims for the balance of 50% of the price which is still outstanding.

This counterclaim is governed by Part 20.

Another common scenario is where the defendant wishes to pass the blame, either in whole or in part, on to a third party. The defendant may be seeking a full indemnity from the third party, or a contribution towards any damages he has to pay the claimant. A claim for an indemnity often arises where there is a contractual relationship between the defendant and the third party, and the defendant alleges that the third party is obliged by the terms of the contract to indemnify him if he is found liable in respect of the claimant's claim against him. Sometimes a right to an indemnity may arise from statute or by implication of law. An example of a claim for an indemnity is where a consumer sues a retailer in respect of goods which he alleges are not of satisfactory quality, and the retailer alleges that there was an inherent defect in the goods and attempts to pass on liability to the manufacturer. The retailer will claim an indemnity from the manufacturer in respect of any sums that he is ordered to pay to the consumer.

A claim for a contribution often arises where there are joint wrong-doers, and the defendant claims that the third party is partly responsible for the harm that the claimant has suffered. An example of a claim for a contribution is where the claimant claims damages from the defendant as a result of a road traffic accident, and the defendant alleges that another driver was partly to blame for the accident. A defendant will then claim a contribution from the other driver towards the damages which he is ordered to pay to the claimant.

These types of claims are further examples of additional claims.

8.2   Procedure

8.2.1   Counterclaims (r 20.4)

If a defendant wishes to make a counterclaim against a claimant, he should file particulars of the counterclaim with his defence. This should form one document, with the counterclaim following on from the defence.

If a defendant does this, he does not need permission from the court to make the counterclaim. However, if a defendant decides to make a counterclaim after he has already filed his defence, he will need the court's permission. The application for permission should be made on notice.

If he wishes to dispute the counterclaim, the claimant (who does not have the option of acknowledging service) has to file a defence to counterclaim within the usual 14-day period. This will usually be a reply (to the defence) and defence (to the counterclaim) (see **Appendix D(6)**). If the claimant fails to file a defence to the counterclaim, the defendant may enter judgment in default on the counterclaim. Therefore, if the claimant requires more time to file a defence to the counterclaim, he should request an extension of time from the defendant. As already seen (at **6.4**), the parties can agree an extension of up to 28 days in addition to the initial 14-day period.

8.2.2   Contribution or indemnity between co-defendants (r 20.6)

If one defendant wishes to seek a contribution or an indemnity from another defendant, after filing his acknowledgement of service or defence, he may proceed with his claim against his fellow defendant by:

(a)   filing a notice containing a statement of the nature and grounds of his claim; and

(b)   serving the notice on the co-defendant.

No permission is required if he files and serves the notice with the defence or, if the defendant against whom the claim is made is added later, within 28 days of that defendant filing his defence. Permission is required to file and serve the notice at all other times.

8.2.3   Other additional claims (r 20.7)

In other additional claims, such as a claim against a third party, the defendant may make an additional claim without the court's permission by issuing an appropriate claim form before or at the same time as he files a defence. Particulars of the additional claim must be contained in or served with the claim form.

If an additional claim is not issued at that time, the court's permission will be required. The application for permission can be made without notice, unless the court directs otherwise.

8.2.4 Applications for permission to make an additional claim

When the court's permission is required, because the counterclaim or other type of additional claim was not made at the time of filing the defence, the application notice should be filed with a copy of the proposed additional claim. The application for permission must be supported by evidence stating:

(a)   the stage which the proceedings have reached;

(b)   the nature of the claim to be made by the additional claimant, or details of the question or issue which needs to be decided;

(c)   a summary of the facts on which the additional claim is based; and

(d)   the name and address of the proposed additional defendant.

If there has been any delay in making the application, the evidence must also explain the delay. Where possible, the applicant should provide a timetable of the proceedings to date.

Rule 20.9(2) sets out the matters the court takes into account in deciding whether to grant permission, and these include:

(a)   the connection between the additional claim and the claim made by the claimant against the defendant;

(b)   whether the additional claimant is seeking substantially the same remedy which some other party is claiming from him;

(c)   whether the additional claimant wants the court to decide any question connected with the subject matter of the proceedings—

(i)   not only between existing parties but also between existing parties and a person not already a party; or

(ii)   against an existing party not only in a capacity in which he is already a party but also in some further capacity.

The court may permit the additional claim to be made, dismiss it, or require it to be dealt with separately from the claim by the claimant against the defendant.

8.2.5 Service (r 20.8)

If the defendant did not need permission in order to make the additional claim then:

(a)   in the case of a counterclaim, he must serve it on every other party when he serves his defence;

(b)   except for claims for contributions or indemnities from co-defendants, he must serve the additional claim on the new party within 14 days of issue.

If a defendant had to make an application for permission to issue an additional claim, the court will give directions as to service when granting permission to make the claim.

If a defendant serves an additional claim form on a person who is not already a party (such as a third party), he must also serve:

(a)   forms for defending or admitting or acknowledging service of the additional claim;

(b)   copies of every statement of case which has already been served; and

(c)   such other documents as the court may direct.

The defendant must also serve copies of the additional claim form on all existing parties to the proceedings.

8.2.6 Judgment in default on additional claims (r 20.11)

Special rules apply where the additional claim is not a counterclaim or a claim by a defendant for an indemnity or contribution against a co-defendant. In other cases, if the party against whom an additional claim is made fails to acknowledge service or file a defence:

(a)   he is deemed to admit the additional claim and will be bound by any decision in the proceedings between the claimant and the defendant which affects the additional claim; and

(b)   if a default judgment is entered against the additional claimant, he may also enter judgment in respect of the additional claim by filing a request in the relevant practice forms. However, the additional claimant will need permission to enter default judgment (which can be obtained without notice unless the court directs otherwise) if he has not satisfied any default judgment obtained against him; or he is seeking any remedy other than a contribution or an indemnity.

8.2.7   Directions (r 20.13)

If a defence is filed to an additional claim (other than a counterclaim), the court will arrange a hearing to give directions as to the future conduct of the case. In giving directions, the court must ensure that, as far as practicable, the additional claim and the main claim are managed together. At the directions hearing, the court may (see para 5.3 of PD 20):

(1)   treat the hearing as a summary judgment hearing,

(2)   order that the additional claim proceedings be dismissed,

(3)   give directions about the way any claim, question or issue set out in or arising from the additional claim should be dealt with,

(4)   give directions as to the part, if any, the additional defendant will take at the trial of the claim,

(5)   give directions about the extent to which the additional defendant is to be bound by any judgment or decision to be made in the claim.

8.2.8   Title of the proceedings

Paragraphs 7.1–7.6 of PD 20 give information as to how parties to additional claims should be described in the title of the proceedings. The title of every additional claim should include both the full name of each party and his status in the proceedings (ie, claimant, defendant, third party, fourth party).

8.3   Drafting a counterclaim

A defence and counterclaim is essentially just what its title suggests: a defence and a (counter) claim, set out in a single document (see PD 20, para 6.1). The title to the action remains the same but the document should be entitled, 'DEFENCE AND COUNTERCLAIM'. The document itself is then sub-divided into two sections, normally by centred sub-headings of 'DEFENCE' (at the start) and then 'COUNTERCLAIM' (immediately after the defence ends).

It is important to appreciate that, as this is one continuous document, the paragraph numbering therefore runs sequentially from the start of the defence through to the end of the counterclaim. The wording of any summary at the end should be, 'AND THE DEFENDANT COUNTERCLAIMS'.

In drafting terms, the defence and counterclaim is essentially the same as a separate defence and particulars of claim. The counterclaim is a self-standing claim (akin to particulars of claim), and so it must deal with all the material facts and particulars that establish the claim. What if facts that are material to the counterclaim have already been set out in, or admitted in, the defence? Rather than stating these again in full in the counterclaim, all that is needed is to cross-refer to the relevant paragraph or paragraphs of the defence.

It is best practice, as indeed with all statements of case, to plan the structure and content of this document before attempting to draft it. Indeed, it is recommended that you plan the counterclaim first as normal particulars of claim. This will ensure that it is complete. You can then plan the defence and subsequently decide what matters in the counterclaim can be dealt with by simple cross-referencing to the defence, and those which need to be stated in full.

Case Study: Drafting the Defence and Counterclaim

Let us briefly consider how the counterclaim was drafted as part of the statement of case at Appendix D(5). In **Chapter 7** we saw how the defence was planned and drafted. As the defendant wants to bring a claim of his own against the claimants, a counterclaim needs to be added as part of the statement of case. The defendant will not need the permission of the court to bring his counterclaim as long as he files the counterclaim with the defence: see r 20.4(2)(a) at **8.2.1** above.

Practice Direction 20, para 6.1 requires that the defence and counterclaim should be contained in a single document. When planning the content of the counterclaim, the best approach is to start by considering it as a stand-alone claim. The defendant is basing his counterclaim on the duty owed to him by Mr and Mrs Simpson under the Occupiers' Liability Act 1957. So let us first outline a case analysis for this, and then focus on the legal issues and the facts the defendant will be relying on for each element:

Duty of care	That the claimants were occupiers and the defendant a visitor to their property – this is, of course, part of the claimants' own claim (see paras 1 and 2 of the particulars of claim which have been admitted in paras 1 and 2 of the defence).
Breach	That the claimants left glass on the driveway which caused the defendant to lose control of the car resulting in the collision with the extension (see paras 3 and 4 of the defence).
Loss	That the defendant's car is written off, he has suffered property damage (computer and telephone) and consequential financial losses (accommodation, hire car, towing and storage).

So, how should Mr Templar's solicitors have approached drafting the counterclaim in light of this analysis? First, the basic formality of having a sub-heading for the title to this part of the statement of case. If you look at Appendix D(5) you will see that the defence is set out in paras 1 to 6, and that immediately following, in the centre of the page, is the sub-heading 'COUNTERCLAIM'. There is no rule that it needs to be in upper case characters – it just needs to stand out.

As the counterclaim is following the defence there is no need to type out again the facts already stated in the defence that form part of the counterclaim. The first paragraph of the counterclaim simply states that the relevant paragraphs are repeated – see para 7. This establishes the duty of care situation and the allegation of breach. Also note that you do not restart numbering the paragraphs.

So the rest of the counterclaim needs to make the allegations of loss resulting from the claimants' breach – see para 8.

The defendant should seek interest on any damages awarded, and so must include a claim for interest; here, as the claim is unspecified and in the High Court, it will be under s 35A of the SCA 1981 – see para 10.

The counterclaim is then dated and signed in the name of the solicitors' firm that drafted it.

A suitable statement of truth must then be added (see **5.3.1.9**) and the document completed with the usual closing formalities.

8.4   Part 8 claims

8.4.1   Introduction

The Part 8 claim procedure may be used by a claimant where he is seeking the court's decision on a question which is unlikely to involve a substantial dispute of fact, or if a Rule or Practice Direction requires or permits the use of the Part 8 procedure.

Practice Direction 8 lists various types of claim for which the procedure may be used, which include a claim by or against a child or patient which has been settled before the commencement of proceedings and where the sole purpose of the claim is to obtain the approval of the court to the settlement.

8.4.2   Procedure

The claimant issues a Part 8 claim form (Form N208), which must state:

(a)   the question the court is to decide, or the remedy the claimant is seeking;

(b)   any enactment under which the claim is being made;

(c)   the representative capacity (eg, litigation friend) of any of the parties.

Instead of serving particulars of claim, the claimant must file and serve any written evidence, usually in the form of witness statements, with the claim form.

The defendant must then file and serve an acknowledgement of service not more than 14 days after service of the claim form. Again, instead of serving a defence, the defendant has to file and serve his written evidence with the acknowledgement of service.

If the defendant fails to file an acknowledgement of service, the claimant is unable to obtain a default judgment, and the defendant may still attend the hearing of the claim. However, the defendant may not take part in the hearing unless the court gives permission.

The court may give directions, including a hearing date, when the claim form is issued, or otherwise as soon as practicable after the defendant has acknowledged service or the time for acknowledging service has expired.

All Part 8 claims are allocated to the multi-track.

Chapter 9

Case Management and Allocation of Cases

9.1 Introduction

One of the key elements of the CPR 1998 is the notion of case management. As we saw in **Chapter 1**, r 1.4 imposes a duty on the court to manage cases actively.

Part 3 of CPR 1998 gives the court a wide range of case management powers. We shall look first at the court's general powers in r 3.1(2) and then consider the specific power to strike out a party's statement of case in r 3.4(2).

9.2 The court's powers

Rule 3.1(2) sets out a non-exclusive list of the court's powers, which include instructions that the court can:

(a)   extend or shorten the time for compliance with any Rule, Practice Direction or court order (even if an application for extension is made after the time for compliance has expired);

(b)   adjourn or bring forward a hearing;

(c)   require a party or a party's legal representative to attend the court;

(d)   hold a hearing and receive evidence by telephone, or by using any other method of direct oral communication;

(e)   direct that part of any proceedings (such as a counterclaim) be dealt with as separate proceedings;

(f)   stay the whole or part of any proceedings or judgment either generally or until a specified date or event;

(g)   consolidate proceedings;

(h)   try two or more claims on the same occasion;

(i)   direct a separate trial of any issue;

(j)   decide the order in which issues are to be tried;

(k)   exclude an issue from consideration;

(l)   dismiss or give judgment on a claim after a decision on a preliminary issue;

(ll)   order any party to file and serve an estimate of costs;

(m)   take any other step or make any other order for the purpose of managing the case and furthering the overriding objective.

The court may make any order subject to conditions and can specify the consequence of non-compliance. Such conditions can include a requirement for a party to pay a sum of money into court pending the outcome of the proceedings. In particular, by r 3.1(5), the court may order a party to pay a sum of money into court if that party has, without good reason, failed to comply with a Rule, Practice Direction or a relevant pre-action protocol. In exercising its power under r 3.1(5), however, the court must have regard to both the amount in dispute and the costs which the parties have incurred or which they may incur.

By r 3.1(6A), the money paid into court stands as security for any sum payable by that party to any other party in the proceedings.

The court can normally exercise any of its powers of case management on its own initiative. However, before doing so, it must give any person likely to be affected by the order an opportunity to make representations within a specified time and in a specified manner.

If the court proposes to hold a hearing before making an order on its own initiative, it must give the parties at least three days' notice of the hearing.

The court may make a provisional order without notice to the parties. However, any party may then apply to set aside, vary or stay the order within seven days of service of the order on that party (or such other period as the court may specify). The order must notify the parties of this right.

9.3   Striking out a statement of case and other sanctions

Rule 3.4(2) gives the court a specific power to strike out all or part of a statement of case.

The court can exercise this power if it appears to the court:

(a)   that the statement of case discloses no reasonable grounds for bringing or defending the claim;

(b)   that the statement of case is an abuse of the court's process or is otherwise likely to obstruct the just disposal of the proceedings; or

(c)   that there has been a failure to comply with a rule, practice direction or court order.

9.3.1   Inadequate statements of case

Practice Direction 3 gives examples of the types of statement of case which may fall to be struck out within (a) above. These include particulars of claim which set out no facts indicating what the claim is about – for example, 'money owed £5,000' – and particulars of claim which contain a coherent set of facts, but those facts, even if true, do not disclose any legally recognisable claim against the defendant. As far as defences are concerned, it gives examples of a defence which consists of a bare denial or otherwise sets out no coherent statement of facts, or a defence which, whilst coherent, would not, even if true, amount in law to a defence to the claim.

The following is an example of how a judge might use this power.

Example

A claimant issues proceedings for the recovery of a debt. A defence is filed which simply consists of a bare denial that the money is due. The defence has therefore failed to comply with r 16.5 of CPR 1998 (see **Chapter 7**). The judge, when looking at the case, may, as part of his case management powers under Part 3, make an order that unless the defendant files a full defence setting out his reasons for denying that the debt is owed within seven days of service of the order, the defence will be struck out.

Note that the court may, as in the example given, make such an order of its own volition or, alternatively, the claimant in such a case may make an application to the court for an order in similar terms.

If, in the example given above, the defendant did not comply with the order then the claimant would be able to obtain judgment simply by filing a request for judgment. As this was a debt claim, the claimant would be able to obtain judgment for the amount of the debt, together with interest and costs. If it had been a claim for an unspecified sum, the judgment would be for an amount to be decided by the court at a disposal hearing. Note that the request must state that the right to enter judgment has arisen because the court's order has not been obeyed.

Continuing with the above example, if judgment is entered in these circumstances against the defendant, the defendant can apply to the court under r 3.6 for the judgment to be set aside. Such an application must be made not more than 14 days after the judgment has been served. If the judgment had been entered incorrectly (eg, prematurely), the court must set aside the judgment. However, if the judgment was entered correctly, r 3.9 (relief from sanctions) applies (see **9.4**).

9.3.2   Non-compliance with a Rule, Practice Direction or court order

The striking-out sanction is not confined to cases where the statement of case is defective. As stated in **9.3**, the court can also strike out a party's statement of case and enter judgment against him for 'failure to comply with a Rule, Practice Direction or court order'.

Striking out is, however, only one of a number of sanctions that the court can apply (see **9.3.3**). How does the court decide what is appropriate? The starting point for decisions on sanctions for default is *Biguzzi v Rank Leisure plc* [1999] 1 WLR 1926. This was an early post-CPR case where the Court of Appeal emphasised the importance of compliance with the CPR 1998 and court orders, but recognised that, whilst it would, on occasions, be appropriate to deal with non-compliance by striking out, there were less drastic but equally effective ways of dealing with default. In many cases, the use of these other powers would produce a more just result.

Given that there is a range of sanctions that the court can apply, when will it apply the ultimate sanction of striking out? In each case, the court will have to consider all the circumstances, and in particular the factors set out in r 3.9 (relief from sanctions: see **9.4**). However, the case law emphasises that the overriding objective of dealing with cases justly and the duty to ensure fairness will be a central consideration in the exercise of the court's discretion (see, eg, *Necati v Commissioner of Police for the Metropolis* [2001] LTL, 19 January). The court should also bear in mind the observations of the Court of Appeal in *Arrow Nominees Inc v Blackledge* [2000] 1 BCLC 709, that striking out a case purely on the basis of a breach of the rules or an order of the court may infringe Article 6(1) of the ECHR unless the breach itself meant that it may no longer be possible to have a fair trial.

None of the above should, however, be read as a reluctance on the part of the courts to strike out a party's statement of case in appropriate circumstances. Where delay or non-compliance means that it is no longer possible to have a fair trial (see *Habib Bank Ltd v Abbeypearl Ltd and Others* [2001] EWCA Civ 62, [2001] 1 All ER 185), or where the default is so bad that it amounts to an abuse of the court (see *UCB Corporate Services Ltd v Halifax (SW) Ltd* [1999] 1 Lloyd's Rep 154), strike out may be the appropriate response.

Sanctions may also be imposed by the court for non-payment of any court fees. Where a party fails to pay a fee on filing an allocation questionnaire (see **9.5**), or a pre-trial checklist, listing questionnaire (see **9.6.2.6**), the court will serve notice requiring payment of the fee by a specified date. If the claimant does not pay the fee, or make an application for exemption from or remission of the fee within the specified time period, the claim will be struck out with costs.

9.3.3   Sanctions other than striking out

9.3.3.1   Costs

A common sanction is to require the party in default to pay the other party's costs occasioned by the delay on an indemnity basis. The court will make a summary assessment of those costs at the time of the hearing and may order those costs to be paid immediately. The solicitor handling the case would then have to explain to his client why he had been ordered to pay those costs. See generally **10.3** and **14.3.3.2**.

Where the court forms the view that the fault lies not with the party himself but with his legal representative, the court may make a wasted costs order. This obliges the legal representative to pay costs incurred by a party as a result of any improper, unreasonable or negligent act or omission on the part of the legal representative (SCA 1981, s 51). Before making such an order, the court must allow the legal representative a reasonable opportunity to attend a hearing and give reasons why the order should not be granted.

9.3.3.2   Interest

Alternatively, the court may make orders affecting the interest payable on any damages subsequently awarded to the claimant. If the party at fault is the claimant, the court may reduce the amount of interest payable on his damages. If the party in default is the defendant, the interest payable on the claimant's damages at the end of the case may be increased.

9.3.3.3   Limiting the issues

The appropriate sanction may be to limit the issues that are allowed to proceed to trial. See, for example, *AXA Insurance Co Ltd v Swire Fraser* (2000) *The Times*, 19 January.

9.3.4   The unless order

If a party has not taken a step in the proceedings in accordance with a court order, what should the other party do? It will serve the overriding objective (see **1.1**) first to chase up the defaulting party promptly in correspondence. If that does not work, an application should be made to the court for an 'unless order'. This is reflected in fast track and multi-track proceedings, where, for example, a party fails to follow a case management direction. Practice Directions 28 (paras 5.1 and 5.2) and 29 (paras 7.1 and 7.2) both provide in these circumstances that:

> Where a party has failed to comply with a direction given by the court any other party may apply for an order to enforce compliance or for a sanction to be imposed or both of these.

The party entitled to apply for such an order must do so without delay, but should first warn the other party of his intention to do so.

The 'unless order' is not, strictly speaking, a sanction but rather a suspended sanction. The court makes an order that unless a party complies with a particular court order or rule within a specified time, his claim or defence will be struck out.

A party who is subject to an unless order but who cannot make the deadline set should apply to the court before that deadline expires to extend it. Why? Because the strike out takes effect without any further court order (see PD 3, para 1.9).

Example

Although an order of the court required the defendant, D, to serve his witness statements on his opponent, C, by 5 November 2010, D did not do so despite reminders from C. In order to force D to comply, C applies for and obtains an unless order requiring D to serve the witness statements by a new deadline (usually seven or 14 days from the date of the unless order), failing which his defence will be struck out.

9.4   Relief from sanctions

A party's ability to obtain relief from the sanctions imposed by the court is dealt with by rr 3.8 and 3.9.

Where a party has failed to comply with a Rule, Practice Direction or court order, any sanction for failure to comply imposed by the Rule, Practice Direction or court order has effect unless the party in default applies for and obtains relief from the sanction. Note that where the sanction is the payment of costs, the party in default may obtain relief only by appealing against the order for costs.

Where a Rule, Practice Direction or court order requires a party to do something within a specified time, and specifies the consequence of failure to comply, can the time for doing the act in question be extended by agreement between the parties? No, says r 3.8(3).

9.4.1 Relevant factors

Where a party applies for relief from any sanction for failure to comply with any Rule, Practice Direction or court order, the court will consider all the circumstances, including the following (r 3.9(1)):

(a)   the interests of the administration of justice;

(b)   whether the application for relief has been made promptly;

(c)   whether the failure to comply was intentional;

(d)   whether there is a good explanation for the failure;

(e)   the extent to which the party in default has complied with other rules, practice directions, court orders and any relevant pre-action protocol;

(f)   whether the failure to comply was caused by the party or his legal representative;

(g)   whether the trial date or the likely trial date can still be met if relief is granted;

(h)   the effect which the failure to comply had on each party; and

(i)   the effect which the granting of relief would have on each party.

Factor (c) is an important consideration. As Parker LJ stated in *Bournemouth & Boscombe Athletic FC Ltd v Lloyds Bank Plc* [2003] EWCA Civ 1755, [2003] LTL, 10 December:

> A finding of an intentional failure to comply with the CPR in the sense of a deliberate decision not to comply is, inevitably, a highly significant finding in the context of CPR 3.9. Depending on the circumstances of the particular case, it may or may not be decisive of the question whether relief should be granted under that rule; but, to put it no higher, in deciding whether to do so the court will be likely to regard it as a factor of very considerable weight. By comparison, a finding that the failure to comply was due to a mistaken understanding of the effect of the CPR (albeit a mistake for which there may have been little or no excuse) is a much less serious finding, which will be likely to carry correspondingly less weight.

This principle was confirmed in *CIBC Mellon Trust Co v Stolzenberg* [2004] EWCA Civ 827, (2005) *The Times*, 8 June. In this case, even though it was still possible to have a fair trial, the court decided that it was not in the interest of justice to grant relief from sanctions because the defendant had made a conscious decision not to comply with the orders of the court.

Although it is a relevant consideration on an application for relief whether the failure to comply is the failure of the party or his legal representative (r 3.9(1)(f)), the court will generally not be keen to spend time considering separately the conduct of the legal representatives from that which the party himself must be treated as knowing, encouraging or permitting (*Daryanani v Kumar & Co and Another* [2000] LTL, 15 March). After all, the other side will be equally affected whether the shortcomings are those of the party or his representatives. On the other hand, the issue of where the fault lies will be very relevant to the question of whether a wasted costs order is appropriate (see **9.3.3.1**).

An application for relief from sanctions must be supported by evidence, usually a witness statement.

9.4.2 Failure to give notice of CFA and/or AEI

As we saw at **2.4.3.3**, where a party fails to give notice of a CFA and/or an AEI either before or during proceedings then r 44.3(B)(1)(c) imposes the sanction of limiting the recoverability of that additional liability. In what circumstances, if any, should relief from that sanction be given? The court will, of course, have to apply the relevant factors, but Floyd J stated in *Supperstone v Hurst* [2008] EWHC 735 that relief from sanctions should not be granted lightly and any party who fails to comply with the CPR runs a significant risk that he will be refused relief. Thus if a party does not have a good explanation, or the other side is prejudiced by his failure, relief from sanctions will usually be refused. It is vitally important to the administration of justice that the rules of procedure are observed.

That led Master Campbell in *Kutsi v North Middlesex University Hospital NHS Trust* [2008] EWHC 90119 (Costs) to refuse any relief where the notice had not been given at all due to the solicitors being unaware of the need to give it.

9.5　Allocation

Part 26 of CPR 1998 deals with the preliminary stage of case management when cases are allocated to a particular track. This stage of case management arises where a defence has been filed.

Rule 26.2 provides for the automatic transfer of certain types of cases which are defended. If the claim is for a specified amount of money and the defendant is an individual then, if the claim was not commenced in the defendant's 'home court', the court will transfer the proceedings to the defendant's home court when a defence is filed (see **6.5.1**). This Rule also applies in certain circumstances when a defendant admits the claim (see **6.5**), or on an application to set aside a default judgment (see **10.5.1**).

In most cases, the crucial preliminary case management issue is that of allocation.

Where the claim is defended then, on receipt of the defence, the court will serve each party with an allocation questionnaire. This is usually in Form N150 and a copy of this form appears in **Appendix A(8)**. However, if the claim falls within the financial scope of the small claims track, a slightly different allocation questionnaire in Form N149 is sent to the parties. The remainder of this chapter will consider only the usual allocation questionnaire in Form N150.

The questionnaire must be returned by the parties to the court by the date stipulated in the questionnaire, which must be at least 14 days after service of the questionnaire. The claimant must pay a fee when filing his allocation questionnaire. Where there are two or more defendants, the questionnaire will be sent when all the defendants have filed their defence, or (provided at least one defendant files a defence) when the period for filing the last defence has expired, whichever is the sooner. If the matter is going to be automatically transferred to the defendant's home court then the court at which the proceedings were commenced will serve an allocation questionnaire before the proceedings are transferred.

9.5.1　Completing the allocation questionnaire

The allocation questionnaire (Form N150) is a key document in the progress of a case and must be completed carefully by each party and filed by the set date. The parties should consult one another and co-operate in completing the allocation questionnaire, although this must not delay its filing. Indeed, r 26.3(6A) provides that the date for filing cannot be varied by agreement between the parties. The form is divided into nine parts, lettered A to I.

9.5.1.1　Part A

Part A deals with settlement. The parties are reminded that under the CPR 1998 every effort should be made to settle the case and that the court will enquire as to what steps have already been taken in that respect. To assist the court a solicitor must confirm (by ticking a box) if he has explained to the client the need to try to settle, the options available and the possibility of costs sanctions if the client refused to do so. Moreover, it is made clear to the parties that their answers to this part will be taken into account when the court decides who pays costs and the amount of those costs (see **14.3**). The parties must then indicate whether or not they want to attempt to settle at this stage. If a party answers yes, the next question asks the parties if they wish there to be a one-month stay of proceedings so that they can attempt to settle the case. If all the parties request a stay, the court will usually order a stay of one month, or such other specified period as the court considers appropriate. Alternatively, the court, of its own initiative, may order a stay if it considers it appropriate. If a stay is granted and the parties feel they require more time than the initial period granted to try to reach a settlement, any of the parties may, by letter to the court, request an extension of time. More than one extension of the stay may be granted. If a settlement is reached, the claimant must tell the court. If a settlement is not reached, the court will allocate the case and give directions in the usual way. Note that in Part A the parties can request the court to arrange a mediation appointment. What if a party has indicated in Part A that he does not want to attempt to settle the case? That party will have to set out his reasons why he considers it inappropriate at this stage.

9.5.1.2   Part B

Part B asks the parties whether there is any reason why the case needs to be heard at a particular court. If the claim has been issued in the Central Office of the Royal Courts of Justice (RCJ) then each party should state whether he considers the claim should be managed and tried at the RCJ and, if so, why. As set out in para 2.6 of PD 29, claims suitable for trial in the RCJ include:

    (1)   professional negligence claims,

    (2)   Fatal Accident Act claims,

    (3)   fraud or undue influence claims,

    (4)   defamation claims,

    (5)   claims for malicious prosecution or false imprisonment,

    (6)   claims against the police,

    (7)   contentious probate claims.

If a claim does not fall within one of the above categories and has an estimated value of less than £50,000 then it will generally be transferred from the RCJ to a county court. If it has a value of more than £50,000, it will usually be transferred to a District Registry.

9.5.1.3   Part C

Part C of the allocation questionnaire asks the parties to state whether they have complied with the Practice Direction on Pre-Action Conduct or any relevant pre-action protocol and, if not, to explain the reasons why.

9.5.1.4   Part D

Part D asks the parties if they have made an application to the court, including an application for summary judgment (see **Chapter 10**) or to join another party into the proceedings. Any such application should be made as soon as possible. Part D then asks the parties to name the witnesses of fact they will be calling and what facts they are witnesses to. If a party does not wish to, or cannot, 'name names' at this stage, he can simply indicate the number of witnesses he may call on a particular fact. This Part also deals with expert evidence and asks the parties various questions about whether and, if so, how they wish to use expert evidence at the trial (see further **12.3**). Lastly, Part D asks the parties which track they consider is most suitable for their case. As already seen in **Chapter 1**, there are three tracks:

(a)   small claims;

(b)   fast track;

(c)   multi-track.

The basic criteria for allocation to a particular track is the value of the claim which is in dispute, disregarding interest, costs and any question of contributory negligence. If there is a counterclaim or additional claim, in assessing the value the court will not usually aggregate the claims but generally will regard the largest of the claims as determining the financial value of the claim. So, for example, if the original claim was for £20,000, but there is a counterclaim valued at £35,000, the latter figure will usually be the relevant one for allocation purposes (PD 26, para 7.7).

9.5.1.5 Part E

The parties should indicate at Part E any dates on which their expert witnesses or any other essential witness will be unavailable to give evidence. It is advisable also to state why the experts are unavailable on those dates (*Matthews v Tarmac Bricks and Tiles Ltd* [1999] CPLR 463). Part E asks the parties to state how long they estimate the trial or final hearing will take.

9.5.1.6 Part F

In accordance with Part F, the parties should attach a list of directions that are appropriate for the management of the case and indicate whether or not these are agreed. For the fast track, the parties should consider the directions outlined in PD 28 (see **Appendix A(14)**). For the multi-track the parties are referred to the Queen's Bench Division Practice Form, PF52.

9.5.1.7 Part G

Part G requires the parties to provide an estimate of costs incurred to date and the overall costs of the case. In fast track and multi-track cases, a detailed estimate is required (see **9.7**).

9.5.1.8 Part H

Part H reminds the parties that the allocation fee should be paid at this stage.

9.5.1.9 Part I

Part I asks the parties whether they have attached documents to the questionnaire and whether they intend to make any applications in the immediate future. The parties are also asked whether there is any other information which could assist the judge in managing the case.

9.5.2 Failure to file an allocation questionnaire

If none of the parties has filed an allocation questionnaire by the stipulated date, the matter will be referred to a judge for directions and the judge will order that all claims, defences and counterclaims should be struck out unless an allocation questionnaire is filed within seven days of service of the order (PD 26, para 2.5(1)).

If some, but not all, of the parties have filed an allocation questionnaire, the court will allocate the case on the basis of the information available or, if it does not have enough information, it will list an allocation hearing. Otherwise, the court will hold an allocation hearing on its own initiative only if it considers that it is necessary to do so. Where the court does order an allocation hearing to take place, the parties must be given at least seven days' notice of the hearing. Where an allocation hearing does take place then, by para 6.5 of PD 26, the legal representative who attends should, if possible, be the person responsible for the case and must, in any event, be familiar with the case, be able to provide the court with the information it is likely to need to take its decisions about allocation and case management, and have sufficient authority to deal with any issues that are likely to arise.

Paragraph 6.6 of PD 26 sets out the sanctions which the court will usually impose where a party has been in default in connection with the allocation procedure. In particular, where an allocation hearing takes place because a party has failed to file an allocation questionnaire or to provide further information which the court has ordered, the court will usually order that party to pay, on the indemnity basis (see **14.3.3.2**), the costs of any other party who has attended the hearing, summarily assess the amount of those costs (see **10.3**), and order them to be paid immediately or within a stated period. The court may order that if the party does not pay those costs within the time stated, that party's statement of case will be struck out.

These are very severe sanctions and emphasise the fact that the allocation stage is extremely important in the overall case management of the proceedings. It is therefore imperative that the parties return the allocation questionnaires, properly completed and within the requisite time period.

By para 2.4 of PD 26, if a court hearing takes place (eg, on an application for summary judgment under Part 24 – see **Chapter 10**) before the claim is allocated to a track, the court may, at that hearing, either dispense with the need for the parties to file allocation questionnaires, treat the hearing as an allocation hearing, make an order for allocation and give directions for case management, or fix a date for allocation questionnaires to be filed and give other directions. This is an example of the general principle in r 1.4(2)(i) that whenever a case comes for hearing before the court, the court should endeavour to carry out as much case management at that hearing as possible.

9.5.3 Scrutinising your opponent's allocation questionnaire

The parties may exchange questionnaires, but in any event copies are sent out by the court. What should you look for in your opponent's questionnaire? Pay particular attention to Part C and check that the answers are accurate. As to Part D, see how many witnesses of fact your opponent has and if any witnesses have been named. Should you consider interviewing any that are named? Then check your opponent's views on expert evidence. Is anything new revealed? Then check Part G and your opponent's costs estimate (see **9.7**). Finally, see if your opponent supplied any additional information at Part I.

9.6 Allocation to a track

After the filing of the allocation questionnaires or any allocation hearing, or at the end of any stay of proceedings, a case will be allocated to one of the three tracks. Generally, the most important factor in allocation will be the financial value of the claim.

Claims not exceeding £5,000 will normally be allocated to the small claims track.

Claims between £5,000 and £25,000 will normally be allocated to the fast track.

Claims exceeding £25,000 will normally be allocated to the multi-track.

Rule 26.8(1) sets out the factors to which the court must have regard, including:

(a)   the financial value, if any, of the claim;

(b)   the nature of the remedy sought;

(c)   the likely complexity of the facts, law or evidence;

(d)   the number of parties or likely parties;

(e)   the value of any counterclaim or other additional claim and the complexity of any matters relating to it;

(f)   the amount of oral evidence which may be required;

(g)   the importance of the claim to persons who are not parties to the proceedings;

(h)   the views expressed by the parties; and

(i)   the circumstances of the parties.

By r 26.8(2), when the court calculates the value of a money claim, it will disregard:

(a)   any amount not in dispute;

(b)   any claim for interest;

(c)   costs; and

(d)   any contributory negligence.

What if case involves more than one claim for money, eg a claim and counterclaim – should these be added together? No, states PD 26, para 7.7. The court will not generally aggregate the claims. Instead it will usually regard the largest of them as determining the value of the claims for allocation purposes.

Furthermore, the fast track is the normal track for claims with a value exceeding £5,000, but not £25,000, only if the trial is likely to last for no longer than one day; oral expert evidence at trial will be limited to no more than one expert per party in relation to any expert field and there will be expert evidence in no more than two expert fields. For example, if the court at the allocation stage considered that the trial was likely to last two days then the court will usually allocate it to the multi-track.

The court will not allocate proceedings to a particular track if the financial value of any claim in those proceedings exceeds the limit for that track, unless all the parties consent to the allocation of the claim to that track. So, for example, in a straightforward debt case worth £30,000, if one party asked for it to be allocated to the fast track rather than the multi-track, the court could not do this unless the other party consented (r 26.7(3)).

When it has allocated a claim to a track, the court will serve notification on every party. The court may subsequently re-allocate a claim to a different track either on the application of any party, or on its own initiative.

If a party is dissatisfied with the allocation to a particular track, PD 26, para 11 provides that he may:

(a)   appeal, if the order was made at a hearing at which he was present or represented, or of which he was given due notice; or

(b)   in any other case (eg, the case was allocated without an allocation hearing), apply to the court to re-allocate the claim.

9.6.1 Allocation to the small claims track (Part 27)

Part 27 of CPR 1998 deals with allocation to the small claims track. The small claims track is designed to provide a procedure whereby claims of not more than £5,000 in value can be dealt with quickly and at minimal cost to the parties.

Note that PD 26, para 8.1(1) provides that:

(a)   The small claims track is intended to provide a proportionate procedure by which most straightforward claims with a financial value of not more than £5,000 can be decided, without the need for substantial pre-hearing preparation and the formalities of a traditional trial, and without incurring large legal costs.

(b)   The procedures laid down in Part 27 for the preparation of the case and the conduct of the hearing are designed to make it possible for a litigant to conduct his own case without legal representation if he wishes.

(c)   Cases generally suitable for the small claims track will include consumer disputes, accident claims, disputes about the ownership of goods, and most disputes between a landlord and tenant other than those for possession.

(d)   A case involving a disputed allegation of dishonesty will not usually be suitable for the small claims track.

In most small claims cases, after allocation, the court will order standard directions and fix a date for the final hearing. The court does have the power to hold a preliminary hearing, but this will happen only in a very limited number of cases. Certain parts of the CPR 1998 do not apply to small claims, including Part 18 (Further Information), Part 31 (Disclosure and Inspection), Part 32 (Evidence), most of Part 35 (Experts and Assessors) and Part 36 (Offers to Settle), unless the court orders otherwise. But note that by r 27.2(3), the court may of its own initiative order a party to provide further information. The intention is to make the procedure as simple as possible because, in most cases, solicitors will not be involved. The reason for this is that, under r 27.14, the costs which can be recovered by a successful party are extremely limited, and therefore it is usually uneconomic for solicitors to represent the parties in a case proceeding on the small claims track.

The standard directions which the court gives in small claims cases are set out in various forms which are in Appendix B to PD 27 of CPR 1998. The directions vary depending on the type of case, so that there are particular directions for claims arising out of holidays or weddings. The most simple forms of directions as set out in Form A are as follows:

1   Each party shall deliver to every other party and to the court office copies of all documents (including any expert's report) on which he intends to rely at the hearing no later than [   ] [14 days before the hearing].

2   The original documents shall be brought to the hearing.

3   [Notice of hearing date and time allowed.]

4   The court must be informed immediately if the case is settled by agreement before the hearing date.

The hearing itself will be informal and, if all parties agree, the court can deal with the claim without a hearing at all. In other words, a court could make a decision based on the statements of case and documents submitted rather than by hearing oral evidence.

As mentioned earlier, the costs which can be recovered in a small claims case are limited by r 27.14. Generally speaking, the only costs recoverable are the fixed costs attributable to issuing the claim, any court fees paid and sums to represent travelling expenses and loss of earnings or leave. On those (rare) occasions where expert evidence is called, a limited amount may be recovered in respect of the expert's fees. The court does have power to award further costs if a party has behaved unreasonably.

It should be noted, however, that where a claim has been allocated to the small claims track but is subsequently reallocated to another track, the costs rules of the new track will apply from the date of reallocation.

9.6.2 Allocation to the fast track (Part 28)

When a case is allocated to the fast track, the court will give directions as to how the case is to proceed to trial. In most cases, the court will allocate the case to this track without a hearing and order standard directions.

9.6.2.1 Timetable of directions

Paragraph 3.12 of PD 28 (The Fast Track) sets out a typical timetable for case preparation of a case allocated to the fast track:

Disclosure	4 weeks
Exchange of witness statements	10 weeks
Exchange of experts' reports	14 weeks
Court sends pre-trial checklist, listing questionnaires	20 weeks
Parties file pre-trial checklists, listing questionnaires	22 weeks
Trial	30 weeks

These periods will run from the date of allocation.

The trial date will either be a fixed date or a 'trial period', not exceeding three weeks, within which the trial will take place. At this stage, the court is more likely to fix a 'trial period' rather than a fixed date for trial.

The parties may agree directions between themselves, but if they do so, the directions must be approved by the court (which will not necessarily accept them).

Fast track standard directions, dealing with disclosure, etc, are set out in the Appendix to PD 28. A copy appears at **Appendix A(14)**.

9.6.2.2   Varying directions (r 28.4)

Although the parties can vary certain directions by written agreement, for example for disclosure or exchange of witness statements, an application must be made to the court if a party wishes to vary the dates for:

(a)   the return of the allocation questionnaire and the pre-trial checklist;

(b)   the trial; or

(c)   the trial period.

Furthermore, the parties cannot agree to vary any matter if the change would lead to an alteration of any of those dates. For example, it would not be possible to agree to delay the exchange of witness statements until after the date for the return of the pre-trial checklist, since this would inevitably lead to the need to alter the trial date or period.

Practice Direction 28 states that any party who wishes to have a direction varied should take steps to do so as soon as possible (para 4.2(1)). There is an assumption that if an application to vary directions is not made within 14 days of the service of the order then the parties are content that the directions were correct in the circumstances then existing (para 4.2(2)).

A party dissatisfied with a direction or other order given by the court should either:

(a)   appeal, if the direction was given or the order was made at a hearing at which he was present or represented, or of which he had due notice; or

(b)   in any other case, apply to the court to reconsider its decision. Such an application would be heard by the same judge or same level of judge as gave the original decision.

9.6.2.3   Variation by consent (PD 28, para 4.5)

Where the agreement to vary relates to an act which does not need the court's consent, the parties need not file their written agreement to vary (which will usually be recorded in correspondence). In any other case, the party must apply to the court for an order by consent. The parties must file a draft of the order sought and an agreed statement of the reasons why the variation is sought. The court may make an order in the agreed terms, or in other terms, without a hearing, but it may well direct that a hearing is to occur.

9.6.2.4   Failure to comply with directions (PD 28, para 5)

If a party fails to comply with a direction, any other party may apply for an order enforcing compliance and/or for a sanction to be imposed (see **9.3.2**).

The application should be made without delay.

Practice Direction 28 is quite clear that a failure to comply with directions will not normally lead to a postponement of the trial date (see para 5.4(1)). This will not be allowed unless the circumstances of the case are exceptional.

If it is practical, the court will exercise its powers in a manner that enables the case to come up for trial on the date or within the period previously set. In particular, the court will assess what steps each party should take to prepare the case for trial, direct that those steps be taken in the shortest possible time and impose a sanction for non-compliance. Such a sanction may, for example, deprive a party of the right to raise or contest an issue, or to rely on evidence to which the direction relates.

Further, if the court is of the view that one or more issues can be made ready for trial within the time fixed, the court may direct that the trial will proceed on the issues which are, or will then be, ready. The court can also order that no costs will be allowed for any later trial of the remaining issues, or that those costs will be paid by the party in default. If the court has no option but to postpone the trial, it will do so for the shortest possible time and will give directions for the taking of all outstanding necessary steps as rapidly as possible.

It is clear, therefore, that the trial date is sacrosanct and the parties should ensure that they are ready for trial on the due date.

9.6.2.5   Directions as to exchange of witness statements and exchange of expert reports

We shall look in detail at evidence in **Chapter 12**. However, the evidence of those witnesses on whom a party intends to rely at trial must be exchanged in the form of witness statements and experts' reports. The exchange should normally be simultaneous.

So far as expert evidence is concerned, the direction in relation to the evidence will say whether it gives permission for oral evidence, or written reports or both, and will usually name the experts concerned or the fields of expertise. The court will not make a direction giving permission for an expert to give oral evidence unless it believes that it is necessary in the interests of justice to do so. In fast track cases, therefore, the usual provision will be for expert evidence to be given by means of written reports and experts will not be allowed to give oral evidence at the trial. Furthermore, the court may order that a single joint expert be appointed, rather than allowing each party to appoint their own.

9.6.2.6   The pre-trial checklist (PD 28, para 6)

The purpose of the pre-trial checklist is to check that directions have been complied with so that the court can fix a date for the trial (or confirm the date if one has already been fixed).

The directions order will specify a date by which the parties should return the pre-trial checklist. This date will be not later than eight weeks before the trial date or the start of the trial period. The pre-trial checklist will have been sent to the parties at least two weeks before it has to be filed at court. A copy of the pre-trial checklist (Form N170) appears at **Appendix A(13)**. Parties are encouraged to exchange copies of the pre-trial checklist before filing them with the court. A cost estimate (see **9.7**) should also be filed and served.

If no party files a pre-trial checklist, the court will direct that any claim, defence or counterclaim will be struck out unless a pre-trial checklist is filed within seven days. If some, but not all, parties have filed a pre-trial checklist, the court will give its normal listing directions or may hold a hearing (see **9.6.2.7** below).

9.6.2.7   Listing directions (PD 28, para 7)

The court will confirm or fix the date, length and place of the trial. The court will normally give the parties at least three weeks' notice of the trial.

The parties should try to agree directions. The agreed directions should deal with, among other things:

(a)   evidence;

(b)   a trial timetable and time estimate;

(c)   preparation of a trial bundle (see below).

The court may fix a listing hearing on three days' notice if either:

(a)   a party has failed to file the pre-trial checklist; or

(b)   a party has filed an incomplete pre-trial checklist; or

(c)   a hearing is needed to decide what directions for trial are appropriate.

Prior to the trial, the parties should try to agree the contents of the trial bundle (see **14.1.3**) which will contain all documents needed for use at the trial. The standard directions require that this bundle should be lodged with the court by the claimant not more than seven days and not less than three days before the start of the trial. Included in the bundle should be a case summary, not exceeding 250 words, outlining the matters still in issue, and referring, where appropriate, to the relevant documents. This is designed to assist the judge in reading the papers before the trial. The case summary should be agreed by the parties if possible.

9.6.3   Allocation to the multi-track (Part 29)

9.6.3.1   Directions

Cases which have a value of more than £25,000 will, as we have seen, usually be allocated to the multi-track. The multi-track therefore includes an enormously wide range of cases, from the fairly straightforward to the most complex and weighty matters involving claims for millions of pounds and multi-party claims. Case management on the multi-track has to reflect this wide diversity of claims. In straightforward cases, the standard directions which we have already looked at in relation to the fast track may be perfectly adequate, but in more complex cases the court will need to adapt the directions to the particular needs of the case.

When the matter is allocated to the multi-track, the court will either:

(a)   give directions for the management of the case and set a timetable for the steps to be taken between the giving of directions and the trial; or

(b)   fix a case management conference, or a pre-trial review or both and give such directions relating to the management of the case as it sees fit.

The court will fix the trial date or the period in which the trial is to take place as soon as practicable. There is no deadline, however, of 30 weeks as we saw in the fast track (see **9.6.2.1**).

In a fairly straightforward case, the court may well give directions without holding a case management conference. If it does so, then, by para 4.10 of PD 29, its general approach will be:

(1)   to give directions for the filing and service of any further information required to clarify either party's case,

(2)   to direct standard disclosure between the parties,

(3)   to direct the disclosure of witness statements by way of simultaneous exchange,

(4)   to give directions for a single joint expert on any appropriate issue unless there is a good reason not to do so,

(5)   … to direct disclosure of experts' reports by way of simultaneous exchange on those issues where a single joint expert is not directed,

(6)   if experts' reports are not agreed, to direct a discussion between experts …

(7)   to list a case management conference to take place after the date for compliance with the directions,

(8)   to specify a trial period; and

(9)   in such cases as the court thinks appropriate, the court may give directions requiring the parties to consider ADR. Such directions may be, for example, in the following terms:

'The parties shall by [date] consider whether the case is capable of resolution by ADR. If any party considers that the case is unsuitable for resolution by ADR, that party shall be prepared to justify that decision at the conclusion of the trial, should the judge consider that such means of resolution were appropriate, when he is considering the appropriate costs order to make.

The party considering the case unsuitable for ADR shall, not less than 28 days before the commencement of the trial, file with the court a witness statement without prejudice save as to costs, giving reasons upon which they rely for saying that the case was unsuitable.'

Alternatively, the parties themselves may agree directions that deal with these matters.

> **Case Study: Directions Order**
>
> A directions order made in the case study is provided at **Appendix D(9)**. You will note that this sets out a timetable of the steps the parties are required to take to prepare for the trial.

9.6.3.2   The case management conference

In many multi-track cases, the court will hold a case management conference where it feels that more of a 'hands on' approach is needed.

At any case management conference, the court will (by para 5.1 to PD 29):

(1)   review the steps which the parties have taken in the preparation of the case, and in particular their compliance with any directions that the court may have given,

(2)   decide and give directions about the steps which are to be taken to secure the progress of the claim in accordance with the overriding objective, and

(3)   ensure as far as it can that all agreements that can be reached between the parties about the matters in issue and the conduct of the claim are made and recorded.

What topics are the court likely to consider at the case management conference? These are likely to include:

(a)   Whether each party has clearly stated its case, for example has the claimant made clear the claim he is bringing and the amount he is claiming, so that the other party can understand the case he has to meet? As we saw in **Chapter 1**, r 1.4(2)(b) requires the court to identify the issues in dispute at an early stage.

(b)   Whether any amendments are required to the claim form, a statement of case or any other document.

(c)   What disclosure of documents, if any, is necessary.

(d)   What expert evidence is reasonably required, and how and when that evidence should be obtained and disclosed. Note that PD 29, para 5.5(1) provides that the court will not at this stage give permission for any party to rely on expert evidence unless the court can in its order either name an expert or state the relevant field of expertise. The court will also consider whether expert evidence is to be given orally or by the use of a report only at trial.

(e)   What factual evidence should be disclosed.

(f)   What arrangements should be made about the giving or clarification of further information and the putting of questions to experts.

(g)   Whether it will be just and will save costs to order a split trial (eg, on liability and quantum) or the trial of one of more preliminary issues.

In all cases, the court will set a timetable for the steps it decides are necessary to be taken.

9.6.3.3   Who should attend the case management conference?

Rule 29.3(2) provides that where a party has a legal representative, a representative familiar with the case and with sufficient authority to deal with any issues that are likely to arise must attend the case management conference. Practice Direction 29, para 5.2(2) further adds that the representative should be someone who is personally involved in the conduct of the case, and who has both the authority and information available to deal with any matter which may reasonably be expected to be dealt with at the hearing, including the fixing of the timetable, the identification of issues and matters of evidence.

Practice Direction 29, para 5.2(3) warns that where the inadequacy of the person attending, or of his instructions, leads to the adjournment of a hearing, the court will expect to make a wasted costs order, ie the solicitor or his firm will be made personally responsible for paying the costs incurred by other parties in preparing for and attending at the hearing that is adjourned.

The consequences of failing to send a properly prepared legal representative to a directions hearing were considered by the Court of Appeal in *Baron v Lovell* [1999] CPLR 630. The court will usually make an order imposing a sanction (see **9.3.2**) where the inadequacy of the person attending or his instructions leads to the adjournment of the conference. In this case, the court made a wasted costs order against the solicitor concerned personally.

In the case of *Tarajan Overseas Ltd v Kaye* (2002) *The Times*, 22 January, the Court of Appeal stressed that if a judge requires a party to attend a case management conference then the individual must know about the dispute and have authority to make decisions. The Court stressed that it would be 'objectionable … to make an order that a party should attend with a view to putting pressure on the party concerned to drop the proceedings altogether'. The Court also considered what the judge should do if he had ADR in mind. Tuckey LJ said:

> There is no doubt that the court, in exercising its case management powers, can order the attendance of a party: CPR 1998, r 3.1(2)(c). One good reason why this may be appropriate is to facilitate settlement if the court takes the view that the case before it is one which the parties should strive to settle. There would be nothing wrong either in requiring the attendance of a party with a view to making an ADR order which, of course, is not coercive but simply suspends the proceedings to enable the parties to explore (if they agree) the prospect of settlement with the assistance of an experienced mediator. Such an order is one which could be made however, and usually is made, without the attendance of any party.

Practice Direction 29 sets out, at para 5.6, guidelines as to how parties should prepare for the case management conference. They should:

(1)   ensure that all documents that the court is likely to ask to see (including witness statements and experts' reports) are brought to the hearing,

(2)   consider whether the parties should attend,

(3)   consider whether a case summary will be useful, and

(4)   consider what orders each wishes to be made and give notice of them to the other parties.

Any party who wishes to apply for an order which is not usually made at a case management conference should issue and serve his application in plenty of time if he knows that the application will be opposed; and he should warn the court if the time allowed for the case management conference is likely to be insufficient for his application to be heard.

9.6.3.4   Case summary

In most multi-track cases a case summary will be prepared for any case management conference. What are the formalities? These are set out in PD 29, para 5.7(1), as follows.

The case summary:

(a)   should be designed to assist the court to understand and deal with the questions before it;

(b)   should set out a brief chronology of the claim, the issues of fact which are agreed or in dispute and the evidence needed to decide them;

(c)   should not normally exceed 500 words in length; and

(d)   should be prepared by the claimant and agreed with the other parties if possible.

It can be seen that the function of the case summary is to assist the judge to identify the issues in dispute between the parties and so help him determine how the case should progress to trial, eg what issues require expert evidence, what issues might be suitable for ADR, etc.

Remember, that when completing paragraph D of the allocation questionnaire (see **9.5.1**) a party can either give the names of their likely witnesses (expert and/or non-expert) or simply state the number of likely witnesses and any expert's field of expertise. Exactly the same principles apply to the case summary. It may be that some witnesses of fact have yet to be traced or provide a proof of evidence, or the client is uncertain whether to rely on their evidence. It may be that there are so many witnesses that listing all their names is pointless. All the court needs is an indication of their number so it can consider if it is reasonable, give appropriate directions and start to think about the length of the trial. Likewise, a suitable expert may not yet have been found. However, as a bare minimum the likely number of experts and their field or fields of expertise should be given.

A template to help you draft a case summary is set out at **Appendix B(4)**.

> **Case Study: Case Summary**
>
> A case summary for use at a case management conference can be found in the case study at **Appendix D(8)**. You will note that this follows the structure required by PD 29, para 5.7(1)(b). How have the parties formulated the issues in dispute in respect of the claim and counterclaim? They have taken into account the denials and non-admissions made in the defence (**Appendix D(5)**) and defence to counterclaim (**Appendix D(6)**). This skill is analysed at **7.5.1**.

9.6.3.5 Variation of directions (r 29.5)

A party must apply to the court if he wishes to vary the date which the court has fixed for:

(a)   a case management conference;

(b)   a pre-trial review;

(c)   the return of a pre-trial checklist;

(d)   the trial; or

(e)   the trial period.

Just like the fast track, any date set by the court or the rules for doing any act may not be changed by the parties if the change would make it necessary to vary any of the dates mentioned above.

A party who wishes to vary a direction (eg, because of a change of circumstances) must apply as soon as possible. There is an assumption that if an application to vary directions was not made within 14 days of service of the directions order, the parties were content that the directions ordered were correct in the circumstances then existing.

A party who is dissatisfied with the direction may appeal, but if he was not notified of the hearing or was not present when it was made, he must apply for the court to reconsider, and the court will give all parties three days' notice of the hearing.

9.6.3.6 Non-compliance with directions (PD 29, para 7)

If a party fails to comply with a direction, any other party may apply for an order for compliance and/or for the imposition of a sanction. Any delay in making the application will be taken into account by the court.

As we saw in the fast track, the trial date is sacrosanct. The court will not allow failure to comply with directions to lead to the postponement of the trial unless the circumstances are exceptional.

9.6.3.7 The pre-trial checklist (PD 29, para 8)

The date for filing the completed pre-trial checklist will be not later than eight weeks before the trial date or the start of the trial period and the checklists will have been served on the parties at least 14 days before that date. The parties are encouraged to exchange copies of the checklists before they file them. If none of the parties files a checklist, the court will order that the claim, the defence and any counterclaim will be struck out unless any party files a checklist within seven days of service of the order.

If only some of the parties have filed a checklist, the court will usually fix a listing hearing and give directions.

On receipt of the pre-trial checklists, the court may decide that it is necessary to hold a pre-trial review (or may decide to cancel one already listed). The court must give the parties at least seven days' notice of its decision. A pre-trial review will usually occur in any heavy case, particularly when the trial is likely to last longer than 10 days.

As soon as practicable after:

(a)   each party has filed a completed pre-trial checklist;

(b)   the court has held a listing hearing; or

(c)   the court has held a pre-trial review,

the court will:

(a)   set a timetable for the trial, unless a timetable has already been fixed or the court considers that it will be inappropriate to do so; and

(b)   fix the date for the trial or the week within which the trial is to begin (or, if it has already done so, confirm that date).

As with the fast track, the court will also order, on listing, that a trial bundle of documents be prepared.

9.7   Costs estimates

9.7.1   Filed with questionnaires

In fast track and multi-track cases, the parties must file and serve with their allocation and pre-trial checklist an estimate of costs. These are designed to keep the parties informed about their potential liability in respect of costs and in order to assist the court to decide what, if any, order to make about costs and about case management. Under Practice Direction – Costs, an 'estimate of costs' means an estimate of base costs (including disbursements) already incurred; and an estimate of base costs (including disbursements) to be incurred, which a party intends to seek to recover from any other party under an order for costs if he is successful in the case. Base costs are those which do not include any additional liability (ie, the success fee under a conditional fee agreement and/or the amount of an after the event insurance premium). A party who intends to recover an additional liability need not, and should not, reveal the amount of that liability in the estimate.

9.7.2   Format

An estimate of base costs should be substantially in the form illustrated in Precedent H in the Schedule of Costs Precedents annexed to the Practice Direction (a copy of which appears at **Appendix A(9)**).

9.7.3   Practical point

On an assessment of the costs of a party the court may have regard to any estimate previously filed by that party, or by any other party in the same proceedings. Such an estimate may be taken into account as a factor among others, when assessing the reasonableness of any costs claimed: see PD – Costs (Parts 43 to 48), para 6.6, and *Leigh v Michelin Tyres plc* [2003] EWCA Civ 1766 (discussed at **14.3.2.5**).

Chapter 10

Applications to the Court

10.1 Introduction

In this chapter, we shall consider the way in which a party to the case can make an application to the court. We are considering applications made after the issue of proceedings and before the trial. These are known as interim applications.

Part 23 of CPR 1998 sets out the general rules governing applications to the court. These rules are subject to any express provisions which may apply to specific types of application.

We have already considered some possibilities, for example pre-action disclosure (see **3.9**); permission to serve a claim form out of the jurisdiction (see **5.5.7.2**); challenging the court's jurisdiction (see **6.3**); extension of time to serve a claim form or defence (see **5.6** and **6.4** respectively); permission to amend a statement of case (see **7.6.2**); requiring a reply to a Part 18 request (see **7.7.4**); permission to make an additional claim (see **8.2.4**); and relief from a sanction (see **9.4**).

10.2 Applications generally

An application to the court is made by an application notice. Form N244 (see **Appendix A(11)**) should be used.

The party who is making the application is known as the applicant, and the party against whom the order is sought is known as the respondent.

10.2.1 Where to make the application

By r 23.2, the application must be made to the court where the claim has been started, or the court to where the claim has been transferred. If the claim has already been listed for trial, it must be made to the court where the trial is to take place. Most applications will be heard by a master in the RCJ, or a district judge in the county court or a High Court District Registry.

10.2.2 Content of the application notice

By r 23.6, an application notice must state what order the applicant is seeking and, briefly, why the applicant is seeking the order.

If the applicant wishes to rely on matters set out in the application notice as evidence at the hearing, then it must be verified by a statement of truth. This appears on the second page of Form N244.

10.2.3   Draft order

Practice Direction 23 states that, except in the most simple application, the applicant should attach a draft of the order sought. If the case is proceeding in the RCJ and the order is unusually long or complex, it should also be supplied on disk for use by the court office.

10.2.4   Evidence in support of the application

As we shall see at **10.2.9** and **10.6**, certain of the rules set out a specific requirement for evidence in support of a particular application. Apart from that, PD 23 states, at para 9.1, that where there is no specific requirement to provide evidence, it should be borne in mind that, as a practical matter, the court will often need to be satisfied by evidence of the facts that are relied on in support of, or for opposing, the application. The evidence will usually take the form of a witness statement, although a party may also rely on the contents of a statement of case or the application notice itself as evidence, provided it is verified by a statement of truth.

Affidavits (see **10.7**) may be used, but the extra cost of preparing an affidavit over and above that of a witness statement may be disallowed since affidavits are no longer required, except for a limited number of specific applications.

Any evidence relied upon must be filed at the court as well as served on the parties with the application notice. Any evidence in response must be served as soon as possible.

10.2.5   Service of the application notice

Unless the rules relating to a particular type of application specify another time-limit, the application notice must be served at least three clear days before the court is to deal with the application. The court may allow a shorter period of notice if this is appropriate in the circumstances. When served, the application notice must be accompanied by a copy of any supporting written evidence and a copy of any draft order.

10.2.6   Consent orders

If the parties have reached agreement on the order they wish the court to make, they can apply for an order to be made by consent without the need for attendance by the parties. The parties must ensure that they provide the court with any material it needs to be satisfied that it is appropriate to make the order, and usually a letter will suffice.

10.2.7   Orders made without notice

Most applications have to be made on notice (ie, served on the other party so that he can respond and object to the application if he wishes to do so). However, in certain cases it is possible for an application to be made without notice being given to the other side. Paragraph 3 of PD 23 indicates that this may be done in the following circumstances:

(a)   where there is exceptional urgency;

(b)   where the overriding objective is best furthered by doing so;

(c)   by consent of all parties;

(d)   with the permission of court;

(e)   where a date for a hearing has been fixed and the party wishes to make an application at that hearing but he does not have sufficient time to serve an application notice, he should inform the other party and the court of the intended application as soon as possible and make the application orally at the hearing;

(f)   where a court order, Rule or Practice Direction permits.

The most common examples are freezing injunctions and search orders (see **10.6**).

When an order is made on an application without notice to the respondent, a copy of the order must be served on the respondent, together with a copy of the application notice and the supporting evidence. The order must contain a statement of the right of the respondent to make an application to set aside or vary the order. The respondent may then apply to set aside or vary the order within seven days of service of the order on him.

10.2.8 Telephone hearings and video conferencing

Many district registries of the High Court and county courts have facilities to deal with interim applications by telephone conferencing. These are known as 'telephone conference enabled courts'. A list of these courts can be found on HM Court Service website (see **1.5**). By PD 23, para 6.2, the general rule is that at a telephone conference enabled court all allocation hearings (see **9.6**), listing hearings (see **9.6.2.7** and **9.6.3.7**), interim applications, case management conferences (see **9.6.3.2**) and pre-trial reviews (see **9.6.3.7**) with a time estimate of less than one hour will be conducted by telephone. The exceptions are any hearing of an application made without notice to the other party, or where all the parties are unrepresented, or where more than four parties wish to make representations at the hearing (for this purpose, where two or more parties are represented by the same person, they are treated as one party).

Can a party, or a party's legal representative, to an application being heard by telephone attend the judge in person while the application is being heard? No, not unless every other party to the application has agreed. As to the mechanics of how the telephone conference call takes place, see PD 23.

Note that the applicant's legal representative (or failing that a legal representative nominated by the court) must file and serve a case summary and draft order no later than 4 pm on the last working day before the telephone hearing if the claim has been allocated to the multi-track or, in any other case, if the court so directs.

Where the parties wish to use video conferencing facilities, and those facilities are available in the relevant court, they should apply to the master or district judge for directions.

10.2.9 Preparing supporting evidence

Most solicitors will prepare a witness statement in support of, or in opposition to, an interim application. Whilst the Rule under which the application is made may dictate some of the content of that statement, the following general questions must always be answered:

(a) Who should make the statement? It should be the person best able to address the relevant points from personal knowledge. For example, on an application for pre-action disclosure which relies on ground (d)(iii) of r 31.16(3), the person who can quantify and justify the savings in costs (see **3.9**) will probably be best placed to make the witness statement.

(b) What needs to be included? List the important points to be brought to the court's attention. Include all the relevant detailed evidence relied on and anticipate your opponent's case, where appropriate.

(c) How should the statement appear? Divide up the important points into numbered paragraphs. Set out the relevant information in chronological order.

(d) What about hearsay evidence (see **12.9**)? When relying on this, state the source of the information. A witness statement must indicate which of the contents derive from the maker's own knowledge and which are either matters of information he has received from a third party or form the basis of his own belief. The source of any matters of information or belief must also be given. For example, a witness may state, 'I am advised by Laura Smith who inspected the machinery immediately after it broke down that ...'.

(e) What is the key to possible success? Focus on detail and exhibit any relevant supporting documents. A witness statement containing highly relevant details and made by a person with first-hand knowledge of the facts will be very persuasive indeed. If any of the facts arise from or are supported by documents, these should be exhibited.

Should points of law be included? Legal arguments are best left to the advocates at the hearing. However, your client may have to express a legal opinion. For example, when applying for summary judgment (see **10.5.2**) there must be a statement of belief that on the evidence the respondent has no real prospect of succeeding and there is no other compelling reason for a trial.

10.3   Interim costs

10.3.1   Costs of applying for or opposing an application

Any interim application will involve the parties in expense. A party may be involved in collecting evidence, interviewing witnesses, conducting a site visit, negotiating, etc. The applicant will prepare the notice of application (see **10.2**) and supporting witness statement (see **10.2.4**). A court fee is payable for making the application. The respondent will usually prepare a witness statement in response. The more complex the application, the greater the costs involved. Moreover, the cost of travelling to and from the court, and the advocate dealing with the application, must also be taken into account.

10.3.2   'Pay as you go' litigation

At the end of any interim application, the judge may decide that one party should pay the other party's costs. This is often called 'pay as you go' litigation. The general costs rule applies, namely, the loser pays the winner's costs. So if the application is granted, it is normal to order the respondent to pay the applicant's costs. But the type of costs order will depend on the nature of the application, and interim costs orders usually reflect to a large extent the conduct of the parties. For example, a party who wants permission to amend his statement of case (see **7.6**) starts from a weak position, as he wants the court to allow him to do something. Hence, the normal order is that such an applicant pays the respondent's costs of the application, which may include additional costs, eg, if the respondent has to amend, file and serve his own statement of case as a result of the amendment. Such a costs order would be expressed as 'costs of and caused by' (see the table below).

10.3.3   Possible orders

Practice Direction 44 sets out, at para 8.5, the different costs orders which may be made at the end of an interim hearing and the effect of those orders. These include the following:

Term	Effect
[Named party's] costs ([Named party's] costs in any event)	The party named in the order and thereby in whose favour the order is made (eg, claimant's costs) is entitled to the costs in respect of the part of the proceedings to which the order relates, whatever other costs orders are made in the proceedings. These costs are normally summarily assessed and ordered to be paid within 14 days.
Costs in the case (Costs in the application)	In this order, no party is named. At this interim stage no party is able to recover his costs of the interim hearing. The outcome at the end of the proceedings will determine which party recovers these interim costs. The party in whose favour the court makes an order for costs at the end of the proceedings is entitled to his costs of the part of the proceedings to which the order relates.

Term	Effect
[Named party's] costs in case	If the named party is awarded costs at the end of the proceedings, that party is entitled to his costs of the part of the proceedings to which the order relates. So the party not named in the order is never entitled to recover his interim costs of the application. The named party recovers his interim costs of the application only if he is ultimately awarded costs at the conclusion of the proceedings.
[Named party's] costs thrown away	Where, for example, a judgment or order is set aside, the party in whose favour the costs order is made is entitled to the costs which have been incurred as a consequence. This includes the costs of: (a) preparing for and attending any hearing at which the judgment or order which has been set aside was made; (b) preparing for and attending any hearing to set aside the judgment or order in question; (c) preparing for and attending any hearing at which the court orders the proceedings or the part in question to be adjourned; (d) any steps taken to enforce a judgment or order which has subsequently been set aside.
[Named party's] costs of and caused by	Where, for example, the court makes this order on an application to amend a statement of case, the party in whose favour the costs order is made is entitled to the costs of preparing for and attending the application and the costs of any consequential amendment to his own statement of case.
No order as to costs (Each party to pay his own costs)	Each party is to bear his own costs of the part of the proceedings to which the order relates whatever costs order the court makes at the end of the proceedings.

If the order made at the hearing makes no mention of costs, the general rule is none are payable in respect of that application. So it is always vital to ensure that the judge makes some sort of costs order.

10.3.4 Summary assessment

If the court makes an order for costs in favour of one of the parties to the application (eg, 'claimant's costs', or 'claimant's costs thrown away' or 'defendant's costs of and caused by') then the court will make a summary assessment of costs there and then. Any such costs are payable within 14 days, unless the court orders otherwise (r 44.8). In order for the court to be able to assess the costs at the end of the application, the parties are required, not less than 24 hours prior to the hearing, to file and serve a statement of costs. This provides a breakdown of the costs incurred in relation to the application. A model form of the statement of costs (Form N260) appears at **Appendix A(12)**. If a party fails to comply with this requirement without reasonable excuse, this will be taken into account by the court in deciding what costs order to make. To help the judge carry out a summary assessment, he will take into account the guideline rates for solicitors and counsel: see **Appendix A(21)** and **14.3.4.2**.

The parties may well agree the amount of costs at an interim hearing. The judge is likely to reject an agreed figure only if he considers it to be disproportionate.

10.3.5 Fixed costs

On a few occasions, the court may award fixed costs rather than making one of the orders set out above (see, eg, **6.6.3** and **10.5.2.5**). Part 45 sets out the occasions on which fixed costs may be granted and specifies the amount awarded to the receiving party. Where fixed costs are granted there is, of course, no need for a summary assessment.

10.3.6 Costs-capping order (r 44.18)

10.3.6.1 The problem to be addressed

In heavy, complex litigation, costs can build up quickly. If one or more of the parties does not strictly follow the Practice Direction on Pre-action Conduct or any approved pre-action protocol that applies (see **3.7**), a large amount of unnecessary costs may be incurred. In these exceptional circumstances the court may make an order capping the amount of costs recoverable by a party that are incurred after the date of the order. An order does not act retrospectively.

10.3.6.2 Making the application

Any party may apply for a costs-capping order, but normally it is a defendant seeking to cap what the claimant might recover in costs. The application should be made as soon as possible, preferably before or at the first case management conference (see **9.6.3.2**). The evidence in support should set out whether the costs-capping order is in respect of the whole of the litigation or a particular issue which is ordered to be tried separately, and why a costs-capping order should be made. It should be accompanied by an estimate of costs, setting out the costs and disbursements incurred by the applicant to date and those the applicant is likely to incur in the future conduct of the proceedings. The court will normally direct that all other parties file a similar estimate.

10.3.6.3 Grounds for making an order

By r 44.18(5), the court can make a costs-capping order against all or any of the parties, if:

(a)   it is in the interests of justice to do so;

(b)   there is a substantial risk that without such an order costs will be disproportionately incurred; and

(c)   it is not satisfied that the risk in sub-para (b) can be adequately controlled by –

    (i)   case management directions or orders made under Part 3, and

    (ii)   detailed assessment of costs. So where the concerns are that the other side's hourly charges and use of leading counsel are excessive, as in *Peacock v MGN Ltd* [2009] EWHC 769, the order will be refused on the basis that a costs judge can deal with these issues on a detailed assessment (see **14.3**).

In considering whether to exercise its discretion under the rule, the court will consider all the circumstances of the case, including:

(a)   whether there is a substantial imbalance between the financial position of the parties;

(b)   whether the costs of determining the amount of the cap are likely to be proportionate to the overall costs of the litigation;

(c)   the stage which the proceedings have reached; and

(d)   the costs which have been incurred to date and the future costs.

10.3.6.4 Effect of order

A costs-capping order, once made, limits the costs recoverable by the party subject to the order unless that party successfully applies to vary it. However, no such variation will be made by the court unless there has been a material and substantial change of circumstances since the date the order was made, or there is some other compelling reason why a variation should be made.

10.3.7   Conditional fee agreements and the summary assessment of interim application costs

This is dealt with at para 14 of PD 44. The fact that one (or even both) of the parties has entered into a conditional fee agreement (a CFA) will not prevent the costs of the interim application from being summarily assessed if the court has awarded costs in favour of a party.

10.3.7.1   Receiving party CFA funded

Where the receiving party (the party whose costs are to be paid) is CFA funded, the court cannot order payment to be made unless satisfied that the receiving party is immediately liable to his solicitor for the costs of the application under the terms of the CFA. To order otherwise would be contrary to the indemnity principle (see **14.3**). Accordingly, the form of agreement recommended by The Law Society entitles solicitors to payment of costs on all successful interim applications, whatever the outcome of the proceedings at trial.

It should be noted that where the receiving party is on a CFA, the court's summary assessment can deal only with the base costs. The question of whether the paying party should be responsible for the success fee on those costs (and if so to what extent) will not be considered by the court until the conclusion of the case.

10.3.7.2   Paying party CFA funded

A party who is CFA funded may not be in a position to pay interim costs if ordered to do so. Although many CFA clients have the benefit of AEI, it is common for such policies not to cover the payment of interim costs awarded to the other side. The court may, therefore, decide to defer the payment of the interim costs until the end of the proceedings. In considering whether to do so, the court should take into account the unfairness of this on the receiving party.

The topic of CFAs is dealt with at **2.4.2**.

10.4   Appeals against an interim order

The procedure for appeals is set out in Part 52. An appeal from a decision of a district judge in a county court is made to a circuit judge, and from a master or district judge in the High Court to a High Court judge.

Permission to appeal is required and will be granted only if the appeal has a real prospect of success, or there is some other compelling reason for the appeal to be heard (r 52.3(6)). Permission may be sought either at the original hearing, or from the appeal court within 14 days of the original decision. If permission is sought at the original hearing but refused, a further application for permission may be made to the appeal judge.

The appeal hearing will usually be limited to a review of the district judge's or master's original decision and no new evidence will be admitted unless the court orders otherwise (r 52.11). The appeal will be allowed if the original decision was either wrong or unjust because of a serious procedural or other irregularity. If the appeal is allowed, the appeal judge may make a variety of orders (eg, setting aside or varying the original order and ordering a re-hearing).

10.5   Particular types of application

10.5.1   Applications to set aside a default judgment (Part 13)

10.5.1.1   The mandatory grounds

Under r 13.2, the court is obliged to set aside a default judgment that was wrongly entered before the defendant's deadline for filing an acknowledgement of service or a defence (whichever is applicable) expired. The court is also obliged to set aside a default judgment entered after the claim was paid in full.

10.5.1.2   The discretionary grounds

Rule 13.3(1) gives the court the power to set aside or vary a default judgment where:

(a)   the defendant has a real prospect of successfully defending the claim; or

(b)   it appears to the court that there is some other good reason why—

    (i)   the judgment should be set aside or varied; or

    (ii)   the defendant should be allowed to defend the claim.

The court will take account of the promptness of the defendant's application and it is therefore essential that the defendant should issue the application as soon as he becomes aware of the default judgment. The application to the court must be on notice and must be supported by evidence. Although the rule states that only one of the grounds needs to be satisfied, in practice the defendant will usually have to show a defence with a real prospect of success at trial in order to persuade the court to exercise its discretion.

Example 1

A issues a claim form (with particulars of claim) against B, claiming the price of goods sold and delivered to B. B receives the claim form but forgets to deal with it and A is able to enter default judgment.

B then instructs solicitors. They immediately apply to set the default judgment aside. The evidence in support of the application is a witness statement from B in which he seeks to show that the goods were not of satisfactory quality.

If B can show that he has a real prospect of successfully defending the claim, the default judgment will be set aside. He may, however, have to pay the costs of the application, which will be summarily assessed, as he was to blame for the default judgment being entered.

Example 2

Mr and Mrs X buy a dining room table and chairs from Y Ltd. There is a dispute about the quality of the wood used in the construction of the furniture. Mr and Mrs X refuse to pay Y Ltd. Whilst they are away on holiday, Y Ltd issue proceedings for the price of the furniture, serve the proceedings and enter default judgment when no acknowledgement or defence is filed within the prescribed time. On their return from holiday, Mr and Mrs X open their post and discover the proceedings and default judgment.

Mr and Mrs X have a good reason for asking the court to set aside the default judgment as they were away on holiday when the proceedings were served and default judgment entered. Hence they were unable to respond to the proceedings through no fault of their own. They should immediately ask Y Ltd to agree to the default judgment being set aside, or otherwise make an application to the court. Any application should be supported by evidence to show that they were away on holiday at the material times and that they have acted promptly in making the application once they became aware of the default judgment. Any delay should be explained. They should also state the basis of the defence to the claim and the evidence they have to support that to show that there is a defence with a real prospect of success at trial.

> **Example 3**
>
> What if the claimant posts the proceedings to the defendant's last known residence (see **5.5.3**) and the proceedings are not returned undelivered, but the defendant does not receive the proceedings because he has moved to a new address? These are the facts of *Akram v Adam* [2004] EWCA Civ 1601, (2004) *The Times*, 29 December. In these circumstances the defendant has a good reason for asking the court to set aside the default judgment as he was unable to respond to the proceedings through no fault of his own. He should immediately ask the claimant to agree to the default judgment being set aside, or otherwise make an application to the court. Any application should be supported by evidence to show that that he had moved from and had no connection with the address to which the proceedings were sent, and that he acted promptly in making the application once he became aware of the default judgment. Any delay should be explained. He should also state the basis of the defence to the claim and the evidence he has to support that to show that there is a defence with a real prospect of success at trial.

What about the interim costs (see **10.3**) in Examples 2 and 3? If the court accepts that there is a good reason then, as neither party can be said to be at fault in those circumstances, it is likely that the court will set aside the default judgment and make an order for costs in the case. The court may, or may not, summarily assess these. If, however, the reason is rejected and the default judgment set aside on the ground of a defence with a real prospect of succeeding at trial, the court is likely to order the defendant to pay the claimant's (summarily assessed) costs within 14 days.

If the original claim was for a specified amount of money and the defendant is an individual then, if the judgment was not entered in the defendant's home court, the application to set aside the default judgment will be transferred to the defendant's home court and the case proceeds there (see **9.5**).

10.5.1.3   Orders the court can make

The court may set aside the default judgment, refuse the application or make a conditional order. Where the judgment is set aside, the court usually gives directions for the future management of the case. In respect of a conditional order, the normal condition is that the defendant pays into court the amount of the claim or such amount as he can reasonably afford (within a set time period, otherwise the default judgment stands). The court will usually impose such a condition only if the application was made very late.

10.5.1.4   Costs

The costs order made at the conclusion of the application will depend on the outcome. If the application is granted on a mandatory ground, the claimant will have been at fault for entering judgment when he should not have done so, and therefore normally the claimant is ordered to pay the defendant's costs. Where the defendant establishes the discretionary ground of a good reason for the default then, as neither side is at fault, costs are usually in the case. Where the defendant only establishes the discretionary ground of a defence with a real prospect of success at trial, the defendant is at fault in failing to deal with the proceedings and normally has to pay the claimant's costs. If a conditional order is made due to a very late application then the defendant is normally penalised by being ordered to pay the claimant's costs.

10.5.1.5   Practical point: prepare for all possible outcomes

As the judge will invariably make some sort of costs order at the end of the interim application, it is vital that an advocate is able to deal with it. An advocate needs to prepare for all potential outcomes. These are summarised in the flowchart in **Appendix C(11)**.

10.5.2   Summary judgment (Part 24)

We saw at **9.3** that the court has the power, under its case management powers contained in Part 3 of CPR 1998, to strike out a statement of case if it discloses no reasonable grounds for bringing or defending the claim. The court has similar powers under Part 24 of CPR 1998, which deals with applications for summary judgment. The aim behind the Part 24 procedure is to enable a claimant or defendant to obtain judgment at an early stage without the time and expense involved in proceeding to a full trial.

10.5.2.1   Grounds for the application

Rule 24.2 states that:

> The court may give summary judgment against a claimant or defendant on the whole of the claim or on a particular issue if—
>
> (a)   it considers that—
>
> > (i)   that claimant has no real prospect of succeeding on the claim or issue; or
> >
> > (ii)   that defendant has no real prospect of successfully defending the claim or issue; and
>
> (b)   there is no other compelling reason why the case or issue should be disposed of at trial.

Therefore, either party can make an application for summary judgment (or indeed the court could list the case for a Part 24 hearing on its own initiative). According to para 1.3 of PD 24, the application may be based on:

> (1)   a point of law (including a question of construction of a document),
>
> (2)   the evidence which can reasonably be expected to be available at trial or the lack of it, or
>
> (3)   a combination of these.

The court can give summary judgment against a claimant in any type of proceedings and against the defendant in most types of proceedings, with some exceptions which are beyond the scope of this book.

What cases are not suitable for summary judgment? In *Swain v Hillman* [2001] 1 All ER 91, Lord Woolf MR said:

> Useful though the power is under Part 24, it is important that it is kept to its proper role. It is not meant to dispense with the need for a trial where there are issues which should be investigated at the trial ... the proper disposal of an issue under Part 24 does not involve the judge conducting a mini trial, that is not the object of the provisions; it is to enable cases, where there is no real prospect of success either way, to be disposed of summarily.

What is a compelling reason for the purposes of r 24.2(b)? In *Secretary of State for Health v Norton Healthcare Ltd and Others* [2004] LTL, 25 February, the claimants alleged that the defendants had operated an unlawful price fixing cartel or under an anti-competition arrangement in supplying a particular drug. The seventh defendant applied for summary judgment on the basis that the claim against it was legally and factually flawed. The application was dismissed. The court held that the public interest in controlling pharmaceutical costs and the investigation of a possible cartel was a compelling reason for a trial. In addition, the claim involved allegations of conspiracy between the parties and those accusations could only be properly examined at trial.

In *Kirschel & Others* v *Fladgate Fielder (a firm)* [2000] LTL, 22 December, the court refused applications for summary judgment by both parties for the compelling reason that their contrary submissions raised difficult questions of law, two of which did not appear to be covered by authority and so ought to be tried.

A compelling reason for a trial may be to allow the respondent more time to investigate the matter, particularly if he has a good reason for being unable so far to get in touch with a material witness. Alternatively, the respondent may argue that the claim or defence is of such a highly complicated and/or technical nature that it can only be properly understood if the usual procedural steps are taken and the evidence then given at a full trial subject to cross-examination (see *Three Rivers District Council and Others v Governor and Company of the Bank of England (No 3 bis)* [2001] 2 All ER 513, HL). For example, in *Celador Productions Limited v Melville* [2004] EWHC 2362 (Ch), [2004] LTL, 26 October, the case concerned infringement of a TV game show format. The application for summary judgment was refused. The court held that in order to determine whether similarities between the formats were the result of copying, it was necessary both for standard disclosure (see **Chapter 11**) to be given and for witnesses to be cross-examined at trial (see **14.2.3.2**). Those were compelling reasons for refusing the application.

10.5.2.2   Procedure

The claimant may not apply for summary judgment until the defendant has filed an acknowledgement of service or a defence, unless the court gives permission. The reason for this is that if the defendant fails to file an acknowledgement of service or defence, the claimant can enter a default judgment without having to make an application for summary judgment. If the claimant applies for summary judgment before the defendant has filed a defence, the defendant need not file a defence until after the application for summary judgment has been heard.

The defendant can apply for summary judgment at any time. Irrespective of who makes the application, it should be made without delay and usually prior to, or at the time of, filing of allocation questionnaires (see **9.5.1**).

The respondent to the application must be given at least 14 days' notice of the date fixed for the hearing. A respondent who wishes to rely on written evidence must file and serve this at least seven days before the hearing. An applicant who wishes to rely on written evidence in reply to the respondent's submissions must file and serve it at least three days before the hearing.

The application notice itself must state that it is an application for summary judgment and the application notice or the evidence contained or referred to in it, or served with it, must, as stated in para 2(3) of PD 24:

(a)   identify concisely any point of law or provision in a document on which the applicant relies, and/or

(b)   state that it is made because the applicant believes that on the evidence the respondent has no real prospect of succeeding on the claim or issue, or (as the case may be) of successfully defending the claim or issue to which the application relates,

and and in either case state that the applicant knows of no other reason why the disposal of the claim or issue should await trial.

If the application notice does not contain all the applicant's evidence, it should identify the written evidence (such as a witness statement or statement of case) the applicant intends to rely on. The application notice should also inform the respondent of his right to file and serve written evidence in reply.

10.5.2.3   Orders the court may make on an application for summary judgment

On a Part 24 application the court may order:

(1)   judgment on the claim,

(2)   the striking out or dismissal of the claim,

(3)   the dismissal of the application,

(4)   a conditional order.

(See para 5.1 of PD 24.)

To grant summary judgment, the court will have to come to the conclusion that the claim or defence has no real prospects of succeeding at trial (and there is no other compelling reason for a trial). For example, in the Court of Appeal case of *Peskin v Anderson and Others* [2001] 1 BCLC 372, Mummery LJ described the claimant's case as a 'flight of fancy [that] does not, on the pleaded facts, even make it to the take off point and should be grounded immediately under CPR Part 24'. Simon Brown LJ added that the claim was 'worthless and must fail'. So, summary judgment should be granted where the claim, etc is 'merely fanciful, imaginary, unreal or intrinsically unrealistic' (*per* Otton LJ in *Sinclair v Chief Constable of West Yorkshire and Another* [2000] LTL, 12 December).

Note that the court will grant judgment on the claim under Part 24 only if the claimant makes an application. It will strike out the claim only on a defendant's application. Therefore a defendant who wishes to oppose an application for summary judgment and also to apply for an order striking out the claim must make his own application for summary judgment.

When should the application be dismissed? Pill LJ in *Hussain v Woods and Another* [2001] Lloyd's Rep PN 134 suggested this was appropriate where 'an apparently credible witness says one thing and another apparently credible witness says the opposite, and there is not conclusive circumstantial evidence pointing one way or the other'.

A conditional order is an order which requires a party:

(1)   to pay a sum of money into court, or

(2)   to take a specified step in relation to his claim or defence, as the case may be,

and provides that that party's claim will be dismissed or his statement of case will be struck out if he does not comply. (para 5.2 of PD 24)

The court is likely to make a conditional order where it appears to the court possible that a claim or defence may succeed but improbable that it will do so. See PD 24, para 4. This is a situation where the statement of case might be described as 'shadowy and unsatisfactory' (*per* Sir Richard Scott V-C in *Bates v Microstar Ltd* [2000] LTL, 4 July). For example, where a claimant applies for summary judgment in a debt or damages case, if the court is not satisfied that the defence has a 'real prospect' of success, but none the less considers that success is possible (although improbable), the court may allow the defendant to continue to defend the claim on the condition that he pays the amount of the claim into court or such amount as he can reasonably afford (see *MV Yorke Motors v Edwards* [1982] 1 All ER 1024 and *Training In Compliance Ltd (t/a Matthew Read) v Dewse (t/a Data Research Co)* [2000] LTL, 2 October). The money would remain in court pending the final outcome of the case. If the defendant fails to make the payment into court then the defence would be dismissed and judgment entered for the claimant.

But what financial condition will the judge impose on a claimant where the claim may possibly succeed although it probably will not do so at trial? In the case of *Sweetman v Shepherd* (2000) *The Times*, 29 March, the Court of Appeal indicated that in the absence of financial constraints it would expect a claimant to pay into court a sum of about 75% to 80% of those costs which the defendant could reasonably expect to recover at the end of the claim if it were fully contested. The defendant should produce an estimate of those costs (see **9.7**).

10.5.2.4 Directions

When the court determines a summary judgment application it may:

(a)   give directions as to the filing and serving of a defence, if one has not already been filed; and

(b)   give further directions.

So, where the court dismisses the application or makes an order that does not completely dispose of the claim, the court may well give case management directions as to the future conduct of the case.

10.5.2.5 Costs

The costs order made at the conclusion of the hearing will depend on the type of claim and the outcome of the application. Where a claimant is successful in obtaining summary judgment for a specified sum, the court will usually award fixed costs (see Part 45). The fixed costs are £175 if the judgment exceeds £25 but does not exceed £5,000, and £210 if the judgment exceeds £5,000. In fairly straightforward cases, it is likely that the court will award fixed costs. However, it is open to the successful claimant to ask for costs to be summarily assessed if these are going to be more than the fixed costs. See **10.3**.

What is the effect if a claimant of an unspecified sum is awarded summary judgment? The claimant will have established liability but a later assessment of the quantum of damages will be necessary. The court will normally award the claimant his costs of making the application (claimant's costs) and summarily assess these (see **10.3**). The court will then usually fix a date to assess quantum and deal with the costs of the entire claim ('a disposal hearing'), and may allocate the matter to a track and give case management directions.

What if the defendant secures summary judgment (ie, the claim is struck out)? The court will normally award the defendant his costs of the claim (including pre-action costs) and, unless agreed, these will be subject to a summary assessment.

If a conditional order is made the claimant's application has not been granted, but equally the defendant has not got the application dismissed. Neither side can be said to have won and so the usual order is costs in the case.

10.5.2.6 Practical point: prepare for all possible outcomes

As the judge will invariably make some sort of costs order at the end of the interim application, it is vital that an advocate is able to deal with it. An advocate needs to prepare for all potential outcomes. These are summarised in the flowchart at **Appendix C(12)**.

10.5.3 Application for further information (Part 18)

As we saw in **Chapter 7**, a party may request further information from another party to clarify any matter which is in dispute, or give additional information in relation to any such matter.

If the request is not met, the party can apply for an order from the court.

Provided that the request made complied with para 1 of PD 18 (see **Chapter 7**), and at least 14 days have elapsed and the time stated for a response has expired, the application notice need not be served on the other party and the court may deal with the application without a hearing (PD 18, para 5.5(1)). Otherwise, the application notice must be served on the other party.

10.6 Interim remedies (Part 25)

The court has wide powers to grant parties to a claim, or to a proposed claim, various interim remedies. These are set out in r 25.1.

    (1)   The court may grant the following interim remedies—

        (a)   an interim injunction;

        (b)   an interim declaration;

        (c)   an order—

            (i)   for the detention, custody or preservation of relevant property;

            (ii)   for the inspection of relevant property;

            (iii)   for the taking of a sample of relevant property;

(iv)   for the carrying out of an experiment on or with relevant property;

(v)   for the sale of relevant property which is of a perishable nature or which for any other good reason it is desirable to sell quickly; and

(vi)   for the payment of income from relevant property until a claim is decided;

(d)   an order authorising a person to enter any land or building in the possession of a party to the proceedings for the purposes of carrying out an order under sub-paragraph (c);

(e)   an order under section 4 of the Torts (Interference with Goods) Act 1977 to deliver up goods;

(f)   an order (referred to as a 'freezing injunction')—

(i)   restraining a party from removing from the jurisdiction assets located there; or

(ii)   restraining a party from dealing with any assets whether located within the jurisdiction or not;

(g)   an order directing a party to provide information about the location of relevant property or assets or to provide information about relevant property or assets which are or may be the subject of an application for a freezing injunction;

(h)   an order (referred to as a 'search order') under section 7 of the Civil Procedure Act 1997 (order requiring a party to admit another party to premises for the purpose of preserving evidence etc);

(i)   an order under section 33 of the Supreme Court Act 1981 or section 52 of the County Courts Act 1984 (order for disclosure of documents or inspection of property before a claim has been made);

(j)   an order under section 34 of the Supreme Court Act 1981 or section 53 of the County Courts Act 1984 (order in certain proceedings for disclosure of documents or inspection of property against a non-party);

(k)   an order (referred to as an order for interim payment) under rule 25.6 for payment by a defendant on account of any damages, debt or other sum(except costs) which the court may hold the defendant liable to pay;

(l)   an order for a specified fund to be paid into court or otherwise secured, where there is a dispute over a party's right to the fund;

(m)   an order permitting a party seeking to recover personal property to pay money into court pending the outcome of the proceedings and directing that, if he does so, the property shall be given up to him;

(n)   an order directing a party to prepare and file accounts relating to the dispute; and

(o)   an order directing any account to be taken or inquiry to be made by the court.

An interim remedy can be obtained before proceedings are issued (eg, for pre-action disclosure of documents – see **11.16**), during proceedings, or even after judgment has been given. A court can grant a remedy before a claim is issued only if the matter is urgent, or it is otherwise desirable to do so in the interests of justice. Unless the court orders otherwise, a defendant may not apply for one of the orders listed in r 25.1 until he has filed an acknowledgement of service or defence.

A court can grant an interim remedy on an application made without notice if it appears to the court that there are good reasons for not giving notice. Examples of applications which will, by their very nature, be made without notice are freezing injunctions and search orders. A freezing injunction restrains a party from removing his assets from the jurisdiction (ie, England and Wales). If notice was given to the respondent of such an application, the respondent could simply transfer his assets prior to the hearing of the application.

A search order is an order compelling the respondent to allow his premises to be searched by the applicant. It is obtained where the applicant believes that the respondent has documents which, it is usually alleged, belong to the applicant. Again, if notice was given to the respondent in advance, it would be a simple matter for the respondent to hide the documents somewhere else. Because freezing injunctions and search orders can be quite draconian in their impact upon the respondent, such applications must be made to a High Court judge and the evidence in support of these applications must be by way of affidavit. Evidence in support of other applications for interim remedies is by the usual methods:

(a)   witness statements;

(b)   the application notice;

(c)   the statement(s) of case.

The contents of (a) and (c) can be relied on as evidence only where they contain a statement of truth. By their very nature, (a) must contain a statement of truth (see **12.3**).

10.7   Interim payments

One particular type of interim remedy is an interim payment (see r 25.1(1)(k) at **10.6** above). An interim payment is an advance payment on account of any damages, debt or other sum (excluding costs) which a defendant may be held liable to pay. The interim payment procedure enables a claimant who has a strong case on liability to avoid the financial hardship and/or inconvenience which might otherwise be suffered because of any delay during the period between the start of the claim and its final determination.

Before making an application to the court, the claimant should try to negotiate with the defendant or the defendant's insurance company to obtain a voluntary interim payment. If one is not forthcoming, and if the claimant feels he has good grounds for making the application, then the application should be made as soon as possible.

A claimant may not seek an interim payment until after the time for acknowledging service has expired. The claimant may make more than one application.

10.7.1   Procedure

An application notice for an interim payment must be supported by evidence and be served at least 14 days before the hearing date.

The evidence required in support of an interim payment application is set out in para 2.1 of PD 25B – Interim Payments. The evidence must, amongst other matters, deal with:

(a)   the amount of the interim payment being sought;

(b)   the items or matters in respect of which the interim payment is sought;

(c)   the likely amount of the final judgment;

(d)   the reasons for believing that the conditions for an interim payment are satisfied (see **10.7.2** below);

(e)   any other relevant matters.

Any documents in support of the application should be exhibited.

If the respondent wishes to rely on evidence then this should be served at least seven days before the hearing. If the applicant wishes to use evidence in reply to the respondent's evidence, this should be served at least three days before the hearing.

10.7.2   Grounds for making the order

By r 25.7(1), The grounds for the court making an interim payment are as follows:

(a)   the defendant against whom the order is sought has admitted liability to pay damages or some other sum of money to the claimant;

(b)   the claimant has obtained judgment against that defendant for damages to be assessed or for a sum of money (other than costs) to be assessed;

(c)   the court is satisfied that if the claim went to trial the claimant would obtain judgment for a substantial amount of money (other than costs) against the defendant from whom he is seeking an order for an interim payment, whether or not that defendant is the only defendant or one of a number of defendants to the claim;

(d)   the following conditions are satisfied—

    (i)   the claimant is seeking an order for possession of land (whether or not any other order is also sought), and

    (ii)   the court is satisfied that, if the case went to trial, the defendant would be held liable (even if the claim for possession fails) to pay the claimant a sum of money for the defendant's occupation and use of the land while the claim for possession was pending; or

(e)   in a claim in which there are two or more defendants and the order is sought against any one or more of those defendants, the following conditions are satisfied—

    (i)   the court is satisfied that, if the claim went to trial, the claimant would obtain judgment for a substantial amount of money (other than costs) against at least one of the defendants (but the court cannot determine which), and

    (ii)   all the defendants are either—

        (a)   a defendant that is insured in respect of the claim;

        (b)   a defendant whose liability will be met by an insurer under s 151 of the Road Traffic Act 1988, or an insurer acting under the Motor Insurers Bureau Agreement, or the Motor Insurers Bureau where it is acting itself, or

        (c)   a defendant that is a public body.

The rules do not require the applicant to show any need for the interim payment, or that he will suffer prejudice if he does not receive it: see *Stringman v McArdle* [1994] 1 WLR 1653. However, if the delay in assessment of damages is unlikely to be substantial, the court may be reluctant to exercise its discretion to make an order unless the claimant has some special reason for requiring it.

A respondent cannot contest the application on the grounds of poverty. However, the respondent will know from the claimant's evidence how much the claimant is seeking. If the respondent wishes the court to take into account his ability to pay that sum (or indeed any sum) when deciding whether or not to exercise its discretion, sufficient details of the respondent's financial position should be disclosed in his evidence in reply to the application.

The applicant must prove the grounds of application relied upon up to the civil standard of the balance of probabilities. There are degrees of probability within the civil standard and ground (c) has been interpreted as meaning that:

> the burden is a high one within that standard if only because litigation of its nature involves uncertainties. A [claimant] with what may on paper appear to be a strong case may find it fails at trial. If he does then he will have to repay the whole or, to the extent that he fails, part of the interim payment. But ... the [claimant] may spend it ... If he does it may be difficult ... to recover ... Clearly the burden resting on the applicant in those circumstances is towards the top of the flexible scale. (*per* May LJ in *Gibbons v Wall* (1988) *The Times*, 24 February).

As the burden is so high it is not surprising that the court has interpreted ground (c) as meaning that the applicant *will* succeed. It is not enough that the court thinks it likely that the claimant will succeed at trial: see *British and Commonwealth Holdings plc v Quadrex Holdings Inc* [1989] 3 WLR 723.

An application for an interim payment is often combined with an application for summary judgment (see **10.5.2**). Where the respondent satisfies the court only that it is possible that his claim or defence may succeed but improbable that it will do so, the court might be persuaded to order an interim payment rather than make a conditional order.

If the applicant can establish an entitlement to an interim payment the court then has a discretion as to two questions:

(a)   whether to make an order; and

(b)   if so, the amount.

As to question (a), an interim payment may be inappropriate if the issues are complicated, or if difficult questions of law arise which may take many hours and the citation of many authorities to resolve: see *British and Commonwealth Holding plc v Quadrex Holdings Inc*, above.

In respect of question (b), the court must not make an interim payment of more than a 'reasonable proportion of the likely amount of the final judgment' after taking into account contributory negligence and any relevant set-off or counterclaim that would reduce any judgment. In other words, the court will seek to calculate what sum is indisputably due to the claimant and then finally consider what sum the defendant is able to pay. For example, in *British and Commonwealth Holding plc v Quadrex Holdings Inc*, the claim was for over £100 million and the judge made an order for an interim payment of £75 million. The Court of Appeal found that such a payment would have a severe adverse impact on the business of the defendant which would be irremediable. In particular, the repayment of that sum if the defendant's defence succeeded at trial would not remedy the damage caused to it by making an interim payment of that size. In the circumstances the court reduced the amount to £5 million.

10.7.3 Consequences of an interim payment order

If a defendant has made an interim payment which exceeds his total liability under the final judgment, the court may award interest on the overpaid amount from the date of the interim payment.

The trial judge will not be told about any interim payment until after he has decided all issues of liability and quantum, unless the defendant consents.

10.8 Security for costs (r 25.12)

10.8.1 Introduction

We have seen at **3.12** that the time and expense involved in dealing with prospective and actual litigation, including defending a claim, are often considerable. Even if the claim is defeated and the defendant obtains an order for his costs, the full amount spent on the litigation will never be recovered. Even worse, the claimant may be unable or unwilling to honour the costs order, leaving the defendant with the unenviable choice between bearing his own costs or investing further time and money in trying to enforce the order.

The provisions in Part 25 about security for costs may be of assistance. If one of the grounds in Part 25 applies, the defendant (including a defendant to an additional claim under Part 20: see **8.1**) can ask the court to exercise its discretion to order the claimant (or even some other person) to provide security for the costs that the defendant is likely to be awarded if he defeats the claim.

10.8.2 The form and effect of the order

If the court grants the application, it will specify in the order:

(a)   the amount of the security;

(b)   the date by which the claimant must provide it; and

(c)   the form it is to take.

Most commonly, the claimant is required to make a payment into court. Alternatively, the security may be held by the defendant's solicitor, and will sometimes take the form of a banker's draft or a guarantee. On other occasions, the requirement for security is satisfied by the claimant giving a suitable undertaking to the court.

What happens if the claimant fails to provide the security by the date ordered? Part 25 is silent on this point, but in practice the court will frequently order that the claim is to be struck out and the defendant entitled to apply without further order for judgment to be entered with costs to be assessed. Even if this penalty is not set out in the order, the defendant will be entitled to apply for a strike out for non-compliance with a court order under the power in r 3.4(2)(c): see **9.3**.

10.8.3   The grounds on which the defendant may apply

The defendant can obtain an order for security only if he can show that one of the grounds set out in rr 25.13 and 25.14 applies. The grounds set out below are those most often relied upon.

10.8.3.1   Claimant based outside the EU

The defendant may apply where the claimant (whether an individual, a company or an other incorporated body) is ordinarily resident out of the jurisdiction and is not a person against whom a claim can be enforced under the Brussels Regulation (or Brussels and Lugano Conventions: see **2.8**).

This ground recognises the difficulties that the defendant may have in enforcing a costs order outside the EU. For example, in *Al-Koronky and Another v Time-Life Entertainment Group Ltd and Another* [2006] EWCA Civ 1123, the Court of Appeal confirmed that it was quite proper to make an order under this ground where the claimants resided in Sudan and it was unlikely that any eventual award of costs could be enforced there.

10.8.3.2   Impecuniosity

The defendant may apply where the claimant is a company or other body (whether incorporated inside or outside Great Britain) and there is reason to believe that it will be unable to pay the defendant's costs if ordered to do so.

This ground applies not only to limited companies, but also to unlimited companies: see *Jirehouse Capital v Beller* [2008] EWHC 725 (Ch).

10.8.3.3   The evasive claimant

There are a number of grounds which may be used against an evasive claimant. In particular, security may be applied for against a claimant who has taken steps in relation to his assets that would make it difficult to enforce an order for costs against him. This is analogous to the claimant's right to apply for a freezing injunction (see **10.6**) against a defendant.

10.8.3.4   The nominal claimant

The defendant may seek security where the claimant is a nominal claimant (other than as a representative claimant under Part 19) and there is reason to believe that he will be unable to pay the defendant's costs if ordered to do so.

10.8.3.5   Statutory provisions

There are a number of other statutory provisions which permit the court to require security to be given. For example, s 70(6) of the Arbitration Act 1996 enables the court to grant security in relation to various applications to challenge an arbitration award or appeal on a point of law.

10.8.3.6   Security other than from the claimant

The court may order someone other than the claimant to provide security. The defendant has to show that the person against whom security is sought has either:

(a)   assigned the right to the claim to the claimant with a view to avoiding the possibility of a costs order being made against him; or

(b)   contributed to or has agreed to contribute to the claimant's costs in return for a share of any money or property which the claimant may recover in the proceedings.

If the person against whom security is sought is not a party to the proceedings, the defendant must apply to join him as one. It is doubtful that an order against someone other than the claimant would provide for dismissal of the claim without further order if the security is not provided.

In addition to establishing one of the grounds in rr 25.13 or 25.14, the court must be satisfied that it is just to make the order, having regard to all the circumstances of the case.

10.8.4 Factors relevant to the court's exercise of its discretion

In considering whether it is just to make an order, the following matters are likely to be considered important.

10.8.4.1 The strength of the claim and the defence

The less likely the defendant is to win at trial, the less justified he is in seeking security. The court will therefore consider whether the claim has a reasonably good prospect of success. Any open admission or offer of settlement and any Part 36 offer (see **Chapter 13**) made by the defendant will tend to undermine the application. However, the true strength of each party's case may not be easy to assess and a detailed consideration of the merits is discouraged (*Fernhill Mining Ltd v Kier Construction Ltd* [2000] CPLR 23).

10.8.4.2 The claimant's ability to provide security

Where the claimant can show a reasonable prospect of success, the courts will be reluctant to make an order for security with which he cannot comply, since the effect is to stifle the claim. The court must strike a balance between the right of the claimant to pursue a genuine claim and the unfairness to the defendant of allowing the claimant to do so without providing security. It is possible that to make an order which the claimant cannot meet would amount to a breach of his right to a fair trial under Article 6(1) of the European Convention on Human Rights.

An increasing problem for defendants is likely to be the difficulty of persuading the court to order security when the claimant is funding the litigation by a CFA (see **2.4.2**). Where, however, the claimant has purchased AEI (see **2.4.5**) which will cover payment of the defendant's costs if the claim fails, no order for security is likely to be sought.

10.8.4.3 The causes of the claimant's impecuniosity

The claimant may be able to persuade the court that his shortage of money has been caused by or contributed to by the defendant's behaviour.

> **Example**
>
> C Ltd's business is dependent on a few major contracts, including one with D Ltd. As a result of a disagreement, D Ltd breaks off the relationship. C Ltd sues, alleging that D Ltd was not entitled to terminate the contract. D Ltd applies for security, on the basis that C Ltd will be unable to pay its costs if it wins at trial. C Ltd admits it is in financial difficulties, but opposes the application, contending that these are the result of D Ltd's wrongful termination.

10.8.4.4 Property within the jurisdiction

Where the application is made against a claimant ordinarily resident outside the EU, the court is unlikely to grant security if the claimant has substantial property of a permanent or fixed nature within the jurisdiction which would be available to meet the defendant's costs.

The court will not necessarily order security if the claimant does not have property within the jurisdiction. The single criterion is what is just in all the circumstances (*Leyvand v Barasch* (2000) *The Times*, 23 March).

10.8.4.5 The timing of the application

The application should be made as soon as practicable. Where the defendant has delayed for no good reason, the court may be less willing to order security, particularly for costs already incurred. Where the claimant would find it difficult to provide security, a delay in applying which has prejudiced the claimant's ability to raise the necessary funds would be a relevant consideration.

10.8.5 Procedure

An application for security can be made at any time, but, as mentioned at **10.8.4.5**, the defendant would be wise to apply as soon as the facts justifying the application are known. As with other interim applications, the defendant is encouraged, where practicable, to indicate that he intends to apply on the allocation questionnaire (see **9.5.1**), so that the application can be dealt with at any case management conference (see **9.6.3.2**).

Before applying, the defendant should (except in exceptional circumstances, such as the evasive removal of assets) write to the claimant and ask that security be provided voluntarily.

Where an application to the court is necessary, it must be supported by written evidence. This is often provided in the form of a witness statement. The CPR 1998, Part 25 does not prescribe the content of the evidence, but there are three objectives, ie to:

(a)   establish that a ground exists;

(b)   persuade the court that it is just to exercise its discretion in favour of the defendant; and

(c)   justify the amount sought.

The defendant will usually apply both in relation to costs already incurred and estimated future costs, giving details of these in a statement of costs. On a first application, the court may well refuse to grant security to cover the defendant's estimated costs up to and including trial, preferring to order an amount estimated to cover the costs up to a particular stage in the litigation and leaving the defendant to reapply as the claim progresses.

10.8.6 Security under r 3.1(5)

In addition to the powers in Part 25, the court has the power under r 3.1(5) to order a party to make a payment into court if that party has, without good reason, failed to comply with a rule, Practice Direction or pre-action protocol. The money paid in provides security for any sum ordered to be paid to another party in the proceedings.

This power broadens the court's discretion to grant security, since a payment in can be required against a defendant as well as a claimant, and there is no requirement to establish that one of the grounds in r 25.13 applies.

In considering whether to make such an order the court must have regard to the amount in dispute and the costs which the parties have incurred or may incur in the future (r 3.1(6)). The court will doubtless also have in mind the ability of the party against whom the order is made to apply for relief under r 3.9, and will take into account the factors identified in that rule (see **9.4**).

The circumstances in which the courts choose to exercise their power under r 3.1(5) are limited and tend to be occasions where the court considers that the other side needs protection, either because there is a history of repeated breaches of the timetable or court orders, or because of a suspicion that a party is not acting in good faith: see *Mealey Horgan plc v Horgan* (1999) *The Times*, 6 July, cited with approval in *Olatawura v Abiloye* [2003] 1 WLR 275.

Chapter 11

Disclosure and Inspection of Documents – CPR 1998, Part 31

11.1 Purpose of disclosure and inspection

> In plain language, litigation in this country is conducted 'cards face up on the table'. Some people from other lands regard this as incomprehensible. 'Why', they ask, 'should I be expected to provide my opponent with the means of defeating me?' The answer, of course, is that litigation is not a war or even a game. It is designed to do real justice between opposing parties and, if the court does not have *all* the relevant information, it cannot achieve this object. (*per* Sir John Donaldson MR in *Davies v Eli Lilly & Co* [1987] 1 WLR 428)

As we saw in **Chapter 3**, the pre-action protocols require the parties to prospective litigation to share information. However, there is no general obligation on a party to show his opponent the contents of documents, and in particular no requirement to show documents that are adverse to his own position. A party can request that an opponent disclose documents that he would normally show during court proceedings, but the only way to compel that disclosure is by way of court order (see **3.9** and **11.16**). Therefore, prior to a claim form being issued, the parties can to a large extent select those documents they wish to show and keep all the others hidden.

The main purpose of the disclosure and inspection stage(s) of the litigation process are to enable the parties better to evaluate the strength of their opponent's case in advance of the trial. The parties have to reveal to each other the documents which have a bearing on the case. This is the disclosure stage. It is done by each party providing the other with a list of their documents. The parties may then inspect, that is, read, some of the other side's documents. The process is intended to promote settlements and therefore a saving in costs. It ensures that the parties are not taken by surprise at the trial and that the court has all relevant information in order to do justice between the parties. However, inspection is subject to restrictions, and some documents may not have to be shown to the opponent (see **11.11**).

Disclosure is governed by Part 31 of CPR 1998, which applies to all claims save those allocated to the small claims track (see **9.6.1**).

11.2   Definition of 'disclosure' (r 31.2)

'Disclosure' is defined in r 31.2, which states:

> A party discloses a document by stating that the document exists or has existed.

This is done by preparing and serving a list of documents on every other party (see **11.8**). But before we consider how disclosure is given in civil litigation, let us briefly consider how a document can be described. This will then help you understand standard disclosure. There are two ways. Consider the book that you are now reading. I can describe the actual document to you, namely it is the 'the Civil Litigation Textbook published by CLP'. Alternatively, I can just describe it generally as 'a textbook'. However, either way, I have disclosed to you the existence of a document. In the first example you know precisely what document I am referring to; whilst in the second example you only know that it is some sort of textbook. Bear this in mind as you read the rest of this chapter.

11.3   Definition of 'documents' (r 31.4)

'Documents' are defined in r 31.4 as being anything in which information of any description is recorded. 'Documents' therefore include written documents, audiotapes, videotapes and photographs.

Electronic documents, such as e-mails, word-processed documents and databases, are also documents. In addition to documents that are readily accessible from computer systems and other electronic devices and media, the definition includes those documents that are stored on servers and back-up systems, and electronic documents that have been 'deleted'. See further PD 31, para 2A.1.

Whilst it is important to appreciate how wide the definition of a document is under the CPR 1998, it is crucial to your understanding of how to give standard disclosure that you spend some time with this definition. You should focus on three words, namely 'information … is recorded'. It is the information recorded in a document that will determine whether or not it forms part of standard disclosure. The procedure has nothing to do with whether or not the document itself is admissible at trial. It is also irrelevant whether or not a party would wish to rely on the document itself at trial. Remember, it is what a document records that governs whether or not it will form part of standard disclosure.

11.4   Standard disclosure (r 31.6)

When a court makes an order for a party to give disclosure of documents, the order is limited to standard disclosure unless the court directs otherwise. Standard disclosure is defined in r 31.6 and requires a party to disclose:

(a)   the documents on which he relies; and

(b)   the documents which:

    (i)   adversely affect his own case;

    (ii)   adversely affect another party's case; or

    (iii)   support another party's case; and

(c)   the documents which he is required to disclose by a relevant Practice Direction. (At the time of writing, there are none.)

It should not be difficult to identify information in a document that the client relies on, as most clients provide their solicitors with favourable documents from the outset of a case. But that is not always true, and a thorough search for documents – both favourable and unfavourable (wholly or in part) – should be made at Stage 1 (see **Chapters 1** to **3**).

11.4.1 Identify the issues in dispute

As we have just seen, standard disclosure obligations require the parties to disclose the existence of documents which record information that they intend to rely on, or which adversely affect or support another party's 'case'. So what is the 'case'? Remember that we have just reached Stage 3 of Civil Litigation and are dealing with what is normally the first procedural step. At Stage 2 the 'case' should have been set out and defined by the statements of case (see **7.5.1**). So the parties should focus on the issues in dispute and search for documents dealing with those issues. Consider Example 2 at **7.5.1**. The claimant should search for documents concerning the issues identified as being in dispute. There is no need to search for and disclose documents that record only information relating to agreed issues (see Example 1). For instance, there is no need to search for documents dealing with delivery of the Unit in June 2010 as this is not disputed. But as it is not admitted that the claimant installed the Unit in July 2010, documents that record information concerning that matter should be searched for and disclosed.

In many cases both liability and quantum will be the legal issues in dispute. But costs will normally be a live issue at trial, and so documents that record information concerning costs (such as Part 36 or other offers of settlement: see **Chapter 13**) should be included as part of standard disclosure.

11.4.2 Control of documents

The duty of disclosure is limited to documents which are or have been in a party's control (see r 31.8). This means that:

(a)   the document is or was in his physical possession; or

(b)   he has or has had a right to possession of it; or

(c)   he has or has had a right to inspect or take copies of it.

Documents held by a party's agent would therefore be within that party's control.

Note that it is open to the parties to agree in writing to dispense with or limit standard disclosure, but this is not common. Any difficulties in giving disclosure, etc, should be raised at the first opportunity, eg at a case management conference (see **9.6.3.2**).

11.4.3 Practical point

Remember that a document is anything in which *information is recorded* (see **11.3**). You are not concerned at this stage about what use, if any, your client or opponent might make of any particular document at trial. Your task is to scrutinise the contents of documents to see if any fall within the r 31.6 definition.

Case Study: Rule 31.6 Documents

Consider the case study in **Appendix D**. Assume that you act for the claimants. Is the letter before claim (**Appendix D(2)**) a r 31.6 document? By comparing para 3 of the particulars of claim with para 3 of the defence and counterclaim, we know that the defendant denies the legal issue of liability and the factual basis of the claim, ie the allegation in the letter that he 'drove up the drive at excessive speed and without properly controlling the Car'. So the letter before claim records information on which your clients rely. It is therefore a r 31.6 document.

What about the particulars of claim and the defence and counterclaim (**Appendix D(3)** and **(4)**)? Are these r 31.6 documents? The answer is yes. The particulars of claim record information on which your clients rely, ie the legal issues of liability and quantum and their factual bases in paras 3 and 4 respectively. The defence and counterclaim record information adverse to your clients' case and supporting the defendant's case; for example, as to liability, that the collision was caused or contributed to by your clients (para 4). Your clients have denied this in para 2 of the reply and defence to counterclaim (**Appendix D(5)**). So the reply and defence to counterclaim is also a r 31.6 document.

11.5   Disclosure of copies (r 31.9)

A party need not disclose more than one copy of a document unless the copy contains 'a modification, obliteration or other marking or feature' on which the party intends to rely, or which supports another party's case, or which could adversely affect his own or another party's case. In that case, the copy document is treated as a separate document.

The most common example in practice of a document that has been modified so creating another copy is one where handwritten notes have been made on the original.

Example

A managing director of a company receives a letter before action. He forwards it to a colleague to get out any records that might still exist, having written on the letter, 'I remember this person's accident. It was the company's fault but after all this time he probably can't prove it.' What this copy of the letter now records is adverse to the company's case if it does go on to defend the claim. The handwritten notes are a form of admission. So this will meet the r 31.6 definition (see **11.4**) and that copy will be subject to standard disclosure.

11.6   The duty to search (r 31.7)

11.6.1   A reasonable and proportionate search

In order to give standard disclosure, a party must make a reasonable and proportionate search for all documents which could adversely affect his own or another party's case, or which support another party's case.

What is reasonable depends on:

(a)   the number of documents involved;

(b)   the nature and complexity of the proceedings;

(c)   the ease and expense of retrieval of any particular document; and

(d)   the significance of the document.

11.6.2   Electronic documents

As to factor (c) above, PD 31, para 2A.4 sets out the following additional matters to be taken into account when considering a search for electronic documents:

(a)   the accessibility of electronic documents or data, including e-mail communications on computer systems, servers, back-up systems and other electronic devices or media that may contain such documents, taking into account alterations or developments in hardware or software systems used by the disclosing party and/or available to enable access to such documents;

(b)   the location of relevant electronic documents, data, computer systems, servers, back-up systems and other electronic devices or media that may contain such documents;

(c)   the likelihood of locating relevant data;

(d)   the cost of recovering any electronic documents;

(e)   the cost of disclosing and providing inspection of any relevant electronic documents;

(f)   the likelihood that electronic documents will be materially altered in the course of recovery, disclosure or inspection.

11.6.3   Putting limits on a search

If a party has limited the search for certain documents, he must state this in his disclosure statement (see **11.9**). Practice Direction 31 suggests, at para 2, for example, that it may be reasonable to decide not to search for documents coming into existence before some particular date, or to limit the search to documents in some particular place or places, or to documents falling into particular categories.

11.6.4   Practical point: anticipate any potential problems or disputes

Before case management directions are given (see **Chapter 9**), and particularly prior to the first case management conference in a multi-track case (see **9.6.3.2**), the parties should discuss any issues that may arise regarding searches for, and the preservation of, documents. For example, as to electronic documentation, this may involve the parties providing information about the categories of electronic documents within their control, the computer systems, electronic devices and media on which any relevant documents may be held, the storage systems maintained by the parties and their document retention policies. Any difficulties or disagreements that arise should be referred to the court for directions at the earliest practical date. Where key word searches are used, these should be agreed as far as possible between the parties: see *Digicel (St. Lucia) Limited v Cable & Wireless Plc* [2008] EWHC 2522.

11.7   The right of inspection (r 31.3)

Rule 31.3(1) gives a party a right of inspection of a disclosed document, except where:

(a)   the document is no longer in the control of the party who disclosed it (see **11.4**);

(b)   the party disclosing the document has a right or a duty to withhold inspection of it (see **11.11**); or

(c)   a party considers it would be disproportionate to the issues in the case to permit inspection of documents within a category and states in his disclosure statement (see **11.9**) that inspection of those documents will not be permitted on the grounds that to do so would be disproportionate.

By r 31.15, where a party has a right to inspect a document, that party wishing to inspect must give written notice of his wish to inspect and the party who disclosed the document must permit inspection not more than seven days after the date on which he received the notice. Rather than going to inspect the documents personally, a party may also request a copy of the document, provided the party also undertakes to pay reasonable copying costs. In this case, the party who disclosed the document must supply him with a copy not more than seven days after the date on which he received the request.

11.8   Procedure for standard disclosure

Where an order for standard disclosure has been made, each party must make and serve a list of documents using Practice Form N265 (a copy of which appears in the case study at **Appendix D(10)**), which must identify the documents in a convenient order and manner and as concisely as possible. Practice Direction 31, at para 3.2, states that it will normally be necessary to list the documents in date order, to number them consecutively and to give each a concise description (eg, letter, claimant to defendant). It also suggests that where there is a large number of documents all falling into a particular category, the disclosing party may list those documents as a category rather than individually.

The list is in three parts on the final page. The first part of the list sets out the documents within the party's control and which he does not object to the other party inspecting. The second part of the list sets out other documents of which the party has control but where the party objects to the other party inspecting them. The most common reason for objection is that the party claims privilege from inspection in relation to those documents (see **11.11**).

The third part of the list consists of documents which are not privileged from inspection but are no longer in the party's control. The list must state what has happened to these documents.

See further **11.12**.

11.9 The disclosure statement

11.9.1 An individual must sign

It will have been seen from the definition of standard disclosure at **11.4** that a party is under an obligation to disclose documents which might adversely affect his own case or support another party's case. A party is therefore under an obligation to disclose documents which could be very detrimental to that party's chances of success, but which the other party does not know exist until disclosure. It is, therefore, essential that parties comply fully and honestly with the requirements of disclosure. Partly for that reason, the list of documents contains a disclosure statement (see r 31.10(5)). This is a statement made by the party disclosing the documents:

(a)   setting out the extent of the search that has been made to locate documents of which disclosure is required;

(b)   certifying that he understands the duty to disclose documents;

(c)   certifying that, to the best of his knowledge, he has carried out that duty.

Where the party making the disclosure statement is a company, firm, association or other organisation, the statement must also identify the person making the statement, the office or position he holds, and explain why he is considered the appropriate person to make the statement.

In what circumstances can (and should) a solicitor sign a disclosure statement? Obviously if a firm of solicitors is itself a party to proceedings then, as a party, the solicitor in the firm who deals with disclosure should sign. Otherwise, by r 31.10(9), a disclosure statement may be made by a person who is not a party only where this is permitted by a relevant Practice Direction. The only provision in PD 31 is at para 4.7, which provides that 'an insurer or the Motor Insurers' Bureau may sign a disclosure statement on behalf of a party where the insurer or the Motor Insurers' Bureau has a financial interest in the result of proceedings brought wholly or partially by or against that party'. However, remember that the different divisions of the High Court produce their own *Court Guides* (see **5.1**), and these should be consulted for any variation of this general rule.

11.9.2 Contempt of court

Proceedings for contempt of court may be brought against a person if he makes, or causes to be made, a false disclosure statement without an honest belief in its truth. The proceedings require the permission of the court unless they are brought by the Attorney-General.

11.9.3 Solicitors' duties

Practice Direction 31, at para 4.4, also states that if the disclosing party has a legal representative acting for him, the legal representative must endeavour to ensure that the person making the disclosure statement understands the duty of disclosure (see further at **11.18**).

A solicitor therefore is under a clear duty to advise his client as to the requirements of disclosure. The solicitor must ensure as far as possible that all documents which have to be disclosed are preserved and made available for inspection. (See **11.18**.) This is obviously something a solicitor must explain to the client on receiving instructions. It is best practice to confirm that advice in writing.

11.10 Continuing obligation (r 31.11)

Disclosure is an obligation which continues until the proceedings are concluded. If documents to which the duty of disclosure extends come to a party's notice at any time during the proceedings, even though the party has already supplied a list of documents, he must immediately notify every other party.

If a document is found after a party's list of documents has been served and it satisfies the test in r 31.6 (see **11.4**), notice should be given by way of letter or a supplemental list. If the party wishes to rely on the document at trial, either the opponent will have to agree or a successful application made to the court for permission to do so (see **11.13**). Even if permission is given, the opponent may still argue at trial that little weight should be attached to the evidence (see **12.9.3**). Late disclosure of an important document can be highly damaging to a case.

11.11 Withholding inspection

As we have already seen, a party can withhold the right to inspect a document which has been disclosed. The usual reason for this is that a party claims that the documents are privileged from inspection. These privileged documents fall into three classes:

(a)   documents protected by legal professional privilege;

(b)   documents tending to incriminate the party producing them;

(c)   documents privileged on the grounds of public policy.

11.11.1 Legal professional privilege

11.11.1.1 Communications passing between a party and his legal advisers or between a party's legal advisers ('advice privilege')

Letters and other communications passing between a party and his solicitor are privileged from inspection provided they are written by or to the solicitor in his professional capacity and for the sole or dominant purpose of obtaining legal advice or assistance for the client. 'Legal advice' is not confined to telling the client the law; it includes information passed by solicitor to client, or vice versa, so that advice may be sought and given, and it includes advice about what should prudently and sensibly be done in the relevant legal context.

Let us briefly consider an example. In a conveyancing transaction the buyer's solicitor sends a short letter, asking the client to make an appointment to see the solicitor to discuss the contract. The letter contains no legal advice. At that meeting, when legal advice is given, the client makes notes of what his solicitor says and the solicitor subsequently makes an attendance note of the legal advice given. Is the letter to the client, asking him to make an appointment, privileged from inspection? No, as legal advice is not given. However, unless the document meets the test in r 31.6 (see **11.4**) it would not be disclosable. What about the client's and the solicitor's notes of the meeting? As these record legal advice given, they are privileged from inspection.

Privilege, however, does not extend without limit to all solicitor/client communications. The range of assistance given by solicitors to their clients has greatly broadened in recent times; for example, many solicitors now provide investment advice to clients. The scope of legal professional privilege has to be kept within reasonable bounds. See further *Three Rivers*

District Council and Others v Governor and Company of the Bank of England [2004] UKHL 48, [2004] 3 WLR 1274.

The privilege extends to communications between a party and his solicitor's employee or agent, and also to communications between a party and a solicitor in his service, for example a solicitor to a government department or in a legal department of a commercial enterprise.

The privilege also covers instructions and briefs to counsel, counsel's opinions, and counsel's drafts and notes.

11.11.1.2 Communications passing between the solicitor and a third party ('litigation privilege')

Communications passing between the solicitor and a third party are privileged from inspection only if:

(a)   they come into existence after litigation is contemplated or commenced; and

(b)   they are made with a view to the litigation, either for the sole or dominant purpose of obtaining or giving advice in regard to it, or for obtaining evidence to be used in it.

Examples of documents which may come within this head of privilege are a report from an expert obtained by a solicitor with a view to advising his client about existing or contemplated litigation, or witness statements obtained by a solicitor for the purpose of existing or contemplated litigation.

11.11.1.3 Communications between the client and a third party ('litigation privilege')

Documents which have passed between the client and a third party are privileged if the sole or dominant purpose for which they were produced was to obtain legal advice in respect of existing or contemplated litigation, or to conduct, or aid in the conduct of, such litigation, usually to have as evidence. It must be the case that litigation was reasonably in prospect at the time when the document was created, and that the sole or dominant reason for obtaining the document was either to enable solicitors to advise as to whether a claim should be made or resisted, or to have as evidence.

In order to determine whether the document is privileged, one must look at the dominant purpose at the time when it came into existence. So if a client asks an expert to prepare a report, it is the client's intention that is relevant. If the document is subsequently used by solicitors for the purposes of litigation, that will not mean that it is privileged if the original purpose of the document was something different.

Example

In *Waugh v British Railways Board* [1980] AC 521, the claimant's husband, an employee of the defendant Board, was killed in an accident while working on the railways. In accordance with the defendant's usual practice, a report on the accident was prepared by two of its officers very shortly after the accident. Although the report was headed 'For the information of the Board's solicitor', the defendant accepted that it had been prepared for two purposes. First, to establish the cause of the accident so that appropriate safety measures could be taken. Secondly, to enable the defendant's solicitor to advise in the litigation that was almost certain to follow. Whilst the first purpose was more immediate than the second, the defendant stated that both were of equal importance. The House of Lords held that as preparing the report for use in anticipated litigation was merely one of the purposes and not the dominant purpose for which it was prepared, the report was not privileged from inspection.

Where a client is not an individual, this form of privilege is also applied to communications between individuals within that organisation. Thus, a memorandum sent by one partner of a firm to another would be privileged if it was prepared for the dominant purpose of obtaining legal advice in respect of existing or contemplated litigation, or to aid the conduct of such litigation.

11.11.1.4 Waiver of privilege

The privilege is the client's and not the solicitor's, and therefore it may be waived by the client. Once a copy of a privileged document is served on the other side, the privilege is waived.

Note that subsequent to disclosure and inspection, each party is required by the court to serve on the other(s) copies of the witness statements and expert reports upon which he intends to rely at trial (see further **Chapter 12**). This waives the privilege in these documents, unless it had been waived earlier.

Special considerations apply to the written instructions given by a solicitor to an expert whose report is relied upon at trial (see **12.13.3**).

11.11.2 Documents tending to incriminate the party who would produce them

A party is entitled to claim privilege for documents which will tend to incriminate either him or his spouse. This rule applies to criminal liability or penal proceedings under the law of any part of the UK. The details are beyond the scope of this book.

11.11.3 Documents privileged on the ground of public policy

If producing a copy of a document would be injurious to the public interest, it may be withheld on the ground of public policy.

The judge has to consider whether the withholding of the documents is necessary for the proper functioning of the public service. Examples of documents which have been withheld from production on this ground are documents dealing with matters of national defence, information as to ill-treatment of children given to the NSPCC, local authority social work records, probation service records, and evidence which might reveal the identity of a police informant.

11.11.4 Challenging a claim to privilege (r 31.19)

A party who wishes to challenge his opponent's claim to privilege can apply for the court to decide whether the claim to privilege should be upheld. In any case where there is a claim to privilege, the court may require the party claiming privilege to produce the document to the court and may invite any person, even if they are not a party, to make representation. See, for example, *Atos Consulting Ltd v Avis plc (No 2)* [2007] EWHC 323.

11.11.5 Inadvertent disclosure of privileged documents

11.11.5.1 An obvious mistake

If privileged documents are mistakenly listed in part 1 of a party's list (instead of part 2), no harm is done if the error is spotted before the other side inspects the document since the list may be amended and re-served.

But what if inspection of privileged material is allowed inadvertently, for example where copies of privileged documents have been sent in error to the other side's solicitor? Under r 31.20, the receiving party is not permitted to use the documents or their contents without the permission of the court. If the receiving party does not seek that permission, the disclosing party may be able to persuade the court to grant an injunction requiring the receiving party and his solicitor to return the documents, without retaining a photocopy and restraining the use of the privileged material in the litigation. The court has a discretion whether to grant an injunction and will do so only if satisfied that the mistake was evident to the solicitor receiving the documents, or, if not, that it would have been obvious to a hypothetical reasonable solicitor that disclosure had occurred as a result of an obvious mistake (*IBM Corporation and Another v Phoenix International (Computers) Ltd* [1995] 1 All ER 413).

Where the mistake is less than obvious, there is no obligation on the solicitor receiving the documents to make enquiries of the sending party: see *Norman Roger Breeze v John Stacy & Sons Ltd* (1999) *The Times*, 8 July.

11.11.5.2   Practical point

The Solicitors' Code of Conduct makes it clear that as soon as a solicitor who receives privileged documents realises that the sender has made an obvious mistake, he should immediately stop reading the documents, inform the other side and return the documents. See guidance note 20(c) to r 4.

11.11.6   Without prejudice correspondence

As we saw at **3.10.1,** without prejudice correspondence will record information as part of a party's genuine attempt to settle a case. The correspondence will probably therefore satisfy the r 31.6 definition, as it is likely to set out the strengths of a party's case, and indeed may contain concessions that are adverse to that case and support the opponent. You should remember that it is irrelevant to standard disclosure that the recipient of a document has already seen it. So without prejudice correspondence, just like the other common correspondence between parties that meets the r 31.6 test, should be disclosed and no privilege from inspection claimed. This is because when the letters were being drafted by a solicitor and before being sent to the other party, the letters were privileged from inspection; but the privilege was waived by sending them to the other side.

The only time privilege from inspection is relevant to without prejudice correspondence is in multi-party litigation where not all the parties are involved in that correspondence. So what does that mean if, for example, C sues D1 and D2, but C has without prejudice correspondence only with D1? As between C and D1, that correspondence will go in the first part of their respective list of documents as not being privileged from inspection. However, as between C and D2, that correspondence will go in the second part of C's list of documents as it is privileged from inspection by D2. The correspondence will not, of course, appear in D2's list of documents as D2 never received it.

11.12   Disclosing the existence of documents: the list

A party discloses a document by stating that the document exists or has existed. As we saw at **11.2**, there are two possible ways of disclosing the existence of a document, namely by identifying either:

(a)   the actual document itself; or

(b)   the type of document.

11.12.1   Part 1 of the list

In the first part of the list of documents, the actual documents are identified so that the other parties can decide whether or not they wish to inspect them. Remember that these are documents in the party's control which he does not object to being inspected.

11.12.2   Part 2 of the list

In the second part of the list of documents the party should disclose the type of documents for which he is claiming privilege from inspection, for example 'confidential correspondence between the claimant and his solicitors'; 'various experts' reports and witness statements', etc. It is quite proper to do this. The existence of the document has been disclosed and so the duty to give disclosure is thereby discharged. However, the general description as to the type of document ensures that the contents are not indirectly revealed. The objections to inspection must then be stated. A legitimate ground must be claimed. It is *not* a ground of objection that the document is adverse to the party's case or is confidential. For examples of different possible grounds, see **11.11**.

In practice, the most common objection is based on legal professional privilege. For advice privilege, the objection to inspection is that the documents are communications between the party and his solicitor that were created for the sole (or dominant) purpose of obtaining legal advice. For litigation privilege, there are two matters to include: (i) when the document was created, and (ii) why it was created. An example might be: 'Expert's report obtained by the Claimant's solicitors when this litigation was pending for the sole purpose of having as evidence to be used in this litigation.'

If different grounds are relied on for different documents, they should be arranged and listed separately.

11.12.3 Part 3 of the list

In the third part of the list of documents the party must state the actual (non-privileged) documents that he once had, but no longer has, in his control. This often comprises little more than the original letters, written by or on behalf of the party, copies of which have already been detailed in the first part of the list. In respect of each document it is necessary to state when it was last in the party's control and where it is now. The purpose is to enable the parties receiving the list to continue their investigations elsewhere. If they can locate the present whereabouts of the documents they may be able to obtain copies on an application for disclosure by a non-party (see **11.17**).

Case Study: Claimants' List of Documents

The claimants' list of documents can be found by way of example in the case study at **Appendix D(10)**. You will note that this is on the prescribed form, N265. The first two pages are taken up mostly with the disclosure statement. Did you spot how the claimants limited their search? Then the final page contains the three parts of the list. Note how each document in the first part is explicitly described so that the defendant can identify it and decide whether or not to inspect it. Contrast that with the second part of the list. Here, the documents are identified only generally but, most importantly, the claim to privilege from inspection is described in full. Look closely at the wording used. Lastly, the third part records the fact that the claimants once had in their possession the originals of the copy documents listed in the first part of their list.

11.13 Failure to disclose (r 31.21)

A party who fails to disclose a document or fails to allow inspection of a document may not rely on that document at trial unless the court permits. Note importantly, however, that a party who fails to disclose a document which harms his case may find that his case is struck out as a result of failure to comply with an order for specific disclosure (see **11.15**).

A party who fails to give disclosure properly may be penalised financially. For example, in *Earles v Barclays Bank Plc* [2009] EWHC 2500 the court held that the successful defendant should recover only one half of its costs because of its failure to conduct disclosure adequately.

11.14 Subsequent use of disclosed documents (r 31.22)

Where a document has been disclosed to a party, he may use that document only for the purposes of the case in which it has been disclosed unless:

(a)   the document has been read or referred to during a public hearing (eg, at trial); or

(b)   the court grants permission; or

(c)   the party who disclosed the document and the person to whom the document belongs consent.

Where (a) applies, the court may make an order restricting or prohibiting the use of the document.

11.15   Applying for specific disclosure (r 31.12)

If a party is dissatisfied with disclosure provided by the other party and believes it is inadequate then he may make an application for an order for specific disclosure. The application notice must specify the order the applicant wants the court to make, and the grounds of the application must be set out in the application notice or in the supporting evidence. For example, in a claim arising out of the supply of allegedly defective goods sold by the defendant to the claimant, the claimant may suspect that the defendant should have quality control records. If these have not been disclosed then an application for specific disclosure may be justified.

Before making such an application, a party should write to the other side explaining why he believes the documents are disclosable and asking the other party to comply properly with the order for disclosure. If a satisfactory response is not forthcoming then it would be appropriate to issue the application.

An application will require a witness statement in support. This should detail the date of the order for standard disclosure and the document or documents that the applicant believes should have been included in the list. If it is not obvious, the witness statement should explain how these documents satisfy the definition of standard disclosure and why the applicant believes they exist. A reference to the request for the documents and the respondent's response should be made to show that the applicant has complied with the overriding objective by trying to avoid making an application.

An order for specific disclosure can require a party to:

(a)   disclose specified documents or classes of documents;

(b)   carry out a search as specified by the order and disclose any documents located as a result of that search.

When deciding whether to make an order for specific disclosure, the court will take into account all the circumstances of the case and, if satisfied that the respondent has failed adequately to comply with the obligations imposed by the order for disclosure, will usually make such order as is necessary to make sure those obligations are adequately complied with. For example, the order will often be made in the form of an 'unless' order (see **9.3.4**). The applicant would also seek an order that the respondent pay the applicant's costs.

A party can also apply for an order for specific inspection, which would require a party to permit inspection of documents which he omitted from his disclosure statement on the grounds that inspection would be disproportionate (see **11.7**).

11.16   Disclosure before proceedings start (r 31.16)

As we saw at **3.9**, a party may make an application for pre-action disclosure.

This procedure will normally be used where a party is unsure whether he has a good case against another party and, therefore, does not know whether to issue proceedings. The party could, therefore, apply for pre-action disclosure against the intended defendant so that he can then make an informed decision as to whether or not to issue proceedings against that person.

11.17 Non-party disclosure (r 31.17)

Where proceedings are already in existence, a party to the proceedings can apply for disclosure against a non-party. For an example, see *Secretary of State for Transport v Pell Frischmann Consultants Ltd* [2006] EWHC 2756.

The application must be supported by evidence.

The court may order non-party disclosure only if:

(a)   the documents in question are likely to support the applicant's case or adversely affect the case of another party; and

(b)   disclosure is necessary to dispose fairly of the case or to save costs.

The order must:

(a)   specify the documents or classes of documents to be disclosed; and

(b)   require the non-party to specify which documents are no longer in his control and which are privileged.

The order may specify a time and place for disclosure and inspection, and may require the non-party to indicate what has happened to the documents which are no longer in his control.

This procedure enables a party to proceedings which are already in existence to obtain disclosure of documents from a non-party if it is going to help resolve the issues in the case.

The most common application of this procedure would be where a party indicates in his list of documents that he no longer has a document in his possession. He also indicates that X now has possession of that document. The other party may then write to X asking for a copy of the document. If X refuses to supply that copy voluntarily, the other party could then apply for an order for non-party disclosure against X.

11.18 Disclosure obligations and solicitors' duties

Rule 11.01 of the Solicitors' Code of Conduct provides that a solicitor must never deceive or knowingly mislead the court. Guidance note 13(d) suggests that the rule might be broken if a solicitor does not immediately disclose a document that he becomes aware of during the course of a case, which should have been, but was not, disclosed. Obviously, this situation may arise after the client's list of documents has been served. The solicitor needs to advise the client to disclose it and determine how the document should be disclosed. A supplemental list is probably appropriate. If the document is privileged from inspection, it should be listed in the second part of the list. If it is not privileged from inspection, it should be listed in the first part, and, of course, the opponent may then wish to inspect it. If a client refuses to allow disclosure, the solicitor should withdraw from the case. In order to keep client confidentiality (see r 4), the solicitor should not inform any other party (or the court) of the reasons for ceasing to act.

A solicitor must ensure that his client understands the duties to conduct a reasonable and proper search and then give full and frank disclosure. The client must also appreciate that disclosure is an ongoing obligation. As an officer of the court a solicitor has a duty to ensure disclosure is properly given and that the court is not misled. Moreover, the client should sign the disclosure statement only after receiving legal advice. Remember, that statement includes the following:

> I certify that I understand the duty of disclosure and that to the best of my knowledge I have carried out that duty. I further certify that the list of documents set out in or attached to this form, is a complete list of all documents which are or have been in my control and which I am obliged under the order to disclose. I understand that I must inform the court and the other parties immediately if any further document required to be disclosed by Rule 31.6 comes into my control at any time before conclusion of the case.

So during the first three Stages of Civil Litigation the client must be made aware of the extent of his disclosure obligations and the importance of not destroying documents that might have to be disclosed. A solicitor should advise a client that if he destroys disclosable documents deliberately and contumaciously, or such that a fair trial is rendered impossible, his statement of case is likely to be struck out.

Woods v Martin's Bank [1959] 1 QB 55 imposes a duty on a solicitor to the court to examine his client's documents himself in order to ensure that proper disclosure is made. *Myers v Elman* [1940] AC 282 provides that if the client will not permit this, or insists on giving imperfect disclosure, the solicitor must withdraw from the case, as otherwise he will be participating in a deception of the court.

11.19 Summary of key points

11.19.1 Giving standard disclosure

Broadly, standard disclosure involves a party taking the following steps:

(1)   Identify the issues in dispute between the parties.

(2)   Decide who should carry out the search for r 31.6 documents and how this should be done, eg whether there should be any limitations placed on the search in relation to the age, location and/or categories of documents.

(3)   Carry out a reasonable and proportionate search for r 31.6 documents. Identify the words in each document that make it a r 31.6 document, namely those that record information which:

  (a)   the party intends to rely on; or

  (b)   adversely affects that party's case; or

  (c)   adversely affects another party's case; or

  (d)   supports another party's case.

(4)   Consider each and every r 31.6 document in your client's control, or formerly in his control. It is irrelevant for listing purposes that:

  (a)   the same or similar information is recorded in another document;

  (b)   the document has already been seen by the opponent (but remember that if the document had attracted privilege from inspection then by sending it to the opponent that privilege was waived);

  (c)   the document came from your opponent (but remember that if the document had attracted privilege from inspection then by sending it to you the opponent waived that privilege).

(5)   Prepare a list of documents in Form N265. On the final page, decide where each r 31.6 document should appear.

  (a)   The document should appear in the first part of the list if it is in the party's control and is not privileged from inspection. The actual document should be described (ie the name of the author (and recipient, if appropriate) and date: for example, 'Letter from Claimant to Defendant dated 8 September 2008').

  (b)   The document should appear in the second part of the list if it is currently privileged from inspection. The actual document must not be described, as that will allow the other parties to identify it. Two things must be done. First, describe the document generally, for example: 'instructions to counsel', 'proof of evidence', 'correspondence between the claimant and the claimant's solicitors', 'expert's report', etc. This discloses the existence of the document and so standard disclosure is given. However, secondly, the relevant privilege from inspection must be claimed. Remember that there are two facts to include: when the document was created; and why it was created. For example (expert's report) 'obtained by the claimant when this litigation was reasonably contemplated for the sole purpose of taking legal advice'.

(c)   A document that is not privileged from inspection but is no longer in the party's control should appear in the third part of the list, for example, 'Bundle of invoices concerning the onward sale of the goods in question, all dated 2007, destroyed in a flood at the claimant's premises on 6 February 2008'.

(6)   If a r 31.6 document is discovered after the list of documents has been served, a supplemental list should be served on the opponent. If the party serving the supplemental list wants to rely on the document at trial, either the opponent will have to agree or the court must give permission (see **11.10**).

11.19.2 Responding to standard disclosure

What should a party do on receipt of the opponent's list of documents? Consider the following:

(1)   Check the disclosure statement. Are any limits placed on the search reasonable? (See **11.9**.)

(2)   Check Part 1. What documents need to be inspected (see **11.7**)? Is the list complete? Is a request for specific disclosure justified (see **11.15**)?

(3)   Check Part 2. Are all claims to privilege from inspection legitimate (see **11.11.4**)?

(4)   Check Part 3. If a document was not in Part 1, is it here? Is there any document worth tracing to obtain a copy (see **11.17**)?

Chapter 12

Evidence

12.1 Introduction

12.1.1 Relevance

Any evidence, to be admissible, must be relevant. Contested trials last long enough as it is without spending time on evidence which is irrelevant and cannot affect the outcome. Relevance must, and can only, be judged by reference to the issue which the court is called upon to decide. (*per* Lord Bingham of Cornhill in *O'Brien v Chief Constable of South Wales Police* [2005] UKHL 26, (2005) *The Times*, 29 April).

12.1.2 Judicial control

The rules on evidence are contained primarily within Parts 32 and 33 of the CPR 1998. These rules do not change the law on the admissibility of evidence save for the fact that the court, as might be expected through its court management powers, can control the evidence brought before the court.

Rule 32.1 states:

(1)   The court may control the evidence by giving directions as to—

    (a)   the issues on which it requires evidence;

    (b)   the nature of the evidence which it requires to decide those issues; and

    (c)   the way in which the evidence is to be placed before the court.

(2)   The court may use its power under this rule to exclude evidence that would otherwise be admissible.

(3)   The court may limit cross-examination.

In exercising its powers under this Rule, the court will bear in mind the overriding objective in r 1.1 and will attempt to define and identify the issues between the parties. For example, the court may decide, prior to the trial, that a particular issue which has been raised is no longer important and make an order excluding any evidence which the parties intended to use in relation to that particular issue.

12.1.3   Factual and expert evidence

Evidence falls into two broad types. First, factual evidence from a witness (see **12.2** to **12.9**). Secondly, expert evidence from a suitably qualified expert (see **12.13**).

12.2   Witness evidence

12.2.1   General rule

Under r 32.2(1), the general rule is that any fact which needs to be proved is to be proved at trial by oral evidence given in public, and at any other hearing by evidence in writing. The Rules also provide that the court may allow a witness to give evidence by any means, including a video link.

12.2.2   Pre-trial exchange

As already seen in **Chapter 9**, when giving directions for trial, the court will usually order witness statements to be exchanged. Rule 32.4(2) states that the court will order a party to serve on the other parties any witness statement of the oral evidence which the party serving the statement intends to rely upon in relation to any issue of fact to be decided at the trial. As outlined at **12.6**, where a witness statement is not served, the witness will be allowed to give evidence at trial only with the court's permission.

The court can give directions as to the order in which witness statements are to be served. Usually the court will order simultaneous exchange, but exceptionally it may order one party (usually the claimant) to serve first (sequential exchange). Once a witness statement is served, it ceases to be privileged (see further **11.11.1.4**).

12.2.3   Objections to contents

By r 32.4(1), a witness statement is a written statement signed by a person that contains the evidence which that person would be allowed to give orally. So what should you do if, after exchanging witness statements, you object to the relevance or admissibility of material contained in your opponent's statements? Best practice is to notify the other party of your objection immediately and seek to resolve the dispute. Failing that, raise the matter at any pre-trial review or at the beginning of the trial itself.

12.2.4   Additional evidence

What if, after the exchange of witness statements, a party wants a witness to give additional evidence? It may well be that a witness needs to deal with events occurring, or matters discovered, after the exchange, or in response to matters dealt with by another party's witness. The answer is to prepare and serve a supplemental witness statement dealing with these points as soon as possible. The other party should be asked to agree to the evidence being adduced at trial. Failing that, an application for permission to rely on the evidence should be made at any pre-trial review or at the beginning of the trial itself.

12.3   Form of witness statements

12.3.1   Structure and contents

Rules relating to the form of witness statements are set out in paras 17–20 of PD 32.

By para 17.1 the witness statement should be headed in the same way as any other court document, and by para 17.2 the top right-hand corner should state:

(a)   the party on whose behalf the statement is filed (eg Claimant);

(b)   the initials and surname of the witness (eg MJ Brownlow);

(c)   the number of the statement in relation to that witness (eg 1st);

(d)   the identifying initials and number of each exhibit referred to (eg MJB1); and

(e)   the date the statement was made (eg 16/05/10).

The statement is required to be set out in numbered paragraphs and will generally outline the relevant events chronologically. Dates and any other numbers should be expressed in figures, not words (see also **7.1.4**).

The statement should be in the witness's own words as far as practicable. It should be in the first person and state:

(a)   the full name of the witness;

(b)   where he lives or, if the statement is made as part of his employment or business, where he works, his position in the business and the name of the business;

(c)   his occupation or description; and

(d)   (if so) that he is a party or an employee of a party.

12.3.2 Witness's own words

In the case of *Alex Lawrie Factors Ltd v Morgan, Morgan and Turner* (1999) *The Times*, 18 August, the Court of Appeal held that the purpose of a witness statement was for the witness to say, in his or her own words, what the relevant evidence was. It was not to be used by the lawyer who prepared it as a vehicle for complex legal argument to which the witness would not be readily able to speak if cross-examined on the document. In this case, the second defendant, Mrs Morgan, was seeking to avoid liability to the claimant under a deed of indemnity. She had averred that the reason why her signature appeared on the deed was due to her former husband's fraudulent actions and misrepresentations. The claimant applied for summary judgment (see **10.5.2**) and, in her evidence in reply, Mrs Morgan stated that she had had the opportunity of studying the decision of the House of Lords in *Barclays Bank plc v O'Brien* [1994] 1 AC 180 in some detail. She made a number of points in reliance on that decision. The judge said that Mrs Morgan was clearly, from her evidence, an intelligent woman. He concluded that her evidence as to how she came to sign the deed of indemnity was simply not credible and he awarded summary judgment.

On the appeal, Mrs Morgan's counsel sought permission to put in new evidence going to her intelligence. The court allowed such because the situation was susceptible of injustice if the matter proceeded on the basis on which the judge had considered it, which would derive from his interpretation of the kind of woman Mrs Morgan must be from a perusal of her evidence. The court said that the case was a very good warning of the grave dangers which could occur when lawyers put into witnesses' mouths a sophisticated legal argument which, in effect, represented the lawyers' arguments in the case, to which the witnesses themselves would not be able to speak if cross-examined. Having had the benefit of further evidence, the court did not consider that this was a case in which it was appropriate to disregard Mrs Morgan's evidence as incredible and it allowed the appeal.

12.3.3 Sources of information and belief (PD 32, para 18.2)

The statement must indicate which of the statements are based on the witness's own knowledge and which are matters of information or belief, and the source of his information and belief.

12.3.4 Exhibits (PD 32, paras 18.3 and 18.6)

Any exhibit used in connection with a witness statement should be verified and identified by the witness and remain separate from the statement. Exhibits should be numbered and, where a witness makes more than one statement in which there are exhibits in the same proceedings, the numbering of the exhibits should run consecutively throughout and not start again with each witness statement.

12.3.5   Statement of truth (PD 32, para 20.2)

The witness statement must contain a statement of truth in the following words:

> I believe that the facts stated in this witness statement are true.

The statement of truth must be signed by the witness himself. Proceedings for contempt of court may be brought against a person who makes a false statement in a witness statement without an honest belief in its truth.

12.3.6   Template

A template to help you draft a witness statement is set out at **Appendix B(5)**.

> **Case Study: Witness Statement**
>
> An example of a witness statement to be used at trial may be found in the case study at **Appendix D(11)**. This witness statement, filed on behalf of the Defendant, would have been exchanged by the Defendant's solicitors in accordance with the directions order (see **9.6.3.1** and **Appendix D(9)**).

12.4   Use of witness statements at trial

Having served a witness statement on the other side, the witness will usually be called to give oral evidence at trial, unless the court orders otherwise or the party uses the statement as hearsay evidence (see **12.9**).

The witness statement will stand as the evidence-in-chief of the witness (see **14.2.3.2**) unless the court orders otherwise. When preparing a witness statement to be used at trial, it is, therefore, essential to ensure that the statement is comprehensive. By r 32.5(3), a witness may amplify his statement or give evidence of matters which have arisen since he served his witness statement, or in response to matters dealt with by another party's witness, but only if the court gives permission. The court will not do so unless it considers that there is good reason why the evidence was not dealt with by the witness in his witness statement. Pursuant to the overriding objective, a court will usually allow amplification or additional examination-in-chief where admitting that evidence will not cause any other party injustice. For example, additional expense to a party caused by a late, unjustified change of tack by his opponent may see an application under r 32.5(3) refused.

If a party who has served a witness statement does not call the witness or use the statement as hearsay evidence, any other party may use the witness statement as hearsay evidence (r 32.5(5)).

As the witness statement will usually stand as the evidence-in-chief, the witness will normally simply be asked to confirm that it is true and will then be subject to cross-examination by the other side. It is because it is subject to cross-examination that oral evidence from witnesses is considered to be the 'best' form of evidence as it has been tested in court.

Because a witness statement normally stands as the witness's evidence-in-chief, the trial judge will have read it before the trial starts, and all witnesses are expected to have re-read their witness statements shortly before they are called to give evidence.

12.5   Witness summaries (r 32.9)

Sometimes it will be very difficult to persuade a witness to give a witness statement. As we shall see at **14.1.2**, the means exist to compel a witness to come to court, but it is obviously risky to do that if you do not know what the witness is going to say and, of course, as no witness statement will have been exchanged, permission of the court will be necessary anyway before the witness can give oral evidence.

> **Example**
>
> Fred is suing his former employers for damages arising out of an accident he suffered at work. Fred believes that his former colleague, Mark, could give evidence about poor safety practices within the firm, but Mark has refused to give a witness statement to Fred's solicitors as he is worried that if he does he might be dismissed.

Rule 32.9 provides that Fred's solicitors can apply to court without notice for an order to serve a 'witness summary'. This provision applies where a party is required to serve a witness statement for trial but cannot obtain one. The witness summary must contain:

(a)   the evidence which would otherwise go in a witness statement; or

(b)   if the party serving the summary does not know what evidence will be given, the areas about which he proposes to question the witness; and

(c)   the witness's name and address.

Unless the court orders otherwise, the summary must be served on the other side at the same time as the witness statements.

12.6   Sanctions for not serving a witness statement (r 32.10)

If a party does not serve a witness statement or witness summary within the proper time-limit, the witness cannot give oral evidence unless the court gives permission.

What if a party knows that it will not make the deadline to exchange? As soon as that becomes clear, he should contact all other parties and seek an agreement to an extension. He must try to ascertain when the witness's signed statement is going to be available. Any agreement reached must be recorded in writing, but it must be remembered that the parties cannot alter the key case management dates set in fast track or multi-track cases (see **9.6.2.2** and **9.6.3.5**). If no agreement is reached, or if a key case management date will not be met, an immediate application to the court should be made.

What if a party is ready to exchange within the deadline but his opponent is not? If a good reason is given for an extension it should be agreed, subject to the above comments. But what if there has been no request or application for an extension? If the party complies with the direction and serves the statements on the opponent then that party potentially gains an advantage in that he will see the evidence first and could tailor his own evidence accordingly. The usual practice in these circumstances is for the party to file the statements with the court and explain the situation in a covering letter. Subsequently, an application might be made to strike out the opponent's case for failing to complying with the court order (see **9.3**).

Will the court allow an application to serve a witness statement late or to rely on a witness at trial without having previously served a statement? All will turn on the circumstances of the case and the application of the overriding objective. What if a party discovers a new, favourable witness after witness statements have already been exchanged? At an interim application before trial, will the court's permission be given to serve the statement in order that the party can rely on the evidence at trial? The court will scrutinise why the discovery was made so late in the day, and only in exceptional cases is it likely that the party will be successful: see *Stroh v London Borough of Haringey* [1999] LTL, 13 July, where the Court of Appeal upheld the refusal of permission as it was clear that the judge had had in mind the overriding objective and he was entitled to conclude that the prejudice to the respondent outweighed the prejudice to the applicant.

12.7   Affidavits

Affidavits are sworn statements of evidence (ie, the maker of the affidavit has to swear before a solicitor (not his own), or other authorised person, that the contents of the affidavit are true).

Prior to the CPR 1998 coming into force, affidavits were the usual means of submitting evidence at interim applications. As we have seen, however, evidence at such applications is now given by witness statements, the statement of case itself or the application notice provided it contains a statement of truth.

In the great majority of cases, therefore, there is no need to go to the extra expense (an oath fee) of using sworn affidavits as evidence. Indeed, if you do, it is very unlikely that the court would allow you to recoup the extra cost from the other side.

On some occasions, however, it is still necessary to use affidavits. The Rules provide that if you are applying for a freezing injunction or search order (see **10.6**), the evidence in support of such an application must be by way of affidavit rather than a witness statement.

12.8 Opinion evidence

12.8.1 Relevant facts personally perceived

The general rule is that opinion evidence is not admissible. The function of a witness is to relate the facts to the court so that the court can draw its own conclusions. There are some situations in which it may be difficult for a witness to separate fact and opinion. A typical example is speed. If a witness gives evidence that a vehicle was being driven at 'about 60 mph', that is only the witness's opinion. Nevertheless, it is difficult to see how else the witness could express what he saw unless he restricted himself to describing the speed as 'fast'. Accordingly, whilst the cogency of the witness's assessment of the speed might be challenged, it would usually be admissible. Similarly, a witness may be permitted to express a view that 'John was drunk'. Properly, the witness should relate the physical characteristics he observed which led to that conclusion (eg, slurred speech, glazed eyes, an unsteadiness of gait, breath smelling of alcohol, etc). However, the witness's opinion, whilst it might be challenged, will be admissible. This is confirmed by s 3(2) of the Civil Evidence Act 1972, which states that:

> … where a person is called as a witness in any civil proceedings, a statement of opinion by him on any relevant matter on which he is not qualified to give expert evidence, if made as a way of conveying relevant facts personally perceived by him, is admissible as evidence of what he perceived.

12.8.2 Practical point

When a solicitor prepares a witness statement, it is vital that any relevant opinions expressed are based firmly on what the witness personally perceived. Assume that you act for a claimant in negligence proceedings against the defendant, Mr X. When you interview a former personal assistant of Mr X, she tells you, 'Mr X was always very disorganised'. That is a conclusion she has drawn. What you want to know is what did the witness see or hear that led her to that conclusion. Was it that Mr X's office was untidy, with the files on the floor and not in the cabinet? That Mr X did not keep his diary up to date and missed appointments? That Mr X told her at least once a week that he had been late for a meeting?

12.8.3 Expert evidence

As is indicated in s 3(1), the other main exception to the inadmissibility of opinion evidence concerns expert evidence (see **12.13**).

12.9 Hearsay evidence

Special considerations apply where hearsay evidence is to be used. Before looking at these, it is necessary to understand what is meant by 'hearsay'.

12.9.1 Definition

Hearsay evidence is defined in s 1(2)(a) of the Civil Evidence Act 1995 as 'a statement made otherwise than by a person while giving oral evidence in the proceedings which is tendered as evidence of the matters stated'.

Hearsay evidence may be an oral or a written statement made outside the courtroom which is repeated to the court in order to prove the truth of the matter stated out of court.

Note that s 13 of the 1995 Act defines a 'statement' as 'any representation of fact or opinion'.

The statement that constitutes the hearsay evidence must itself constitute admissible evidence. So any fact must be relevant (see **12.1**). Likewise, any opinion must be that of a non-expert based on that person's perception (see **12.8.1**).

Therefore, in considering whether evidence is admissible hearsay, the following three questions must be answered in the affirmative:

(a)   Does the evidence consist of an oral or written statement made outside the courtroom?

(b)   Is that statement being presented to the court in order to prove that it is true? If the previous statement is being related, for example, to show a person's state of mind or simply to show that the statement was made, it will not be hearsay.

(c)   Is the statement an admissible statement of fact or opinion?

Example 1

Richard is giving evidence. He says in his evidence, 'Dave told me that Peter had stolen a car'. Richard is repeating what someone else said outside the courtroom, so the first part of the definition of hearsay is satisfied. But consider why Richard is giving this evidence. If it is as part of a case against Peter where it is relevant to show that Peter did, indeed, steal a car, then it will be hearsay. On the other hand, if Richard is giving evidence in a defamation claim brought by Peter against Dave then it will not be hearsay, as Richard is not giving the evidence to show that Peter stole a car. Indeed, this would be exactly what Peter does not want to show! Richard is relating the evidence simply to show that the statement was made.

Example 2

Michael booked a holiday with Fancy Tours Ltd. When booking, the agent assured him that the hotel would be quiet and peaceful, close to the beach and with its own swimming pool. However, the hotel was noisy, some distance away from the beach, and did not have a swimming pool. Michael is now suing for misrepresentation and wishes to repeat in evidence the oral statements made to him by the agent. This will be relevant evidence on the issue of liability but it will not be hearsay because it is not being related to show the truth of those statements. It is being related to show the effect that the statements had on his state of mind, namely that he relied on them and was misled by the misrepresentations.

Example 3

Clive arrives at the scene of an accident shortly after the claimant, Anna, a pedestrian, was knocked over by a motorbike ridden by the defendant, Matthew. The accident takes place in a 30 miles per hour zone. The defendant denies liability, alleging that he was not speeding and that Anna ran out in front of him. Clive's evidence is, 'When I arrived at the accident a woman I know only as Liz came up to me and said, "That pedestrian was knocked over by the motorbike that was going at at least 45 miles per hour. It was the bike rider's fault"'. Assume Clive is called as a witness by Anna. Her solicitor's attempts to trace Liz fail. Clive can repeat what Liz told him about the pedestrian being knocked over by the motorbike and that in Liz's opinion the motorbike was travelling at at least 45 miles per hour. That would be admissible evidence if given by Liz in court. It is relevant to the issue of liability and based on what Liz perceived. But Clive cannot repeat Liz's opinion that the accident was the defendant's fault. Liz would be a winess of fact in court. A witness of fact cannot give evidence beyond relevant facts and perceptions. This would be inadmissible opinion evidence from Liz. So it cannot be admissible as hearsay evidence for Clive to repeat it.

Hearsay evidence may be either first-hand or multiple.

Example 1

Sara gives evidence of something that she was told by John (in order to prove the truth of John's statement). Sara's evidence is first-hand hearsay.

Example 2

Sara also gives evidence of something that John was told by Michelle (in order to prove the truth of what Michelle said). This evidence is multiple hearsay.

Example 3

Sara keeps a diary. She records what she saw one day. Sara's diary is used at a trial to prove the truth of its contents. That evidence is first-hand hearsay.

Example 4

Sara keeps a diary. She records what she was told by John one day. Sara's diary is used at a trial to prove the truth of what John said. That evidence is multiple hearsay.

12.9.2 Using hearsay evidence

12.9.2.1 Notice requirements

Section 1 of the Civil Evidence Act 1995 provides that, in civil proceedings, evidence shall not be excluded on the ground that it is hearsay. Therefore, hearsay evidence is admissible in civil proceedings. Section 2 of the Act provides that a party proposing to bring hearsay evidence must notify any other party of that fact and, on request, give particulars of, or relating to, the evidence. This must be read in conjunction with Part 33 of the CPR 1998 which sets out the rules relating to how hearsay evidence can be used.

Rule 33.2 states:

(1)   Where a party intends to rely on hearsay evidence at trial and either—

    (a)   that evidence is to be given by a witness giving oral evidence; or

    (b)   that evidence is contained in a witness statement of a person who is not being called to give oral evidence;

that party complies with section 2(1)(a) of the Civil Evidence Act 1995 by serving a witness statement on the other parties in accordance with the court's order.

(2)   Where paragraph (1)(b) applies, the party intending to rely on the hearsay evidence must, when he serves the witness statement—

(a)   inform the other parties that the witness is not being called to give oral evidence; and

(b)   give the reason why the witness will not be called.

(3)   In all other cases where a party intends to rely on hearsay evidence at trial, that party complies with section 2(1)(a) of the Civil Evidence Act 1995 by serving a notice on the other parties which—

(a)   identifies the hearsay evidence;

(b)   states that the party serving the notice proposes to rely on the hearsay evidence at trial; and

(c)   gives the reason why the witness will not be called.

(4)   The party proposing to rely on the hearsay evidence must—

(a)   serve the notice no later than the latest date for serving witness statements; and

(b)   if the hearsay evidence is to be in a document, supply a copy to any party who requests him to do so.

12.9.2.2   Practical points

Therefore, if a party serves a witness statement of Mr X which contains hearsay evidence, but intends to call Mr X to give evidence at trial, simply serving the statement on the other party complies with the notice requirements of the Civil Evidence Act 1995. However, if a party does not intend to call a witness but instead intends to rely on the statement itself as hearsay evidence, that party must inform the other side when he serves the witness statement that he is not calling the witness to give oral evidence and give the reason why, if any, the witness will not be called.

Note that by s 2(4), a party's failure to comply with the notice requirement does not affect the admissibility of the evidence but it may be taken into account by the court as a matter adversely affecting the weight to be given to the evidence in accordance with s 4 (see **12.9.3.1**) and/or when the court makes a costs order at the end of the trial (see **14.3**).

Notice of intention to rely on hearsay evidence is only required for evidence to be used at a trial.

A template to help you draft a hearsay notice is set out at **Appendix B(6)**.

12.9.3   Weight to be attached to hearsay evidence

12.9.3.1   'Second best' evidence

Whilst hearsay evidence is admissible, it is important to remember that it is not normally the best evidence of a fact. Out-of-court statements are not made on oath or with any form of affirmation. It is not uncommon for a person to lie or make ill-considered statements which are inaccurate. The greater the number of times a statement is repeated, the more likely there is to be an error in the transmission process. Therefore hearsay statements may be less likely to be true or accurate.

The memory or power of observation of the maker of a hearsay statement may be defective, but such weaknesses cannot be directly revealed by cross-examination. The trial judge cannot assess the reliability of the statement by observing the witness's demeanour as he is not giving evidence. But are there any safeguards? If X tells the court what Y said, then even though Y cannot be cross-examined as to his means of knowledge and reliability, X can be cross-examined both about his own reliability and about his view of Y's reliability. As to the latter, that depends on how well X knows Y, if at all, and how accurately and honestly X is prepared to give his views about Y. Although this is undoubtedly inferior to cross-examination of Y, Y's reliability can be tested to some degree. But if X tells the court what Y told him Z said, there is not even this indirect check on Z's reliability (when neither Y nor Z is called to give evidence).

12.9.3.2 Judicial approach

A trial judge will normally start to assess the probative value of any hearsay evidence by answering these questions:

(a)   What issue, if any, does the hearsay evidence address?

(b)   How important is that issue in the case?

(c)   What other evidence is available on the same issue?

(d)   Is the hearsay evidence more probative than any other evidence which the proponent could procure through reasonable efforts?

12.9.3.3 Statutory guidelines

Section 4 of the Civil Evidence Act 1995 provides guidelines for the courts to assist them in assessing the weight they should attach to hearsay evidence. It provides that the court is to have regard to any circumstances from which any inference can reasonably be drawn as to the reliability or otherwise of the evidence, and, in particular, to the following:

(a)   Whether it would have been reasonable and practicable for the party adducing the evidence to have called the person who made the original statement as a witness. How credible is any reason? Is the maker of the statement dead, or abroad and unwilling or unable to return, or unfit to attend trial, or untraceable, or unlikely to remember the details of his statement? What if the maker of the statement is the opponent or the opponent's spouse?

So where a party chooses to rely on hearsay evidence on a key issue when the maker of the statement is readily available to give oral evidence, you can expect the other side to comment adversely on this in its closing speech, and the trial judge may well decide to give it little or no weight. The inference is that such evidence, if called, would have been unfavourable to the party and so it has relied on hearsay instead.

(b)   Whether the original statement was made contemporaneously with the events in question. Was the statement made at a time when the facts referred to in it were fresh in the memory of the person making it? Since the accuracy and completeness of recollection decrease rapidly as time passes, an out-of-court statement made soon after an event is likely to be more reliable than the testimony of the maker of the statement given days, weeks, months, or even years later. What is likely to be more reliable: a note a witness makes of a car registration number immediately after the car drives off, or such a note made by the witness the next day?

(c)   Whether the evidence involves multiple hearsay. For example, Anne says to Brian, 'I saw an accident in Bow Street today involving a lorry and a red taxi'. The next day Brian says to Chris, 'Anne said to me yesterday that she saw an accident in Bow Road where a red lorry hit a taxi'. For Chris to repeat in court what Brian informed him Anne had said about the accident would be multiple hearsay. The danger with multiple hearsay is that it may become less and less reliable. Note that Brian tells Chris something slightly different from what Anne told him. Chris's version could become even less like what Anne originally said. There is always the danger of mishearing, exaggeration, unclear reporting and general inaccuracy through repetition.

(d)   Whether any person involved had any motive to conceal or misrepresent matters. Was the maker of the statement employed by the party who now relies on it? Did the employee make the statement with a view to pleasing his employer?

(e)   Whether the original statement was edited, or was made in collaboration with someone else or for a particular purpose. Is a statement made by a person who is trained to make it or record it more or less reliable than a statement made by, or to, someone not so trained?

(f)   Whether the circumstances suggest an attempt to prevent proper evaluation of the weight of the evidence. Was notice given of the intention to adduce the hearsay evidence and, if so, was that notice given sufficiently in advance of the trial to permit the party affected by it a fair opportunity to respond to it? If notice was given, did the other side object? Note that by s 2(4) of the 1995 Act, this guideline includes any failure to comply with the notice requirements (see **12.9.2**)

12.9.4   Right of the opposing party to cross-examine the person who originally made the statement

Section 3 of the Civil Evidence Act 1995 provides that where a party adduces hearsay evidence from a person whom he does not call as a witness, any other party may, with the permission of the court, call that person as a witness and cross-examine him. An application for such permission must be made not later than 14 days after service of the hearsay notice (CPR 1998, r 33.4).

12.9.5   Competence (Civil Evidence Act 1995, s 5)

Hearsay evidence is not admissible if the original statement was made by a person who was not competent as a witness because of his mental or physical infirmity or lack of understanding.

12.9.6   Credibility (Civil Evidence Act 1995, s 5)

Where hearsay evidence is adduced and the person who made the original statement is not called as a witness, evidence is still admissible to attack or support his credibility, or to show that he has made another, inconsistent statement. The party wishing to call such evidence must give notice to the other party not later than 14 days after service of the hearsay evidence (CPR 1998, r 33.5).

Although notice may have been given under s 5, how will the party actually adduce the discrediting evidence (such as an allegation of bias, previous convictions or a previous inconsistent statement) at trial? It is now too late to include such allegations in any witness statements as they have already been served pursuant to the directions order. The opponent's agreement, or otherwise the court's permission, should be sought to rely on the evidence. An application to the court should be made at any pre-trial review or trial. If done at a pre-trial review then permission should be requested to serve a supplemental witness statement dealing with the evidence.

12.9.7   Previous inconsistent statements (Civil Evidence Act 1995, s 6)

The effect of this provision is that, where a party calls a witness to give evidence at the trial, the opposing party may cross-examine the witness about a previous inconsistent statement provided that he has complied with the requirements of the Civil Evidence Act 1995 concerning the use of hearsay evidence. For example, in *Fifield v Denton Hall Legal Services* [2006] EWCA Civ 169, the claimant's doctor, during a consultation, wrote down certain facts that the claimant told him about how she sustained her injuries. The defendants contended that the facts in the doctor's record were inconsistent with the facts advanced by the claimant in her own evidence. So in the circumstances the doctor's record was hearsay evidence and notice should have been given by the defendants to the claimant. If the court concludes that the inconsistent statement was made, it is unclear whether the earlier inconsistent statement itself can be treated as evidence of its contents, or if it only affects the credibility of the witness.

This provision does not prevent a person's witness statement that has been exchanged in accordance with a case management order from being treated as his evidence-in-chief. Indeed, the judge at the trial can, and usually will, order that a witness statement which was served before the trial shall stand as the evidence-in-chief of that witness. The witness will, of course, be present at the trial, and will be subject to cross-examination. In these circumstances, his witness statement is not treated as hearsay evidence.

12.10 Use of plans, photographs and models as evidence (r 33.6)

Where evidence such as a plan, photograph, model or the records of a business or public authority is to be given in evidence and it is not:

(a)   contained in a witness statement, affidavit, or expert's report;

(b)   to be given orally at the trial; or

(c)   the subject of a hearsay notice;

the evidence will not be admissible unless the party intending to use it has disclosed his intention to use such evidence within the deadline for serving witness statements.

He must disclose his intention at least 21 days before the hearing, if:

(a)   there are not to be witness statements; or

(b)   he intends to use the evidence solely to disprove an allegation made in a witness statement.

If the evidence forms part of an expert's report, he must disclose his intention when he serves his expert's report.

Where a party has given notice of his intention to put in the evidence, he must give every other party an opportunity to inspect it and to agree to its admission without further proof.

12.11 Notice to admit facts (r 32.18)

In order to try to avoid the expense of proving a particular fact at trial, a party may serve on another party a notice requiring him to admit certain facts or a certain part of his case, as specified in the notice. Form N266 should be used. A copy is set out at **Appendix A(7)**.

Such a notice must be served no later than 21 days before the trial.

If the party upon whom the notice is served refuses to admit the relevant fact(s), the other party will still be required to prove the fact(s) at trial. Where, however, he does so, the court may take this into account when considering the issue of costs. Effectively, this means that the party who served the notice will usually recover the cost of proving the facts in question (even if he loses the case).

12.12 Notice to admit or prove documents (r 32.19)

A party is deemed to admit that any document disclosed in a list of documents served under Part 31 (see **Chapter 11**) is genuine unless he serves notice that he wants the document to be proved at trial.

A notice to prove a document must be served by the later of the following:

(a)   the latest date for serving witness statements; or

(b)   within seven days of disclosure of the document.

12.13 Expert evidence (Part 35)

As we saw at **3.4**, in many cases a party may wish to instruct an expert and rely upon expert evidence. However, parties do not have an unfettered right to use expert evidence and, as part of its case management powers, the court will restrict expert evidence to that which is reasonably required to resolve the proceedings, bearing in mind the overriding objective and particularly the issue of proportionality.

By s 3(1) of the Civil Evidence Act 1972, subject to the rules of court, 'where a person is called as a witness in any civil proceedings, his opinion on any relevant matter on which he is qualified to give expert evidence shall be admissible in evidence.'

See the Protocol for the Instruction of Experts (**Appendix A(20)**) for a detailed consideration of the duties of experts, their appointment, etc.

Part 35 of the CPR governs the use of experts by parties only during court proceedings. This is because an expert is defined by r 35.2 as a person who has been instructed to give or prepare expert evidence for the purpose of the proceedings.

12.13.1 The duty of an expert

Although in many cases an expert is instructed by one particular party, r 35.3 makes it clear that the duty of an expert is to help the court on the matters within his expertise, and this duty overrides any obligation to the person from whom he has received instructions or by whom he is paid. If the expert is unsure of the nature of these obligations, he may file a request for directions from the court. Experts should, therefore, be completely objective and unbiased in the way in which they provide their opinion for the benefit of the court (see *Stevens v Gullis* [1999] BLR 394).

An expert is not disqualified by the fact of being employed by one of the parties, although the court will need to be satisfied that the expert was sufficiently aware of his responsibilities to the court (*Field v Leeds City Council* [2000] 1 EGLR 54). Given the risk of the appearance of bias, parties will generally prefer to instruct an expert who is independent.

An expert who behaves improperly is likely to be reported to his governing body by the trial judge at the end of the hearing, as suggested in *Pearce v Ove Arup Partnership* [2001] LTL 8 November and *Meadow v General Medical Council* [2006] EWCA Civ 1390.

12.13.2 The court's power to restrict expert evidence

Rule 35.1 provides that expert evidence must be restricted to that which is reasonably required to resolve the proceedings, and r 35.4 provides that no party may call an expert or put in evidence an expert's report without the court's permission. Permission is usually granted at the directions stage, and the party applying for permission must identify both the field in which he wishes to rely on expert evidence and, where practicable, the name of the expert in that field on whose evidence he wishes to rely. As we saw in **Chapter 9**, this information should normally be provided in the allocation questionnaire.

The options available to the court in giving directions on expert evidence include:

(a) directing that no expert evidence is to be adduced at all, or no expert evidence of a particular type or relating to a particular issue;

(b) limiting the number of expert witnesses which each party may call, either generally or in a given speciality;

(c) directing that evidence is to be given by one or more experts chosen by agreement between the parties or, where they cannot agree, chosen by such other manner as the court may direct.

The court will also decide whether it is necessary for experts to give oral evidence at trial. This is probably going to be the case in multi-track proceedings, but in fast track proceedings, the normal position is that expert evidence will be given in the form of a written report or reports rather than by way of oral evidence (see **Chapter 9**).

The court also has the power to limit the amount of the expert's fees and expenses that the party who wishes to rely on the expert may recover from any other party.

12.13.3 Instructions to an expert witness

One would normally expect the instructions from a solicitor to an expert witness to be privileged from inspection by other parties (see **11.11**). However, r 35.10(4) states:

> The instructions referred to in paragraph (3) [the substance of all material instructions, written or oral, on which the report is based] shall not be privileged against disclosure but the court will not, in relation to those instructions—
>
> (a)   order disclosure of any specific document; or
>
> (b)   permit any questioning in court other than by the party who instructed the expert,
>
> unless it is satisfied that there are reasonable grounds to consider the statement of instructions given under paragraph (3) to be inaccurate or incomplete.

As we shall see at **12.13.5**, the report itself must contain the substance of all material instructions received.

So has legal professional privilege in relation to instructions to an expert gone? The answer appears to be that it has not. Rule 35.10(4) is qualified by PD 35, para 3, which provides that such cross-examination will be permitted only where it is in the 'interests of justice'. Arguably the instructions remain privileged from inspection unless and until the court makes an order under the Rule. Such an order will be made only if there are reasonable grounds for believing that the expert's statement of instructions is inaccurate or incomplete: *Lucas v Barking, Havering and Redbridge Hospitals NHS Trust* [2003] EWCA Civ 1102.

Of course, a party can always waive privilege if he wishes to do so. Indeed, there are many occasions when solicitors might use a standard format for instructions to an expert, especially where recommended by a pre-action protocol. In such a case there should be no objection to the expert exhibiting those to his report. However, there is no question of confidential information concerning the merits of the case having to be disclosed. The court will not readily entertain any applications for disclosure or cross-examination in this context. After reports have been exchanged it should be routine for a party to send a copy of the other side's report to their own expert for comment. Obviously one point that can be looked for is whether any report is based on inaccurate or incomplete instructions. If there are doubts the matter should be raised in correspondence and/or an interim application made for directions concerning the 'suspicious' report.

12.13.4 Form of expert evidence

Expert evidence is to be given in a written report unless the court directs otherwise, and, if the party wishes to rely on the expert evidence at trial, the report must be disclosed to the other party in accordance with the directions given by the court. The usual order is for simultaneous mutual exchange on or before a set date.

When first obtained, an expert's report which has been prepared for the sole or dominant purpose of the litigation is a privileged document. A copy must be given to the other party only if the party who commissioned it wishes to rely on it at trial. If he decides not to rely on the report (perhaps because it is unfavourable) he does not have to allow the other side to inspect it. It is, however, disclosable in part 2 of the list of documents. See further **Chapter 11**.

12.13.5 Contents of the report

Rule 35.10 and PD 35, paras 3.1 and 3.2 give the following detailed instructions on the contents of an expert's report:

> 3.1   An expert's report should be addressed to the court and not to the party from whom the expert has received his instructions.

3.2   An expert's report must:

(1)   give details of the expert's qualifications;

(2)   give details of any literature or other material which the expert has relied on in making the report;

(3)   contain a statement setting out the substance of all facts and instructions given to the expert which are material to the opinions expressed in the report or upon which those opinions are based;

(4)   make clear which of the facts stated in the report are within the expert's own knowledge;

(5)   say who carried out any examination, measurement, test or experiment which the expert has used for the report, give the qualifications of that person, and say whether or not the test or experiment has been carried out under the expert's supervision;

(6)   where there is a range of opinion on the matters dealt with in the report—

(a)   summarise the range of opinion, and

(b)   give reasons for his own opinion;

(7)   contain a summary of the conclusions reached;

(8)   if the expert is not able to give his opinion without qualification, state the qualification; and

(9)   contain a statement that the expert:

(a)   understands their duty to the court, and has complied with that duty; and

(b)   is aware of the requirements of Part 35, this practice direction and the Protocol for Instruction of Experts to give Evidence in Civil Claims.

The report must also be supported by a statement of truth that states:

I confirm that I have made clear which facts and matters referred to in this report are within my knowledge and which are not. Those that are within my own knowledge I confirm to be true. The opinions I have expressed represent my true and complete professional opinions on the matters to which they refer.

These formalities do not address the question of any potential or actual conflict of interest. In *Toth v Jarman* [2006] EWCA Civ 1028, [2006] 4 All ER 1276, the Court of Appeal held that whilst the presence of a conflict of interest does not automatically disqualify an expert, the key question is whether the expert's opinion is independent. So where an expert has a material or significant conflict of interest, the court is likely to refuse the party permission to rely on that evidence, or otherwise the trial judge may well decline to accept it. It is therefore important that a party who wishes to call an expert with a potential conflict of interest should disclose details of that conflict at as early a stage in the proceedings as possible. In any event, an expert should produce his *curriculum vitae* when he provides his report, and this should give details of any employment or activity that raises a possible conflict of interest.

12.13.6   Questions to the expert

After an expert's report has been disclosed, the party who did not instruct the expert may put written questions to the expert about his report. Where a party sends a written question or questions direct to an expert, a copy of the question(s) should, at the same time, be sent to the other party or parties.

Such written questions:

(a)   may be put once only;

(b)   must be put within 28 days of service of the report;

(c)   must be to clarify the report, unless the court permits or the other party agrees to allow questions for a different purpose.

The answers will be treated as part of the expert's report.

12.13.7   Discussion between experts (r 35.12)

12.13.7.1   Court direction

The court will often direct that the parties' experts should meet and have a without prejudice discussion. Rule 35.12(4) confirms that the content of the discussion between the experts shall not be referred to at the trial unless the parties agree.

The purpose of the discussion is not for the experts to settle the case but to agree and narrow the issues. Practice Direction 35, para 9.2 states that the experts should identify:

(i)   the extent of the agreement between them;

(ii)   the points of and short reasons for any disagreement;

(iii)   action, if any, which may be taken to resolve any outstanding points of disagreement; and

(iv)   any further material issues not raised and the extent to which these issues are agreed.

Before the experts meet, the parties must discuss and if possible agree whether an agenda is necessary, and if so attempt to agree one that helps the experts to focus on the issues which need to be discussed. The agenda must not be in the form of leading questions or hostile in tone (PD 35, para 9.3).

Should the parties and/or their legal representatives attend an experts' discussion? No – unless all the parties and the experts agree or the court allows that. Practice Direction 35, para 9.5 provides that if legal representatives do attend, they should not normally intervene in the discussion except to answer questions put to them by the experts or to advise on the law; and the experts may if they so wish hold part of their discussions in the absence of the legal representatives.

12.13.7.2   Written joint statement

Following the discussion, a statement must be prepared by the experts dealing with the points raised in PD 35, para 9.2(i)–(iv) above. Individual copies of the statements must be signed by the experts at the conclusion of the discussion, or as soon thereafter as practicable, and in any event within seven days. Copies of the statements must be provided to the parties no later than 14 days after signing.

Practice Direction 35, para 9.7 makes it clear that the experts must give their own opinions to assist the court and do not require the authority of the parties to sign a joint statement.

What if an expert significantly alters an opinion as a result of the discussion? The joint statement must include a note or an addendum by that expert, explaining the change of opinion (PD 35, para 9.8).

Note that r 35.12(5) makes it clear that where the experts reach agreement on an issue during their discussions, the agreement does not bind the parties unless the parties expressly agree to be bound by the agreement.

Case Study: Experts' Without Prejudice Meeting Statement

The experts' without prejudice meeting statement in the case study is at **Appendix D(12)**. You will note that this sets out the issues that are agreed and those that remain in dispute. The parties are likely to adopt this position, and so the disputed issues will be taken forward to trial.

12.13.7.3   Changing experts

If a party has permission to rely on an expert but that expert changes his opinion on certain issues following the without prejudice meeting, can that party now obtain the court's permission to rely upon additional expert evidence? This was the question in *Stallwood v David* [2006] EWHC 2600. Teare J observed that as an agreement between experts does not bind the parties unless they expressly agree to be bound by it (see r 35.12(5)), so a modification of an expert's opinion also cannot bind the party who instructed him. But at trial, when the experts' evidence is given, it will be rare that a party will have any prospect of persuading the court not to follow the agreed opinion of the experts. The party will have to demonstrate a good reason to rely upon additional expert evidence. This might include that his expert's change of mind was based on unsound reasons or a mistaken view of the facts, or that his expert acted outside his area of expertise or instructions. As Teare J stressed in the case, the starting point is normally for the party to ask his expert why he changed his mind, if this is not clear from the joint statement.

12.13.8   The single joint expert (r 35.7)

12.13.8.1   When appropriate?

Whether it is appropriate for each party to call its own expert evidence depends on the issues raised in each particular case. However, in a fast track case the general approach of the court is to order a single joint expert unless there is good reason not to do so (see para 3.9 of PD 28). A joint expert is less likely to be ordered in a multi-track case. Even where the court is willing to allow the parties to call their own expert evidence on the issue of liability, it may order a joint expert on any quantum issues that require expert evidence.

Note that PD 35, para 7 provides as follows:

> When considering whether to give permission for the parties to rely on expert evidence and whether that evidence should be from a single joint expert the court will take into account all the circumstances in particular, whether:
>
> (a)   it is proportionate to have separate experts for each party on a particular issue with reference to–
>
>   (i)   the amount in dispute;
>
>   (ii)   the importance to the parties; and
>
>   (iii)   the complexity of the issue;
>
> (b)   the instruction of a single joint expert is likely to assist the parties and the court to resolve the issue more speedily and in a more cost-effective way than separately instructed experts;
>
> (c)   expert evidence is to be given on the issue of liability, causation or quantum;
>
> (d)   the expert evidence falls within a substantially established area of knowledge which is unlikely to be in dispute or there is likely to be a range of expert opinion;
>
> (e)   a party has already instructed an expert on the issue in question and whether or not that was done in compliance with any practice direction or relevant pre-action protocol;
>
> (f)   questions put in accordance with rule 35.6 are likely to remove the need for the other party to instruct an expert if one party has already instructed an expert;
>
> (g)   questions put to a single joint expert may not conclusively deal with all issues that may require testing prior to trial;
>
> (h)   a conference may be required with the legal representatives, experts and other witnesses which may make instruction of a single joint expert impractical; and
>
> (i)   a claim to privilege makes the instruction of any expert as a single joint expert inappropriate.

Both the Queen's Bench Division and the Chancery Court Guides provide that:

> In very many cases it is possible for the question of expert evidence to be dealt with by a single expert. Single experts are, for example, often appropriate to deal with questions of quantum in cases where the primary issues are as to liability. Likewise, where expert evidence is required in order to acquaint the court with matters of expert fact, as opposed to opinion, a single expert will usually be appropriate. There remains, however, a body of cases where liability will turn upon expert opinion evidence and where it will be appropriate for the parties to instruct their own experts. For example, in cases where the issue for determination is as to whether a party acted in accordance with proper professional standards, it will often be of value to the court to hear the

opinions of more than one expert as to the proper standard in order that the court becomes acquainted with the range of views existing upon the question and in order that the evidence can be tested in cross examination.

12.13.8.2   Court direction

Where the court orders a single joint expert it will usually direct that:

(a)   the parties should prepare joint instructions for the expert;

(b)   the expert's fees should be paid jointly by the parties; and

(c)   if the parties have been unable by a set date to agree on the identity of the expert, further directions should be obtained from the court.

It is less likely in the case of a single joint expert that the court will think it appropriate to allow oral evidence at trial.

Where there is an order for a single joint expert there is, of course, no need for a direction that reports be exchanged.

12.13.8.3   Practical points

Note that the parties have a duty to assist the court to further the overriding objective (see **1.1.1**) by spotting any manifest ambiguities or errors in the report of a single joint expert and resolving these by asking one or more suitable questions: see *Woolley v Essex CC* [2006] EWCA Civ 753. By analogy, there is a corresponding duty to point out such errors in a report prepared by an opponent's expert.

There is useful guidance from the Court of Appeal in relation to dealing with problems with a single joint expert in the case of *Daniels v Walker* [2000] 1 WLR 1382:

(a)   where the parties cannot agree joint instructions for the expert, it is perfectly proper for one party to give separate or supplemental instructions;

(b)   where a party is dissatisfied with the expert's report, he should first submit questions to the expert;

(c)   if this does not resolve the problem, the dissatisfied party can apply to the court for permission to call another expert. This application will be granted if the court is satisfied that it would be unjust, having regard to the overriding objective, to refuse to allow the further evidence to be called;

(d)   where the dissatisfied party has already obtained its own expert's report, the court should not grant permission for that evidence to be used at trial until the experts have met to resolve their differences. Permission for oral evidence to be given at trial is a last resort.

Further, where a single joint expert is appointed by the parties pursuant to a court order, neither party should meet that expert without the other party being present. See *Peet v Mid-Kent Healthcare Trust (Practice Note)* [2001] EWCA Civ 1703, [2002] 3 All ER 688. Likewise, it is wholly improper for one party to have any discussion with a joint expert without the other party being present. It might be possible if the absent party gives fully-informed consent: see *Childs v Vernon* [2007] EWCA Civ 305, [2007] LTL, 16 March.

12.13.9   Summary: the admissibility of expert evidence at trial

To be admissible at trial, an expert's evidence must be:

(a)   relevant and within the expertise of the expert (see **12.13**);

(b)   in the correct format by way of a report that complies with Part 35 (see **12.13.5**); and

(c)   permitted by the court which has given a direction allowing either a named expert or an expert in a specified field of expertise to give evidence.

That evidence, as directed by the court, may be given orally or in the form of a written report (see **12.13.2**).

12.14 Professional negligence cases: the defendant's own evidence

Rather uniquely, in professional negligence claims a defendant is allowed to give his own expert opinion on what he did or did not do that is said to amount to negligence. There is no need for this to be in the format of a Part 35 report. The defendant's witness statement will suffice. Why? In *DN v London Borough of Greenwich* [2004] EWCA Civ 1659, the Court of Appeal explained this exception to the general rule as follows.

> It very often happens in professional negligence cases that a defendant will give evidence to a judge which constitutes the reason why he considers that his conduct did not fall below the standard of care reasonably to be expected of him. He may do this by reference to the professional literature that was reasonably available to him as a busy practitioner or by reference to the reasonable limits of his professional experience; or he may seek to rebut, as one professional man against another, the criticisms made of him by the claimant's expert(s). Such evidence is common, and it is certainly admissible …
>
> Of course a defendant's evidence on matters of this kind may lack the objectivity to be accorded to the evidence of an independent expert, but this consideration goes to the cogency of the evidence, not to its admissibility. (*per* Brooke LJ at paras 25 and 26)

12.15 Assessors (r 35.15)

In some cases of a technical nature, the court may seek the assistance of someone with technical knowledge in the relevant field. Such a person is known as an assessor, and he has a judicial role in that he is instructed to assist the court. He is not an expert witness and cannot be cross-examined by any of the parties. His function is to 'educate' the judge and to enable the judge to reach a properly informed decision.

By r 35.15, the assessor shall take such part in the proceedings as the court may direct. The court may direct the assessor to prepare a report and/or direct the assessor to attend the trial. Any report prepared by an assessor will be sent to the parties.

The use of assessors is rare.

Chapter 13
Settlement

Most disputes are resolved not by a judgment of the court but by the parties reaching a settlement. This can happen at any stage from before the issue of proceedings to during the trial. Settlement may be achieved as a result of negotiations, which will often involve the use of the procedures set out in Part 36, or (less commonly) the use of alternative dispute resolution (ADR).

In this chapter we start by considering how the parties' solicitors might negotiate a settlement and then safeguard their clients' respective positions by formally recording that agreement. The main part of this chapter looks at the CPR 1998, Part 36. This is often described as a negotiation tool, as it gives the parties the ability to make offers of settlement that may have financial penalties for the opponent if rejected. The chapter ends with the procedure known as discontinuance. This is where a claimant abandons his claim. Unless this is negotiated on terms that are favourable to the claimant, discontinuance will mean the claimant having to pay the defendant's costs of the proceedings.

13.1 Negotiations

13.1.1 Solicitor's authority

The scope of the solicitor's authority to negotiate on his client's behalf depends on whether or not proceedings have been issued. Prior to issue, the solicitor has no implied authority to settle the client's claim. Acceptance of any offer can, therefore, only be subject to the client's approval. Where the client wishes to accept, it is advisable for the solicitor to obtain written confirmation of this.

Once proceedings have been issued, the solicitor has implied authority to compromise a claim. However, in practice it is, of course, essential to seek the client's express instructions.

13.1.2 Basis on which to conduct negotiations

Negotiations may be conducted either orally or in writing. Whichever method is adopted, care should be taken to ensure that the negotiations proceed on a 'without prejudice' basis. This ensures that the negotiations cannot be referred to in court at a later date except to prove the terms of any settlement reached (see further **3.10.1**).

Negotiation is dealt with further in *Skills for Lawyers*, **Chapter 12**.

13.2 Pre-action settlements

13.2.1 Costs and interest

Where a settlement is reached prior to the issue of proceedings, the prospective claimant will not be entitled to recover his legal costs unless this has been agreed. Neither will he be entitled to interest on any sum agreed under s 69 of the CCA 1984, or s 35A of the SCA 1981. There may, however, be an entitlement to interest under contract or the Late Payment of Commercial Debts (Interest) Act 1998, and such should be taken into account during any negotiations and as part of any settlement. The topic of interest is dealt with at **2.7.2**. Whatever the position, it is important that the parties are clear whether any amount for costs and/or interest is included in the terms being proposed.

13.2.2   Recording a pre-action settlement

It is equally important that once settlement terms have been agreed, they are clearly and accurately recorded in writing, so that the agreement can be enforced if one of the parties defaults.

It may be sufficient for a settlement reached before the issue of proceedings to be recorded in an exchange of correspondence. Commonly, there will be a letter from the potential defendant setting out the terms being offered 'in full and final settlement' of all claims which the prospective claimant may have, and a reply accepting these terms. More complicated settlements should normally be recorded in a formal settlement agreement.

13.3   Settlements reached after the issue of proceedings

It is preferable for the settlement to be recorded in a court order or judgment, since this will make enforcement easier if the agreement is not honoured. In particular, enforcement proceedings (see **Chapter 15**) may be commenced to recover any money due under the settlement (including costs). The date by which payment of any debt or damages is due must, however, be specified in the judgment or order.

Unless the settlement provides otherwise, interest is not payable on costs until judgment is entered (see **15.2**).

13.3.1   Consent orders or judgments

Where none of the parties is a litigant in person, it will often be possible to avoid an application to the court by drawing up a consent order or judgment for sealing by a court officer under r 40.6. Although in theory the court retains the power not to approve the proposed order, it will in practice be referred to a judge only if it appears to be incorrect or unclear.

The formalities for a consent order are set out in r 40.6(7) as follows:

(a)   the order which is agreed by the parties must be drawn up in the terms agreed;

(b)   it must be expressed as being 'By Consent';

(c)   it must be signed by the legal representative acting for each of the parties to whom the order relates.

> **Case Study**
>
> An example of a consent order appears in the case study at **Appendix D(15)**. The claimants have agreed to accept £170,000 in settlement of their claim. Provided that is paid in accordance with para 1, then under para 2 both the claim and counterclaim will come to an end. What if it is not paid? Interest will run (see **15.2**) and the claimants can take enforcement proceedings (see generally **Chapter 15**). What about costs? You will see that by para 3, each side has agreed to pay its own costs.

It is important to note two things. First, the terms of a consent order will be open to public inspection. Secondly, the terms agreed must be within the powers of a court to order, eg the payment of a sum of money, specific performance of a contract and the dismissal of a claim. If the parties want any terms to be confidential and/or beyond the powers of a court to order, they should use a special form of consent order known as the *Tomlin* order (see **13.3.2** below).

13.3.2 *Tomlin* orders

A *Tomlin* order stays the claim on agreed terms that are set out in a schedule to the order. The basic formalities are in r 40.6(7) (see **13.3.1**). But the key to drafting a *Tomlin* order correctly is to appreciate that certain terms must appear in the order itself, whilst others can be put in the schedule. This is because PD 40B provides as follows:

> Where the parties draw up a consent order in the form of a stay of proceedings on agreed terms, disposing of the proceedings, and where the terms are recorded in a schedule to the order, any direction for:
>
> (1)   payment of money out of court, or
>
> (2)   payment and assessment of costs
>
> should be contained in the body of the order and not in the schedule.

A direction for the payment of money held by the court will be rare. It is most likely to occur where a party has had to pay a sum into court under a previous order, eg a conditional order made on a summary judgment application (see **10.5.2.3**). Where one party is to pay another party's costs and/or the parties want the amount of those costs assessed by the court (known as a detailed assessment: see **14.3**), that direction must go in the order.

Moreover, because there is a possibility that a party may not perform its part of the agreement, the order should include a provision that any party is at liberty to apply for the stay to be lifted so that the court can enforce the settlement. This means that it is not necessary to start new proceedings to enforce the terms.

The schedule may contain any agreed term. Often this will be for the payment of a sum of money. When this is not in the order, a provision should be made for interest to run on any late payment. The schedule must also record any agreed terms that the court cannot impose, eg that the parties enter into a particular contract, or that in future dealings one party gives the other a discount.

The following table summarises the main points to consider when drafting the order and schedule.

Order	Schedule
'By Consent'	Include any agreed term that court could not order
Stay of proceedings	Any payment of money should include provision for interest on late payment
Liberty to apply	
Payment of money out of court	
Payment of costs	
Detailed assessment of costs	
Signed by the parties' solicitors	

An example of a *Tomlin* order follows. You will see that the order is made 'By Consent', the proceedings are stayed, there is liberty to apply and the defendant has agreed to pay £10,000 of the claimant's costs. Then the schedule records at para 1 the settlement payment, at para 2 the provision for interest on any late payment, and at para 3 that the parties have entered into a particular contract as part of the settlement.

Example

IN THE HIGH COURT OF JUSTICE   2010 L 164

QUEEN'S BENCH DIVISION

WEYFORD DISTRICT REGISTRY

BETWEEN

LA BOULE PLC   Claimant

and

CHRISTALINE LIMITED   Defendant

ORDER BY CONSENT

UPON the parties having agreed terms of settlement

BY CONSENT IT IS ORDERED THAT:

1.   All further proceedings in this action shall be stayed upon the terms set out in the attached schedule, except for the purpose of carrying such terms into effect.

2.   Each party shall have liberty to apply to the court if the other party does not give effect to the terms set out in the schedule.

3.   The Defendant do pay the Claimant on or before 14 August 2010 the sum of £10,000 in respect of the Claimant's costs.

Dated: ....

We consent to the making of an order in the above terms.

....

Swallows & Co., Solicitors for the Claimant

....

Singleton Trumper & Co., Solicitors for the Defendant

SCHEDULE

1.   The Defendant shall pay or cause to be paid to the Claimant the sum of £50,000 on or before 14 August 2010 in full and final satisfaction of all claims and counterclaims arising in this action.

2.   In the event of late payment, the Defendant will pay interest on the sum of £50,000 or any part remaining due at a daily rate equal to 10% above the Bank of England base rate as at 14 August 2010.

3.   The Claimant and the Defendant have entered into a distribution agreement dated 3 August 2010 as part of the compromise of this action.

13.4   Part 36

As we saw in **Chapter 3**, before litigation starts the parties are encouraged to negotiate and settle the claim. It is open to the parties to make 'without prejudice' offers to settle (see generally **3.10.1**). If proceedings are issued, the parties should continually review the case and consider making offers to settle it. By r 36.3(2), a Part 36 offer can be made both before and during proceedings (including appeal proceedings).

A party can make an offer to settle in whatever way he chooses. By r 44.3, the court will take into account when deciding the issue of costs any admissible offer to settle that has been made. So what are the advantages of making an offer to settle in accordance with the formalities required by Part 36? First, by r 36.13(1), a Part 36 offer will be treated as 'without prejudice except as to costs'. So the fact that a Part 36 offer has been made must not be communicated to the trial judge (or to any judge allocated in advance to conduct the trial) until the case has been decided, ie the issues of liability and quantum have been adjudicated on. Secondly, if a defendant makes a Part 36 offer and the claimant fails to obtain a judgment more advantageous than that offer, the claimant will usually suffer severe financial penalties (see **13.4.5**). Likewise, if a claimant makes a Part 36 offer and the judgment against the defendant is at least as advantageous to the claimant as the proposals contained in his Part 36 offer, the defendant will usually suffer severe financial penalties (see **13.4.6**).

13.4.1   Form and content of a Part 36 offer

For clarity (and consistent with the definition in r 36.3), in the rest of this chapter we will refer to a party who makes a Part 36 offer as 'the offeror' and to the party to whom the offer is made as 'the offeree'.

13.4.1.1   Formalities

Pursuant to r 36.2(2), to be a valid Part 36 offer, the offer must:

(a)   be in writing;

(b)   state on its face that it is intended to have the consequences of Part 36;

(c)   specify a period of not less than 21 days within which the offeree may decide to accept it (known as 'the relevant period');

(d)   state whether it relates to the whole of the claim or to part of it, or to an issue that arises in it, and if so to which part or issue; and

(e)   state whether it takes into account any counterclaim.

The offer can be made using Form N242A (see **Appendix A(10)**). However, many practitioners set out the terms in a letter. A template to help you draft a Part 36 offer letter is set out at **Appendix B(7)**.

Most commonly, Part 36 offers are made by a claimant and/or a defendant in a monetary claim to settle the claim on payment of a lump sum. However, in a non-monetary claim, such as an injunction, an offeror can set out the terms that he would accept. Also, by r 36.2(5), an offeror can make a Part 36 offer solely in relation to the issue of liability.

Note that by r 36.4, a Part 36 offer by a defendant to pay a sum of money in settlement of a claim must be an offer to pay a single sum of money. Moreover, the defendant must be prepared to pay that sum to the claimant within 14 days of the claimant accepting the defendant's offer (see further **13.4.4.2**).

Does an offeror have to set out separately in his Part 36 offer (i) the sum that he is willing to pay or accept, and (ii) the amount of interest to be paid on that sum? The answer is no. By r 36.3(3), a Part 36 offer which offers to pay, or offers to accept, a sum of money is treated as inclusive of all interest until the relevant period expires.

13.4.1.2   Making more than one offer

An offeror can make more than one Part 36 offer. For example, a claimant making a monetary claim might start with a Part 36 offer to the defendant of, say, £100,000, and subsequently be prepared to reduce that to £95,000 and later £90,000. Of course, the lower the claimant goes, the more chance there is that the defendant might accept one of the offers and put an end to the case. But if none is accepted, the financial consequences of r 36.14 (see **13.4.6**) will be imposed on the defendant should the claimant secure a judgment that is at least as advantageous to him as the proposals contained in one of his Part 36 offers. Equally, a defendant facing a monetary claim might start with a Part 36 offer to the claimant of, say, £65,000, and subsequently be prepared to increase that to £70,000 and later £75,000. Of course, the higher the defendant goes, the more chance there is that the claimant might accept one of the offers and put an end to the case. But if none is accepted, the financial consequences of r 36.14 (see **13.4.5**) will be imposed on the claimant should the claimant fail to obtain a judgment more advantageous than one of the defendant's offers. Here we have considered a change in the terms of an offer that are more favourable to the offeree. If the terms become less advantageous, see **13.4.2**.

13.4.1.3   Offers made close to trial

As the relevant period is a minimum of 21 days, can an offer be made less than 21 days before the start of a trial? The answer is yes. By r 36.3(1)(c), in those circumstances the relevant period is the period up to the end of the trial or such other period as the court orders. Note that by r 36.3(3)(b), such an offer is deemed inclusive of interest up to a date 21 days after the offer was made. If the trial starts then, by r 36.9(3), the offeree will need the court's permission to accept the Part 36 offer. Generally no party should leave making a Part 36 offer so late. This is especially so as the financial benefits under r 36.14(2) or (3) (see **13.4.5** and **13.4.6**) will not apply to a Part 36 offer made less than 21 days before trial unless the court has abridged the relevant period.

13.4.1.4   Offer made when served

Rule 36.7(1) provides that a Part 36 offer is made when it is *served* on the offeree. If the offeree is legally represented, the offer must be served on his solicitors. As the offer has to be served, it appears the usual rules on deemed service (see **5.7.2**) apply. So, for example, if the offer is posted, first class, to the offeree on Monday, 1 June 2009, it will be deemed to have been made on Wednesday, 3 June 2009 (ie the second business day after it was posted). If the offer has the usual 21 days limit to accept, the last day of the relevant period (day 21) will be Wednesday, 24 June 2009.

> **Case Study: Claimant's Part 36 Offer**
>
> The claimant's Part 36 offer in the case study is at **Appendix D(13)**. You will note that this sets out the offer, and in particular how it complies with the formalities at **13.4.1.1**. Whilst it is not necessary to refer to the provisions of the CPR 1998, r 36.2(2) in the offer letter, we take the view that it should help to prevent any ambiguity and so the need for the offeree to ask for any clarification. In addition, whilst the offer is deemed by r 36.3(3) to be inclusive of interest, confirmation that that is what the offeror is proposing should again ensure there is no uncertainty. Why is the letter headed up 'without prejudice save as to costs' when that is the effect of a Part 36 offer under the CPR 1998, r 36.13(1)? Again, it is simply to make it clear to the offeree that a Part 36 offer is being made.

13.4.2   Withdrawal of a Part 36 offer or change in its terms

Can an offeror either withdraw his offer, or change its terms so that the offer is less advantageous to the offeree, during the relevant period? By r 36.3(5), that will be possible only if the court gives its permission. However, after expiry of the relevant period, either step can be taken without the court's permission, provided, of course, that the offeree has not previously served notice of acceptance of that offer. The offeror must serve written notice of the withdrawal or change of terms on the offeree. This can be done by letter. There is no prescribed form.

Where a claimant reduces the amount he is prepared to accept, or a defendant increases the amount he is willing to pay, the offeror will not bother to withdraw the earlier offer. But a Part 36 offer may be accepted at any time (see **13.4.4**), whether or not the offeree has subsequently made a different offer, *unless* the offeror has served notice of withdrawal of that offer on the offeree. So a claimant who wishes to increase the sum he was previously prepared to accept, or a defendant who wishes to decrease the amount he previously offered, must serve written notice withdrawing the first offer so that it is no longer capable of acceptance. The new Part 36 offer can be served at the same time. It would make sense in correspondence to explain why this step is being taken, in case evidence needs to be put before the court in due course.

It is vital that an offeror understands the effect of withdrawing or reducing the terms of his offer. By r 36.14(6), where a Part 36 offer is withdrawn or its terms made less advantageous to the offeree, it no longer constitutes a Part 36 offer and the financial consequences of r 36.14 (see **13.4.5** and **13.4.6**) will not apply to it.

13.4.3   Clarification of a Part 36 offer

In most cases the terms of a Part 36 offer should not be ambiguous, particularly where the only claim or claims concern a sum or sums of money. But where monetary and/or non-monetary remedies are sought, it is possible that an offeree may not be clear about the terms proposed. By r 36.8, an offeree may, within seven days of receiving a Part 36 offer, request clarification from the offeror. Although the rule is silent on the point, best practice is to make the request in writing. If the offeror does not give the clarification requested, the offeree can (unless the trial has already started) apply to the court for an order that he does so.

Remember that usually 21 days (sometimes more) is given to an offeree to accept a Part 36 offer (the relevant period: see **13.4.1**). After that the offeree may accept the offer but suffer a costs penalty (see **13.4.4.3**), or proceed to trial where he is at risk of suffering the financial consequences of r 36.14 (see **13.4.5** and **13.4.6**). So when making any clarification order, the court will also specify the date when the relevant period is treated as having started.

13.4.4   Acceptance of a Part 36 offer

A Part 36 offer may be accepted at any time, whether or not the offeree has subsequently made a different offer, unless the offeror has served notice of withdrawal of that offer on the offeree (see **13.4.2**).

So whilst a Part 36 offer must specify a period of not less than 21 days within which the offeree may decide to accept it (the relevant period: see **13.4.1**), the offeree can still accept that offer even after the relevant period has expired. However, there may be adverse costs consequences of such late acceptance (see **13.4.4.3**).

13.4.4.1   How to accept

An offeree can accept a Part 36 offer by serving written notice of the acceptance on the offeror. This can be done by letter. There is no prescribed form. If proceedings have started, PD 36, para 3.1 provides that the notice of acceptance must also be filed with the court where the case is proceeding.

Note that r 21.10 provides that acceptance on behalf of a child or patient is not valid unless the court has approved the settlement (see **5.4.1.4**). If the matter concerns a pre-action Part 36 offer, the application for approval should be made under CPR Part 8 (see **8.3**).

13.4.4.2   Practical consequences of acceptance

When a Part 36 offer is accepted, the claim is stayed. However, that does not affect the power of the court to enforce the terms of a Part 36 offer and to deal with any question of costs (including interest on costs) relating to the proceedings.

Where a claimant accepts a defendant's Part 36 offer that is, or includes, an offer to pay a single sum of money, that sum must be paid to the claimant within 14 days of the date of acceptance (unless the parties agree otherwise in writing). If the accepted sum is not paid within 14 days (or such other period as has been agreed), the claimant may enter judgment for the unpaid sum. In respect of any other kind of Part 36 offer, any party who has accepted it, but considers that the other party has not honoured its terms, may apply to the court in any existing proceedings to enforce the terms of the offer.

13.4.4.3   Costs consequences of acceptance

Acceptance within relevant period

Where a defendant's Part 36 offer is accepted by the claimant within the relevant period, the claimant is entitled to his costs of the proceedings up to the date on which notice of acceptance is served on the defendant. Those costs should be agreed by the parties or otherwise will be assessed by the court on the standard basis (see **14.3.3.1**). This is summarised in the flowchart at **Appendix C(13)**.

Where a claimant's Part 36 offer is accepted by the defendant within the relevant period, the claimant is entitled to his costs of the proceedings up to the date on which notice of acceptance is served on the claimant. Those costs should be agreed by the parties or otherwise will be assessed by the court on the standard basis (see **14.3.3.1**). This is summarised in the flowchart at **Appendix C(14)**.

Late acceptance

What is the outcome if the offeree accepts late, ie after the relevant period as specified in the offer has expired? If the parties cannot agree who pays costs, the court will make an order. What costs order will the court make? By r 36.10(5), unless the court considers otherwise:

(a)   the defendant will be ordered to pay the claimant's costs of the proceedings up to the date on which the relevant period expired; and

(b)   the offeree will be ordered to pay the offeror's costs for the period from the date of expiry of the relevant period to the date of acceptance.

So where a defendant's Part 36 offer is accepted late by the claimant, if the parties cannot agree on costs, the court will usually order that:

(a)   the defendant pay the claimant's costs of the proceedings up to the date on which the relevant period expired; and

(b)   the claimant pay the defendant's costs from the date of expiry of the relevant period to the date of acceptance.

This is summarised in the flowchart at **Appendix C(15)**.

As you would expect, where a claimant's Part 36 offer is accepted late by the defendant, if the parties cannot agree on costs, the court will usually order that the defendant pay the claimant's costs of the proceedings up to the date of acceptance.

For these purposes the claimant's costs include any costs incurred in dealing with a defendant's counterclaim if the Part 36 offer states that it takes that into account.

If the parties cannot agree costs when late acceptance occurs, the court will assess costs on the standard basis (see **14.3.3.1**).

13.4.5   Part 36 consequences at trial of a defendant's offer

If the claimant at trial (or earlier by way of summary judgment) obtains a judgment that is more advantageous than a defendant's Part 36 offer, the claimant can be seen to have been justified in not accepting the offer. In those circumstances, the defendant will have to pay the amount of the judgment (damages plus interest in a monetary claim) and will normally be ordered to pay the claimant's costs on the standard basis (see **14.3.3.1**). Note that interest is payable on those costs only from the date of judgment (see **15.2**).

But what if a claimant fails to obtain a judgment that is more advantageous than the defendant's Part 36 offer? The court will, unless it considers it unjust to do so (see **13.4.8**), make what is commonly called a 'split costs' order under r 36.14(2). This penalises the claimant financially for proceeding with the claim but failing to secure a judgment that is any better for him than the defendant's Part 36 offer.

13.4.5.1   The 'like with like' comparison

Before we look at r 36.14(2), we need to answer this question: how can the court tell if the claimant has been awarded a judgment that is not more advantageous to him than the earlier defendant's Part 36 offer? Where the claimant has made a money claim the judgment will be for a capital sum plus interest awarded at the trial judge's discretion, usually from when the loss was sustained up to judgment given at the end of the trial, or subsequently if judgment is reserved (see **2.7.2.3**). If the judge has made an award of interest it is necessary for him to be provided with a calculation of the amount of interest he would have awarded had the judgment been given at the date the relevant period for the Part 36 offer expired.

To make a 'like with like' comparison you should:

(a)   calculate the interest that would have accrued on the sum awarded by the judge from the date interest becomes payable (see **2.7.2.3**) up to and including the last date for acceptance of the Part 36 offer (ie the end of the relevant period, normally day 21);

(b)   add the figure in (a) to the amount of the judgment; and

(c)   if the figure in (b) is less than or the same as the amount offered by D, C has failed to obtain a judgment more advantageous than D's Part 36 offer and r 36.14(2) should apply. See also **13.4.7**.

Example

C instructs solicitors in April 2007. A letter before claim is sent in May 2007 seeking £70,000 damages plus interest in respect of a contract that was broken in July 2006 (when the loss was sustained).

In July 2009, C commences High Court proceedings which include a claim for interest under s 35A of the SCA 1981. C is served with a Part 36 offer from D in the sum of £55,000 (inclusive of interest) on 5 January 2010. The last day to accept that sum is 26 January 2010. C does not accept the sum.

At trial in July 2011 C is awarded £38,000 plus interest up to that date of approximately £11,400 (five years at approximately 1% over base rate). C has been awarded £49,400 in total. But has C secured a judgment more advantageous than D's Part 36 offer made back in January 2010? To decide that we must compare like with like and so calculate the amount of interest that would be awarded on £38,000 from July 2006 to 26 January 2010. That is approximately three and a half years, totalling £7,980 in interest. Hence, at January 2010 C would have been awarded a total of approximately £45,980 and so has not secured a judgment more advantageous than D's Part 36 offer. Hindsight has shown that C should have accepted the offer in January 2010, and in effect C has wasted the time and money of D and the court ever since.

13.4.5.2   What is a split costs order?

So what is a r 36.14(2) 'split costs' order? The rule provides that 'the court will, unless it considers it unjust to do so, order that the defendant is entitled to (a) his costs from the date on which the relevant period expired; and (b) interest on those costs.' *Remember, the usual costs order is that the losing party should pay the winning party's costs and that interest on costs is normally only payable from the date of judgment.* The claimant is the 'winner' of the proceedings, having secured a judgment for the defendant to pay him a sum of money, but he has in these circumstances not been awarded more than the defendant's Part 36 offer. In hindsight the claimant should have accepted that offer. By failing to do so he has, since the relevant period expired, wasted the time and money of both the defendant and court.

The effect of r 36.14(2) is as follows:

(a)   the defendant pays the claimant's costs from when those costs were first incurred until the relevant period expired (usually day 21). The defendant does not pay the claimant any interest on those costs. Those costs should be agreed by the parties or otherwise will be assessed by the court on the standard basis (see **14.3.3.1**); and

(b)   the claimant pays the defendant's costs from expiry of the relevant period (usually day 22) until judgment. Those costs should be agreed by the parties or otherwise will be assessed by the court on the standard basis (see **14.3.3.1**). But in addition the claimant pays interest on those costs from when each item was incurred. How much interest? The rule is silent on the point. Interest on costs is not normally payable until after judgment (see **15.2**). The Court of Appeal, in *Bim Kemi AB v Blackburn Chemical* [2003] EWCA Civ 889, gave guidance on when it may be appropriate to award interest on costs before judgment. In the case the Court indicated that an award of 1% over base rate will usually be the appropriate rate of interest.

The effect of r 36.14(2) is summarised in the flowchart at **Appendix C(16)**.

Trial outcomes summary

In the example in **13.4.5.1**, there are three possible trial outcomes. The table that follows considers each.

Result at trial	Likely costs order (subject to the court's discretion)
Judgment **more** advantageous than D's offer.	C awarded his costs of the claim to be paid by D on the standard basis.
Judgment not as advantageous as D's offer.	The court will make a split costs order: D ordered to pay C's costs on the standard basis from April 2007 up to and including 26 January 2010. C ordered to pay D's costs on the standard basis from and including 27 January 2010 until judgment in July 2011 plus interest on those costs.
C **loses** at trial.	C ordered to pay D's costs of defending the claim on the standard basis plus interest on costs incurred from and including 27 January 2010 to judgment in July 2011.

13.4.5.3   Financial consequences of r 36.14(2) order

Let us consider a very simple example to show the potential financial effect on the parties of a r 36.14(2) 'split costs' order. The first step is to ascertain the last day for acceptance of the defendant's Part 36 offer (ie the end of the relevant period). In the example we call this the 'split date'.

Example

Assume that C is awarded £45,000 damages (inclusive of interest) at trial. Before the split date C's costs are in the region of £10,000 and D's approximately £8,500. After the split date C's costs are in the region of £15,500 and D's approximately £13,250. Who pays what?

D will pay C:

(a)   the £45,000 damages; and

(b)   C's costs of £10,000 up to the split date; and

(c)   his own costs of £8,500 to his solicitors.

After the split date:

(a)   C pays D's costs of £13,250 plus interest on those costs; and

(b)   his own costs of £15,500 to his solicitors.

	C receives: £	C pays out: £
Damages	45,000	
Costs before split date	10,000	
TOTAL	55,000	
Own legal costs		25,500
D's costs from split date		13,250 (plus interest)
TOTAL		38,750
BALANCE	**16,250**	

What is the overall effect on C?

C recovers £45,000 damages and £10,000 costs, a total of £55,000.

C pays out his own costs of £25,500 and D's costs of £13,250 (exclusive of interest), a total of £38,750 plus the interest on D's costs.

C receives the balance.

What is the overall effect on D?

	D receives: £	D pays out: £
Damages		45,000
C's costs before split date		10,000
Own legal costs		21,750
TOTAL		76,750
Costs from split date	13,250 (plus interest)	
TOTAL	13,250 (plus interest)	
BALANCE		63,500

D pays C £45,000 damages and £10,000 costs and D pays his own costs of £21,750, a total of £76,750.

> D receives from C costs of £13,250 plus interest on those costs.
>
> D is out of pocket by £63,500 (less the interest recovered on costs from the split date).

As to the assessment of the amount of costs payable under a court order, see **14.3**.

13.4.5.4   Rule 36.14(2) and a claimant who loses at trial

What if at trial the claimant fails to establish liability and so is awarded no sum of money whatsoever? This may seem an unlikely outcome where a defendant has made a Part 36 offer, but it has occurred in practice and no doubt will do so again albeit very occasionally. The normal court order would be for the claimant as the loser to pay the defendant's costs from when those were first incurred by the defendant to judgment. Interest would normally be payable on those costs only from the date of judgment (see **15.2**). However, in these circumstances, a defendant should argue that r 36.14(2) applies. After all, the claimant has failed to obtain a judgment more advantageous than the defendant's Part 36 offer. If the court agrees then the claimant should start paying interest on the defendant's costs (arguably at 1% over base rate) from when the relevant period for acceptance of that offer expired. This is summarised in the flowchart at **Appendix C(17)**.

13.4.5.5   Tactical considerations

From the point of view of a defendant who considers himself at risk on liability, a Part 36 offer can provide a useful mechanism for pressurising the claimant to accept a reasonable settlement and will often be used tactically as part of settlement discussions. Of course, the defendant has to make a careful assessment of how much to offer. An over-generous offer will be snapped up by a claimant eager to receive more than the true value of the claim. An unrealistically low offer will impose no real pressure, since the claimant will feel confident of beating it at trial. The wise defendant will aim to pitch his offer at a level that is just high enough for the claimant to feel that it would be unsafe not to accept.

Also important is the stage in the litigation at which a Part 36 offer is made. The earlier this is done, the greater the potential costs protection for the defendant and the greater the pressure placed on the claimant. Thus, the vulnerable defendant should make an offer as soon as he has enough information to judge its amount accurately.

13.4.6   Part 36 consequences at trial of a claimant offer

13.4.6.1   Claimant's failure to beat his Part 36 offer

No specific penalty is imposed on the claimant if he fails at trial (or earlier summary judgment) to do better than the proposals in his Part 36 offer, although the making of the offer may be taken into account by the court in exercising its general discretion as to costs, especially if the claimant has exaggerated his claim.

13.4.6.2   Judgment is at least as advantageous to the claimant as his Part 36 offer

If the judgment against the defendant is at least as advantageous to the claimant as the proposals contained in the claimant's Part 36 offer, r 36.14(3) provides that the court will, unless it considers it unjust to do so, order that the claimant:

(a)   be awarded interest on the whole or part of any sum awarded to him (excluding interest already awarded) at a rate not exceeding 10% pa above the Bank of England's base rate for some or all of the period starting with the date on which the relevant period expired; and/or

(b)   recover his costs on the indemnity basis (see **14.3.3**) from the date on which the relevant period expired; and/or

(c)   be awarded interest on those indemnity costs from when each item of cost was incurred at up to 10% pa above base rate.

Did you spot the difference in wording between (a) and (b) as to when interest on damages and indemnity costs start to be payable? Do not worry if you did not, as it appears the point is not taken in practice. Technically, under (a), the interest on damages at up to 10% pa above base rate can start *on* the date the relevant period expires, ie usually day 21. Under (b), the entitlement to indemnity costs starts *from* when the relevant period expires, ie usually day 22. We take the view that a commonsense reading and interpretation of this provision is that under both (a) and (b) the payment is from and including the day after the relevant period expires, ie usually day 22. After all, the defendant had up until the very last day of the relevant period to accept the offer, ie usually day 21. So any financial penalty should start to be paid only from the next day.

Why is an order under r 36.14(3)(a), (b) and (c) a financial penalty for the defendant? Remember that the usual order would be that the defendant pays the claimant interest on damages awarded at 1% pa above base rate in a commercial case or 8% pa in a non-commercial case (see **2.7.2.3**). Under (a), that rate can be increased up to 10% over base rate for the period from day 22 to judgment. Then the usual costs order would be for the defendant to pay the claimant's costs on the standard basis. Interest is not normally payable on those costs before judgment. However, under (b), the defendant has to pay the costs incurred by the claimant from day 22 to judgment at a penalty rate, the indemnity basis, plus under (c) interest on those indemnity costs from when each was incurred until judgment at up to 10% pa above base rate. See the flowchart at **Appendix C(18)**.

13.4.6.3 The 'like with like' comparison

Before we look at r 36.14(3), we need to answer this question: how can the court tell if the judgment is at least as advantageous to the claimant as the claimant's Part 36 offer? Where the claimant has made a money claim the judgment will be for a capital sum plus interest awarded at the trial judge's discretion, usually from when the loss was sustained up to trial. If the judge has made an award of interest, it is necessary for him to be provided with a calculation of the amount of interest he would have awarded had the judgment been given at the date the claimant's Part 36 offer expired. So the process is similar to that described at **13.4.5.1**.

13.4.6.4 Calculating the amount of 'enhanced interest' to be awarded and indemnity costs

Enhanced interest on damages

There is a cap on the amount of interest that can be awarded on damages by the trial judge generally and under r 36.14(3). This is set out in r 36.14(5), which provides that 'where the court awards interest under [r 36.14(3)] and also awards interest on the same sum and for the same period under any other power, the total rate of interest may not exceed 10% above base rate'.

This award of interest on damages under r 36.14(3) is often called 'enhanced interest'. But how much should the court award? David Foskett QC, when sitting as a deputy High Court judge in the case of *Little and Others v George Little Sebire & Co* [2001] EWCA Civ 894, [2001] STC 1065, indicated that the court should take as the starting point 10% above base. However, Lord Woolf MR in *Petrotrade Inc v Texaco Ltd* [2001] 1 WLR 947 said that he did not endorse that approach. In *Mann and Holt v Lexington Insurance Co* [2001] 1 Lloyd's Rep 1, Waller LJ said in the unreported post-judgment discussion:

> What the rule provides for is a rate not exceeding 10%. The object of the rule must be to provide the court with a weapon to punish parties who have failed to take and accept a Part 36 offer and have really behaved badly in the context of litigation as a whole. The ten per cent must be reserved for the worst cases.

Interest on indemnity costs

If indemnity costs are awarded, how much interest should be awarded on those indemnity costs? In *Rowlands v Bryn Alyn Community (Holdings) Ltd* [2003] EWCA Civ 383, [2003] 3 WLR 107, the Court of Appeal indicated that, as a norm, the rate of interest should reflect the cost of borrowing money. The court put this at 4% over base rate. The court justified potentially having a different interest figure from that for enhanced interest on damages, saying that the latter compensates also for the general impact of proceedings on the claimant.

How do you calculate interest on the indemnity costs? According to the Court of Appeal in *McPhilemy v Times Newspapers Ltd (No 2)* [2001] EWCA Civ 933, [2001] 4 All ER 861, interest runs on the indemnity costs from the date upon which the work was done or liability for the disbursement was incurred.

Note that according to the *McPhilemy* case, both enhanced interest on damages and interest on indemnity costs runs under r 36.14(3) only until judgment. Thereafter interest is payable on damages and costs ordered to be paid under a judgment pursuant to either s 17 of the Judgments Act 1838 or the County Courts (Interest on Judgment Debts) Order 1991 (see **14.2.8.2**).

Example

In order to understand in full the implications of r 36.14(3) in a particular case, you need to identify these key dates:

(a)   The date interest on damages starts to be payable: this is normally when the damage was suffered (see **2.7.2.3**).

(b)   The date the claimant first incurred costs: this is often the first time he instructs solicitors.

(c)   The relevant period (see **13.4.1.1**): see **13.4.1.4** for how to calculate the date of service of a Part 36 offer. The relevant period expires 21 days after service of the offer. It is from the 22nd day that the financial penalties under r 36.14(3) can be imposed.

Assume C alleges a breach of contract by D, which occurred on 16 March 2007 when C sustained loss. He first instructs solicitors on 31 July 2007.

C issues proceedings in December 2008, claiming damages estimated at £75,000 plus interest. In March 2009, C serves a Part 36 offer of £60,000. The relevant period (ie the deadline for acceptance) expires on 27 March 2009. D does not accept, the case proceeds to trial and judgment is given on 21 September 2011.

(i)   If C wins but fails to obtain a judgment at least as advantageous as his own Part 36 offer

Here Part 36 will have no effect and the court will usually award C his costs of the claim on the standard basis. C will not usually be penalised for having made a Part 36 offer, albeit unsuccessful, neither will he gain any advantage. C first instructed solicitors on 31 July 2007, so he may receive his costs incurred from that date until judgment on 21 September 2011. Do not forget that C will receive the damages plus any interest awarded on those by the court (usually 8% if a non-commercial claim, or 1% over base rate if a commercial claim). The interest will start to run from the date loss was suffered on 16 March 2007 and will continue until judgment on 21 September 2011.

(ii)   If C wins and obtains a judgment at least as advantageous as his own Part 36 offer

Here, the court will, unless it considers it unjust, impose the financial penalties under r 36.14(3). So D will pay C:

•   interest on the damages awarded from 16 March 2007 (when loss suffered) until and including 27 March 2009 (when relevant period expired), plus

> • enhanced interest on the damages awarded from and including 28 March 2009 (day 22) to judgment on 21 September 2011 at no more than 10% pa above the base rate, plus
>
> • the costs incurred by C from 31 July 2007 (first incurred) up to and including 27 March 2009 on the standard basis, plus
>
> • the costs incurred by C from and including 28 March 2009 to judgment on 21 September 2011 on the indemnity basis, plus
>
> • interest on those indemnity basis costs from when each item was incurred until judgment on 21 September 2011 at a maximum of 10% pa above base rate.
>
> *(iii)   If D wins*
>
> C will usually be ordered to pay D's costs of defending the claim on the standard basis.

13.4.6.5   Tactical considerations

Where the defendant does not accept a claimant's Part 36 offer and the claimant obtains a judgment that is at least as advantageous as his own Part 36 offer, the defendant is likely to pay a heavy price. In contrast, we have seen that a claimant who fails to achieve such a judgment is usually in no worse position than if his offer had not been made. The result is that, whereas there is no downside for the claimant in making such an offer, a reasonable proposal will place the defendant under considerable pressure.

Since the penalties in r 36.14(3) are imposed as from the expiry of the relevant period, the earlier the claimant makes his offer, the greater the pressure on the defendant. It is tactically sensible for a claimant to make an offer as soon as there is enough information to judge its amount and prior to issuing proceedings where practicable.

If a claimant's Part 36 offer is too high and/or a defendant's Part 36 offer too low, Part 36 has no effect (see the flowchart in **Appendix C(19)**).

13.4.7   What does 'advantageous' mean in r 36.14?

Rule 36.14(1) states that:

(1)   This rule applies where upon judgment being entered–

    (a)   a claimant fails to obtain a judgment more advantageous than a defendant's Part 36 offer; or

    (b)   judgment against the defendant is at least as advantageous to the claimant as the proposals contained in a claimant's Part 36 offer.

In a money claim, do (a) and (b) require just a mathematical comparison of the figures, or can the court look at all the circumstances of the case in deciding where the balance of advantage lies? In *Carver v BAA plc* [2008] EWCA Civ 412 Ward LJ posed this question: if a claimant beats a defendant's Part 36 offer in a money claim by a modest amount, even £1, has he obtained a judgment more advantageous than the defendant's Part 36 offer so that (a) does not apply? The Court said the only way to answer that question was to look at all the circumstances of the case. Here, the claimant was awarded £4,686.26. That was only £51 more than the defendant had previously offered under Part 36. Mathematically the claimant had obtained a judgment greater in amount than the sum offered under Part 36. But the Court held that the claimant had failed to obtain a judgment that was more advantageous than that offer. Why? Ward LJ observed as follows:

> The Civil Procedure Rules, and Part 36 in particular, encourage both sides to make offers to settle. Compromise is seen as an object worthy of promotion for compromise is better than contest, both for the litigants concerned, for the court and for the administration of justice as a whole. Litigation is time consuming and it comes at a cost, emotional as well as financial. Those are,

therefore, appropriate factors to take into account in deciding whether the battle was worth it. Money is not the sole governing criterion.

It follows that [the trial judge] was correct in looking at the case broadly. He was entitled to take into account that the extra £51 gained was more than off set by the irrecoverable cost incurred by the claimant in continuing to contest the case for as long as she did. He was entitled to take into account the added stress to her as she waited for the trial and the stress of the trial process itself. No reasonable litigant would have embarked upon this campaign for a gain of £51. (paras 31 and 32)

13.4.8   When an order under r 36.14(2) or (3) might be unjust

As we have seen, a well-judged offer that is not accepted will lead to an order under r 36.14(2) or (3) unless it would be unjust for the court to make that order.

In considering whether it would be unjust to make the orders referred to in r 36.14(2) or (3) (see **13.4.5** and **13.4.6**), the court will take into account all the circumstances of the case including:

(a)   the terms of the Part 36 offer;

(b)   the stage in the proceedings when the Part 36 offer was made, including in particular how long before the trial started the offer was made;

(c)   the information available to the parties at the time when the Part 36 offer was made; and

(d)   the conduct of the parties with regard to the giving of or refusal to give information for the purposes of enabling the offer to be made or evaluated.

In *Ford v GKR Construction Ltd* [2000] 1 WLR 1397, the Court of Appeal indicated that the court should take into account such matters as late disclosure, late service of evidence or the development of unanticipated contentions, and the stage in the litigation when these events occur, as well as their nature and effect on the outcome of the litigation. Lord Woolf observed that

If a party has not enabled another party to properly assess whether or not to make an offer, or whether or not to accept an offer which is made, because of non-disclosure to the other party of material matters, or if a party comes to a decision which is different from that which would have been reached if there had been proper disclosure, that is a material matter for a court to take into account in considering what orders it should make.

In *Huntley v Simmonds* [2009] EWHC 406, Underhill J indicated that when looking at the terms of the offer, technical errors under r 36.2(2) as to form and content (see **13.4.1**) that cause no real uncertainty or other prejudice to the offeree are unlikely to make the order unjust. However, a significant error, such as failing to state on the face of an offer letter that it was intended to have the consequences of Part 36, might make it unjust.

13.4.9   Rule 36.14(2) and a CFA

What if a claimant who has entered into a CFA (see **2.4.2**) with his solicitors establishes liability but is awarded damages that only equal or are less than a defendant's Part 36 offer? In those circumstances, how will an order under r 36.14(2) affect the CFA success fee? The answer will have to be found in the wording of the CFA. The usual provisions are as follows. If the claimant rejected the offer on the basis of advice from the solicitors or counsel, the success fee is not payable by the client on charges incurred after the date the relevant period to accept the offer expired (day 22). The firm's normal charges and disbursements will remain payable. However, if the client rejected the offer against the advice of the solicitors or counsel, the success fee remains payable (as well as the firm's normal charges and disbursements).

13.4.10   Secrecy

Except in very limited circumstances, a Part 36 offer should not be revealed to the trial judge until all questions of liability and quantum have been decided.

What if a Part 36 offer is made known to the trial judge? In *Garratt v Saxby* [2004] LTL, 18 February, the Court of Appeal indicated that the judge had to determine whether the disclosure of the offer made a fair trial possible, or whether justice required the judge to withdraw from the case. The judge in exercising that discretion was entitled to take into account the additional time, cost and difficulty involved for all concerned if the hearing were to be aborted.

13.4.11 Part 36 offer in respect of a counterclaim

If a defendant makes a Part 36 offer in respect of his counterclaim and at trial obtains a judgment on that counterclaim that is at least as advantageous as his Part 36 offer, can the court impose financial penalties on the claimant under r 36.14(3)? Yes, held the Court of Appeal in *AF v BG* [2009] EWCA Civ 757.

13.5 Claims involving children and protected parties

Where a claim is made by or on behalf of a child or protected party, or against a child or protected party, no settlement of that claim is valid without the approval of the court. Thus, a Part 36 offer may not be accepted without the court's approval.

Approval is required even if a compromise is reached before the issue of proceedings. In such a case the application for approval should be made under Part 8 (see **8.3**).

13.6 Discontinuance (Part 38)

13.6.1 General provisions

A claimant may decide not to pursue his claim, even though no settlement has been reached. For example, he may conclude that his chances of succeeding at trial or of recovering any money from the defendant are so slim that he would be better to discontinue. A claimant may discontinue a claim at any time and, if there are co-defendants, he may do so against all or any of them. The claimant will need the court's permission to discontinue a claim where:

(a) the court has granted an interim injunction; or

(b) any party has given an undertaking to the court.

If an interim payment has been made, the claimant may discontinue only if:

(a) the defendant who made the payment consents in writing; or

(b) the court gives permission.

Where there are two or more claimants, a claimant may discontinue only if:

(a) all the other claimants consent in writing; or

(b) the court gives permission.

13.6.2 Procedure

The claimant must file and serve a notice of discontinuance on all other parties. If the claimant needs the consent of another party in order to discontinue, a copy of that consent must be attached to the notice.

If the claimant discontinues in a case where consent or the court's permission was not required, any defendant may apply to set aside the notice of discontinuance. The application must be made within 28 days.

13.6.3 Liability for costs

A claimant who discontinues is liable for the defendant's costs on the standard basis (see **14.3.3.1**) unless the court orders otherwise. It is therefore vital that a solicitor acting for a potential claimant explains this to the client. Note that in the case of *Noorani v Calver (No 2/ Costs)* [2009] EWHC 592, the discontinuing claimant was ordered to pay the defendant's costs on the penalty, indemnity basis (see **14.3.3.2**) because of the claimant's unreasonable conduct both before and during the litigation.

If proceedings are only partly discontinued, the claimant is liable only for the costs of the part of the claim he is discontinuing, and those costs must not be assessed until the rest of the case is over unless the court orders otherwise.

Chapter 14

Final Preparations for Trial, Trial and Assessment of Costs

14.1 Final preparations for trial

14.1.1 Briefing counsel

If the solicitor intends to brief counsel to deal with the trial, counsel should be instructed well in advance of the trial date. Very often, of course, counsel will already have been instructed in a case to advise, draft a statement of case or appear at a case management conference. Moreover, the trial date or period will have been known since allocation. The brief to counsel should contain copies of all relevant documents which will be required at the trial.

The content of the brief should deal in detail with the facts still in issue and how they are to be proved. Even though the barrister may be familiar with the case, the solicitor should nevertheless take the time to set matters out fully in the brief in case it is passed on to another barrister at a later stage. Occasionally, the barrister originally instructed may be unable to attend the trial, in which case the brief will be handed over to another barrister at short notice.

Practice varies as to whether there will be a conference with counsel before the hearing. This will depend on the extent to which there have already been conferences, and the value, importance and complexity of the case.

When acting for a private or commercial client, it is for the solicitor to negotiate the brief fee with counsel's clerk following delivery of the brief. In a fast track case, you should try to restrict the brief fee to the maximum amount allowed for the advocacy in a fast track case (see **14.3.6**).

In a multi-track case, the fee covers only one day unless agreed otherwise. If the case takes more than one day, counsel will be entitled to charge a 'refresher fee' for each subsequent day. For example, the brief fee (to cover preparation for trial and the first day) might be £5,000 for a fairly complex High Court case, with a refresher fee of £1,500.

A brief to counsel can be found in the multi-track case study at **Appendix D(14)**.

14.1.2 Attendance of witnesses (Part 34)

14.1.2.1 Witnesses in general

All witnesses should be kept fully informed of the expected trial date and, once the date has been fixed, should be told of that date without delay. It is essential that, at an early stage, witnesses are asked whether any particular periods would be inconvenient for them to attend the trial. Details of a witness's availability have to be given to the court on the allocation and pre-trial checklists, listing questionnaires (see **Chapter 9**).

Even where witnesses have been kept fully informed and involved, it is unwise to rely on the assumption that they will attend court voluntarily. Instead, their attendance should be encouraged by serving them with a witness summons. This is a document issued by the court requiring a witness to:

(a)   attend court to give evidence; and/or

(b)   produce documents to the court.

A witness summons should be served at least seven days before the date on which the witness is required to attend court. It will then be binding upon the witness, and if the witness fails to attend court, he will be in contempt. If a party wishes to issue a summons less than seven days before the date of the trial, permission from the court must be obtained.

The witness summons will normally be served by the court, unless the party on whose behalf it is issued indicates that he wishes to serve it himself.

At the time of service of a witness summons the witness must be offered or paid:

(a)   a sum reasonably sufficient to cover his expenses in travelling to and from the court; and

(b)   such sum by way of compensation for loss of time as may be specified by the court.

The danger in not serving a witness with a witness summons is that if he fails to attend the trial, the first question the judge will ask the solicitor or barrister conducting the case is why a witness summons was not served. If a witness summons had been served, there is a greater possibility that the court will be sympathetic enough to grant an adjournment of the trial if that is required because of the crucial nature of the missing witness's evidence.

Police officers must always be served with a witness summons, because they will not give evidence in a civil matter on behalf of either party unless they are under an obligation to do so.

14.1.2.2   Expert witnesses

Paragraph 19 of the Protocol for the Instruction of Experts (see **Appendix A(20)**) deals with the attendance of experts at court. Experts are expected to keep those instructing them informed of their availability and make every effort to ensure that they are available to attend court if required. A witness summons to require the attendance of an expert at trial should be used only if required by the expert.

14.1.3   Preparing trial bundles (Part 39)

14.1.3.1   What to include

Unless the court orders otherwise, the claimant must file the trial bundle not more than seven days and not less than three days before the start of the trial. By para 3.2 of PD 39 – Miscellaneous Provisions Relating to Hearings, unless the court orders otherwise, the trial bundle should include a copy of:

(1)   the claim form and all statements of case,

(2)   a case summary and/or chronology where appropriate,

(3)   requests for further information and responses to the requests,

(4)   all witness statements to be relied on as evidence,

(5)   any witness summaries,

(6)   any notices of intention to rely on hearsay evidence under rule 33.2,

(7)   any notices of intention to rely on evidence (such as a plan, photograph etc) under rule 33.6 which is not—

    (a)   contained in a witness statement, affidavit or expert's report,

    (b)   being given orally at trial,

    (c)   hearsay evidence under rule 33.2,

(8)   any medical reports and responses to them,

(9)   any expert's reports and responses to them,

(10) any order giving directions as to the conduct of the trial, and

(11) any other necessary documents.

Paragraph 3.9 of PD 39 provides that the contents of the trial bundle should be agreed where possible. The parties should also agree where possible that the documents contained in the bundle are authentic even if not disclosed under Part 31, and that documents in the bundle may be treated as evidence of the facts stated in them even if a notice under the Civil Evidence Act 1995 has not been served. Where it is not possible to agree the contents of the bundle, a summary of the points on which the parties are unable to agree should be included.

The party filing the trial bundle should supply identical bundles to all the parties to the proceedings and for the use of the witnesses.

14.1.3.2 Case summary (skeleton argument)

Each party should prepare a case summary (often called a 'skeleton argument') to use at trial. This is designed to assist both the court and the parties by indicating what points are or are not in issue, and the nature of the argument about the disputed matters. It should also assist the court in its advance reading. As a general rule a case summary should therefore:

(a) concisely review the party's submissions of fact in relation to each of the issues with reference to the evidence;

(b) concisely set out the propositions of law advanced with reference to the main authorities relied on;

(c) be divided into numbered paragraphs and paginated consecutively; and

(d) identify any key documents which the trial judge should, if possible, read before the trial starts.

Templates to help you draft case summaries for use at a fast track or multi-track trial are set out at **Appendices B(8)** and **B(9)**.

In *Tombstone Ltd v Raja* [2008] EWCA Civ 1444, the Court of Appeal stressed that the case summary or skeleton argument should assist the court, as well as the parties, by improving preparations for, and the efficiency of, adversarial oral hearings. The Court reminded practitioners that

> skeleton arguments should not be prepared as verbatim scripts to be read out in public or as footnoted theses to be read in private. Good skeleton arguments are tools with practical uses: an agenda for the hearing, a summary of the main points, propositions and arguments to be developed orally, a useful way of noting citations and references, a convenient place for making cross references, a time-saving means of avoiding unnecessary dictation to the court and laborious and pointless note-taking by the court. Skeleton arguments are aids to oral advocacy. (*per* Mummery LJ, at paras 126 and 127)

14.1.3.3 Time estimates and core bundles

The trial bundle should be accompanied by an estimated length of reading time and an agreed estimate of the likely length of the hearing. If the trial bundle is very large, a 'core' bundle of key documents, to be read by the trial judge, should be prepared.

14.2 Trial

14.2.1 Venue

Most county courts belong to a group, with one court being designated the trial centre. The trial of the case, whether fast track or multi-track, will usually take place at that trial centre, which may therefore not be the same court that managed the case.

14.2.2   Timetable

In most cases, in both the fast track and multi-track, a trial timetable will have been fixed after filing the pre-trial checklists (listing questionnaires). The timetable may, for example, limit the time for cross-examination and re-examination of each particular witness. For example, in *Three Rivers DC v The Governor and Company of the Bank of England* [2005] EWCA Civ 889, the trial judge (upheld by the Court of Appeal) limited the cross-examination of a key witness which was projected to last 12 weeks to seven weeks instead. In a complex and long multi-track case, the timetable is usually set at the pre-trial review.

14.2.2.1   Trial timetable

At the trial, the judge may confirm or vary any timetable given previously, or, if none has been given, set his own.

The judge will generally have read the papers in the trial bundle (which, as we saw at **14.1.3**, will have been filed with the court prior to the hearing).

A fast track trial should usually be completed within one day. However, if it lasts more than one day, the judge will normally sit on the next court day to complete the trial. A typical fast track timetable for a day's trial is as follows:

Opening speeches:	20 minutes
Cross-examination and re-examination of claimant's witnesses:	90 minutes
Cross-examination and re-examination of defendant's witnesses:	90 minutes
Defendant's closing submissions:	15 minutes
Claimant's closing submissions:	15 minutes
Judge preparing and delivering judgment:	30 minutes
Summary assessment of costs:	30 minutes

In multi-track cases, the judge will normally sit on consecutive court days until it has been completed.

14.2.2.2   Professional conduct

Rule 11.01(1) of the Solicitors' Code of Conduct provides that a solicitor must never deceive, or knowingly or recklessly mislead, the court. A solicitor might fall foul of this rule at a trial by, for example:

(a)   submitting inaccurate information or allowing a witness to do so;

(b)   indicating agreement with information that a witness has put forward which the solicitor knows is false;

(c)   calling a witness whose evidence the solicitor knows is untrue.

Clearly, a solicitor would be deceiving a court if he constructed facts supporting his client's case (see r 11.01(3)).

Where a client admits to his solicitor that he has committed perjury or misled the court in any material matter relating to the proceedings, the solicitor must not act further in those proceedings unless the client agrees to disclose the truth to the court (see guidance note 16). If the client refuses to do so, the solicitor should cease to act for the client. In order to keep client confidentiality (see r 4), the solicitor should not inform the court or any other party of the reasons for ceasing to act.

There are some types of information which a solicitor is obliged to disclose to the court, whether or not it is in the best interests of the client to do so (see guidance note 18). Failure to disclose this information could amount to a breach of r 11.01(1). For example, the advocates on both sides must advise the court of relevant cases and statutory provisions. If one of them omits a case or provision or makes an incorrect reference to a case or provision, it is the duty of the other to draw attention to it even if that assists the opponent's case.

What if a solicitor knows of facts which, or of a witness who, would assist the opponent? Is the solicitor under any duty to inform the opponent, or indeed the court, of this to the prejudice of his own client? The answer is no (see guidance note 18(b)).

Rule 11.05 flags up particular duties when acting as an advocate. When appearing as an advocate, a solicitor:

(a)   must not say anything which is merely scandalous or intended only to insult a witness or any other person;

(b)   must avoid naming in open court any third party whose character would thereby be called into question, unless it is necessary for the proper conduct of the case;

(c)   must not call into question the character of a witness they have cross-examined unless the witness has had the opportunity to answer the allegations during cross-examination; and

(d)   must not suggest that any person is guilty of a crime, fraud or misconduct unless such allegations go to a matter in issue which is material to the client's case and appear to be supported by reasonable grounds.

However, guidance note 25 makes it clear that it is not the intention of this rule to prevent a solicitor robustly defending his client's position.

14.2.3   Order of proceedings

14.2.3.1   Preliminary issues

Before the case formally commences, a party may wish to raise a preliminary issue with the trial judge. These will normally concern procedural matters. But bear in mind that most of these issues should have been dealt with if a pre-trial review occurred.

Possible preliminary issues include:

(a)   Permission to amend a statement of case (see **7.6**). This would be a very late application liable to fail, and prior notice to the other side would be essential.

(b)   Permission to adduce more evidence by way of examination-in-chief from a witness under r 32.5(3) (see **12.4**). However, the trial judge may prefer to deal with this application immediately after the witness in question has been sworn.

(c)   An application to strike out part of an opponent's witness statement (see **12.2**).

14.2.3.2   The claimant

If allowed by the judge, the claimant may make an opening speech setting out the background to the case and the facts which remain in issue. If this is allowed by the timetable set by the court, it must be very concise. The claimant's advocate will use the case summary (or skeleton argument) filed with the trial bundle (see **14.1.3**).

THE EVIDENCE

Examination-in-chief

The claimant and his witnesses will then give evidence. In most cases, the witness statements will stand as the evidence-in-chief. If that is the case then, after being sworn, the witness may simply be asked to confirm that his statement is correct. He will be able to amplify what is in his witness statement only if allowed to do so by the judge. If some form of limited examination-in-chief is allowed by the judge then the usual rule is that a witness cannot be asked leading questions by his own advocate to encourage him to relate the story. It is difficult to define a leading question. Basically, it is one which suggests the answer or assumes a fact which has not yet been proved. For example, a question to the claimant in a breach of contract case, 'did the defendant supply your firm with goods which did not match the sample?' suggests that the goods did not match the sample. It is therefore an objectionable leading question. Instead, the claimant should be asked in general terms, 'describe to the court the condition of the goods when they arrived as compared to the sample provided earlier'.

Cross-examination

The next stage is the cross-examination of the witness. There is no bar on leading questions. The purpose of cross-examination is to extract favourable evidence and to discredit the person being cross-examined in order to make their evidence appear less believable either on the case overall, or in relation to a specific element of it. There are many ways in which this may be done. It may involve highlighting inconsistencies in the evidence given by the witness, or the improbability of the witness's version of events. It may involve alleging that the witness is biased in some way. If the witness has previous convictions, it is even possible for the advocate to cross-examine on these to show the witness's character generally in a bad light.

As all the evidence to be used at trial has been seen by the parties before the trial starts, you can prepare your line of cross-examination questions in advance. Think about the submissions you will wish to make in your closing speech about the evidence of any particular witness. Ensure that you cover all those points with that witness. The trial judge cannot make any particular finding of fact based on the evidence of a witness if that point did not come out in the examination of the witness.

Sometimes, the witness's evidence will be inconsistent with an earlier statement. This will then give the advocate scope to cross-examine on the previous inconsistent statement to show the court how the witness has given different versions of events at different times and therefore should not be believed. See further **12.9.7**.

However, cross-examination does not always involve an aggressive attack on the witness and his credibility. Cross-examination can be conducted in a more subtle fashion and often the best results are achieved by a less confrontational approach.

In addition to the above, however, there is one mandatory rule concerning cross-examination. This is that the cross-examining advocate must put his own party's case to the witness he is cross-examining. Thus, the claimant's advocate must put the claimant's case to the defendant in cross-examination. For example, perhaps the claimant has given evidence that he made known to the defendant a particular purpose for the goods he has bought. The defendant denies this in his witness statement/ examination-in-chief. It must be put to the defendant in cross-examination that the defendant did know of this particular purpose.

It is highly unlikely that the witness being cross-examined in this way will change his story as a result of the allegation being put to him. Nevertheless, it is essential that the cross-examining advocate puts his own client's case to the witness in this way as failure to challenge the opponent's evidence implies acceptance of that evidence.

Re-examination

Following cross-examination, the advocate is given the opportunity to ask further questions of his own witness. However, re-examination is strictly limited to matters arising out of the cross-examination. It is not possible to introduce new issues at this stage. Accordingly, if some ambiguity has been left as a result of the cross-examination, this might be an opportunity to resolve it and try to restore the witness's credibility on that point. For example, perhaps cross-examination has established that the witness normally wears glasses but that he was not wearing them on the day of the incident in question. In so far as this detracts from his credibility in implying that perhaps he did not see what he thought he saw, re-examination would be an opportunity to clarify the fact that the witness wears glasses only for reading. As with examination-in-chief, the advocate cannot ask a leading question.

Problem witnesses

One problem that can arise with the evidence of a witness is the possibility of the witness unexpectedly being unfavourable to the party who has called him. For example, a witness might change his story during cross-examination. If he does this, there is little that the advocate who called the witness can do to remedy the situation. It is not possible for a party's advocate to cross-examine a witness he has himself called.

However, sometimes matters proceed further than this and the witness proves not merely to be unfavourable to the party who called him, but actually proves to be hostile in giving his evidence. It is difficult to be precise as to when a witness can be said to have passed from merely being unfavourable to being hostile, but it would probably be apparent from the witness's demeanour and lack of co-operation that he has no desire either to see justice done, or to give his evidence fairly. One indicator would be the extent to which the witness's evidence is inconsistent with the statement previously given to the party calling him. It is then for that party to make an application to the court for the witness to be declared hostile; if he is, the party who called him can then (contrary to the usual rule) cross-examine that witness on the facts of the case and on the previous inconsistent statements. The witness's general character cannot, however, be attacked by the party who called him, neither can the witness be cross-examined about any previous convictions. Having a witness declared hostile should be regarded as a damage limitation exercise. Whilst it may allow the advocate to retain some control over the case, he is clearly not going to win it unless the damage done can be repaired by evidence from another witness. Strictly, by virtue of s 4 of the Civil Evidence Act 1995 (see **12.9.3.3**), it would be open to the court to attach weight to the previous inconsistent statement as evidence. In practice, however, the court is more likely to take the view that this witness is not someone who can be relied upon.

14.2.3.3   The defendant

The defence will present its evidence in exactly the same way as the claimant.

14.2.4   Children as witnesses

A child who understands the nature of an oath will give sworn evidence. Otherwise, s 96(2) of the Children Act 1989 provides that:

> The child's evidence may be heard by the court if, in its opinion—
>
> (a)   he understands that it is his duty to speak the truth; and
>
> (b)   he has sufficient understanding to justify his evidence being heard.

A child for these purposes is a person under the age of 18.

It is for the judge to decide whether the child can give evidence and, if so, whether it will be given on oath. As a general rule, it will be assumed that children over the age of 14 can give sworn evidence, and the judge will make enquiries of children under that age in order to form an opinion.

The judge will speak to the child to discover whether he appreciates the solemnity of the occasion and the added responsibility to tell the truth which is involved in taking an oath, over and above the ordinary social duty to be truthful. If so, the child can give sworn evidence. If not, but nevertheless the conditions in s 96(2) are satisfied, the child can give unsworn evidence.

14.2.5   Closing speeches

After the evidence has been given, usually the defence advocate will make a closing speech followed by the claimant's advocate.

14.2.6   The judgment

The judge will either deliver his judgment immediately, perhaps after a short adjournment if he requires time to collect his thoughts, or (if the case is complex) judgment may be reserved to be delivered at a later date. If the court gives judgment on both the claim and counterclaim then, if there is a balance in favour of one of the parties, the court will order the party whose judgment is for the lesser amount to pay the balance.

A judgment will normally address the following matters:

(a)   *Liability.* Has the claimant established a cause of action? The judge will review the evidence and should give reasons.

(b)   *Quantum.* In a claim for a specified amount of money, the judge will deal with the figure work, eg any counterclaim established may be set off against the claim. With an unspecified claim the judge will deal with the heads of damage.

(c)   *Interest.* This topic is dealt with in detail at **2.7.2** (and also see **7.2.1** and **14.2.8** below). Once the trial judge has indicated that he will award interest, the rate of such and the period, it is for the advocates to work out the figures.

(d)   *Costs.* By r 44.3(2)(a), the general rule is that the unsuccessful party will be ordered to pay the costs of the successful party, but the court may make a different order. See **14.3**. At the end of a fast track trial, the trial judge will not only make a costs order but he will assess the amount payable (see **14.3.6**). However, at the end of a multi-track trial, the trial judge will only determine who should pay costs. A different judge (known as a costs judge) will determine the amount (failing any agreement of the parties) at a later ('detailed assessment') hearing (see **14.3.7**).

14.2.7   Part 36

A claimant should now apply for an order under r 36.14(3) and a defendant pursuant to r 36.14(2), if appropriate (see **13.4**).

14.2.8   Interest

14.2.8.1   Interest up to the date of judgment

Interest will normally be awarded, provided it has been claimed in the particulars of claim. In the absence of any contractual provision to the contrary, or entitlement to interest under the Late Payment of Commercial Debts (Interest) Act 1998, interest on the damages will usually be awarded by the judge in his discretion (under SCA 1981, s 35A or CCA 1984, s 69) from the date the loss was sustained until the date of judgment. See further **2.7.2**.

Interest is a discretionary matter and the judge might choose to award at a different rate or for a different period. For example, if the claimant has been very slow about pursuing the claim then the judge may disallow interest for a period, even if the claimant eventually succeeds in his claim.

14.2.8.2   Interest after judgment

Once judgment has been given different rules apply. In the High Court, interest is payable under s 17 of the Judgments Act 1838 at a rate of 8% per annum (unless there is a contractual right to more). In a county court, interest is payable at 8% per annum under the County Courts (Interest on Judgment Debts) Order 1991 (SI 1991/1184), provided the judgment was for at least £5,000 (or, if less, that the Late Payment of Commercial Debts (Interest) Act 1998 applies). In neither case is the interest discretionary and it accrues on both the judgment and on costs.

It should be noted that whilst judgment interest cannot accrue on damages until they have been quantified, interest is payable on costs from the date of judgment even if the amount to be paid has yet to be assessed (*Hunt v RM Douglas (Roofing) Ltd* [1990] 1 AC 398). As a result, it is in the interests of the party paying costs to make a payment on account as soon as possible, even if an interim order requiring such a payment is not made by the court (see **14.3.7.11**).

14.2.9 Register of Judgments Orders and Fines

Judgments of the High Court and county court are officially recorded on the Register of Judgments Orders and Fines. Usually the registration lasts for six years and can affect a judgment debtor's creditworthiness. Normally a judgment can be removed only if it is set aside or paid in full within a month. Any later payment in full will be marked as 'satisfied'.

14.3 Costs

14.3.1 The indemnity principle

Although the court has a wide discretion, the general rule is that the loser in litigation will be ordered to pay the winner's costs (r 44.3(2)(a)). Note that the winner (the receiving party) is entitled to an 'indemnity' in respect of the costs he has incurred. In other words, he cannot make a profit out of the paying party by seeking more than his solicitor and client costs. This is known as the indemnity principle (not to be confused with the indemnity basis: see **14.3.3**).

The word 'indemnity' is misleading. In reality, the receiving party will not receive a full indemnity in respect of his costs. The paying party will invariably challenge particular items, arguing that the work was unnecessary or was performed in an unnecessarily expensive way (eg, at too high a charge-out rate).

14.3.2 General provisions about costs (Part 44)

At the end of the trial, under r 44.3(1) the court has a discretion as to:

    (a)   whether the costs are payable by one party to another;

    (b)   the amount of those costs; and

    (c)   when they are to be paid.

14.3.2.1 What are costs?

By r 43.2(1) 'costs' include fees, charges, disbursements, expenses and remuneration. These therefore include the charges of solicitors, barristers, experts, etc. Are pre-action costs included? Yes – see r 44.3(6)(d). Additionally, the success fee under a CFA and/or the insurance premium for AEI are within the definition of costs: see further **2.6**.

14.3.2.2 Interest on costs

Is interest payable on costs before judgment? The general rule is that it is not. We have already seen that an exception is when r 36.14(3) applies: see **13.4.5**. Also note that by r 44.3(6)(g) the court has a discretion when awarding costs to award interest on such from any date it sees fit, including before judgment.

14.3.2.3 Factors

Whilst the general rule is that the court will order the unsuccessful party to pay the costs of the successful party, this is only a starting point and the court can make a different order for costs if it thinks it appropriate to do so.

All the circumstances will be considered, including:

(a)   the conduct of all the parties;

(b)   whether a party has succeeded on part of his case, even if he has not been wholly successful; and

(c)   any admissible offer to settle made by a party which is drawn to the court's attention (and which is not an offer to which costs consequences under Part 36 apply).

14.3.2.4   Conduct of the parties

Note that the conduct of the parties includes:

(a)   conduct before, as well as during, the proceedings, and in particular the extent to which the parties followed any relevant pre-action protocol;

(b)   whether it was reasonable for a party to raise, pursue or contest a particular allegation or issue;

(c)   the manner in which a party has pursued or defended his case or a particular allegation or issue; and

(d)   whether a claimant who has succeeded in his claim, in whole or in part, exaggerated his claim.

An example of conduct being taken into account in making a decision on costs is the decision of Jacob J in *Mars UK Ltd v Teknowledge Ltd (No 2)* [1999] Masons CLR 322, ChD. In that case, he indicated that the successful claimant would be likely to receive only 40% of the costs because of the heavy-handed way in which it had rushed into court proceedings against a smaller opponent who had been genuinely attempting to achieve a negotiated settlement. Likewise, parties who make fraudulent claims (see *Shah v Ul-Haq* [2009] EWCA Civ 542) or exaggerated claims (see *Widlake v BAA Ltd* [2009] EWCA Civ 1256) can expect that conduct to be taken into account.

14.3.2.5   Previous costs estimates

What if a costs estimate filed by a party with the allocation questionnaire and/or pre-trial checklist, listing questionnaire (see **9.7**) was inaccurate? Should that party be able to recover only the estimated amount? In *Leigh v Michelin Tyres plc* [2003] EWCA Civ 1766, the Court of Appeal indicated that if there was a substantial difference between the estimated costs and the costs claimed then that difference called for an explanation. What is a 'substantial difference'? The Costs Practice Direction, para 6.5A, states that if there is a difference of 20% or more between the base costs claimed by a receiving party on a detailed assessment and the costs shown in an estimate of costs filed by that party, the receiving party must provide a statement of the reasons for the difference with his bill of costs. If a paying party claims that he reasonably relied on an estimate of costs filed by a receiving party, or wishes to rely upon the costs shown in the estimate in order to dispute the reasonableness or proportionality of the costs claimed, the paying party must serve a statement setting out his case in this regard in his points of dispute (see **14.3.7.6**). Note also that by para 6.6 of the Costs Practice Direction, where there is a difference of 20% or more between the base costs claimed by a receiving party and the costs shown in an estimate of costs filed by that party, and it appears to the court that the receiving party has not provided a satisfactory explanation for that difference; or the paying party reasonably relied on the estimate of costs, the court may regard the difference between the costs claimed and the costs shown in the estimate as evidence that the costs claimed are unreasonable or disproportionate.

14.3.2.6   Different types of orders

The order may reflect the decision on particular issues by providing for payment of, for example:

(a)   a proportion of a party's costs;

(b)   a specified amount of a party's costs;

(c)   costs for a particular period;

(d)   costs incurred before the proceedings began;

(e)   costs of a particular step;

(f)   costs of a distinct part of the proceedings;

(g)   interest on costs from or until a certain date, including a date before judgment.

Orders whereby the winner receives only part of his costs are becoming increasingly common, and a party who raises a number of issues but who succeeds on only some of them can no longer expect to recover the whole of his costs. For example, where both claim and counterclaim succeed, the court may well set off the costs payable on each and direct only payment of the balance.

14.3.3   The basis of assessment (r 44.4)

When the court assesses costs, it will assess those costs either on the standard basis or on the indemnity basis. So, what is the difference?

14.3.3.1   The standard basis

The standard basis will apply unless the court orders otherwise. Costs on this basis must be:

(a)   proportionately and reasonably incurred; and

(b)   proportionate and reasonable in amount.

Any benefit of the doubt is given to the paying party.

The proportionality test on the standard basis determines whether or the not usual test of reasonableness in respect of costs being incurred applies, or whether a stricter test of necessity applies instead. The Court of Appeal, in *Lownds v Home Office: Practice Note* [2002] EWCA Civ 365, [2002] 1 WLR 2450 held that a two-stage approach should be taken on an assessment. First a global approach to the entire costs claimed (ie base costs ignoring VAT), followed by an item-by-item approach. This amounts to taking the following steps and applying the following tests:

(a)   If appropriate, as a preliminary issue, the judge should determine if the receiving party's costs claimed in total are disproportionate. This global approach will indicate whether the total sum claimed is, or appears to be, disproportionate having particular regard to whether the appropriate level of fee earner or counsel was deployed, whether offers to settle had been made, whether unnecessary experts had been instructed, whether an approved pre-action protocol or the Practice Direction on Pre-action Conduct was followed, and the other matters set out in CPR 1998, r 44.5(3) (see **14.3.4**).

Whether the costs incurred were proportionate should be decided having regard to what it was reasonable for the receiving party to believe might be recovered. So the proportionality of the costs incurred by a claimant should be determined having regard to the sum that it was reasonable for him to believe that he might recover at the time he made his claim. The proportionality of the costs incurred by a defendant should be determined having regard to the sum that it was reasonable for him to believe that the claimant might recover, should the claim succeed. This is likely to be the amount that the claimant has claimed, for a defendant will normally be entitled to take a claim at its face value.

So, for example, in the case of *Craven Textile Engineers Ltd v Batley Football Club Ltd* [2000] LTL, 7 July, the claim was for about £9,000. D's costs were put at £6,000 and C's at £17,000. The Court of Appeal commented that C's costs were 'wholly disproportionate'.

(b)   If the costs as a whole are proportionate, all that is normally required is that each item should have been reasonably incurred and that the cost for that item should be reasonable.

So, for example, whilst it would be reasonable to use and incur the cost of counsel at a Court of Appeal hearing, if the issues and evidence were well within the grasp of a competent junior counsel, then only junior counsel's fees would be allowed on an assessment (see *Habib Bank Ltd v Ahmed* [2004] EWCA Civ 805, [2004] BPIR 864, where a leading Queen's Counsel was used).

(c)   If, on the other hand, the costs as a whole appear disproportionate then the court will want to be satisfied that the work in relation to each item was necessary and, if necessary, that the cost of the item was reasonable.

The Court in *Lownds* emphasised that a sensible standard of necessity has to be adopted. This is a standard which takes fully into account the need to make allowances for the different judgments which those responsible for litigation can sensibly come to as to what is required. The danger of setting too high a standard with the benefit of hindsight has to be avoided. While the threshold required to meet necessity is higher than that of reasonableness, it is still a standard that a competent practitioner should be able to achieve without undue difficulty. When a practitioner incurs expenses which are reasonable but not necessary, he may be able to recover those fees and disbursements from his client, but the extra expense which results from conducting litigation in a disproportionate manner cannot be recovered from the other party.

So, for example, in the *Lownds* case, the Court indicated that it had not been necessary for the claimant's solicitors to visit him in prison the eight times that they did and that four visits would have been ample. So the cost of the four unnecessary visits would be disallowed. It was not necessary to incur those costs. Of the four necessary visits, the costs would be recoverable only to the extent that they were reasonable.

In deciding what is necessary, the conduct of the other party is highly relevant. The other party by cooperation can reduce costs; by being uncooperative he can increase costs. If he is uncooperative, that may render necessary costs which would otherwise be unnecessary, and that he should pay the costs for the expense which he has made necessary is perfectly acceptable. Access to justice would be impeded if lawyers felt they could not afford to do what is necessary to conduct the litigation.

14.3.3.2   The indemnity basis

Costs on the indemnity basis are awarded as a penalty, usually to reflect the court's displeasure with the manner in which a party has behaved either pre-action and/or during proceedings. Costs on this basis must be:

(a)   reasonably incurred; and

(b)   reasonable in amount.

Any benefit of the doubt is given to the party receiving the costs.

14.3.3.3   The difference between the two bases

Where there is no doubt over the reasonableness of costs, the difference between the two bases is that in assessing on the standard basis the court will allow only those costs that are proportionate to the matters in issue.

In assessing what is proportionate the court should have regard to:

(a)   the amount of money involved;

(b)   the importance of the case;

(c)   the complexity of the issues and the financial position of each party;

(d)   the factors in r 44.5 (see **14.3.4** below).

As the Costs Practice Direction, para 11.1 makes clear:

In applying the test of proportionality the court will have regard to rule 1.1(2)(c). The relationship between the total of the costs incurred and the financial value of the claim may not be a reliable guide. A fixed percentage cannot be applied in all cases to the value of the claim in order to ascertain whether or not the costs are proportionate.

In addition para 11.2 provides that

In any proceedings there will be costs which will inevitably be incurred and which are necessary for the successful conduct of the case. Solicitors are not required to conduct litigation at rates which are uneconomic. Thus in a modest claim the proportion of costs is likely to be higher than in a large claim, and may even equal or possibly exceed the amount in dispute.

Paragraph 11.3 also recognises that:

Where a trial takes place, the time taken by the court in dealing with a particular issue may not be an accurate guide to the amount of time properly spent by the legal or other representatives in preparation for the trial of that issue.

The great majority of costs orders are awarded on the standard basis. An award on the indemnity basis is usually reserved for occasions where there has been culpable behaviour on the part of the paying party (for example, pursuing an unjustified claim or defence, or where there has been non-compliance with court orders). We also saw it applied at **13.4.6** in respect of r 36.14(3). Where the court does not specify in its order which basis is to apply, the standard basis is used.

14.3.3.4 Summary of the standard basis

Consider the following questions in order to identify and apply the correct tests on a standard basis assessment:

Question 1: are the entire costs claimed by the receiving party proportionate?
- If yes, go to question 2.
- If no, go to question 4.

Question 2: as to each item claimed, was it reasonable to incur the cost?
- If yes, go to question 3.
- If no, the cost is not recoverable from the paying party.

Question 3: is the item reasonable in amount?
- If yes, it is recoverable in that sum.
- If no, it is recoverable from the paying party only in the sum the costs judge determines as reasonable.

Question 4: where the entire costs claimed by the receiving party are disproportionate, as to each item claimed, was it necessary to incur the cost?
- If yes, go to question 5.
- If no, the cost is not recoverable from the paying party.

Question 5: is the item reasonable in amount?
- If yes, it is recoverable in that sum.
- If no, it is recoverable from the paying party only in the sum the costs judge determines as reasonable.

Also see the flowchart in **Appendix C(20)**.

14.3.4 Relevant factors in assessing the amount of costs (r 44.5)

As well as the basis (ie, standard or indemnity) on which the court is assessing costs, the court must also take into account the following factors in deciding the amount of costs the receiving party is entitled to:

(a)   the conduct of all the parties, including conduct before as well as during the proceedings and the efforts made, if any, before and during the proceedings in order to try to resolve the dispute;

(b)   the amount or value of any money or property involved;

(c)   the importance of the matter to all the parties;

(d)   the particular complexity of the matter or the difficulty or novelty of the questions raised;

(e)   the skill, effort, specialised knowledge and responsibility involved;

(f)   the time spent on the case;

(g)   the place where and the circumstances in which work or any part of it was done.

14.3.4.1   Conduct and ADR

As to factor (a), parties must seriously consider ADR proposals made by the other side. In *Dunnett v Railtrack plc (in Railway Administration)* [2002] EWCA Civ 303, [2002] 2 All ER 850, the Court of Appeal deprived the successful party of its costs because it unreasonably refused to mediate before the appeal was heard. The Court of Appeal in *Halsey v Milton Keynes General NHS Trust* [2004] EWCA Civ 576, [2004] 4 All ER 920, laid down guidelines in this area. It held that there is no presumption in favour of mediation. The question whether a party has acted unreasonably in refusing ADR must be determined having regard to all the circumstances of the particular case, including:

(i)   the nature of the dispute;

(ii)   the merits of the case;

(iii)   the extent to which other settlement methods have been attempted;

(iv)   whether the costs of the ADR would be disproportionately high;

(v)   whether any delay in setting up and attending the ADR would have been prejudicial; and

(vi)   whether the ADR had a reasonable prospect of success.

It is not always easy to decide when mediation should occur. This was recognised in *Nigel Witham Ltd v Smith* [2008] EWHC 12. The court accepted that a premature mediation simply wastes time. It can also sometimes lead to a hardening of positions on both sides which makes any subsequent attempt at settlement doomed to fail. Conversely, a delay in any mediation until after full particulars and documents have been exchanged can mean that the costs incurred become the principal obstacle to a successful mediation. The solution is to identify the point when the detail of the claim and the response are known to both sides, but before the costs that are incurred in reaching that stage become so great that a settlement is no longer possible. Note that in an exceptional case where mediation occurs very late and its chances of success are very poor, if the successful party in the litigation unreasonably delayed in consenting to the mediation then this may lead to an adverse costs order. See further **3.7**.

Is a party who agrees to mediation but then causes the mediation to fail by taking an unreasonable position to be treated the same as a party who unreasonably refuses to mediate? Yes, held Jack J in *Earl of Malmesbury v Strutt & Parker* [2008] EWHC 424.

14.3.4.2   Time is money

As to factor (f) at **14.3.4** above, regional hourly guideline figures (for a summary assessment) are normally agreed annually between the Law Society and the Supreme Court Costs Office. Examples appear at **Appendix A(21)**.

Judges bring a vast experience to an assessment of costs. A judge will be familiar with the typical charges imposed by local solicitors, counsel, experts, etc. Even on a detailed assessment, the examples given at **Appendix A(21)** may at least be a useful starting point. The complete guidance (to be found on the Court Service website – see **1.5**) has some specific examples that give a flavour of how a judge would assess the reasonableness of certain costs. In relation to a contested case management directions hearing, the following guidance is given:

> If these hearings are attended by solicitor and Counsel the number of hours which it is reasonable to presume that the solicitor will undertake (in respect of preparation, attendance, travel in Central London and waiting) is 4 hours for a one hour appointment and 7.5 hours for a half day appointment. It is reasonable to presume that Counsel who has between 5 and 10 years' experience merits a fee of approximately £550 (exclusive of VAT) for a one hour appointment and merits a fee of approximately £880 (exclusive of VAT) for a half day appointment.

> If these hearings were attended by a solicitor without Counsel it is reasonable to presume that the total number of hours the solicitor will spend (in respect of preparation, attendance, travel in Central London and waiting) is 5 hours for a one hour appointment and 10 hours for a half day appointment.

14.3.5 Procedure for assessing costs

Where the court orders one party to pay costs to another, the court will either make a summary assessment of costs there and then, or order detailed assessment of the costs by the costs officer. (The costs officer is the district judge or, in London, the costs judge.)

The general rule is that the court should, unless there is good reason not to do so (eg, where the paying party shows substantial grounds for disputing the sum claimed for costs that cannot be dealt with summarily, or there is insufficient time to carry out a summary assessment), make a summary assessment of the costs:

(a)   at the conclusion of the trial of a case which has been dealt with on the fast track, in which case the order will deal with the costs of the whole claim; and

(b)   at the conclusion of any other hearing, which has lasted not more than one day, in which case the order will deal with the costs of the application or matter to which the hearing related. If this hearing disposes of the claim, the order may deal with the costs of the whole claim;

(c)   in certain hearings in the Court of Appeal.

To assist the court to make a summary assessment, the parties must file and serve at least 24 hours before an interim hearing a breakdown of their costs – see Costs Form N260 Statement of Costs for Summary Assessment at **Appendix A(13)**.

14.3.6 Fast track costs (Part 46)

14.3.6.1 Trial costs

In fast track cases, there is a specified figure for the advocate for preparing for and appearing at the trial.

Value of the claim	Amount of fast track trial costs which the court may award
Up to £3,000	£485
More than £3,000 but not more than £10,000	£690
More than £10,000 but not more than £15,000	£1,035
More than £15,000	£1,650

The court may not award more or less than the amount shown except in limited circumstances. For example, an additional £345 may be awarded where it is necessary for a legal representative to attend to assist the advocate. Therefore, if a barrister is instructed to conduct the fast track trial and a representative from the solicitor's office attends court with the barrister, £345 may be awarded for that attendance provided the court thinks that it was necessary.

14.3.6.2   Valuing the claim

If the claimant succeeds then the value of the claim is based on the amount awarded, excluding any interest or reduction for contributory negligence.

If the defendant was successful then the value of the claim is based on the amount claimed by the claimant.

Improper or unreasonable behaviour by one of the parties may lead to a departure from the specified figure.

If there is more than one claimant or defendant but the successful parties used only one advocate, there will be only one award. If the successful parties used separate advocates, there will be a separate award for each party.

14.3.6.3   Summary assessment of other fast track costs

The fast track trial costs are in addition to the rest of the costs in bringing the claim. The usual practice on fast track cases is for these to be summarily assessed at the end of the case. In fast track cases, therefore, the party should always file and serve a statement of costs (see **10.3.4**) at least 48 hours prior to the hearing. Because the costs of the entire case are being summarily assessed by the court there and then, and because counsel will not be familiar with the way in which solicitors' costs are incurred in preparing the case for trial, there is a strong argument for using a solicitor advocate rather than counsel at the trial of a fast track claim. Where the receiving party has funded the litigation by way of a CFA the court will as part of its summary assessment assess whether the paying party should pay some or all of any success fee due to the winner's solicitor and any AEI premium that was paid (see **14.3.8**).

14.3.7   Multi-track cases

14.3.7.1   Procedure

In multi-track cases there are no specified trial costs. Although the judge does have the power to make a summary assessment of costs, in multi-track cases the court will usually order detailed assessment.

Detailed assessment proceedings are commenced by the receiving party serving on the paying party:

(a)   notice of commencement in Form N252 (see **Appendix A(15)**); and

(b)   a copy of the bill of costs.

This action must be taken within three months of the date of the judgment or order.

14.3.7.2   Bill of costs

The bill of costs is a rather complex document, which should be prepared in the form described by section 4 of the Costs Practice Direction. A copy of an example of a bill of costs appears at **Appendix A(16)**. Preparing a bill of costs is a specialist task, usually undertaken by either an in-house costs draftsman, or a firm of independent costs draftsmen. A claim can be included for the reasonable costs of preparing and checking the bill.

The first part of the bill sets out background information, including a brief description of the history of the claim and a statement of the grade of fee earner(s) involved (together with the hourly charge-out rate claimed for each). If the litigation was funded by way of a CFA this will be stated, together with the success fee that was agreed. Similarly, if the receiving party has been publicly funded, the relevant details must be set out in the background information.

14.3.7.3   Categories of work

The main body of the bill comprises a breakdown of the work performed, divided into different categories of work as set out in para 4.6 of the Costs Practice Direction:

(1)   attendances on the court and counsel;

(2)   attendances on and communications with the receiving party;

(3)   attendances on and communications with witnesses including any expert witness;

(4)   attendances to inspect any property or place for the purposes of the proceedings;

(5)   attendances on and with other persons;

(6)   communications with the court and with counsel;

(7)   work done on documents: preparing and considering documentation, including documentation relating to pre-action protocols where appropriate, work done in connection with arithmetical calculations of compensation and/or interest and time spent collating documents;

(8)   work done in connection with negotiations with a view to settlement (if not already covered under another head);

(9)   attendances on and communications with agents and work done by them;

(10) other work done which was of or incidental to the proceedings and which is not already covered above.

The work done within each of these heads is set out chronologically in numbered items. As can be seen from the model bill at **Appendix A(16)**, the information is presented in columns, with the amount claimed for profit costs, disbursements and VAT being shown separately.

'Communications', in the context of para 4.6, means letters out, e-mails out and telephone calls. Most will be classed as routine and charged at a standard rate of six minutes (thus a routine letter drafted by an assistant solicitor charging a rate of £140 per hour would be charged at £14). Where letters out, e-mails out or telephone calls are sufficiently complex and/or lengthy not to be classed as routine, they may be charged according to the time actually spent on them. Letters in and e-mails received are not charged for separately.

Local travelling expenses (generally train or taxi fares, petrol costs, etc, within a 10-mile radius of the court) cannot be claimed, but the solicitor is entitled to claim at up to the hourly rate for time spent travelling and waiting (depending on the amount he charged his client).

The cost of postage, couriers, out-going telephone calls, fax and telex messages will in general not be allowed, but the court may exceptionally in its discretion allow such expenses in unusual circumstances or where the cost is unusually heavy.

14.3.7.4   Costs associated with detailed assessment

Note that the bill of costs must not contain any claims in respect of costs or court fees which relate solely to the detailed assessment proceedings. A claim may only be made for the reasonable costs of preparing and checking the bill of costs. The award of costs at a detailed assessment is made at its conclusion.

14.3.7.5   Late commencement of the assessment process

Permission is not required to commence detailed assessment proceedings out of time, but if the receiving party does not commence the process within three months, the court may disallow all or part of the costs, or disallow all or part of any interest accruing on the costs. Since interest will be accumulating on the costs even though they have not yet been quantified, the usual sanction, however, is to disallow all or part of the interest that would otherwise be payable to the receiving party (r 47.8). For a case where both costs and interest were disallowed, see *Haji-Ioannou v Frangos* [2006] EWCA Civ 1663.

It is open to the paying party to apply for an order that the receiving party lose their right to costs unless detailed assessment proceedings are commenced by a certain date.

14.3.7.6 Challenging the bill

The paying party has 21 days from service of the notice of commencement to serve points of dispute on the receiving party (r 47.9). A specimen can be found at **Appendix A(17)**. If he does not do so, the receiving party can apply for a default costs certificate which will include an order to pay the costs. The default costs certificate will be set aside only if good reason is shown by the paying party. If the paying party serves the points of dispute late (but before the default certificate is issued), the paying party may not be heard further unless the court gives permission.

On service of the points of dispute, the receiving party may serve a reply within 21 days (r 47.13). The receiving party must file a request for an assessment hearing within three months of the expiry of the period for commencing detailed assessment proceedings.

There will then be a detailed assessment hearing, at which the court will decide what costs are to be paid. The receiving party must, within 14 days of the hearing, file a completed bill showing the amount of costs finally due.

The receiving party will normally be entitled to the costs of the detailed assessment proceedings, but the court may take into account:

(a)   the conduct of the parties;

(b)   the amount of any reduction from the original amount claimed;

(c)   the reasonableness of claiming or challenging any particular item.

The court must also take into account any written offer expressed to be 'without prejudice save as to the costs of the detailed assessment proceedings' (see **14.3.7.10**).

No time is specified for service of such an offer, but any offer made more than 14 days after:

(a)   service of the notice of commencement (paying party);

(b)   service of the points of dispute (receiving party),

will be given less weight unless good reason is shown.

14.3.7.7 At the assessment

Typically at an assessment, the following areas of costs are targeted by a paying party.

The hourly charging rate

A paying party will often argue for a reduction in the receiving party's solicitors' hourly charges if these exceed the guideline figures – see **Appendix A(21)**. Whilst the guideline rates are general approximations rather than scale figures, they are often the starting and finish points.

If the receiving party's solicitors are from an area that has higher hourly charging rates than the court where the case is proceeding, the paying party will argue for a reduction. The receiving party will have to show that it was reasonable to use those solicitors rather than a local, cheaper firm (see *Truscott v Truscott, Wraith v Sheffield Forgemasters* [1998] 1 WLR 132).

The status of the fee earner who did the work

A paying party will often accept that it was necessary or reasonable (as appropriate) for work to have been done, but will argue that the lawyer used was too senior, eg a partner should not prepare a simple list of documents, that could have been done by an assistant solicitor.

So the grade of fee earner used has to be justified as being reasonable. The grades are set out in the guideline charges (see above). Therefore, in a straightforward case the paying party may well argue that a Grade A or B fee earner can be justified only for a small amount of time to supervise and oversee the case, and that most of the work should have been done by a Grade C or D fee earner.

The length of time it took to do the work

A paying party will often argue that the time it took for a piece of work to be completed was excessive, eg in a very simple case with only a small number of documents, you would not expect preparation of a list of documents to take more than one hour.

No entitlement under CPR

Note that other, somewhat technical points can sometimes be made. Often this will be a challenge to an item that the paying party argues is not allowed under the Costs Practice Direction, para 4.16, which provides as follows:

(1) Routine letters out, routine e-mails out and routine telephone calls will in general be allowed on a unit basis of 6 minutes each, the charge being calculated by reference to the appropriate hourly rate. The unit charge for letters out and e-mails out in will include perusing and considering the relevant letters in or e-mails in and accordingly no separate charge is to be made for in-coming letters.

(2) The court may, in its discretion, allow an actual time charge for preparation of electronic communications other than e-mails sent by solicitors, which properly amount to attendances provided that the time taken has been recorded.

(3) Local travelling expenses incurred by solicitors will not be allowed. The definition of 'local' is a matter for the discretion of the court. While no absolute rule can be laid down, as a matter of guidance, 'local' will, in general, be taken to mean within a radius of 10 miles from the court dealing with the case at the relevant time. Where travelling and waiting time is claimed, this should be allowed at the rate agreed with the client unless this is more than the hourly rate on the assessment.

(4) The cost of postage, couriers, out-going telephone calls, fax and telex messages will in general not be allowed but the court may exceptionally in its discretion allow such expenses in unusual circumstances or where the cost is unusually heavy.

(5) The cost of making copies of documents will not in general be allowed but the court may exceptionally in its discretion make an allowance for copying in unusual circumstances or where the documents copied are unusually numerous in relation to the nature of the case. Where this discretion is invoked the number of copies made, their purpose and the costs claimed for them must be set out in the bill.

(6) Agency charges as between principal solicitors and their agents will be dealt with on the principle that such charges, where appropriate, form part of the principal solicitor's charges.

14.3.7.8   Appeals

Where the assessment was by a judge, the appeals process is governed by Part 52. An appeal from a detailed or summary assessment by a district judge is made to a circuit judge. An appeal from an assessment by a circuit judge is made to a High Court judge. Permission to appeal is required either from the original court, or from the appeal court. If permission is not sought at the original assessment, it must be sought from the appeal court within 14 days. The appeal takes the form of a review of the original decision, rather than a re-hearing.

Part 52 does not apply where the detailed assessment was performed by an officer of the court. In this case, r 47.20 applies (as supplemented by paras 47 and 48 of PD 47). Permission to appeal is not required and the appeal takes the form of a rehearing, either by a costs judge or a district judge of the High Court.

14.3.7.9   Agreeing costs

Rather than go through the detailed assessment procedure, it is always open to the parties to agree the figure for costs payable by one side to another. Very often, the parties will attempt to agree a figure for costs, and proceed to a detailed assessment only if they are unable to reach agreement.

14.3.7.10   Offers to settle a detailed assessment

Costs of a detailed assessment can be significant. A receiving or a paying party can make a written offer to settle under r 47.19(1). The offer must be expressed to be without prejudice save as to the costs of the detailed assessment proceedings. The fact of the offer must not be communicated to the costs judge until the question of costs of the detailed assessment proceedings falls to be decided. The court will take such an offer into account in deciding who should pay the costs of those proceedings. So if a paying party offers to pay a total of £20,000 costs which is refused, but on the detailed assessment the receiving party is awarded less than that amount, the receiving party will usually be ordered to pay the paying party's costs of dealing with the detailed assessment.

14.3.7.11   Interim orders

The detailed assessment of costs procedure initially means that there will be some delay in the successful party receiving their costs from the unsuccessful party. Rule 44.3(8) of CPR 1998 allows the court at trial or on a later application to order an interim payment of part of these costs, and in *Mars UK Ltd v Teknowledge Ltd (No 2)* [1999] Masons CLR 322, Jacob J indicated that the court should make an order for the interim payment of costs in most cases.

14.3.8   Conditional fee agreements and after-the-event insurance

A winning party who has funded the litigation by a CFA is likely to have agreed to pay his solicitor a success fee, and may also have paid a premium for AEI. Where a costs order is made in that party's favour, the costs payable include the success fee and premium. These items are referred to as the 'additional liability' to distinguish them from the base costs.

14.3.8.1   Limits on recoverability

Rule 44.3B sets out a number of limits on the recovery of the additional liability, including that the following may not be recovered:

(a)   Any proportion of the success fee that compensates the solicitor for costs resulting from the postponement of the payment of his fees and expenses. For example, the solicitor will sometimes have funded the disbursements by way of a loan. Any part of the success fee intended to compensate the solicitor for the interest payable on the loan is not recoverable from the paying party.

(b)   The success fee and/or AEI premium applicable to any period during which the required notice of funding had not been filed (see **2.4.3.3**).

(c)   Any success fee and/or AEI premium if the receiving party has failed to disclose the required risk assessment information (see below).

Where (b) or (c) applies the receiving party may apply for relief from the sanction (see **9.4.2**).

14.3.8.2   Reasonableness

In addition, the paying party is, of course, liable for the success fee and AEI premium only to the extent that these are reasonable and (where the standard basis applies) proportionate. The costs judge must take into account the facts and circumstances as they reasonably appeared to the receiving party's solicitors when the CFA and/or AEI policy were/was entered into. Section 11 of the Costs Practice Direction makes clear, however, that the success fee should not be reduced simply because when it is added to the base costs the total appears disproportionate.

Relevant factors include the extent of the risk that the fees and expenses would not be payable, whether the solicitor was liable under the CFA for any disbursements and what other methods of financing the case were available.

When is it reasonable to incur an AEI policy premium? In *Burgess v J Breheny Contracts Ltd* [2009] EWHC 90131, Master Howorth indicated that when the policy was taken out there must be real risks against which it is proper to insure. In the case, although the defendant had admitted primary liability, causation was still in issue. The Master found that it was proper for the claimant to insure against such matters as the claimant failing to establish causation, the risk of the defendant withdrawing its admission of breach of duty and the risk of the defendant making a Part 36 offer which the claimant did not accept and failed to beat. If it is reasonable to incur a premium, how should a paying party set about challenging the amount? In the *Burgess* case the Master stressed that, like many judges, he did not have the expertise to assess the reasonableness of the size of the AEI premium and that to do so the paying party should adduce expert evidence.

14.3.8.3   Formalities

Where the court has ordered a detailed assessment, the receiving party must on commencing those proceedings file and serve on the paying party relevant details of the additional liability, including a statement of the reasons for the success fee, together with a copy of the AEI certificate giving details of the extent of the cover provided and the premium paid (see section 32 of the Costs Practice Direction).

Where the court decides to perform a summary assessment of the additional liability, the party must make available:

(a)   the Form N251;

(b)   all estimates and statements of costs that have been filed during the course of the claim (since the court can take these into account when deciding the reasonableness of the bill); and

(c)   a copy of the risk assessment prepared when the CFA was entered into (see section 14 of the Costs Practice Direction).

Under section 20 of the Costs Practice Direction, any amount of the success fee which is disallowed on assessment ceases to be payable by the receiving party unless the court orders otherwise.

14.3.9   Costs only proceedings

What if the parties to a dispute:

(a)   have reached an agreement on all issues (including which party is to pay the costs);

(b)   made or confirmed that agreement in writing;

(c)   but have failed to agree the amount of those costs; and

(d)   no proceedings have been started?

The answer is provided by r 44.12A. Either party to the agreement may start proceedings by issuing a claim form in accordance with Part 8 (see **8.3**). The claim form must contain or be accompanied by the agreement or confirmation.

14.3.10   As a paying party, what should you look for in the opponent's bill of costs?

When scrutinising an opponent's bill of costs, consider the following:

(1)   Check the scope of the costs order – are there any limits (see **14.3.2.6**)?

(2)   What is the basis of assessment – standard or indemnity (see **14.3.3**)? Where standard, consider overall proportionality first and identify the correct tests (see **14.3.3.4**).

(3)   What is the effect, if any, of any interim costs orders (see **10.3**)?

(4)   Was any CFA and/or AEI notice given pre-action and/or during proceedings (see **14.3.8.1** and **2.4.3.3**)?

(5)   Check the costs estimates. Is there a 20% or more difference (see **14.3.2.5**)?

(6)   As a rough guide, compare solicitors' hourly rates and counsels' fees with the summary assessment rates (see **14.3.4.2** and **Appendix A(21)**).

(7)   Check compliance with the Costs Practice Direction as to content. Are all items claimed allowable (see **14.3.7**)?

Chapter 15

Enforcement of Money Judgments

15.1 Introduction

Once a party has obtained a judgment against his opponent, the opponent will usually pay the amount he has been ordered to pay without any further action being necessary. If, however, the losing party fails to pay the amount he has been ordered to pay, the winning party will have to take steps to enforce the judgment debt. The judgment will not be enforced by the court automatically – unless the winning party takes enforcement action, he will not receive the money that he was awarded. The winning party will have to consider with his solicitor the best method of enforcing payment.

Where the opponent is not insured, the question of enforcement is one which should be considered before proceedings are ever commenced, because it is obviously not worth obtaining a judgment against a party who does not have the means to pay. The solicitor should be satisfied that the defendant's whereabouts are known, that prima facie he has the means to pay the amount in issue, and that he has assets which can be taken from him to enforce payment if necessary.

The CPR 1998 themselves do not yet deal fully with all enforcement methods and so it is occasionally necessary to look at the 'old' High Court and county court rules, contained respectively in Schs 1 and 2 to the CPR 1998.

15.1.1 Enforcing a judgment against partnership property

Practice Direction 70, para 6A.1 provides that a judgment made against a partnership may be enforced against any property of the partnership within the jurisdiction.

A judgment against a partnership can also be enforced against any person who is not a limited partner and who either:

(a) acknowledged service of the claim form as a partner; or

(b) having been served as a partner with the claim form, failed to acknowledge service of it; or

(c) admitted in his statement of case that he is or was a partner at a material time; or

(d) was found by the court to have been a partner at a material time.

Can proceedings be taken against partnership property for a partner's separate judgment debt? Yes – see s 23 of the Partnership Act 1890.

15.2   Interest on judgment debts

15.2.1   High Court judgments

Under the Judgments Act 1838, interest accrues on all High Court judgments from the date judgment is pronounced. The current rate of interest is 8% per annum. Where judgment is entered for damages to be assessed, interest begins to run from the date when damages are finally assessed or agreed (ie, the date of the final judgment). Interest on an order for the payment of costs runs from the date of the judgment, not from the date of the final costs certificate following a detailed assessment (see **14.3.7**). Therefore, interest is accruing on the costs before the paying party knows how much he has to pay in costs. He can alleviate the situation by making a payment on account of costs.

15.2.2   County court judgments

Under s 74 of the CCA 1984, interest accrues on county court judgments of £5,000 or more. The current rate of interest is 8% per annum.

Where, under the terms of the judgment, payment is deferred, or to be in instalments, interest will not accrue until that date, or until an instalment falls due.

Where enforcement proceedings are taken, the judgment debt ceases to carry interest unless the enforcement proceedings fail to produce any payment, in which case interest will continue to accrue on the judgment debt as if the enforcement proceedings had never been issued. 'Enforcement proceedings' include an application for an order to obtain information from the judgment debtor (see **15.4.2**). If an attachment of earnings order is in force, interest does not accrue.

Care needs to be taken as regards interest in the county court. If enforcement proceedings are taken and anything at all is recovered, the balance of the debt will become interest free.

When applying to enforce interest in the county court, a party must supply a certificate setting out the amount of interest claimed, the sum on which it is claimed, the dates from and to which interest has accrued, and the rate of interest applied.

15.3   Tracing the other party

There are a number of methods of enforcement available, but before commencing enforcement proceedings the other party's whereabouts need to be established. If the other party's whereabouts are not known, consideration should be given to employing an enquiry agent to trace him. If this is to be done, the enquiry agent should be given as much information as possible to assist his enquiries (eg, the other party's last known address, his last known employer, details of any known relatives). A limit should be placed on the costs which may be incurred by the enquiry agent, so that a disproportionate amount of money is not wasted in attempts to trace the defendant, which might be unsuccessful in the end. In practice, these enquiries are likely to have been made at the outset of the case, since there is little point in suing a defendant you cannot trace (see **15.1** above).

15.4   Investigating the judgment debtor's means

The next thing to consider is what assets the judgment debtor has, since the method of enforcement chosen will depend upon what type of assets are available to pay the judgment debt. The winning party may already have enough information about his opponent for a decision to be taken, otherwise further enquiries will have to be made.

There are two main ways to investigate the judgment debtor's assets: the winning party can either instruct an enquiry agent to make investigations; or he can apply to the court for an order to obtain information from the judgment debtor. However, do not forget that pre-action it is usual to make a bankruptcy search against an individual and a company search against a company (see **2.6.1.2**). Those should be updated now.

15.4.1 Instructing an enquiry agent

The enquiry agent should be given as much information as possible to assist his enquiries, and a limit should be placed on the amount of costs to be incurred, to avoid spending a disproportionate amount on these preliminary enquiries. Even so, this method of carrying out the investigations is likely to be more expensive than applying to the court for an order to obtain information from the judgment debtor. However, the enquiry agent may be able to discover assets which are not disclosed at the hearing, and may produce results more quickly, depending on the speed with which the hearing can take place at the court.

15.4.2 Obtaining information from judgment debtor (Part 71)

An order to obtain information from a judgment debtor is a court order requiring the judgment debtor to attend before an officer of the court to be examined on oath as to his means. The judgment creditor obtains the order by making an application without notice. The purpose of the order is to assist the judgment creditor in deciding on the most appropriate method for enforcing the judgment.

15.4.2.1 How to make the application – PD 71

(a)   The judgment creditor must complete and file an application notice in Form N316 if the debtor is an individual, and N316A if an officer of a company or other corporation is to be questioned. The application notice must contain a statement of truth.

(b)   Practice Direction 71, para 1 sets out the matters to be contained in the application notice. These include the name and address of the judgment debtor, the judgment or order the creditor is seeking to enforce and the amount presently owed. If the creditor wishes the examination to be conducted by a judge this must be stated in the application notice, together with reasons. If the creditor wishes the debtor to bring any specific documents to court these must be identified.

(c)   Rules 71.3 and 71.4 set out the procedure for service of the order and for payment of the judgment debtor's travelling expenses to court.

15.4.2.2 The hearing

(a)   The hearing will usually take place in the court for the area where the debtor resides or carries on business.

(b)   The examination will be conducted by an officer of the court, or a judge if considered appropriate.

(c)   Where the examination is conducted by a court officer, standard questions to be asked are set out in Appendices A and B to PD 71. The judgment creditor may attend the hearing. If the judgment creditor wishes to ask any additional questions these should be set out in the application notice. The officer will make a written record of the responses given by the debtor, who will be invited to read and sign it at the end of the hearing. If a solicitor attends the hearing, fixed costs may be awarded (r 45.6).

(d)   Where the hearing is to be conducted before a judge the standard questions are not used. The questions will be asked by the judgment creditor and the hearing will be tape-recorded. The judge may make a summary assessment of costs at the end of the hearing (r 45.6).

(e)   If the debtor fails to attend court, or having attended court refuses to take an oath or affirm or answer questions, a committal order may be made against him.

15.5 Methods of enforcement

There are four common methods of enforcement to choose from:

(a)   execution (ie, seizure and sale of the debtor's goods);

(b)   charging order (ie, a charge on the debtor's land or securities);

(c)   third party debt order (ie, an order requiring a third party who owes money to the debtor to pay it directly to the creditor);

(d)   attachment of earnings order (ie, an order requiring the debtor's employer to make deductions from his earnings and pay them to the creditor).

The solicitor must decide, in the light of the information he has obtained about the judgment debtor, which method of enforcement is most suitable.

Each method of enforcement mentioned is now considered in more detail.

15.5.1   Execution (RSC Ord 46 and 47; CCR Ord 26, r 1)

This process enables a High Court Enforcement Officer (HCEO) or court bailiff (county court) to seize and sell the debtor's goods to pay the judgment debt and costs, and the costs of enforcement. The items seized are sold by public auction. After deducting the expenses of sale, the judgment debt and costs are paid, and any surplus proceeds are returned to the debtor.

As a general rule the HCEO or bailiff cannot force entry to a debtor's home, although he may be able to break into business premises if there is no living accommodation attached and he believes the debtor's goods are inside. Second-hand furniture and electrical items are normally taken only if they are likely to sell well at auction. In addition to the usual contents of a home or business premises (although note certain items are exempt: see **15.5.1.4**), any money, banknotes, bills of exchange, promissory notes, bonds, specialties or securities for money belonging to the debtor can be taken.

15.5.1.1   Choice of court

High Court

A party who has obtained a judgment in the High Court may issue a writ of fieri facias in that court, regardless of the amount to be enforced.

County court

Where a party has obtained judgment in a county court, and the amount to be enforced by execution is £5,000 or more, it must be enforced in the High Court unless the proceedings originated under the Consumer Credit Act 1974.

Where the sum to be enforced is less than £600, it must be enforced in a county court.

In the case of county court judgments of £600 or more but less than £5,000, the judgment creditor can choose whether to issue execution in the High Court or the county court. If he chooses to use the High Court, the county court judgment must first be transferred to the High Court. The advantage of this is that interest then accrues on the judgment debt.

A party with a county court judgment for £5,000 or more will be able to issue a part warrant in that court, for example where an instalment order or the final balance is less than £5,000.

15.5.1.2   Procedure in the High Court

(a)   The judgment creditor completes two copies of a writ of fieri facias and a praecipe for a writ of fieri facias.

(b)   He delivers these documents to the court office, together with the judgment and the costs officer's certificate where the enforcement relates to costs.

(c)   The court seals the writ and returns one copy of it to the judgment creditor.

(d)   The judgment creditor forwards the sealed copy writ to the HCEO for the county where the debtor resides or carries on business, to be executed.

15.5.1.3   Procedure in the county court

(a)   The judgment creditor completes the form of request for a warrant of execution.

(b)   The judgment creditor files this at court, together with the fee.

(c)   The warrant is executed by the bailiff of the county court for the district where the debtor resides or carries on business.

15.5.1.4   Items exempt from seizure

Certain items cannot be seized. These are:

(a)   goods on hire or hire-purchase;

(b)   tools, books, vehicles and other items of equipment which are necessary to the debtor for use personally in his job or business;

(c)   clothing, bedding, furniture, household equipment and provisions which are necessary for satisfying the basic domestic needs of the debtor and his family.

'Necessary items' are items which are so essential that without them a debtor could not continue his existing job or business. This is not always clear-cut. For example, in *Brookes v Harris* [1995] 1 WLR 918, the defendant had a substantial collection of records, tapes and compact discs. He was the presenter of musical programmes on radio and television, and it was held that his collection constituted tools of his trade and was therefore exempt from execution.

Motor vehicles

It should be the exception rather than the rule that a debtor is allowed to retain a motor vehicle as a necessary item. It is for the debtor to satisfy the HCEO or bailiff that the vehicle is necessary to allow him to continue his job or business. The fact that a debtor claims to need a vehicle to get to and from his place of work should not by itself be considered grounds to exempt the vehicle. The HCEO or bailiff must be satisfied that no reasonable alternative is available.

Household items

Items such as stereo equipment, televisions, videos, or microwave ovens where there is also a conventional cooker, are not considered to be necessary for satisfying the basic domestic needs of the debtor and his family.

Execution can be levied against goods owned by the judgment debtor jointly with another person(s). This power is derived from the common law (see *Farrar v Beswick* (1836) 1 M & W 682) and in these circumstances the HCEO or bailiff will account to any joint owner(s) for their share of the proceeds of sale.

It is always helpful to inform the HCEO or bailiff of specific items which could be seized, for example tell him the make, type and registration number of the debtor's car.

15.5.1.5   'Walking possession'

In practice, the debtor's goods are not usually removed immediately. The debtor and the HCEO or bailiff will enter into an agreement for 'walking possession'. This means that the HCEO or bailiff agrees not to remove the goods at once and, in return, the debtor agrees not to dispose of them or permit them to be moved. This gives the debtor a further opportunity to pay the sum due, and he may apply for suspension of the writ or warrant. If this is granted, it means that the writ of fieri facias/warrant of execution is suspended on condition that the debtor pays the sum due by specified instalments.

The HCEO or bailiff must not effect a forcible entry to any residential premises and must not take goods from the debtor's person.

15.5.2 Charging order on land (Part 73)

A judgment creditor may apply to the court for an order charging the judgment debtor's land with the amount due under a judgment. A charging order can also be made in respect of land which the debtor owns jointly with another person, in which case the order is a charge upon the debtor's beneficial interest, rather than upon the land itself.

15.5.2.1 Restrictions on making a charging order

Where the court has made an order for payment of the sum due by instalments, a charging order will not be made as long as the debtor is up to date with the instalment payments.

15.5.2.2 Registration of the charging order

Once a charging order has been made, it should be registered if possible.

If the judgment debtor is the sole owner of the land, the charging order can be registered at the Land Charges Department as an order affecting land if the title is unregistered, or at HM Land Registry as a notice if the land is registered.

Where the land is jointly owned, the debtor technically has an interest only in the proceeds of sale under the trust for sale, rather than an interest in the land itself. Therefore, in the case of unregistered land, the charging order is not registrable because it is not an order relating to land. In the case of registered land, the charging order can be protected by entry of a restriction on the register.

If the creditor does not know whether the land is registered, he should make an Index Map Search before applying for a charging order. If the creditor does not know whether the land is jointly owned, he should make a search of the title in the case of registered land, again before applying for a charging order.

15.5.2.3 Notice

Whether or not the charging order is registered, written notice of it should be given to any prior chargee(s) to prevent any tacking of later advances. A search may be necessary at HM Land Registry (registered land) or the Land Charges Department (unregistered land) to discover the existence of prior incumbrances.

Once this has been done, the creditor has security for the debt, but he still has not obtained the sum due.

15.5.2.4 Order for sale

In order to obtain the money, the creditor can apply to the court for an order for sale of the land charged. The judgment will then be satisfied out of the proceeds of sale.

15.5.2.5 Choice of court

The rules specify the court in which the application should be made. This will usually be the court in which the order being enforced was made.

15.5.2.6 Procedure

(a) The judgment creditor must file an application notice in the prescribed form (N379) containing the information specified in PD 73, para 1.2. This includes details of the judgment debt, the land over which the charging order is sought, and the names and addresses of any other person on whom the interim order will be served. This will include parties with a prior charge over the property. The application notice must be verified by a statement of truth.

(b) The judgment creditor must also file a draft interim charging order.

(c) The district judge considers the application in the absence of the parties and, if satisfied, makes the interim charging order.

(d) The interim charging order should be registered either at the Land Charges Department, or at HM Land Registry if registration is possible.

(e) The interim charging order, indorsed with a hearing date, together with a copy of the supporting affidavit or witness statement, must be served on the judgment debtor at least 21 days before the return day. Ordinary service is required.

(f) At the hearing the court can make a final charging order confirming the interim charging order, discharge the interim order, deal with issues in dispute between the parties or direct a trial of any such issues – r 73.8. Fixed costs are payable on the making of the final order – r 45.6.

(g) The creditor now has a charge on the debtor's land which can be enforced by an order for sale of the property.

(h) In order to enforce the charging order by sale of the property charged, fresh proceedings would have to be commenced, normally in the same court that made the final charging order.

15.5.3 Charging order on securities (Part 73)

A judgment creditor can also obtain a charging order on a judgment debtor's beneficial interest in certain specified securities.

The procedure is similar to the procedure for obtaining a charging order on land. An application notice in the prescribed form (N380) must be completed.

15.5.4 Third party debt orders (Part 72)

Where a third party owes money to the judgment debtor, the court can make an order requiring that third party to pay the judgment creditor the whole of that debt, or such part of it as is sufficient to satisfy the judgment debt and costs. This is known as a third party debt order. A bank account or building society account is often the target of such an order. Judgment debtors who are self-employed often have trade debts due to them. It is possible to find out at the hearing of an order to obtain information from a judgment debtor what these debts are and then to take these proceedings accordingly.

The debt must belong to the judgment debtor solely and beneficially. An order cannot be made against joint debts unless all the people owed the debt are joint judgment debtors. This means, for example, that the judgment creditor cannot get an order over the husband and wife's joint bank account if the husband alone is the judgment debtor (*Hirschon v Evans* [1938] 2 KB 801).

Also note that the third party must be within the jurisdiction.

15.5.4.1 Choice of court

The application should be issued in the court which made the order which is being enforced.

15.5.4.2 Procedure

(a) The application is made without notice on the prescribed form (N349). The contents of the application notice are set out in para 1 of PD 72.

(b) The hearing will be before a judge. If successful the judge will make an interim third party debt order. He will also fix a hearing for the final third party debt order, which will be not less than 28 days after the interim order is made.

(c) The interim order is served on the third party not less than 21 days before the hearing date for the final order, and on the judgment debtor within seven days of service on the third party. In practice the interim order will be served as soon as possible as it will not be effective and binding on the third party until served.

(d)   Once the third party has been served with the interim order the third party is required to disclose certain information to the judgment creditor pursuant to r 72.6(2).

(e)   Before the third party debt order is made final the court will consider any objections made by either the third party, or the judgment debtor or anyone else claiming to have a prior interest in the money: see r 72.8.

(f)   Once a final order is made the third party is required to pay the money held to the judgment creditor. Fixed enforcement costs are also payable – r 45.6.

(g)   The rules enable the judgment debtor to apply for the order to be discharged in cases of hardship.

15.5.4.3   Third party debt proceedings against a deposit taking institution

A bank or building society account, provided it is in credit, is an ideal target for third party debt proceedings. Once the interim third party debt order is served, the account is frozen (up to the amount outstanding under the judgment or order) and, upon the making of the final order, the money in the account (or amount required to discharge the judgment) must be paid over to the judgment creditor.

There are some special points to bear in mind when third party debt proceedings are taken against a deposit taking institution, namely:

(a)   The application notice must state (if known) the name and address of the branch at which the account is believed to be held and the account number.

(b)   An order against a building society or credit union cannot require payment which would reduce the balance in the account to a sum less than £1.

(c)   Before paying the judgment creditor, the deposit taking institution is entitled to deduct a prescribed sum in respect of administration expenses.

15.5.4.4   Costs

The costs of a successful application are fixed (see Part 45) and may be retained by the judgment creditor out of the money recovered from the third party in priority to the judgment debt. If the application is unsuccessful the court will exercise its discretion in deciding what, if any, costs order to make.

15.5.5   Attachment of earnings (CCR Ord 27)

An attachment of earnings order is an order which compels the judgment debtor's employer to make regular deductions from the debtor's earnings and pay them into court. The High Court has no power to make an attachment of earnings order. If the judgment has been obtained in the High Court, the proceedings will have to be transferred to the county court before this method of enforcement can be used. The amount remaining due under the judgment must be at least £50 for an attachment of earnings application to be made. Also, the debtor must be employed; an order cannot be made if the debtor is unemployed or self-employed. The judgment debtor must be an individual. An order cannot be made against a partnership or corporate judgment debtor.

15.5.5.1   Procedure

(a)   The judgment creditor completes the prescribed application form and files it at court.

(b)   The court informs the debtor of the application and requires him either to pay the sum due, or to file a statement of means in the prescribed form. The court will make a diary entry for return of the form.

(c)   If the debtor returns the form, the court staff will make an attachment of earnings order. The court staff will fix the repayment rate by applying certain guidelines which they are given to the debtor's statement of means. If necessary, the application will be referred to the district judge. The order will specify the 'normal deduction rate' and the 'protected earnings rate'. The latter is the amount which the debtor is allowed to retain out of his earnings in any event. If his earnings for a particular week are equal to or less than the 'protected earnings rate', the creditor will receive nothing that week.

(d)   The order will be sent to the parties, and to the debtor's employer, with instructions to deduct the amount ordered from the debtor's pay and forward it to the court. The employer is entitled to deduct a small additional sum in respect of his administrative costs for each deduction which he makes in accordance with the order.

(e)   If either party objects to the order which has been made, he can apply for the matter to be reconsidered by the district judge. If such an application is made, there will be a hearing before the district judge. In the meantime, the employer will be required to make deductions as ordered unless and until the order is varied.

(f)   If the debtor informs the court that he is unemployed or self-employed, the application will be dismissed.

(g)   If the debtor does not respond to the initial notice sent to him by the court, an order to produce a statement of means will be served on him personally by the court bailiff. This order is automatically issued by the court. If the creditor has provided the name and address of the debtor's employer, the employer will also be contacted at this stage for a statement of earnings.

(h)   If the debtor still does not respond when the order is served on him by the court bailiff, the court will automatically issue a notice to show cause. This will be served on the debtor by the court bailiff, and it will give notice of a hearing before the district judge which the debtor is required to attend. Failure to attend will lead to his committal to prison.

15.5.6 Insolvency

15.5.6.1 Bankruptcy

Where the judgment debt is for £750 or more, the judgment creditor may decide to petition for bankruptcy of the judgment debtor. However, he will not be able to do this if he has already registered a charging order because he is then in the position of a secured creditor, and a secured creditor cannot petition for bankruptcy unless he gives up his security.

Bankruptcy procedure is not dealt with in detail here (for more detail, please refer to *Business Law and Practice*). Briefly, the first step is for the judgment creditor to serve on the judgment debtor a statutory demand in the prescribed form, unless execution has been levied and remains unsatisfied, in whole or in part, in which case there is no need for a statutory demand. Three weeks after service of the statutory demand, the petitioner may file the bankruptcy petition. In addition, an affidavit is required to verify the truth of the petition. The court will issue the petition indorsed with the date and place of hearing. The petition must be served on the debtor at least 14 days before the hearing. At the hearing, the judgment creditor must prove that the debt is still outstanding, and the court will usually then make a bankruptcy order, although the petition may be dismissed, stayed or adjourned. If a bankruptcy order is made, all the debtor's property vests in the trustee in bankruptcy.

15.5.6.2 Winding up

If the judgment debtor is a company, the judgment creditor may consider winding up the company. The procedure for this is very similar to the bankruptcy procedure for individuals.

15.5.7 Enforcement outside the jurisdiction (Part 74)

The methods of enforcing English judgments abroad, or enforcing a foreign judgment in England, depend on the arrangements made with the foreign country in question by EC Council Regulation, Treaty or Convention. These arrangments are as follows.

15.5.7.1 The EU and the Lugano Convention

The reciprocal rules relating to enforcement in all EU countries apart from Denmark are set out in Council Regulation 44/2001 ('the Regulation'). Similar provisions for Denmark, Norway, Switzerland and Iceland are set out in the Lugano Convention ('the Convention').

In order to enforce a judgment obtained in an EU country the party must obtain a certificate of enforcement by applying to the relevant court. The application should be accompanied by a copy of the judgment.

Articles 38 to 56 of the Regulation set out the procedure to be followed in making an application.

Similar provisions as to obtaining a certificate of judgment and forwarding it to the court of the country where enforcement is sought apply to judgments in countries governed by the Convention.

Enforcement proceedings may be stayed on the application of the judgment debtor to the court in which the certificate of enforcement has been sought.

15.5.7.2 Countries outside the EU and the Convention

Similar provisions to those outlined at **15.5.7.1** above apply to countries covered by the Administration of Justice Act 1920 and the Foreign Judgments (Reciprocal Enforcement) Act 1933. The countries covered by these Acts are mainly Commonwealth States.

For countries not covered by these Acts, such as the USA, enforcement of judgments of the courts of these countries is covered by common law. Usually, the creditor will treat the foreign judgment as a contract containing an implied promise to pay the judgment debt. He will issue proceedings in England alleging breaches of that contract, and if the debtor attempts to defend those proceedings, will apply for summary judgment under Part 24 of CPR 1998.

Enforcement abroad is a matter for the law and courts of the country where the creditor is seeking to enforce an English judgment.

15.6 Summary of key points

When considering enforcement proceedings, take the following points into account:

(1) What is the most cost-efficient way of investigating the judgment debtor's means and enforcing the judgment?

(2) Execution against the judgment debtor's goods. Where are the goods? What goods are exempt? Remember that goods owned with another person can be executed against.

(3) A charging order can be made over any beneficial interest the judgment debtor has in land or certain specified securities.

(4) A third party debt order can only be made against a bank account or building society account in the sole name of the judgment debtor, or against a joint account where it is in the names of all the co-judgment debtors but no one else.

(5) A third party debt order can only be made against a trade debt owed solely to the judgment debtor, or against a joint debt where it is owed to all the co-judgment debtors but no one else.

(6) Is the judgment debtor employed so that an attachment of earnings order might be made?

Appendix A
Court Forms, Protocols and Guidelines

A(1)   Forms N1 and N1A – Claim Form and Notes for Claimant

Claim Form

In the

	for court use only
Claim No.	
Issue date	

Claimant

SEAL

Defendant(s)

Brief details of claim

Value

Defendant's name and address			£	
		Amount claimed	
		Court fee	
		Solicitor's costs	
		Total amount	

The court office at

is open between 10 am and 4 pm Monday to Friday. When corresponding with the court, please address forms or letters to the Court Manager and quote the claim number.

N1 Claim form (CPR Part 7) (01.02)   *Printed on behalf of The Court Service*

	Claim No.	

Does, or will, your claim include any issues under the Human Rights Act 1998? ☐ Yes ☐ No

Particulars of Claim (attached)(to follow)

Statement of Truth
*(I believe)(The Claimant believes) that the facts stated in these particulars of claim are true.
* I am duly authorised by the claimant to sign this statement

Full name _____

Name of claimant's solicitor's firm _____

signed _____ position or office held_____
*(Claimant)(Litigation friend)(Claimant's solicitor)   (if signing on behalf of firm or company)
*delete as appropriate

Claimant's or claimant's solicitor's address to which documents or payments should be sent if different from overleaf including (if appropriate) details of DX, fax or e-mail.

Notes for claimant on completing a claim form

Before you begin completing the claim form

- You must think about whether alternative dispute resolution (ADR) is a better way to reach an agreement before going to court. The leaflet 'Making a claim? - Some questions to ask yourself' explains more about ADR and how you can attempt to settle your claim.

- Please read all of these guidance notes. The notes follow the order in which information is required on the form.

- If you are filling in the claim form by hand, please use black ink and write in block capitals.

- Copy the completed claim form and the defendant's notes for guidance so that you have one copy for yourself, one copy for the court and one copy for each defendant. Send or take the forms to the court office with the appropriate fee. The court will tell you how much this is.

- Court staff can help you fill in the claim form and give information about procedure once it has been issued. But they cannot give legal advice. If you need legal advice, for example, about the likely success of your claim or the evidence you need to prove it, you should contact a solicitor or a Citizens Advice Bureau.

Further information may be obtained from the court in a series of free leaflets.

Notes on completing the claim form

Heading

You must fill in the heading of the form to indicate the name of the court where you want the claim to be issued.

The claimant and defendant

As the person issuing the claim, you are called the 'claimant'; the person you are suing is called the 'defendant'. Claimants who are under 18 years old (unless otherwise permitted by the court) and patients within the meaning of the Mental Health Act 1983, must have a litigation friend to issue and conduct court proceedings on their behalf. Court staff will tell you more about what you need to do if this applies to you.

Providing information about yourself and the defendant

full address including postcode

You should provide the full address including postcode for yourself and the defendant. The postcode for any address in the United Kingdom may be obtained free from the Royal Mail Address Management Guide, or their website at www.royalmail.com.

If an address does not have a postcode you will need to ask the judge for permission to serve the claim with this information missing. There is no additional fee for this, but if you omit a postcode and fail to ask permission of the judge the court will not allow your claim to be served on the defendant until you supply the missing postcode or a judge permits service without it.

You must provide the following information about yourself and the defendant according to the capacity in which you are suing and in which the defendant is being sued.

When suing or being sued as:-

an individual:

You must enter his or her full unabbreviated name where known, including their first name and any middle name, their last name and the title by which she or he is known (i.e. Mr., Mrs., Ms., Dr., etc.) and residential address (including postcode and telephone number). Where the defendant is a proprietor of a business, a partner in a firm or an individual sued in the name of a club or other unincorporated association, the address for service should be the usual or last known place of residence or principal place of business of the company, firm or club or other unincorporated association.

Where the individual is:

trading under another name

you must enter his or her full unabbreviated name where known, and the title by which he or she is known and the full name under which he or she is trading, e.g. 'Mr. John Smith trading as Smith's Groceries'.

suing or being sued in a representative capacity

you must say what that capacity is e.g. 'Mr Joe Bloggs as the representative of Mrs Sharon Bloggs (deceased)'.

suing or being sued in the name of a club or other unincorporated association

add the words 'suing/sued on behalf of' followed by the name of the club or other unincorporated association.

an unincorporated business - a firm

In the case of a partnership (other than a limited liability partnership) you must enter the full name of the business followed by the suffix 'a firm'.

Enter the name of the firm followed by the words 'a firm' e.g. 'Bandbox - a firm' and an address including postcode for service. This may either be one of the partners residential addresses or the principal or last known place of business of the firm.

a company registered in England and Wales or a Limited Liability Partnership

In the case of a registered company or limited liability partnership, you must enter the full name of the company or partnership followed by the appropriate suffix, i.e. Ltd, Plc, LLP. You must provide an address, including postcode which is either the company's registered office or any place of business in England and Wales that has a real, or the most, connection with the claim e.g. a shop where goods were bought.

a corporation (other than a company)

enter the full name of the corporation and any suffix if appropriate and the address including postcode in England and Wales which is either its principal office or any other place where the corporation carries on activities and which has a real connection with the claim.

an overseas company (defined by s744 of the Companies Act 1985)

You must enter the company's full name and any suffix if appropriate and address including postcode. The address must either be the registered address under s691 of the Act or the address of the place of business having a real, or the most, connection with the claim.

under 18 write '(a child by Mr Joe Bloggs his litigation friend)' after the name. If the child is conducting proceedings on their own behalf write '(a child)' after the child's name.

a patient within the meaning of the Mental Health Act 1983 write '(by Mr Joe Bloggs his litigation friend)' after the patient's name.

Brief details of claim

You must set out under **this** heading:

- a concise statement of the nature of your claim
- the remedy you are seeking e.g. payment of money;

Value

If you are claiming a **fixed amount of money** (a 'specified amount') write the amount in the box at the bottom right-hand corner of the claim form against 'amount claimed'.

If you are not claiming a fixed amount of money (an 'unspecified amount') under 'Value' write "I expect to recover" followed by whichever of the following applies to your claim:

- 'not more than £5,000' **or**
- 'more than £5,000 but not more than £15,000' **or**
- 'more than £15,000'

If you are **not able** to put a value on your claim, write 'I cannot say how much I expect to recover'.

Personal injuries

If your claim is for 'not more than £5,000' and includes a claim for personal injuries, you must also

write 'My claim includes a claim for personal injuries and the amount I expect to recover as damages for pain, suffering and loss of amenity is' followed by either:

- 'not more than £1,000' **or**
- 'more than £1,000'

Housing disrepair

If your claim is for 'not more than £5,000' and includes a claim for housing disrepair relating to residential premises, you must also write 'My claim includes a claim against my landlord for housing disrepair relating to residential premises. The cost of the repairs or other work is estimated to be' followed by either:

- 'not more than £1,000' **or**
- 'more than £1,000'

If within this claim, you are making a claim for other damages, you must also write:

'I expect to recover as damages' followed by either:

- 'not more than £1,000' **or**
- 'more than £1,000'

Defendant's name and address

Enter in this box the title, full names, address and postcode of the defendant receiving the claim form (ie. one claim form for each defendant). If the defendant is to be served outside England and Wales, you may need to obtain the court's permission.

Particulars of claim

You must set out under this heading:

- a concise statement of the facts on which you rely
- a statement (if applicable) to the effect that you are seeking aggravated damages or exemplary damages
- details of any interest which you are claiming
- any other matters required for your type of claim as set out in the relevant practice direction

Statement of truth

This must be signed by you, or by your solicitor or your litigation friend, if appropriate.

Where the claimant is a registered company or a corporation the claim must be signed by either the director, treasurer, secretary, chief executive, manager or other officer of the company or (in the case of a corporation) the mayor, chairman, president or town clerk.

Address for documents

Insert in this box the address at which you wish to receive documents and/or payments, if different from the address you have already given under the heading 'Claimant'. The address must be in England or Wales. If you are willing to accept service by DX, fax or e-mail, add details.

A(2)   Form N1C – Notes for Defendant on Replying to the Claim Form

Notes for defendant on replying to the claim form
Please read these notes carefully - they will help you decide what to do about this claim.
Further information may be obtained from the court in a series of free leaflets

- If this claim form was received with the particulars of claim completed or attached, you must reply within 14 days of the date it was served on you. If the words 'particulars of claim to follow' are written in the particulars of claim box, you should not reply until after you are served with the particulars of claim (which should be no more than 14 days after you received the claim form). If the claim was sent by post, the date of service is taken as the second day after posting (see post mark). If the claim form was delivered or left at your address, the date of service will be the day after it was delivered.
- You may either:
  - pay the total amount i.e. the amount claimed, the court fee, and solicitor's costs (if any)
  - admit that you owe all or part of the claim and ask for time to pay or
  - dispute the claim
- If you do not reply, judgment may be entered against you.
- The notes below tell you what to do.
- The response pack will tell you which forms to use for your reply. (The pack will accompany the particulars of claim if they are served after the claim form).
- Court staff can help you complete the forms of reply and tell you about court procedures. But they cannot give legal advice. If you need legal advice, for example about the likely success of disputing the claim, you should contact a solicitor or a Citizens Advice Bureau immediately.

Registration of Judgments: If this claim results in a judgment against you, details will be entered in a public register, the Register of Judgments, Orders and Fines. They will then be passed to credit reference agencies which will then supply them to credit grantors and others seeking information on your financial standing. **This will make it difficult for you to get credit.** A list of credit reference agencies is available from Registry Trust Ltd, 173/175 Cleveland Street, London W1T 6QR.

Costs and Interest: Additional costs and interest may be added to the amount claimed on the front of the claim form if judgment is entered against you. In a county court, if judgment is for £5,000 or more, or is in respect of a debt which attracts contractual or statutory interest for late payment, the claimant may be entitled to further interest.

Your response and what happens next

How to pay

Do not bring any payments to the court - they will not be accepted.

When making payments to the claimant, quote the claimant's reference (if any) and the claim number.

Make sure that you keep records and can account for any payments made. Proof may be required if there is any disagreement. It is not safe to send cash unless you use registered post.

Admitting the Claim

Claim for specified amount

If you admit all the claim, take or send the money, including the court fee, any interest and costs, to the claimant at the address given for payment on the claim form, within 14 days.

If you admit all the claim and you are asking for time to pay, complete Form N9A and send it to the claimant at the address given for payment on the claim form, within 14 days. The claimant will decide whether to accept your proposal for payment. If it is accepted, the claimant may request the court to enter judgment against you and you will be sent an order to pay. If your offer is not accepted, the court will decide how you should pay.

If you admit only part of the claim, complete Form N9A and Form N9B (see 'Disputing the Claim' overleaf) and send them to the court within 14 days. The claimant will decide whether to accept your part admission. If it is accepted, the claimant may request the court to enter judgment against you and the court will send you an order to pay. If your part admission is not accepted, the case will proceed as a defended claim.

Claim for unspecified amount

If you admit liability for the whole claim but do not make an offer to satisfy the claim, complete Form N9C and send it to the court within 14 days. A copy will be sent to the claimant who may request the court to enter judgment against you for an amount to be decided by the court, and costs. The court will enter judgment and refer the court file to a judge for directions for management of the case. You and the claimant will be sent a copy of the court's order.

If you admit liability for the claim and offer an amount of money to satisfy the claim, complete Form N9C and send it to the court within 14 days.

N1C Notes for defendant (04.06)   HMCS

The claimant will be sent a copy and asked if the offer is acceptable. The claimant must reply to the court within 14 days and send you a copy. If a reply is not received, the claim will be stayed. If the amount you have offered is **accepted -**

- the claimant may request the court to enter judgment against you for that amount.

- if you have requested time to pay which is not accepted by the claimant, the rate of payment will be decided by the court.

If your offer in satisfaction is **not accepted -**

- the claimant may request the court to enter judgment against you for an amount to be decided by the court, and costs; and

- the court will enter judgment and refer the court file to a judge for directions for management of the case. You and the claimant will be sent a copy of the court's order.

Disputing the claim

If you are being sued as an individual for a specified amount of money and you dispute the claim, the claim may be transferred to a local court i.e. the one nearest to or where you live or carry on business if different from the court where the claim was issued.

If you need longer than 14 days to prepare your defence or to contest the court's jurisdiction to try the claim, complete the Acknowledgment of Service form and send it to the court within 14 days. This will allow you 28 days from the date of service of the particulars of claim to file your defence or make an application to contest the court's jurisdiction. The court will tell the claimant that your Acknowledgment of Service has been received.

If the case proceeds as a defended claim, you and the claimant will be sent an Allocation Questionnaire. You will be told the date by which it must be returned to the court. The information you give on the form will help a judge decide whether your case should be dealt with in the small claims track, fast track or multi-track. After a judge has considered the completed questionnaires, you will be sent a notice of allocation setting out the judge's decision. The notice will tell you the track to which the claim has been allocated and what you have to do to prepare for the hearing or trial. **Leaflets telling you more about the tracks are available from the court office.**

Claim for specified amount

If you wish to dispute the full amount claimed or wish to claim against the claimant (a counterclaim), complete Form N9B and send it to the court within 14 days.

If you admit part of the claim, complete the Defence Form N9B <u>and</u> the Admission Form N9A

and send them both to the court within 14 days. The claimant will decide whether to accept your part admission in satisfaction of the claim (see under 'Admitting the Claim - specified amount'). If the claimant does not accept the amount you have admitted, the case will proceed as a defended claim.

If you dispute the claim because you have already paid it, complete Form N9B and send it to the court within 14 days. The claimant will have to decide whether to proceed with the claim or withdraw it and notify the court and you within 28 days. If the claimant wishes to proceed, the case will proceed as a defended claim.

Claim for unspecified amount/return of goods/non-money claims

If you dispute the claim or wish to claim against the claimant (counterclaim), complete Form N9D and send it to the court within 14 days.

Personal injuries claims:

If the claim is for personal injuries and the claimant has attached a medical report to the particulars of claim, in your defence you should state whether you:

- agree with the report **or**
- dispute all or part of the report **and** give your reasons for doing so **or**
- neither agree nor dispute the report **or** have no knowledge of the report

Where you have obtained your own medical report, you should attach it to your defence.

If the claim is for personal injuries and the claimant has attached a schedule of past and future expenses and losses, in your defence you must state which of the items you:

- agree **or**
- dispute **and** supply alternative figures where appropriate **or**
- neither agree nor dispute or have no knowledge of

Address where notices can be sent

This must be either your solicitor's address, your own residential or business address in England and Wales or (if you live elsewhere) some other address within England and Wales.

Statement of truth

This must be signed by you, by your solicitor or your litigation friend, as appropriate.

Where the defendant is **a registered company or a corporation** the response must be signed by either the director, treasurer, secretary, chief executive, manager or other officer of the company **or** (in the case of a corporation) the mayor, chairman, president or town clerk

A(3)   Form N9, Including Forms N9A–N9D – Response Pack

Response Pack

You should read the 'notes for defendant' attached to the claim form which will tell you when and where to send the forms

Included in this pack are:

- either **Admission Form N9A** (if the claim is for a specified amount) or **Admission Form N9C** (if the claim is for an unspecified amount or is not a claim for money)

- either **Defence and Counterclaim Form N9B** (if the claim is for a specified amount) or **Defence and Counterclaim Form N9D** (if the claim is for an unspecified amount or is not a claim for money)

- **Acknowledgment of service** (see below)

Complete

If you admit the claim or the amount claimed and/or you want time to pay	▶ the admission form
If you admit part of the claim	▶ the admission form and the defence form
If you dispute the whole claim or wish to make a claim (a counterclaim) against the claimant	▶ the defence form
If you need 28 days (rather than 14) from the date of service to prepare your defence, or wish to contest the court's jurisdiction	▶ the acknowledgment of service
If you do nothing, judgment may be entered against you	

Acknowledgment of Service

Defendant's full name if different from the name given on the claim form

In the	
Claim No.	
Claimant (including ref.)	
Defendant	

Address to which documents about this claim should be sent (including reference if appropriate)

	if applicable
fax no.	
DX no.	
Ref. no.	
e-mail	

Tel. no.   Postcode

Tick the appropriate box

1.   I intend to defend all of this claim ☐

2.   I intend to defend part of this claim ☐

3.   I intend to contest jurisdiction ☐

(My) (Defendant's) date of birth is | D | D | M | M | Y | Y | Y | Y |

If you file an acknowledgment of service but do not file a defence within 28 days of the date of service of the claim form, or particulars of claim if served separately, judgment may be entered against you.

If you do not file an application to dispute the jurisdiction of the court within 14 days of the date of filing this acknowledgment of service, it will be assumed that you accept the court's jurisdiction and judgment may be entered against you.

Signed _____

Position or office held _____

(Defendant)(Defendant's solicitor)(Litigation friend)

(if signing on behalf of firm or company)

Date

The court office at

is open between 10 am and 4 pm Monday to Friday. When corresponding with the court, please address forms or letters to the Court Manager and quote the claim number.

Admission (specified amount)

- You have a limited number of days to complete and return this form
- Before completing this form, please read the notes for guidance attached to the claim form

Name of court	
Claim No.	
Claimant (including ref.)	
Defendant	

When to fill in this form

Only fill in this form if:
- you are admitting all of the claim **and** you are asking for time to pay; or
- you are admitting part of the claim. (You should also complete form N9B)

How to fill in this form

- Tick the correct boxes and give as much information as you can. **Then sign and date the form.** If necessary provide details on a separate sheet, add the claim number and attach it to this form.
- Make your offer of payment in box 11 on the back of this form. **If you make no offer the claimant will decide how much and when you should pay.**
- If you are not an individual, you should ensure that you provide sufficient details about the assets and liabilities of your firm, company or corporation to support any offer of payment made in box 11.
- You can get help to complete this form at **any** county court office or Citizens Advice Bureau.

Where to send this form

- **If you admit the claim in full**
  Send the completed form to the address shown on the claim form as one to which documents should be sent.
- **If you admit only part of the claim**
  Send the form **to the court** at the address given on the claim form, together with the defence form (N9B).

How much of the claim do you admit?

☐ I admit the full amount claimed as shown on the claim form   **or**

☐ I admit the amount of   £ _____

1   Personal details

Surname _____

Forename _____

☐ Mr   ☐ Mrs   ☐ Miss   ☐ Ms

☐ Married   ☐ Single   ☐ Other *(specify)* _____

Date of birth   D D M M Y Y Y Y

Address _____

Postcode _____

Tel. no. _____

2   Dependants   *(people you look after financially)*

Number of children in each age group

under 11 ☐   11-15 ☐   16-17 ☐   18 & over ☐

Other dependants *(give details)* _____

3   Employment

☐ **I am employed as a** _____

My employer is _____

Jobs other than main job *(give details)* _____

☐ **I am self employed as a** _____

Annual turnover is........................... £ _____

☐ **I am not** in arrears with my national insurance contributions, income tax and VAT

☐ **I am** in arrears and I owe........... £ _____

Give details of:
(a) contracts and other work in hand
(b) any sums due for work done _____

☐ **I have been unemployed for**   years   months

☐ **I am a pensioner**

4   Bank account and savings

☐ **I have a bank account**

☐ The account is in credit by........ £ _____

☐ The account is overdrawn by.... £ _____

☐ **I have a savings or building society account**

The amount in the account is.......... £ _____

5   Residence

I live in   ☐ my own house   ☐ lodgings

☐ my jointly owned house   ☐ council accommodation

☐ rented accommodation

6 Income

	£	per
My usual take home pay *(including overtime, commission, bonuses etc)*	£	per
Income support	£	per
Child benefit(s)	£	per
Other state benefit(s)	£	per
My pension(s)	£	per
Others living in my home give me	£	per
Other income *(give details below)*		
	£	per
	£	per
	£	per
Total income	**£**	**per**

7 Expenses

(Do not include any payments made by other members of the household out of their own income)

I have regular expenses as follows:

	£	per
Mortgage *(including second mortgage)*	£	per
Rent	£	per
Council tax	£	per
Gas	£	per
Electricity	£	per
Water charges	£	per
TV rental and licence	£	per
HP repayments	£	per
Mail order	£	per
Housekeeping, food, school meals	£	per
Travelling expenses	£	per
Children's clothing	£	per
Maintenance payments	£	per
Others *(not court orders or credit debts listed in boxes 9 and 10)*		
	£	per
	£	per
	£	per
Total expenses	**£**	**per**

8 Priority debts

(This section is for arrears only. Do not include regular expenses listed in box 7.)

	£	per
Rent arrears	£	per
Mortgage arrears	£	per
Council tax/Community Charge arrears	£	per
Water charges arrears	£	per
Fuel debts: Gas	£	per
Electricity	£	per
Other	£	per
Maintenance arrears	£	per
Others *(give details below)*		
	£	per
	£	per
Total priority debts	**£**	**per**

9 Court orders

Court	Claim No.	£	per

Total court order instalments	**£**	**per**

Of the payments above, I am behind with payments to *(please list)*

10 Credit debts

Loans and credit card debts *(please list)*

	£	per
	£	per
	£	per

Of the payments above, I am behind with payments to *(please list)*

11 Offer of payment

☐ I can pay the amount admitted on

or

☐ I can pay by monthly instalments of   £

If you cannot pay immediately, please give brief reasons below

12 Declaration   I declare that the details I have given above are true to the best of my knowledge

Signed

Date

Position or office held *(if signing on behalf of firm or company)*

Defence and Counterclaim (specified amount)

Name of court	
Claim No.	
Claimant (including ref.)	
Defendant	

- Fill in this form if you wish to dispute all or part of the claim and/or make a claim against the claimant (counterclaim).
- You have a limited number of days to complete and return this form to the court.
- Before completing this form, please read the notes for guidance attached to the claim form.
- Please ensure that all boxes at the top right of this form are completed. You can obtain the correct names and number from the claim form. The court cannot trace your case without this information.

How to fill in this form

- Complete sections 1 and 2. Tick the correct boxes and give the other details asked for.
- Set out your defence in section 3. If necessary continue on a separate piece of paper making sure that the claim number is clearly shown on it. In your defence you must state which allegations in the particulars of claim you deny and your reasons for doing so. **If you fail to deny an allegation it may be taken that you admit it.**
- If you dispute only some of the allegations you must
  - specify which you admit and which you deny; and
  - give your own version of events if different from the claimant's.

- If you wish to make a claim against the claimant (a counterclaim) complete section 4.
- Complete and sign section 5 before sending this form to the court. Keep a copy of the claim form and this form.

Community Legal Service Fund (CLSF)

You may qualify for assistance from the CLSF (this used to be called 'legal aid') to meet some or all of your legal costs. Ask about the CLSF at any county court office or any information or help point which displays this logo.

Community Legal Service

1. How much of the claim do you dispute?

☐ I dispute the full amount claimed as shown on the claim form

or

☐ I admit the amount of £ _____

If you dispute only part of the claim you must **either**:

- pay the amount admitted to the person named at the address for payment on the claim form (see How to Pay in the notes on the back of, or attached to, the claim form). Then send this defence to the court

  or

- complete the admission form **and** this defence form and send them to the court.

  ☐ I paid the amount admitted on (*date*) _____

  or

  ☐ I enclose the completed form of admission

  (*go to section 2*)

2. Do you dispute this claim because you have already paid it? *Tick whichever applies*

☐ **No** (*go to section 3*)

☐ **Yes** I paid £ _____ to the claimant

on _____ *(before the claim form was issued)*

Give details of where and how you paid it in the box below *(then go to section 5)*

3. Defence

Defence (continued)

Claim No. [   ]

4. If you wish to make a claim against the claimant (a counterclaim)

If your claim is for a specific sum of money, how much are you claiming?   £ [   ]

I enclose the counterclaim fee of   £ [   ]

My claim is for *(please specify nature of claim)*

[   ]

- To start your counterclaim, you will have to pay a fee. Court staff can tell you how much you have to pay.

- You may not be able to make a counterclaim where the claimant is the Crown (e.g. a Government Department). Ask at your local county court office for further information.

What are your reasons for making the counterclaim?
If you need to continue on a separate sheet put the claim number in the top right hand corner

[   ]

5. Signed
(To be signed by you or by your solicitor or litigation friend)

*(I believe)(The defendant believes) that the facts stated in this form are true. *I am duly authorised by the defendant to sign this statement

*delete as appropriate

Position or office held
(if signing on behalf of firm or company)

[   ]

Defendant's date of birth, if an individual   [D D M M Y Y Y Y]

Date [   ]

Give an address to which notices about this case can be sent to you

[   ]

Postcode

Tel. no. [   ]

if applicable

fax no. [   ]

DX no. [   ]

e-mail [   ]

Admission (unspecified amount, non-money and return of goods claims)

- Before completing this form please read the notes for guidance attached to the claim form. If necessary provide details on a separate sheet, add the claim number and attach it to this form.
- If you are not an individual, you should ensure that you provide sufficient details about the assets and liabilities of your firm, company or corporation to support any offer of payment made.

In the	
Claim No.	
Claimant (including ref.)	
Defendant	

In non-money claims only

☐ I admit liability for the whole claim
(Complete section 11)

In return of goods cases only

Are the goods still in your possession?

☐ Yes   ☐ No

Part A Response to claim *(tick one box only)*

☐ I admit liability for the whole claim but want the court to decide the amount I should pay / value of the goods

OR

☐ I admit liability for the claim and offer to pay [_____] in satisfaction of the claim
(Complete part B and sections 1 - 11)

Part B How are you going to pay the amount you have admitted? *(tick one box only)*

☐ I offer to pay on (date) [_____]

OR

☐ I cannot pay the amount immediately because *(state reason)*

[_____]

AND

I offer to pay by instalments of £ [_____]
per (week)(month)

starting *(date)* [_____]

1 Personal details

Surname [_____]

Forename [_____]

☐ Mr   ☐ Mrs   ☐ Miss   ☐ Ms

☐ Married   ☐ Single   ☐ Other *(specify)* [_____]

Date of birth [D D M M Y Y Y Y]

Address [_____]

Postcode [_____]

Tel. no. [_____]

2 Dependants *(people you look after financially)*

Number of children in each age group

under 11 [__]   11-15 [__]   16-17 [__]   18 & over [__]

Other dependants *(give details)* [_____]

3 Employment

☐ **I am employed as a** [_____]

My employer is [_____]

Jobs other than main job *(give details)* [_____]

☐ **I am self employed as a** [_____]

Annual turnover is.......................... £ [_____]

☐ **I am not** in arrears with my national insurance contributions, income tax and VAT

☐ **I am** in arrears and I owe........... £ [_____]

Give details of:
(a) contracts and other work in hand [_____]
(b) any sums due for work done [_____]

☐ **I have been unemployed for** [years] [months]

☐ **I am a pensioner**

4 Bank account and savings

☐ **I have a bank account**

☐ The account is in credit by........ £ [_____]

☐ The account is overdrawn by.... £ [_____]

☐ **I have a savings or building society account**

The amount in the account is.......... £ [_____]

5 Residence

I live in   ☐ my own property   ☐ lodgings

☐ jointly owned house   ☐ rented property

☐ council accommodation

N9C Admission (unspecified amount and non-money claims) (04.06)   HMCS

6 Income

My usual take home pay *(including overtime, commission, bonuses etc)*	£	per
Income support	£	per
Child benefit(s)	£	per
Other state benefit(s)	£	per
My pension(s)	£	per
Others living in my home give me	£	per
Other income *(give details below)*		
	£	per
	£	per
	£	per
Total income	**£**	**per**

8 Priority debts *(This section is for arrears only. Do not include regular expenses listed in section 7)*

Rent arrears	£	per
Mortgage arrears	£	per
Council tax/Community Charge arrears	£	per
Water charges arrears	£	per
Fuel debts: Gas	£	per
Electricity	£	per
Other	£	per
Maintenance arrears	£	per
Others *(give details below)*		
	£	per
	£	per
Total priority debts	**£**	**per**

7 Expenses

(Do not include any payments made by other members of the household out of their own income)

I have regular expenses as follows:

Mortgate *(including second mortgage)*	£	per
Rent	£	per
Council tax	£	per
Gas	£	per
Electricity	£	per
Water charges	£	per
TV rental and licence	£	per
HP repayments	£	per
Mail order	£	per
Housekeeping, food, school meals	£	per
Travelling expenses	£	per
Children's clothing	£	per
Maintenance payments	£	per
Others *(not court orders or credit debts listed in sections 9 and 10)*		
	£	per
	£	per
	£	per
Total expenses	**£**	**per**

9 Court orders

Court	Claim No.	£	per
Total court order instalments		**£**	**per**

Of the payments above, I am behind with payments to *(please list)*	

10 Credit debts

Loans and credit card debts *(please list)*

	£	per
	£	per
	£	per

Of the payments above, I am behind with payments to *(please list)*	

11 Declaration   I declare that the details I have given above are true to the best of my knowledge

Signed		Position or office held
Date		*(if signing on behalf of firm or company)*

Defence and Counterclaim
(unspecified amount, non-money and return of goods claims)

- Fill in this form if you wish to dispute all or part of the claim and/or make a claim against the claimant (a counterclaim)
- You have a limited number of days to complete and return this form to the court.
- Before completing this form, please read the notes for guidance attached to the claim form.
- Please ensure that all the boxes at the top right of this form are completed. You can obtain the correct names and number from the claim form. The court cannot trace your case without this information.

How to fill in this form
- Set out your defence in section 1. If necessary continue on a separate piece of paper making sure that the claim number is clearly shown on it. In your defence you must state which allegations in the particulars of claim you deny and your reasons for doing so. **If you fail to deny an allegation it may be taken that you admit it.**
- If you dispute only some of the allegations you must
  - specify which you admit and which you deny; and
  - give your own version of events if different from the claimant's.

In the	
Claim No.	
Claimant (including ref.)	
Defendant	

- If the claim is for money and you dispute the claimant's statement of value, you must say why and if possible give your own statement of value.
- If you wish to make a claim against the claimant (a counterclaim) complete section 2.
- Complete and sign section 3 before returning this form.

Where to send this form
- send or take this form immediately to the court at the address given on the claim form.
- Keep a copy of the claim form and the defence form.

Community Legal Service Fund (CLSF)
You may qualify for assistance from the CLSF (this used to be called 'legal aid') to meet some or all of your legal costs. Ask about the CLSF at any county court office or any information or help point which displays this logo.

1. Defence

Defence (continued)   Claim No. [   ]

**2. If you wish to make a claim against the
   claimant (a counterclaim)**

If your claim is for a specific sum of
money, how much are you claiming? £ [   ]   • To start your counterclaim, you will have to pay a fee.
                                                            Court staff can tell you how much you have to pay.

I enclose the counterclaim fee of   £ [   ]

My claim is for *(please specify)*   • You may not be able to make a counterclaim where the
                                                            claimant is the Crown (e.g. a Government Department).
[   ]   Ask at your local county court office for further
                                                            information.

What are your reasons for making the counterclaim?
If you need to continue on a separate sheet put the claim number in the top right hand corner

[   ]

3. Signed   *(I believe)(The defendant believes) that the facts   **Position or**
(To be signed   stated in this form are true. *I am duly authorised by   **office held**
by you or by   the defendant to sign this statement   (if signing on
your solicitor or   behalf of firm
litigation friend*)*   or company)

                          *delete as appropriate

Defendant's date of   [D D M M Y Y Y Y]   **Date** [   ]
birth, if an individual

Give an   [if applicable   ]
address to
which notices   fax no. [   ]
about this case
can be sent to you   DX no. [   ]
                                        Postcode
                                                                                   e-mail [   ]
                          Tel. no. [   ]

A(4) Form N251 – Notice of Funding

Notice of funding of case or claim

Notice of funding by means of a conditional fee agreement, insurance policy or undertaking given by a prescribed body should be given to the court and all other parties to the case:
- on commencement of proceedings
- on filing an acknowledgment of service, defence or other first document; and
- at any later time that such an arrangement is entered into, changed or terminated.

In the	
The court office is open between 10 am and 4 pm Monday to Friday. When writing to the court, please address forms or letters to the Court Manager and quote the claim number.	
Claim No.	
Claimant (include Ref.)	
Defendant (include Ref.)	

Take notice that in respect of

☐ all claims herein

☐ the following claims

☐ the case of *(specify name of party)*

[is now][was] being funded by:

(Please tick those boxes which apply)

☐ a conditional fee agreement
  ┌Dated

  which provides for a success fee

☐ an insurance policy issued on
  ┌Date   ┌Policy no.

  ┌Name and address of insurer

☐ an undertaking given on
  ┌Date

  by
  ┌Name of prescribed body

  in the following terms

The funding of the case has now changed:

☐ the above funding has now ceased

☐ the conditional fee agreement has been terminated

☐ a conditional fee agreement
  ┌Dated

  which provides for a success fee has been entered into;

☐ an insurance policy
  ┌Date

  has been cancelled

☐ an insurance policy has been issued on
  ┌Date   ┌Policy no.

  ┌Name and address of insurer

☐ an undertaking given on
  ┌Date

  has been terminated

☐ an undertaking has been given on
  ┌Date

  ┌Name of prescribed body

  in the following terms

┌Signed   ┌Dated

Solicitor for the (claimant) (defendant)
(Part 20 defendant) (respondent) (appellant)

A(5)   Form N215 – Certificate of Service

Certificate of service

Name of court	Claim No.
Name of Claimant	
Name of Defendant	

On the .   .*(insert date)*

the   *(insert title or description of documents served)*

a copy of which is attached to this notice was served on *(insert name of person served, including position i.e. partner, director if appropriate)*

Tick as appropriate

☐ by first class post or (with effect from 6th April 2006) an alternative service which provides for delivery on the next working day.

☐ by Document Exchange

☐ by delivering to or leaving at a permitted place *(see notes overleaf)*

☐ by personally handing it to or leaving it with *(please specify)*

☐ by fax machine (.   .time sent) *(you may want to enclose a copy of the transmission sheet)*

☐ by other electronic means *(please specify)*

☐ by other means permitted by the court (please specify)

at *(insert address where service effected, include fax or DX number, e-mail address or other electronic identification)*

being the   ☐ claimant's   ☐ defendant's   ☐ solicitor's   ☐ litigation friend:

☐ usual residence

☐ principal office of the corporation

☐ last known residence

☐ principal office of the company

☐ place of business

☐ other *(please specify)*

☐ principal place of business

☐ last known place of business

The date of service is therefore deemed to be .   *(insert date - see overleaf for guidance)*

I believe that the facts stated in this Certificate are true.	
Full name	
Signed	**Position or office held**
(Claimant)(Defendant)('s solicitor)('s litigation friend)	(if signing on behalf of firm or company)
Date [ ]	

Notes for guidance
Please note that these notes are only a guide and are not exhaustive
If you are in doubt you should refer to Part 6 of the rules

Where to serve

Nature of party to be served	Permitted place of service
Individual	• Usual or last known residence
Proprietor of business	• Usual or last known residence; or • Place of business or last known place of business
Individual who is suing or being sued in the name of a firm	• Usual or last known residence; or • Principal or last known place of business of the firm
Corporation (incorporated in England and Wales) other than a company	• Principal office of the corporation; or • any place of within the jurisdiction where the corporation carries on its activities and which has a real connection with the claim
Company registered in England and Wales	• Principal office of the company or corporation; or • any place of business of the company within the jurisdiction which has a real connection with the claim

Personal Service - A document is served personally on an individual by leaving it with that individual. A document is served personally on a company or other corporation by leaving it with a person holding a senior position within the company or corporation. In the case of a partnership, you must leave it with either a partner or a person having control or management at the principal place of business. Where a solicitor is authorised to accept service on behalf of a party, service must be effected on the solicitor, unless otherwise ordered.

Deemed Service - Part 6.7(1). A document which is served in accordance with these rules or any relevant practice direction shall be deemed to be served on the day shown in the following table.

Method of service	Deemed day of service
First class post or (with effect from 6th April 2006) an alternative service which provides for delivery on the next working day.	The second day after it was posted
Document exchange	The second day after it was left at the document exchange
Delivering the document to or leaving it at a permitted address	The day after it was delivered to or left at the permitted address
Fax	If it is transmitted on a business day before 4 p.m., on that day, or otherwise on the business day after the day on which it was transmitted
Other electronic method	The second day after the day on which it was transmitted

• If a document is served personally after 5 p.m. on a business day, or at any time on a Saturday, Sunday or a bank holiday, the document shall, for the purpose of calculating any period of time after service of the document, be treated as having been served on the next business day.

• In this context "business day" means any day except Saturday, Sunday or a bank holiday; and "bank holiday" includes Christmas Day and Good Friday.

Service of documents on children and patients - The rules relating to service on children and patients are contained in Part 6.6 of the rules.

Claim Forms - The general rules about service are subject to the special rules about service of claim forms contained in rules 6.12 to 6.16.

A(6)   Form N218 – Notice of Service on Partner

Notice of service on partner

In the	
Claim No.	
Claimant (including ref.)	
Defendant	

The (claim form) (particulars of claim) served with this notice (is) (are) served on you

(tick only one box)

☐   as a partner of the business

☐   as a person having control or management of the partnership business

☐   as both a partner and as a person having control or management of the partnership business

named in the claim form (particulars of claim).

Signed _____   **Date** _____

Claimant ('s solicitor)

A(7)   Form N266 – Notice to Admit Facts

Notice to admit facts

In the	
Claim No.	
Claimant (include Ref.)	
Defendant (include Ref.)	

I (We) give notice that you are requested to admit the following facts or part of case in this claim:

I (We) confirm that any admission of fact(s) or part of case will only be used in this claim.

Signed [_____]

(Claimant)(Defendant)('s Solicitor)

Position or office held [_____]

(If signing on behalf of firm or company)

Date [_____]

- -

Admission of facts

I (We) admit the facts or part of case (set out above)(in the attached schedule) for the purposes of this claim only and on the basis that the admission will not be used on any other occasion or by any other person.

Signed [_____]

(Claimant)(Defendant)('s Solicitor)

Position or office held [_____]

(If signing on behalf of firm or company)

Date [_____]

The court office at

is open between 10 am and 4 pm Monday to Friday. Address all communication to the Court Manager quoting the claim number

N266 - w3 Notice to admit facts (4.99)

Printed on behalf of The Court Service

A(8)   Form N150 – Allocation Questionnaire

Allocation questionnaire

To be completed by, or on behalf of,

who is [1ˢᵗ][2ⁿᵈ][3ʳᵈ][   ][Claimant][Defendant]
[Part 20 claimant] in this claim

Name of court
Claim No.	
Last date for filing with court office	

Please read the notes on page six before completing the questionnaire.

You should note the date by which it must be returned and the name of the court it should be returned to since this may be different from the court where the proceedings were issued.

If you have settled this claim (or if you settle it on a future date) and do not need to have it heard or tried, you must let the court know immediately.

Have you sent a copy of this completed form to the other party(ies)?   ☐ Yes   ☐ No

---

A   Settlement

Under the Civil Procedure Rules parties should make every effort to settle their case before the hearing. This could be by discussion or negotiation (such as a roundtable meeting or settlement conference) or by a more formal process such as mediation. The court will want to know what steps have been taken. Settling the case early can save costs, including court hearing fees.

For legal representatives only

I confirm that I have explained to my client the need to try to settle; the options available; and the possibility of costs sanctions if they refuse to try to settle.   ☐

For all

Your answers to these questions may be considered by the court when it deals with the questions of costs: see Civil Procedure Rules Part 44.3 (4).

1. Given that the rules require you to try to settle the claim before the hearing, do you want to attempt to settle at this stage?   ☐ Yes   ☐ No

2. If Yes, do you want a one month stay?   ☐ Yes   ☐ No

3. Would you like the court to arrange a mediation appointment?   ☐ Yes   ☐ No
   (A fee will be payable to the mediation provider appointed by the National Mediation Helpline.)

4. If you answered 'No' to question 1, please state below the reasons why you consider it inappropriate to try to settle the claim at this stage.

Reasons:

B   Location of trial

Is there any reason why your claim needs to be heard at a particular court?   ☐ Yes   ☐ No

If Yes, say which court and why?

C   Pre-action protocols

You are expected to comply with the relevant pre-action protocol.

Have you done so?   ☐ Yes   ☐ No

If No, explain why?

D   Case management information

What amount of the claim is in dispute?   £

Applications

Have you made any application(s) in this claim?   ☐ Yes   ☐ No

If Yes, what for?
(e.g. summary judgment,
add another party)

For hearing on

Witnesses

So far as you know at this stage, what witnesses of fact do you intend to call at the trial or final hearing including, if appropriate, yourself?

Witness name	Witness to which facts

Experts

Do you wish to use expert evidence at the trial or final hearing?   ☐ Yes   ☐ No

Have you already copied any experts' report(s) to the other party(ies)?

☐ None yet obtained
☐ Yes   ☐ No

Do you consider the case suitable for a single joint expert in any field?   ☐ Yes   ☐ No

Please list any single joint experts you propose to use and any other experts you wish to rely on. Identify single joint experts with the initials 'SJ' after their name(s).

Expert's name	Field of expertise (eg. orthopaedic surgeon, surveyor, engineer)

Do you want your expert(s) to give evidence orally at the trial or final hearing?   ☐ Yes   ☐ No

If Yes, give the reasons why you think oral evidence is necessary:

Track

Which track do you consider is most suitable for your claim? Tick one box

☐ small claims track
☐ fast track
☐ multi-track

If you have indicated a track which would not be the normal track for the claim, please give brief reasons for your choice

E   Trial or final hearing

How long do you estimate the trial or final hearing will take?

days	hours	minutes

Are there any days when you, an expert or an essential witness will not be able to attend court for the trial or final hearing?   ☐ Yes   ☐ No

If Yes, please give details

Name	Dates not available

F   Proposed directions *(Parties should agree directions wherever possible)*

Have you attached a list of the directions you think appropriate for the management of the claim?   ☐ Yes   ☐ No

If Yes, have they been agreed with the other party(ies)?   ☐ Yes   ☐ No

G   Costs

*Do **not** complete this section if you have suggested your case is suitable for the small claims track **or** you have suggested one of the other tracks and you do not have a solicitor acting for you.*

What is your estimate of your costs incurred to date?   £

What do you estimate your overall costs are likely to be?   £

In substantial cases these questions should be answered in compliance with CPR Part 43

H   Fee

Have you attached the fee for filing this allocation questionnaire?   ☐ Yes   ☐ No

An allocation fee is payable if your claim or counterclaim exceeds £1,500.

Additional fees will be payable at further stages of the court process.

I   Other information

Have you attached documents to this questionnaire?   ☐ Yes   ☐ No

Have you sent these documents to the other party(ies)?   ☐ Yes   ☐ No

If Yes, when did they receive them?

Do you intend to make any applications in the immediate future?   ☐ Yes   ☐ No

If Yes, what for?

In the space below, set out any other information you consider will help the judge to manage the claim.

Signed

[Counsel] [Solicitor] [for the][1st][2nd][3rd][   ]
[Claimant] [Defendant] [Part 20 claimant]

Date

Please enter your name, reference number and full postal address including (if appropriate) details of telephone, DX, fax or e-mail

	If applicable	
	Telephone no.	
	Fax no.	
	DX no.	
Postcode	Your ref.	

E-mail

Notes for completing an allocation questionnaire

- If the claim is not settled, a judge must allocate it to an appropriate case management track. To help the judge choose the most just and cost-effective track, you must now complete the attached questionnaire.
- If you fail to return the allocation questionnaire by the date given, the judge may make an order which leads to your claim or defence being struck out, or hold an allocation hearing. If there is an allocation hearing the judge may order any party who has not filed their questionnaire to pay, immediately, the costs of that hearing.
- Use a separate sheet if you need more space for your answers marking clearly which section the information refers to. You should write the claim number on it, and on any other documents you send with your allocation questionnaire. Please ensure they are firmly attached to it.
- The letters below refer to the sections of the questionnaire and tell you what information is needed.

A Settlement

Under the Civil Procedure Rules parties should make every effort to settle their case before the hearing. This could be by discussion or negotiation (such as a roundtable meeting or settlement conference) or by a more formal process such as mediation. The court will want to know what steps have been taken. If you think that it would be worthwhile you and the other party trying to negotiate a settlement at this stage you should tick the 'Yes' box. The court may order a stay, whether or not all the other parties to the claim agree. Even if you are requesting a stay, you should still complete the rest of the questionnaire.

More information about settlement options is available in the Legal Services Commission leaflet 'Alternatives to Court' free from any county court or the LSC leaflet line on 0845 3000 343. If you would like to find out more about mediation, and the fees charged, contact the National Mediation Helpline on 0845 60 30 809 or go to www.nationalmediationhelpline.com. Although you may appoint a mediator of your choice, if you would like the court to arrange a mediation for you please tick 'Yes'. By ticking this box you are consenting to your contact details being passed via the Helpline to an accredited external mediation provider.

B Location of trial

High Court cases are usually heard at the Royal Courts of Justice or certain Civil Trial Centres. Fast or multi-track trials may be dealt with at a Civil Trial Centre or at the court where the claim is proceeding.

C Pre-action protocols

Before any claim is started, the court expects you to have complied with the relevant pre-action protocol, and to have exchanged information and documents relevant to the claim to assist in settling it. To find out which protocol is relevant to your claim see: http://www.justice.gov.uk/civil/procrules_fin/menus/protocol.htm

D Case management information

Applications

It is important for the court to know if you have already made any applications in the claim, what they are for and when they will be heard. The outcome of the applications may affect the case management directions the court gives.

Witnesses

Remember to include yourself as a witness of fact, if you will be giving evidence.

Experts

Oral or written expert evidence will only be allowed at the trial or final hearing with the court's permission. The judge will decide what permission it seems appropriate to give when the claim is allocated to track. Permission in small claims track cases will only be given exceptionally.

Track

The basic guide by which claims are normally allocated to a track is the amount in dispute, although other factors such as the complexity of the case will also be considered. Leaflet EX305 - The Fast Track and the Multi-track, explains this in greater detail.

E Trial or final hearing

You should enter only those dates when you, your expert(s) or essential witness(es) will not be able to attend court because of holiday or other commitments.

F Proposed directions

Attach the list of directions, if any, you believe will be appropriate to be given for the management of the claim. Agreed directions on fast and multi-track cases should be based on the forms of standard directions set out in the practice direction to CPR Part 28 and form PF52.

G Costs

Only complete this section if you are a solicitor and have suggested the claim is suitable for allocation to the fast or multi-track.

H Fee

For more information about court fees please go our website www.hmcourts-service.gov.uk or pick up a fees leaflet EX50 from any county court. If you cannot afford the fee, you may be eligible for remission of the fee. More details can be found in the leaflet EX160A, which can be downloaded from our website or you can pick up a copy from any county court.

I Other Information

Answer the questions in this section. Decide if there is any other information you consider will help the judge to manage the claim. Give details in the space provided referring to any documents you have attached to support what you are saying.

A(9)   Precedent H – Estimate of Costs

SCHEDULE OF COSTS PRECEDENTS
PRECEDENT H

IN THE HIGH COURT OF JUSTICE   2000 - B - 9999

QUEEN'S BENCH DIVISION

BRIGHTON DISTRICT REGISTRY

BETWEEN

                              AB   Claimant

                              and

                              CD   Defendant

ESTIMATE OF CLAIMANT'S COSTS DATED 12th APRIL 2001

The claimant instructed E F & Co under a conditional fee agreement dated 8th July 2000 in respect of which the following hourly rates are recoverable as base costs

Partner - £180 per hour plus VAT
Assistant Solicitor - £140 per hour plus VAT
Other fee earners - £85 per hour plus VAT

Item No.	Description of work done	V.A.T.	Disburse-ments	Profit Costs
	PART 1: BASE COSTS ALREADY INCURRED			
	8th July 2000 - EF & Co instructed			
	7th October 2000 - Claim issued			
1	Issue fee	-	£ 400.00	
	21st October 2000 - Particulars of claim served			
	25th November 2000 - Time for service of defence extended by agreement to 14th January 2001			
2	Fee on allocation	-	£ 80.00	
	20th January 2001 - case allocated to multi-track			
	9th February 2001 - Case management conference at which costs were awarded to the claimant and the base costs were summarily assessed at £400 (paid on 24th February 2001)			-
	23rd February 2001 - Claimant's list of documents			
	ATTENDANCES, COMMUNICATIONS AND WORK DONE			
3	**Claimant** 0.75 hours at £180			£ 135.00
4	4.4 hours at £140			£ 616.00
	To Summary	£ -	£ 480.00	£ 751.00

Item No.	Description of work done	V.A.T.	Disburse-ments	Profit Costs
5	**Witnesses of Fact** 3.8 hours at £140			£ 532.00
6	Paid travelling on 9th October 2000	£ 4.02	£ 22.96	
7	**Medical expert (Dr. IJ)** 1.5 hours at £140			£ 210.00
8	Dr. IJ''s fee for report		£ 350.00	
9	**Defendant and his solicitor** 2.5 hours at £140			£ 350.00
10	**Court (communications only)** 0.4 hours at £140			£ 56.00
11	**Documents** 0.75 hours at £180 and 22.25 hours at £140			£3,250.00
12	**Negotiations** 2.75 hours at £140			£ 385.00
13	VAT on solicitor's base fees	£ 968.45		
	To Summary	£ 972.47	£ 372.96	£4,783.00
	PART2: BASE COSTS TO BE INCURRED			
14	Fee on listing -		£ 400.00	
15	Attendance at pre-trial review 5 hours at £140			£ 700.00
16	Counsel's base fee for pre-trial review		£ 750.00	
17	Attendance at trial 20 hours at £140			£2,800.00
18	Counsel's base fee for trial including refresher		£3,000.00	
19	Fee of expert witness (Dr. IJ)	-	£1,000.00	
20	Expenses of witnesses of fact	-	£ 150.00	
	ATTENDANCES, COMMUNICATIONS AND WORK TO BE DONE			
21	**Claimant** 1 hour at £180			£ 180.00
22	8 hours at £140			£1,120.00
23	**Witnesses of fact** 5 hours at £140			£ 700.00
24	**Medical expert (Dr. IJ)** 1 hour at £140			£ 140.00
25	**Defendant and his solicitor** 2 hours at £140			£ 280.00
	To Summary	£ -	£ 5,300.00	£5,920.00

Item No.	Description of work done	V.A.T.	Disburse-ments	Profit Costs
26	**Court (communications only)** 1 hour at £140			£ 140.00
27	**Counsel (communications only)** 3 hours at £140			£ 420.00
28	**Documents** 1 hour at £180, 25 hours at £140 and 15 hours at £85			£4,995.00
29	**Negotiations** 5 hours at £140			£ 700.00
30	**Other work** 5 hours at £140			£ 700.00
31	VAT on solicitor's base fees	£2,253.13		
	To Summary	£2,253.13	£ -	£ 6,955.00
	SUMMARY			
	Part 1 Page 1 Page 2	£ - £ 972.47	£ 480.00 £ 372.96	£ 751.00 £4,783.00
	Total base costs already incurred	£ 972.47	£ 852.96	£5,534.00
	Part 2 Page 2 Page 3	£ - £2,253.13	£ 5,300.00 £ -	£5,920.00 £6,955.00
	Total base costs to be incurred	£2,253.13	£5,300.00	£12,875.00
	Total of base costs	£3,225.60	£6,152.96	£18,409.00
	Grand total			£27,787.56

A(10)   Form N242A – Notice of Offer to Settle – Part 36

Notice of offer to settle - Part 36

Name of court *(If proceedings have started)*	
Claim No. (or other ref)	
Claimant (including ref)	
Defendant (including ref)	

To the Offeree ('s Solicitor) *(Insert name and address)*

Take notice the (defendant)(claimant) offers to settle the claim. This offer is intended to have the consequences of Part 36. If the offer is accepted within _____ days (must be at least 21 days) of service of this notice the defendant will be liable for the claimant's costs in accordance with Rule 36.10 of the Civil Procedure Rules.

The offer is to settle:

(tick as appropriate)

☐ the whole of the claim

☐ part of the claim *(give details below)*

☐ a certain issue or issues in the claim *(give details below)*

The offer is:

(Insert details - expand box as necessary)

Note: Rule 36.5 specifies details that must be included in an offer including periodical payments of damages for future pecuniary loss.

Rule 36.11 requires that an offer by a defendant to pay a sum of money (other than periodical payments) must be paid within 14 days of acceptance.

☐ It (does)(does not) take into account all(part) of the following counterclaim:

(give details of the counterclaim)

Include only if claim for provisional damages

☐ The offer is made in satisfaction of the claim on the assumption that the claimant will not [develop (state the disease)] **OR** [suffer (state type of deterioration)].

But if that does occur, the claimant will be entitled to claim further damages at any time before (insert date).

OR

☐ This offer does not include an offer in respect of the claim for provisional damages.

To be completed by defendants only

☐ This offer is made without regard to any liability for recoverable benefits under the Social Security (Recovery of Benefits Act) 1997.

OR

☐ This offer is intended to include any relevant deductible benefits for which I am liable under the Social Security (Recovery of Benefits Act) 1997.

The amount of [£   ] is offered by way of gross compensation.

[I have not yet received a certificate of recoverable benefits]

OR

[The following amounts in respect of the following benefits are to be deducted (insert details).

Type of benefit   **Amount**

The net amount offered is therefore [£   ]]

Signed ⬚ Offeror('s solicitor)

Position held (If signing on behalf of a firm or company) ⬚

Date ⬚

A(11)   Form N244 – Application Notice

Application notice

For help in completing this form please read
the notes for guidance form N244Notes.

Name of court	
Claim no.	
Warrant no. (if applicable)	
Claimant's name (including ref.)	
Defendant's name (including ref.)	
Date	

1. What is your name or, if you are a solicitor, the name of your firm?

2. Are you a   ☐ Claimant   ☐ Defendant   ☐ Solicitor

   ☐ Other *(please specify)*

   If you are a solicitor whom do you represent?

3. What order are you asking the court to make and why?

4. Have you attached a draft of the order you are applying for?   ☐ Yes   ☐ No

5. How do you want to have this application dealt with?   ☐ at a hearing   ☐ without a hearing

   ☐ at a telephone hearing

6. How long do you think the hearing will last?   ☐ Hours   ☐ Minutes

   Is this time estimate agreed by all parties?   ☐ Yes   ☐ No

7. Give details of any fixed trial date or period

8. What level of Judge does your hearing need?

9. Who should be served with this application?

10. What information will you be relying on, in support of your application?

☐ the attached witness statement

☐ the statement of case

☐ the evidence set out in the box below

If necessary, please continue on a separate sheet.

Statement of Truth

(I believe) (The applicant believes) that the facts stated in this section (and any continuation sheets) are true.

Signed _____   Dated _____

Applicant('s Solicitor)('s litigation friend)

Full name _____

Name of applicant's solicitor's firm _____

Position or office held _____
(if signing on behalf of firm or company)

11. Signature and address details

Signed _____   Dated _____

Applicant('s Solicitor)('s litigation friend)

Position or office held _____
(if signing on behalf of firm or company)

Applicant's address to which documents about this application should be sent

	If applicable	
	Phone no.	
	Fax no.	
Postcode	DX no.	
	Ref no.	

E-mail address	

Application Notice (Form N244) – Notes for Guidance

Court Staff cannot give legal advice. If you need information or advice on a legal problem you can contact Community Legal Service Direct on 0845 345 4 345 or www.clsdirect.org.uk, or a Citizens Advice Bureau. Details of your local offices and contact numbers are available via their website www.citizensadvice.org.uk

Paying the court fee

A court fee is payable depending on the type of application you are making. For example:

- To apply for judgment to be set aside

- To apply to vary a judgment or suspend enforcement

- To apply for a summons or order for a witness to attend

- To apply by consent, or without service of the application notice, for a judgment or order.

No fee is payable for an application by consent for an adjournment of a hearing if it is received by the court at least 14 days before the date of the hearing.

What if I cannot afford the fee?

If you show that a payment of a court fee would involve undue hardship to you, you may be eligible for a fee concession.

For further information, or to apply for a fee concession, ask court staff for a copy of the combined booklet and form EX160A - Court fees - Do I have to pay them? This is also available from any county court office, or a copy of the leaflet can be downloaded from our website www.hmcourts-service.gov.uk

Completing the form

Question 3

Set out what order you are applying for and why; e.g. to adjourn the hearing because..., to set aside a judgment against me because... etc.

Question 5

Most applications will require a hearing and you will be expected to attend. The court will allocate a hearing date and time for the application. Please indicate in a covering letter any dates that you are unavailable within the next six weeks.

The court will only deal with the application 'without a hearing' in the following circumstances.

- Where all the parties agree to the terms of the order being asked for;

- Where all the parties agree that the court should deal with the application without a hearing, or

- Where the court does not consider that a hearing would be appropriate.

Telephone hearings are only available in applications where at least one of the parties involved in the case is legally represented. Not all applications will be suitable for a telephone hearing and the court may refuse your request.

Question 6

If you do not know how long the hearing will take do not guess but leave these boxes blank.

Question 7

If your case has already been allocated a hearing date or trial period please insert details of those dates in the box.

Question 8

If your case is being heard in the High Court or a District Registry please indicate whether it is to be dealt with by a Master, District Judge or Judge.

Question 9

Please indicate in the box provided who you want the court to send a copy of the application to.

Question 10

In this section please set out the information you want the court to take account of in support of the application you are making.
If you wish to rely on:

- **a witness statement,** tick the first box and attach the statement to the application notice. A witness statement form is available on request from the court office.

- **a statement of case,** tick the second box if you intend to rely on your particulars of claim or defence in support of your application.

- **written evidence** on this form, tick the third box and enter details in the space provided. You must also complete the statement of truth. Proceedings for contempt of court may be brought against a person who signs a statement of truth without an honest belief in its truth.

Question 11

The application must be signed and include your current address and contact details. If you agree that the court and the other parties may communicate with you by Document Exchange, telephone, facsimile or email, complete the details

Before returning your form to the court

Have you:
- signed the form on page 2,
- enclosed the correct fee or an application for fee concession,
- made sufficient copies of your application and supporting documentation. You will need to submit one copy for each party to be served and one copy for the court.

A(12)   Form N260 – Statement of Costs for Summary Assessment

Statement of Costs
(summary assessment)

In the	
	Court
Case Reference	

Judge/Master

Case Title

[Party]'s Statement of Costs for the hearing on *(date)*   **(interim application/fast track trial)**

Description of fee earners*
    (a)   *(name) (grade) (hourly rate claimed)*
    (b)   *(name) (grade) (hourly rate claimed)*

Attendances on   *(party)*

    (a) *(number)*   hours at £   £   0.00
    (b) *(number)*   hours at £   £   0.00

Attendances on opponents
    (a) *(number)*   hours at £   £   0.00
    (b) *(number)*   hours at £   £   0.00

Attendance on others
    (a) *(number)*   hours at £   £   0.00
    (b) *(number)*   hours at £   £   0.00

Site inspections etc
    (a) *(number)*   hours at £   £   0.00
    (b) *(number)*   hours at £   £   0.00

Work done on negotiations
    (a) *(number)*   hours at £   £   0.00
    (b) *(number)*   hours at £   £   0.00

Other work, not covered above
    (a) *(number)*   hours at £   £   0.00
    (b) *(number)*   hours at £   £   0.00

Work done on documents
    (a) *(number)*   hours at £   £   0.00
    (b) *(number)*   hours at £   £   0.00

Attendance at hearing
    (a) *(number)*   hours at £   £   0.00
    (b) *(number)*   hours at £   £   0.00

    (a) *(number)*   hours travel and waiting at £   £   0.00
    (b) *(number)*   hours travel and waiting at £   £   0.00

    Sub Total   £   0.00

Brought forward £ [0.00]

Counsel's fees *(name) (year of call)* [　　　　]

　　　　Fee for [advice/conference/documents] £ [　　]

　　　　Fee for hearing £ [　　]

Other expenses

　　　　[court fees] £ [　　]

　　　　Others £ [　　]

　　　　(give brief description) [　　　　]

　　　　Total £ [0.00]

Amount of VAT claimed

　　　　on solicitors and counsel's fees £ [　　]

　　　　on other expenses £ [　　]

Grand Total £ [0.00]

The costs estimated above do not exceed the costs which the *(party)* [　　　　] is liable to pay in respect of the work which this estimate covers.

Dated [　　　　]　Signed [　　　　]

Name of firm of solicitors [partner] for the *(party)* [　　　　]

* 4 grades of fee earner are suggested:

(A) Solicitors with over eight years post qualification experience including at least eight years litigation experience.

(B) Solicitors and legal executives with over four years post qualification experience including at least four years litigation experience.

(C) Other solicitors and legal executives and fee earners of equivalent experience.

(D) Trainee solicitors, para legals and other fee earners.

"Legal Executive" means a Fellow of the Institute of Legal Executives. Those who are not Fellows of the Institute are not entitled to call themselves legal executives and in principle are therefore not entitled to the same hourly rate as a legal executive.

In respect of each fee earner communications should be treated as attendances and routine communications should be claimed at one tenth of the hourly rate.

A(13)   Form N170 – Pre-trial Checklist

Listing questionnaire
(Pre-trial checklist)

In the

To be completed by, or on behalf of,

Claim No.	
Last date for filing with court office	
Date(s) fixed for trial or trial period	

who is [1ˢᵗ][2ⁿᵈ][3ʳᵈ][   ][Claimant][Defendant]
[Part 20 claimant][Part 20 defendant] in this claim

This form must be **completed** and **returned** to the court no later than the date given above. If not, your statement of case may be struck out or some other sanction imposed.

If the claim has settled, or settles before the trial date, you must let the court know immediately.

Legal representatives only: You must **attach** estimates of costs incurred to date, and of your likely overall costs. In substantial cases, these should be provided in compliance with CPR Part 43.

For multi-track claims only, you must also **attach** a proposed timetable for the trial itself.

A Confirmation of compliance with directions

1. I confirm that I have complied with those directions already given which require action by me.   ☐Yes ☐No

If you are unable to give confirmation, state which directions you have still to comply with and the date by which this will be done.

Directions	Date

2. I believe that additional directions are necessary before the trial takes place.   ☐Yes ☐No

If Yes, you should attach an application and a draft order.

*Include in your application all directions needed to enable the claim **to be tried on the date, or within the trial period, already fixed.** These should include any issues relating to experts and their evidence, and any orders needed in respect of directions still requiring action by any other party.*

3. Have you agreed the additional directions you are seeking with the other party(ies)?   ☐Yes ☐No

B Witnesses

1. How many witnesses (including yourself) will be giving evidence on your behalf at the trial? *(Do not include experts - see Section C)*   ☐

Continued over ⟳

Witnesses continued

2. If the trial date is not yet fixed, are there any days within the trial period you or your witnesses would wish to avoid if possible? *(Do not include experts - see Section C)*

Please give details

Name of witness	Dates to be avoided, if possible	Reason

Please specify any special facilities or arrangements needed at court for the party or any witness (e.g. witness with a disability).

3. Will you be providing an interpreter for any of your witnesses? ☐Yes ☐No

C Experts

You are reminded that you may not use an expert's report or have your expert give oral evidence unless the court has given permission. If you do not have permission, you must make an application (see section A2 above)

1. Please give the information requested for your expert(s)

Name	Field of expertise	Joint expert?	Is report agreed?	Has permission been given for oral evidence?
		☐Yes ☐No	☐Yes ☐No	☐Yes ☐No
		☐Yes ☐No	☐Yes ☐No	☐Yes ☐No
		☐Yes ☐No	☐Yes ☐No	☐Yes ☐No

2. Has there been discussion between experts? ☐Yes ☐No

3. Have the experts signed a joint statement? ☐Yes ☐No

4. If your expert is giving oral evidence and the trial date is not yet fixed, is there any day within the trial period which the expert would wish to avoid, if possible? ☐Yes ☐No

If Yes, please give details

Name	Dates to be avoided, if possible	Reason

D Legal representation

1. Who will be presenting your case at the trial?   ☐ You   ☐ Solicitor   ☐ Counsel

2. If the trial date is not yet fixed, is there any day within the trial
   period that the person presenting your case would wish to avoid,
   if possible?   ☐ Yes   ☐ No

If Yes, please give details

Name	Dates to be avoided, if possible	Reason

E The trial

1. Has the estimate of the time needed for trial changed?   ☐ Yes   ☐ No

   If Yes, say how long you estimate the whole trial will take, including
   both parties' cross-examination and closing arguments   ☐ days   ☐ hours   ☐ minutes

2. If different from original estimate have you agreed with the other
   party(ies) that this is now the **total** time needed?   ☐ Yes   ☐ No

3. Is the timetable for trial you have attached agreed with the
   other party(ies)?   ☐ Yes   ☐ No

Fast track cases only

The court will normally give you 3 weeks notice of the date fixed for a fast track trial unless, in
exceptional circumstances, the court directs that shorter notice will be given.

Would you be prepared to accept shorter notice of the date
fixed for trial?   ☐ Yes   ☐ No

F Document and fee checklist

Tick as appropriate

I attach to this questionnaire -

☐ An application and fee for additional directions   ☐ A proposed timetable for trial

☐ A draft order   ☐ An estimate of costs

☐ Listing fee

Signed	Please enter your [firm's] name, reference number and full postal address including (if appropriate) details of DX, fax or e-mail
[Counsel][Solicitor][for the][1st][2nd][3rd][ ] [Claimant][Defendant] [Part 20 claimant][Part 20 defendant]	
Date	Postcode

Tel. no.		DX no.		E-mail	
Fax no.		Ref. no.			

A(14)   Appendix to Part 28

Fast Track Standard Directions

Further Statements of Case

The   must file a   and serve a copy on   no later than   .

Requests for Further Information

Any request for clarification or further information based on another party's statement of case shall be served no later than

[Any such request shall be dealt with no later than   ].

Disclosure of Documents

[No disclosure of documents is required]

[[Each party] [The   ] shall give [to the   ] [to every other party] standard disclosure of documents [relating to   ] by serving copies together with a disclosure statement no later than   ]

[Disclosure shall take place as follows:

[Each party shall give standard discovery to every other party by list]

[Disclosure is limited to [standard] [disclosure by the   to the   ] [of documents relating to damage] [the following documents   ]

[The latest date for delivery of the lists is   ]

[The latest date for service of any request to inspect or for a copy of a document is   ]]

Witnesses of Fact

Each party shall serve on every other party the witness statements of all witnesses of fact on whom he intends to rely.

There shall be simultaneous exchange of such statements no later than   .

Expert Evidence

[No expert evidence being necessary, no party has permission to call or rely on expert evidence].

[On it appearing to the court that expert evidence is necessary on the issue of [   ] and that that evidence should be given by the report of a single expert instructed jointly by the parties, the   shall no later than   inform the court whether or not such an expert has been instructed].

[The expert evidence on the issue of   shall be limited to a single expert jointly instructed by the parties.

If the parties cannot agree by   who that expert is to be and about the payment of his fees either party may apply for further directions.

Unless the parties agree in writing or the court orders otherwise, the fees and expenses of such an expert shall be paid to him [by the parties equally] [   ] and be limited to £   .

[The report of the expert shall be filed at the court no later than   ].

[No party shall be entitled to recover by way of costs from any other party more than £   for the fees or   expenses of an expert].

The parties shall exchange reports setting out the substance of any expert evidence on which they intend to rely.

[The exchange shall take place simultaneously no later than   ].

[The   shall serve his report(s) no later than the   and the   shall serve his reports no later than the
].

[The exchange of reports relating to [causation] [   ] shall take place simultaneously no later than
. The   shall serve his report(s) relating to [damage] [   ] no later than   and the
shall serve his reports relating to it no later than   ].

Reports shall be agreed if possible no later than [days after service] [   ].

[If the reports are not agreed within that time there shall be a without prejudice discussion between the relevant experts no later than   to identify the issues between them and to reach agreement if possible.

The experts shall prepare for the court a statement of the issues on which they agree and on which they disagree with a summary of their reasons, and that statement shall be filed with the court [no later than   ] [with] [no later than the date for filing] [the listing questionnaire].

[Each party has permission to use [   ] as expert witness(es) to give [oral] evidence [in the form of a report] at the trial in the field of   provided that the substance of the evidence to be given has been disclosed as above and has not been agreed].

[Each party has permission to use in evidence   experts' report(s) [and the court will consider when the claim is listed for trial whether expert oral evidence will be allowed].]

Questions to Experts

The time for service on another party of any question addressed to an expert instructed by that party is not later than   days after service of that expert's report.

Any such question shall be answered within   days of service.

Requests for Information etc.

Each party shall serve any request for clarification or further information based on any document disclosed or statement served by another party no later than   days after disclosure or service.

Any such request shall be dealt with within   days of service.

Documents to be Filed with Listing Questionnaires

The parties must file with their listing questionnaires copies of [their experts' reports] [witness statements] [replies to requests for further information]

Dates for Filing Listing Questionnaires and the Trial

Each party must file a completed listing questionnaire no later than   .

The trial of this case will take place [on] [on a date to be fixed between and   ].

Directions Following Filing of Listing Questionnaire

Expert Evidence

The parties have permission to rely at the trial on expert evidence as follows:

The claimant   Oral evidence

                      Written evidence

The defendant: Oral evidence

                      Written evidence

Trial Timetable

The time allowed for the trial is

[The timetable for the trial may be agreed by the parties, subject to the approval of the trial judge].

[The timetable for the trial (subject to the approval of the trial judge) will be that   ].

[The evidence in chief for each party will be contained in witness statements and reports, the time allowed for cross-examination by the defendant is limited to   and the time allowed for cross-examination by the claimant is limited to   ].

[The time allowed for the claimant's evidence is   . The time allowed for the defendant's evidence is   ].

The time allowed for the submissions on behalf of each party is   .

The remainder of the time allowed for the trial (being   ) is reserved for the judge to consider and give the judgment and to deal with costs].

Trial Bundle etc

The claimant shall lodge an indexed bundle of documents contained in a ring binder and with each page clearly numbered at the court not more than 7 days and not less than 3 days before the start of the trial.

[A case summary (which should not exceed 250 words) outlining the matters still in issue, and referring where appropriate to the relevant documents shall be included in the bundle for the assistance of the judge in reading the papers before the trial].

[The parties shall seek to agree the contents of the trial bundle and the case summary].

Settlement

Each party must inform the court immediately if the claim is settled whether or not it is then possible to file a draft consent order to give effect to their agreement.

A(15)   Form N252 – Notice of Commencement of Assessment of Bill of Costs

Notice of commencement of assessment of bill of costs

In the	
Claim No.	
Claimant (include Ref.)	
Defendant (include Ref.)	

To the claimant(defendant)

Following an .... *(insert name of document eg. order, judgment)* dated ....
(copy attached) I have prepared my Bill of Costs for assessment. The Bill totals *£ .... If you choose to
dispute this bill and your objections are not upheld at the assessment hearing, the full amount payable (including the
assessment fee) will be £ .... (together with interest *(see note below)*). I shall also seek the costs of the
assessment hearing

Your points of dispute must include

- details of the items in the bill of costs which are disputed

- concise details of the nature and grounds of the dispute for each item and, if you seek a reduction in
  those items, suggest, where practicable, a reduced figure

You must serve your points of dispute by .... *(insert date 21 days from the date of service
of this notice)* on me at:- *(give full name and address for service including any DX number or reference)*

You must also serve copies of your points of dispute on all other parties to the assessment identified below *(you do not
need to serve your points of dispute on the court).*

I certify that I have also served the following person(s) with a copy of this notice and my Bill of Costs:- *(give details of
persons served)*

If I have not received your points of dispute by the above date, I will ask the court to issue a default costs certificate
for the full amount of my bill *(see above*)* plus fixed costs and court fee in the total amount of £ ....

Signed .... **Date** ....
(Claimant)(Defendant)('s solicitor)

Note: Interest may be added to all High Court judgments and certain county court judgments of £5,000 or more under the
Judgments Act 1838 and the County Courts Act 1984.

The court office at

is open between 10 am and 4 pm Monday to Friday. When corresponding with the court, please address forms or letters to the Court Manager and quote the claim number.

N252 Notice of commencement of assessment of bill of costs (12.99)   *The Court Service Publications Unit*

A(16)   Precedent A – Bill of Costs

SCHEDULE OF COSTS PRECEDENTS
PRECEDENT A

IN THE HIGH COURT OF JUSTICE   2000 - B - 9999

QUEEN'S BENCH DIVISION

BRIGHTON DISTRICT REGISTRY

BETWEEN

AB   Claimant

- and -

CD   Defendant

**CLAIMANT'S BILL OF COSTS TO BE ASSESSED PURSUANT
TO THE ORDER DATED 26th JULY 2000**

V.A.T. No. 33 4404 90

In these proceedings the claimant sought compensation for personal injuries and other losses suffered in a road accident which occurred on Friday 1st January 1999 near the junction between Bolingbroke Lane and Regency Road, Brighton, East Sussex. The claimant had been travelling as a front seat passenger in a car driven by the defendant. The claimant suffered severe injuries when, because of the defendant's negligence, the car left the road and collided with a brick wall.

The defendant was later convicted of various offences arising out of the accident including careless driving and driving under the influence of drink or drugs.

In the civil action the defendant alleged that immediately before the car journey began the claimant had known that the defendant was under the influence of alcohol and therefore consented to the risk of injury or was contributorily negligent as to it. It was also alleged that, immediately before the accident occurred, the claimant wrongfully took control of the steering wheel so causing the accident to occur.

The claimant first instructed solicitors, E F & Co, in this matter in July 2000. The claim form was issued in October 2000 and in February 2001 the proceedings were listed for a two day trial commencing 25th July 2001. At the trial the defendant was found liable but the compensation was reduced by 25% to take account of contributory negligence by the claimant. The claimant was awarded a total of £78,256.83 plus £1,207.16 interest plus costs.

The claimant instructed E F & Co under a conditional fee agreement dated 8th July 2000 which specifies the following base fees and success fees.

    Partner - £180 per hour plus VAT
    Assistant Solicitor - £140 per hour plus VAT
    Other fee earners - £85 per hour plus VAT
    Success fees exclusive of disbursement funding costs: 40%
    Success fee in respect of disbursement funding costs: 7.5% (not claimed in this bill)

Except where the contrary is stated the proceedings were conducted on behalf of the claimant by an assistant solicitor, admitted November 1999.

E F & Co instructed Counsel (Miss GH, called 1992) under a conditional fee agreement dated 5th June 2001 which specifies a success fee of 75% and base fees, payable in various circumstances, of which the following are relevant

Fees for interim hearing whose estimated duration is up to 2 hours: £600
Brief for trial whose estimated duration is 2 days: £2,000
Fee for second and subsequent days: £650 per day

Item No.	Description of work done	V.A.T.	Disburse -ments	Profit Costs
	8th July 2000 - EF & Co instructed			
	22nd July 2000 - AEI with Eastbird Legal Protection Ltd			
1	Premium for policy	-	£ 120.00	
	7th October 2000 - Claim issued			
2	Issue fee	-	£ 400.00	
	21st October 2000 - Particulars of claim served			
	25th November 2000 - Time for service of defence extended by agreement to 14th January 2001			
3	Fee on allocation	-	£ 80.00	
	20th January 2001 - case allocated to multi-track			
	9th February 2001 - Case management conference at which costs were awarded to the claimant and the base costs were summarily assessed at £400 (paid on 24th February 2001)			-
	23rd February 2001 - Claimant's list of documents			
	12th April 2001 - Payment into court of £25,126.33			
	13th April 2001 - Filing pre-trial checklist			
4	Fee on listing	-	£ 400.00	
5	28th June 2001 - Pre trial review: costs in case Engaged 1.5 hours £210.00 Travel and waiting 2.00 hours £280.00 Total solicitor's base fee for attending			£ 490.00
6	Counsel's base fee for pre trial review (Miss GH)		£ 600.00	
7	25th July 2001 - Attending first day of trial: adjourned part heard Engaged in Court 5.00 hours £700.00 Engaged in conference 0.75 hours £105.00 Travel and waiting 1.5 hours £210.00 Total solicitor's base fee for attending			£1,015.00
8	Counsel's base fee for trial (Miss GH)		£2,000.00	
9	Fee of expert witness (Dr. IJ)	-	£ 850.00	
10	Expenses of witnesses of fact	-	£ 84.00	
11	26th July 2001 - Attending second day of trial when judgment was given for the claimant in the sum of £78,256.53 plus £1207.16 interest plus costs Engaged in Court 3.00 hours £420.00 Engaged in conference 1.5 hours £210.00 Travel and waiting 1.5 hours £210.00 Total solicitor's base fee for attending			£ 840.00
12	Counsel's base fee for second day (Miss GH)		£ 650.00	
	To Summary	£ -	£5,184.00	£2,345.00

Item No.	Description of work done	V.A.T.	Disburse -ments	Profit Costs
	Claimant			
13	8th July 2000 - First instructions: 0.75 hours by Partner: base fee			£ 135.00
14	Other timed attendances in person and by telephone - See Schedule 1 Total base fee for Schedule 1 - 7.5 hours			£1,050.00
15	Routine letters out and telephone calls - 29 (17 + 12) total base fee			£ 406.00
16	**Witnesses of Fact** Timed attendances in person, by letter out and by telephone - See Schedule 2 Total base fee for Schedule 2 - 5.2 hours			£ 728.00
17	Routine letters out, e mails and telephone calls - 8 (4 + 2 + 2)total base fee			£ 112.00
18	Paid travelling on 9th October 2000	£ 4.02	£ 22.96	
	Medical expert (Dr. IJ)			
19	11th September 2000 - long letter out 0.33 hours: base fee			£ 46.20
20	30th January 2001 - long letter out 0.25 hours base fee			£ 35.00
21	23rd May 2001 - telephone call 0.2 hours base fee			£ 28.00
22	Routine letters out and telephone calls - 10 (6 + 4) total base fee			£ 140.00
23	Dr. IJ's fee for report	-	£ 350.00	
	Defendant and his solicitor			
24	8th July 2000 - timed letter sent 0.5 hours: base fee			£ 70.00
25	19th February 2001 - telephone call 0.25 hours: base fee			£ 35.00
26	Routine letters out and telephone calls - 24 (18 + 6) total base fee			£ 336.00
27	**Communications with the court** Routine letters out and telephone calls - 9 (8 + 1) total base fee			£ 126.00
28	**Communications with Counsel** Routine letters out, e mails and telephone calls - 19 (4 + 7 + 8) total base fee			£ 266.00
29	**Work done on documents** Timed attendances - See Schedule 3 Total base fees for Schedule 3 - 0.75 hours at £180, 44.5 hours at £140, 12 hours at £85			£7,385.00
30	**Work done on negotiations** 23rd March 2001 - meeting at offices of Solicitors for the Defendant Engaged - 1.5 hours £210.00 Travel and waiting - 1.25 hours £175.00 Total base fee for meeting			£ 385.00
31	**Other work done** Preparing and checking bill Engaged: Solicitor - 1 hour £140.00 Engaged: Costs Draftsman - 4 hours £340.00 Total base fee on other work done			£ 480.00
	To Summary	£ 4.02	£ 372.96	£11,763.20

Item No.	Description of work done	V.A.T.	Disburse-ments	Profit Costs
32	Success fee on solicitor's base fee on interim orders which were summarily assessed (40% of £400) plus VAT at 17.5%	£ 28.00		£ 160.00
33	VAT on solicitor's other base fees (17.5% of £14,108.20)	£ 2,468.94		
34	Success fee on solicitor's other base fees (40% of £14,108.20) plus VAT at 17.5%	£ 987.58		£ 5,643.28
35	VAT on Counsel's base fees (17.5% of £3,250)'	£ 568.75		
36	Success fee on Counsel's base fee (75% of £3,250) plus VAT at 17.5%'	£ 426.57	£ 2,437.50	
	To Summary	£ 4,479.84	£ 2,437.50	£ 5,803.28
	SUMMARY			
	Page 3 £	-	£ 5,184.00	£ 2,345.00
	Page 4 £	4.02	£ 372.96	£ 11,763.20
	Page 5 £	4,479.84	£ 2,437.50	£ 5,803.28
	Totals:	£ 4,483.86	£ 7,994.46	£ 19,911.48
	Grand total:			£ 32,389.80

A(17)   Precedent G – Points of Dispute

SCHEDULE OF COSTS PRECEDENTS
PRECEDENT G

IN THE HIGH COURT OF JUSTICE   2000 B 9999

QUEEN'S BENCH DIVISION

BRIGHTON DISTRICT REGISTRY

B E T W E E N

AB
Claimant

- and -

CD
Defendant

POINTS OF DISPUTE SERVED BY THE DEFENDANT

Item	Dispute	Claimant's Comments
General point	Base rates claimed for the assistant solicitor and other fee earners are excessive. Reduce to £100 and £70 respectively plus VAT. Each item in which these rates are claimed should be recalculated at the reduced rates.	
(1)	The premium claimed is excessive. Reduce to £95.	

Item	Dispute	Claimant's Comments
(14)	The claim for timed attendances on claimant (schedule 1) is excessive. Reduce to 4 hours ie. £400 at reduced rates.	
(29)	The total claim for work done on documents by the assistant solicitor is excessive. A reasonable allowance in respect of documents concerning court and counsel is 8 hours, for documents concerning witnesses and the expert witness, 6.5 hours, for work done on arithmetic, 2.25 hours and for other documents, 5.5 hours. Reduce to 22.25 hours ie. £2,225 at reduced rates (£3,380 in total).	
(31)	The time claimed is excessive. Reduce solicitors time to 0.5 hours ie. to £50 at reduced rates and reduce the costs draftsman's time to three hours ie. £210 (£260 in total).	
(32)	The success fee claimed is excessive. Reduce to 25% ie. £100 plus VAT of £17.50.	
(33)	The total base fees when recalculated on the basis of the above points amount to £7,788, upon which VAT is £1,362.90.	
(34)	The success fee claimed is excessive. Reduce to 25% of £7,788 ie £1,947.50 plus VAT of £340.73.	
(36)	The success fee claimed is excessive.Reduce to 50% ie £1,625 plus VAT of £284.38.	

Served on .... [date] by .... [name] [solicitors for] the Defendant.

A(18)   Practice Direction – Pre-action Conduct

SECTION I – INTRODUCTION

1. Aims

1.1   The aims of this Practice Direction are to –
(1)   enable parties to settle the issue between them without the need to start proceedings (that is, a court claim); and
(2)   support the efficient management by the court and the parties of proceedings that cannot be avoided.

1.2   These aims are to be achieved by encouraging the parties to –
(1)   exchange information about the issue, and
(2)   consider using a form of Alternative Dispute Resolution ('ADR').

2. Scope

2.1   This Practice Direction describes the conduct the court will normally expect of the prospective parties prior to the start of proceedings.

2.2   There are some types of application where the principles in this Practice Direction clearly cannot or should not apply. These include, but are not limited to, for example –
(1)   applications for an order where the parties have agreed between them the terms of the court order to be sought ('consent orders');
(2)   applications for an order where there is no other party for the applicant to engage with;
(3)   most applications for directions by a trustee or other fiduciary;
(4)   applications where telling the other potential party in advance would defeat the purpose of the application (for example, an application for an order to freeze assets).

2.3   Section II deals with the approach of the court in exercising its powers in relation to pre-action conduct. Subject to paragraph 2.2, it applies in relation to all types of proceedings including those governed by the pre-action protocols that have been approved by the Head of Civil Justice and which are listed in paragraph 5.2 of this Practice Direction.

2.4   Section III deals with principles governing the conduct of the parties in cases which are not subject to a pre-action protocol.

2.5   Section III of this Practice Direction is supplemented by two annexes aimed at different types of claimant.
(1)   **Annex A** sets out detailed guidance on a pre-action procedure that is likely to satisfy the court in most circumstances where no pre-action protocol or other formal pre-action procedure applies. It is intended as a guide for parties, particularly those without legal representation, in straightforward claims that are likely to be disputed. It is not intended to apply to debt claims where it is not disputed that the money is owed and where the claimant follows a statutory or other formal pre-action procedure.
(2)   **Annex B** sets out some specific requirements that apply where the claimant is a business and the defendant is an individual. The requirements may be complied with at any time between the claimant first intimating the possibility of court proceedings and the claimant's letter before claim.

2.6   Section IV contains requirements that apply to all cases including those subject to the pre-action protocols (unless a relevant pre-action protocol contains a different provision). It is supplemented by **Annex C**, which sets out guidance on instructing experts.

3. Definitions

3.1   In this Practice Direction together with the Annexes –
(1)   'proceedings' means any proceedings started under Part 7 or Part 8 of the Civil Procedure Rules 1998 ('CPR');
(2)   'claimant' and 'defendant' refer to the respective parties to potential proceedings;
(3)   'ADR' means alternative dispute resolution, and is the collective description of methods of resolving disputes otherwise than through the normal trial process; (see paragraph 8.2 for further information); and
(4)   'compliance' means acting in accordance with, as applicable, the principles set out in Section III of this Practice Direction, the requirements in Section IV and a relevant pre-action protocol. The words 'comply' and 'complied' should be construed accordingly.

SECTION II – THE APPROACH OF THE COURTS

4. Compliance

4.1   The CPR enable the court to take into account the extent of the parties' compliance with this Practice Direction or a relevant pre-action protocol (see paragraph 5.2) when giving directions for the management of claims (see CPR rules 3.1(4) and (5) and 3.9(1)(e)) and when making orders about who should pay costs (see CPR rule 44.3(5)(a)).

4.2   The court will expect the parties to have complied with this Practice Direction or any relevant pre-action protocol. The court may ask the parties to explain what steps were taken to comply prior to the start of the claim. Where there has been a failure of compliance by a party the court may ask that party to provide an explanation.

Assessment of compliance

4.3   When considering compliance the court will –
   (1)   be concerned about whether the parties have complied in substance with the relevant principles and requirements and is not likely to be concerned with minor or technical shortcomings;
   (2)   consider the proportionality of the steps taken compared to the size and importance of the matter;
   (3)   take account of the urgency of the matter. Where a matter is urgent (for example, an application for an injunction) the court will expect the parties to comply only to the extent that it is reasonable to do so. (Paragraph 9.5 and 9.6 of this Practice Direction concern urgency caused by limitation periods.)

Examples of non-compliance

4.4   The court may decide that there has been a failure of compliance by a party because, for example, that party has –
   (1)   not provided sufficient information to enable the other party to understand the issues;
   (2)   not acted within a time limit set out in a relevant pre-action protocol, or, where no specific time limit applies, within a reasonable period;
   (3)   unreasonably refused to consider ADR (paragraph 8 in Part III of this Practice Direction and the pre-action protocols all contain similar provisions about ADR); or
   (4)   without good reason, not disclosed documents requested to be disclosed.

Sanctions for non-compliance

4.5   The court will look at the overall effect of non-compliance on the other party when deciding whether to impose sanctions.

4.6   If, in the opinion of the court, there has been non-compliance, the sanctions which the court may impose include –
   (1)   staying (that is suspending) the proceedings until steps which ought to have been taken have been taken;
   (2)   an order that the party at fault pays the costs, or part of the costs, of the other party or parties (this may include an order under rule 27.14(2)(g) in cases allocated to the small claims track);
   (3)   an order that the party at fault pays those costs on an indemnity basis (rule 44.4(3) sets out the definition of the assessment of costs on an indemnity basis);
   (4)   if the party at fault is the claimant in whose favour an order for the payment of a sum of money is subsequently made, an order that the claimant is deprived of interest on all or part of that sum, and/or that interest is awarded at a lower rate than would otherwise have been awarded;
   (5)   if the party at fault is a defendant, and an order for the payment of a sum of money is subsequently made in favour of the claimant, an order that the defendant pay interest on all or part of that sum at a higher rate, not exceeding 10% above base rate, than would otherwise have been awarded.

5. Commencement of pre-action protocols

5.1   When considering compliance, the court will take account of a relevant pre-action protocol if the proceedings were started after the relevant pre-action protocol came into force.

5.2   The following table sets out the pre-action protocols currently in force and the dates that they came into force –

Pre-Action Protocol	Came into force
Personal Injury	26 April 1999
Clinical Disputes	26 April 1999
Construction and Engineering	2 October 2000
Defamation	2 October 2000
Professional Negligence	16 July 2001
Judicial Review	4 March 2002
Disease and Illness	8 December 2003
Housing Disrepair	8 December 2003
Possession Claims based on rent arrears	2 October 2006
Possession Claims based on Mortgage Arrears etc.	19 November 2008

SECTION III – THE PRINCIPLES GOVERNING THE CONDUCT OF THE PARTIES IN CASES NOT SUBJECT TO A PRE-ACTION PROTOCOL

6. Overview of Principles

6.1   The principles that should govern the conduct of the parties are that, unless the circumstances make it inappropriate, before starting proceedings the parties should –

(1)   exchange sufficient information about the matter to allow them to understand each other's position and make informed decisions about settlement and how to proceed;

(2)   make appropriate attempts to resolve the matter without starting proceedings, and in particular consider the use of an appropriate form of ADR in order to do so.

6.2   The parties should act in a reasonable and proportionate manner in all dealings with one another. In particular, the costs incurred in complying should be proportionate to the complexity of the matter and any money at stake. The parties must not use this Practice Direction as a tactical device to secure an unfair advantage for one party or to generate unnecessary costs.

7. Exchanging Information before starting proceedings

7.1   Before starting proceedings –

(1)   the claimant should set out the details of the matter in writing by sending a letter before claim to the defendant. This letter before claim is not the start of proceedings; and

(2)   the defendant should give a full written response within a reasonable period, preceded, if appropriate, by a written acknowledgment of the letter before claim.

7.2   A 'reasonable period of time' will vary depending on the matter. As a general guide –

(1)   the defendant should send a letter of acknowledgment within 14 days of receipt of the letter before claim (if a full response has not been sent within that period);

(2)   where the matter is straightforward, for example an undisputed debt, then a full response should normally be provided within 14 days;

(3)   where a matter requires the involvement of an insurer or other third party or where there are issues about evidence, then a full response should normally be provided within 30 days;

(4)   where the matter is particularly complex, for example requiring specialist advice, then a period of longer than 30 days may be appropriate;

(5)   a period of longer than 90 days in which to provide a full response will only be considered reasonable in exceptional circumstances.

7.3   Annex A sets out detailed guidance on a pre-action procedure that is likely to satisfy the court in most circumstances where no pre-action protocol applies and where the claimant does not follow any statutory or other formal pre-action procedure.

7.4   Annex B sets out the specific information that should be provided in a debt claim by a claimant who is a business against a defendant who is an individual.

8. Alternative Dispute Resolution

8.1   Starting proceedings should usually be a step of last resort, and proceedings should not normally be started when a settlement is still actively being explored. Although ADR is not compulsory, the parties should consider whether some form of ADR procedure might enable them to settle the matter without starting proceedings. The court may require evidence that the parties considered some form of ADR (see paragraph 4.4(3)).

8.2   It is not practicable in this Practice Direction to address in detail how the parties might decide to resolve a matter. However, some of the options for resolving a matter without starting proceedings are –

(1)   discussion and negotiation;

(2)   mediation (a form of negotiation with the help of an independent person or body);

(3)   early neutral evaluation (where an independent person or body, for example a lawyer or an expert in the subject, gives an opinion on the merits of a dispute); or

(4)   arbitration (where an independent person or body makes a binding decision), many types of business are members of arbitration schemes for resolving disputes with consumers.

8.3   The Legal Services Commission has published a booklet on 'Alternatives to Court', CLS Direct Information Leaflet 23 (www.clsdirect.org.uk) which lists a number of organisations that provide alternative dispute resolution services. The National Mediation Helpline on 0845 603 0809 or at www.nationalmediationhelpline.com can provide information about mediation.

8.4   The parties should continue to consider the possibility of reaching a settlement at all times. This still applies after proceedings have been started, up to and during any trial or final hearing.

SECTION IV – REQUIREMENTS THAT APPLY IN ALL CASES

9. Specific Provisions

9.1   The following requirements (including Annex C) apply in all cases except where a relevant pre-action protocol contains its own provisions about the topic.

Disclosure

9.2   Documents provided by one party to another in the course of complying with this Practice Direction or any relevant pre-action protocol must not be used for any purpose other than resolving the matter, unless the disclosing party agrees in writing.

Information about funding arrangements

9.3   Where a party enters into a funding arrangement within the meaning of rule 43.2(1)(k), that party should inform the other parties about this arrangement as soon as possible.

(CPR rule 44.3B(1)(c) provides that a party may not recover certain additional costs where information about a funding arrangement was not provided.)

Experts

9.4   Where the evidence of an expert is necessary the parties should consider how best to minimise expense. Guidance on instructing experts can be found in Annex C.

Limitation Periods

9.5   There are statutory time limits for starting proceedings ('the limitation period'). If a claimant starts a claim after the limitation period applicable to that type of claim has expired the defendant will be entitled to use that as a defence to the claim.

9.6   In certain instances compliance may not be possible before the expiry of the limitation period. If, for any reason, proceedings are started before the parties have complied, they should seek to agree to apply to the court for an order to stay (i.e. suspend) the proceedings while the parties take steps to comply.

Notifying the court

9.7   Where proceedings are started the claimant should state in the claim form or the particulars of claim whether they have complied with Sections III and IV of this Practice Direction or any relevant protocol.

ANNEX A

Guidance on pre-action procedure where no pre-action protocol or other formal pre-action procedure applies

1. General

1.1   This Annex sets out detailed guidance on a pre-action procedure that is likely to satisfy the court in most circumstances where no pre-action protocol or other formal pre-action procedure applies. It is intended as a guide for parties, particularly those without legal representation, in straightforward claims that are likely to be disputed. It is not intended to apply to debt claims where it is not disputed that the money is owed and where the claimant follows a statutory or other formal pre-action procedure.

2. Claimant's letter before claim

2.1   The claimant's letter should give concise details about the matter. This should enable the defendant to understand and investigate the issues without needing to request further information. The letter should include –

(1)   the claimant's full name and address;

(2)   the basis on which the claim is made (i.e. why the claimant says the defendant is liable);

(3)   a clear summary of the facts on which the claim is based;

(4)   what the claimant wants from the defendant;

(5)   if financial loss is claimed, an explanation of how the amount has been calculated; and

(6)   details of any funding arrangement (within the meaning of rule 43.2(1)(k) of the CPR) that has been entered into by the claimant.

2.2   The letter should also –

(1)   list the essential documents on which the claimant intends to rely;

(2)   set out the form of ADR (if any) that the claimant considers the most suitable and invite the defendant to agree to this;

(3)   state the date by which the claimant considers it reasonable for a full response to be provided by the defendant; and

(4)   identify and ask for copies of any relevant documents not in the claimant's possession and which the claimant wishes to see.

2.3   Unless the defendant is known to be legally represented the letter should –

(1)   refer the defendant to this Practice Direction and in particular draw attention to paragraph 4 concerning the court's powers to impose sanctions for failure to comply with the Practice Direction; and

(2)   inform the defendant that ignoring the letter before claim may lead to the claimant starting proceedings and may increase the defendant's liability for costs.

3. Defendant's acknowledgment of the letter before claim

3.1   Where the defendant is unable to provide a full written response within 14 days of receipt of the letter before claim the defendant should, instead, provide a written acknowledgment within 14 days.

3.2   The acknowledgment –

(1)   should state whether an insurer is or may be involved;

(2)   should state the date by which the defendant (or insurer) will provide a full written response; and

(3)   may request further information to enable the defendant to provide a full response.

3.3   If the date stated under paragraph 3.2(2) of this Annex is longer than the period stated in the letter before claim, the defendant should give reasons why a longer period is needed.

3.4   If the defendant (or insurer) does not provide either a letter of acknowledgment or full response within 14 days, and proceedings are subsequently started, then the court is likely to consider that the claimant has complied.

3.5   Where the defendant is unable to provide a full response within 14 days of receipt of the letter before claim because the defendant intends to seek advice then the written acknowledgment should state –

(1)   that the defendant is seeking advice;

(2)   from whom the defendant is seeking advice; and

(3)   when the defendant expects to have received that advice and be in a position to provide a full response.

3.6   A claimant should allow a reasonable period of time of up to 14 days for a defendant to obtain advice.

4. Defendant's full response

4.1   The defendant's full written response should –

(1)   accept the claim in whole or in part; or

(2)   state that the claim is not accepted.

4.2   Unless the defendant accepts the whole of the claim, the response should –

(1)   give reasons why the claim is not accepted, identifying which facts and which parts of the claim (if any) are accepted and which are disputed, and the basis of that dispute;

(2)   state whether the defendant intends to make a counterclaim against the claimant (and, if so, provide information equivalent to a claimant's letter before claim);

(3)   state whether the defendant alleges that the claimant was wholly or partly to blame for the problem that led to the dispute and, if so, summarise the facts relied on;

(4)   state whether the defendant agrees to the claimant's proposals for ADR and if not, state why not and suggest an alternative form of ADR (or state why none is considered appropriate);

(5)   list the essential documents on which the defendant intends to rely;

(6)   enclose copies of documents requested by the claimant, or explain why they will not be provided; and

(7)   identify and ask for copies of any further relevant documents, not in the defendant's possession and which the defendant wishes to see.

4.3   If the defendant (or insurer) does not provide a full response within the period stated in the claimant's letter before claim (or any longer period stated in the defendant's letter of acknowledgment), and a claim is subsequently started, then the court is likely to consider that the claimant has complied.

4.4   If the claimant starts proceedings before any longer period stated in the defendant's letter of acknowledgment, the court will consider whether or not the longer period requested by the defendant was reasonable.

5. Claimant's reply

5.1   The claimant should provide the documents requested by the defendant within as short a period of time as is practicable or explain in writing why the documents will not be provided.

5.2   If the defendant has made a counterclaim the claimant should provide information equivalent to the defendant's full response (see paragraphs 4.1 to 4.3 above).

6. Taking Stock

6.1   In following the above procedure, the parties will have a genuine opportunity to resolve the matter without needing to start proceedings. At the very least, it should be possible to establish what issues remain outstanding so as to narrow the scope of the proceedings and therefore limit potential costs.

6.2   If having completed the procedure the matter has not been resolved then the parties should undertake a further review of their respective positions to see if proceedings can still be avoided.

ANNEX B

Information to be provided in a debt claim where the claimant is a business and the defendant is an individual

1.   Where paragraph 7.4 of the Practice Direction applies the claimant should –

(1)   provide details of how the money can be paid (for example the method of payment and the address to which it can be sent);

(2)   state that the defendant can contact the claimant to discuss possible repayment options, and provide the relevant contact details; and

(3)   inform the defendant that free independent advice and assistance can be obtained from organisations including those listed in the table below.

INDEPENDENT ADVICE ORGANISATIONS

Organisation	Address	Telephone Number	e-mail Address
National Debtline	Tricorn House 51-53 Hagley Road Edgbaston Birmingham B16 8TP	FREEPHONE 0808 808 4000	www.nationaldebtline.co.uk
Consumer Credit Counselling Service (CCCS)		FREEPHONE 0800 138 1111	www.cccs.co.uk
Citizens Advice	Check your local Yellow Pages or Thomson local directory for address and telephone numbers		www.citizensadvice.org.uk

Community Legal Advice (formerly Community Legal Services Direct)	0845 345 4345	www.clsdirect.org.uk

2.   The information set out in paragraph 1 of this Annex may be provided at any time between the claimant first intimating the possibility of court proceedings and the claimant's letter before claim.

3.   Where the defendant is unable to provide a full response within the time specified in the letter before claim because the defendant intends to seek debt advice then the written acknowledgment should state –

(1)   that the defendant is seeking debt advice;

(2)   who the defendant is seeking advice from; and

(3)   when the defendant expects to have received that advice and be in a position to provide a full response.

4.   A claimant should allow a reasonable period of time of up to 14 days for a defendant to obtain debt advice.

5.   But the claimant need not allow the defendant time to seek debt advice if the claimant knows that–

(1)   the defendant has already received relevant debt advice and the defendant's circumstances have not significantly changed; or

(2)   the defendant has previously asked for time to seek debt advice but has not done so.

ANNEX C

Guidance on instructing experts

1.   The CPR contain extensive provisions which strictly control the use of experts both before and after proceedings are started. These provisions are contained in –

(1)   CPR Part 35;

(2)   the Practice Direction supplementing Part 35; and

(3)   the Protocol for the 'Instruction of Experts to give Evidence in Civil Claims' which is annexed to that Practice Direction.

2.   Parties should be aware that once proceedings have been started –

(1)   expert evidence may not be used in court without the permission of the court;

(2)   a party who instructs an expert will not necessarily be able to recover the cost from another party; and

(3)   (it is the duty of an expert to help the court on the matters within the expert's scope of expertise and this duty overrides any obligation to the person instructing or paying the expert.

3.   Many matters can and should be resolved without the need for advice or evidence from an expert. If an expert is needed, the parties should consider how best to minimise the expense for example by agreeing to instruct –

(1)   a single joint expert (i.e. engaged and paid jointly by the parties whether instructed jointly or separately); or

(2)   an agreed expert (i.e. the parties agree the identity of the expert but only one party instructs the expert and pays the expert's costs).

4.   If the parties do not agree that the nomination of a single joint expert is appropriate, then the party seeking the expert evidence (the first party) should give the other party (the second party) a list of one or more experts in the relevant field of expertise whom the first party would like to instruct.

5.   Within 14 days of receipt of the list of experts, the second party may indicate in writing an objection to one or more of the experts listed. If there remains on the list one or more experts who are acceptable, then the first party should instruct an expert from the list.

6.   If the second party objects to all the listed experts, the first party may then instruct an expert of the first party's own choice. Both parties should bear in mind that if proceedings are started the court will consider whether a party has acted reasonably when instructing (or rejecting) an expert.

A(19)   Professional Negligence Pre-action Protocol

THIS PROTOCOL MERGES THE TWO PROTOCOLS PREVIOUSLY PRODUCED BY THE SOLICITORS INDEMNITY FUND (SIF) AND CLAIMS AGAINST PROFESSIONALS (CAP)

A Introduction

A1. This protocol is designed to apply when a Claimant wishes to claim against a professional (other than construction professionals and healthcare providers) as a result of that professional's alleged negligence or equivalent breach of contract or breach of fiduciary duty. Although these claims will be the usual situation in which the protocol will be used, there may be other claims for which the protocol could be appropriate. For a more detailed explanation of the scope of the protocol see Guidance Note C2.

A2. The aim of this protocol is to establish a framework in which there is an early exchange of information so that the claim can be fully investigated and, if possible, resolved without the need for litigation. This includes:

    (a)   ensuring that the parties are on an equal footing

    (b)   saving expense

    (c)   dealing with the dispute in ways which are proportionate:

        (i)   to the amount of money involved

        (ii)   to the importance of the case

        (iii)   to the complexity of the issues

        (iv)   to the financial position of each party

    (d)   ensuring that it is dealt with expeditiously and fairly.

A3. This protocol is not intended to replace other forms of pre-action dispute resolution (such as internal complaints procedures, the Surveyors and Valuers Arbitration Scheme, etc). Where such procedures are available, parties are encouraged to consider whether they should be used. If, however, these other procedures are used and fail to resolve the dispute, the protocol should be used before litigation is started, adapting it where appropriate. See also Guidance Note C3.

A4. The Courts will be able to treat the standards set in this protocol as the normal reasonable approach. If litigation is started, it will be for the court to decide whether sanctions should be imposed as a result of substantial noncompliance with a protocol. Guidance on the courts' likely approach is given in the Protocols Practice Direction. The Court is likely to disregard minor departures from this protocol and so should the parties as between themselves.

A5. Both in operating the timetable and in requesting and providing information during the protocol period, the parties are expected to act reasonably, in line with the Court's expectations of them. See also Guidance Note C1.2.

B The Protocol

B1. Preliminary Notice (See also Guidance Note C3.1)

B1.1 As soon as the Claimant decides there is a reasonable chance that he will bring a claim against a professional, the Claimant is encouraged to notify the professional in writing.

B1.2 This letter should contain the following information:

    (a)   the identity of the Claimant and any other parties

    (b)   a brief outline of the Claimant's grievance against the professional

(c)   if possible, a general indication of the financial value of the potential claim B1.3 This letter should be addressed to the professional and should ask the professional to inform his professional indemnity insurers, if any, immediately.

B1.4 The professional should acknowledge receipt of the Claimant's letter within 21 days of receiving it. Other than this acknowledgement, the protocol places no obligation upon either party to take any further action.

B2. Letter of Claim

B2.1 As soon as the Claimant decides there are grounds for a claim against the professional, the Claimant should write a detailed Letter of Claim to the professional.

B2.2 The Letter of Claim will normally be an open letter (as opposed to being 'without prejudice') and should include the following:

(a)   The identity of any other parties involved in the dispute or a related dispute.

(b)   A clear chronological summary (including key dates) of the facts on which the claim is based. Key documents should be identified, copied and enclosed.

(c)   The allegations against the professional. What has he done wrong? What has he failed to do?

(d)   An explanation of how the alleged error has caused the loss claimed.

(e)   An estimate of the financial loss suffered by the Claimant and how it is calculated. Supporting documents should be identified, copied and enclosed. If details of the financial loss cannot be supplied, the Claimant should explain why and should state when he will be in a position to provide the details. This information should be sent to the professional as soon as reasonably possible.

   If the Claimant is seeking some form of non-financial redress, this should be made clear.

(f)   Confirmation whether or not an expert has been appointed. If so, providing the identity and discipline of the expert, together with the date upon which the expert was appointed.

(g)   A request that a copy of the Letter of Claim be forwarded immediately to the professional's insurers, if any.

B2.3 The Letter of Claim is not intended to have the same formal status as a Statement of Case. If, however, the Letter of Claim differs materially from the Statement of Case in subsequent proceedings, the Court may decide, in its discretion, to impose sanctions.

B2.4 If the Claimant has sent other Letters of Claim (or equivalent) to any other party in relation to this dispute or related dispute, those letters should be copied to the professional. (If the Claimant is claiming against someone else to whom this protocol does not apply, please see Guidance Note C4.)

B3. The Letter of Acknowledgment

B3.1 The professional should acknowledge receipt of the Letter of Claim within 21 days of receiving it.

B4. Investigations

B4.1 The professional will have three months from the date of the Letter of Acknowledgment to investigate.

B4.2 If the professional is in difficulty in complying with the three month time period, the problem should be explained to the Claimant as soon as possible. The professional should explain what is being done to resolve the problem and when the professional expects to complete the investigations. The Claimant should agree to any reasonable request for an extension of the three month period.

B4.3 The parties should supply promptly, at this stage and throughout, whatever relevant information or documentation is reasonably requested. (Please see Guidance Note C5.)

(If the professional intends to claim against someone who is not currently a party to the dispute, please see Guidance Note C4.)

B5. Letter of Response and Letter of Settlement

B5.1 As soon as the professional has completed his investigations, the professional should send to the Claimant:

    (a)   a Letter of Response, or

    (b)   a Letter of Settlement; or

    (c)   both.

The Letters of Response and Settlement can be contained within a single letter.

The Letter of Response

B5.2 The Letter of Response will normally be an open letter (as opposed to being 'without prejudice') and should be a reasoned answer to the Claimant's allegations:

    (a)   if the claim is admitted the professional should say so in clear terms.

    (b)   if only part of the claim is admitted the professional should make clear which parts of the claim are admitted and which are denied.

    (c)   if the claim is denied in whole or in part, the Letter of Response should include specific comments on the allegations against the professional and, if the Claimant's version of events is disputed, the professional should provide his version of events.

    (d)   if the professional is unable to admit or deny the claim, the professional should identify any further information which is required.

    (e)   if the professional disputes the estimate of the Claimant's financial loss, the Letter of Response should set out the professional's estimate. If an estimate cannot be provided, the professional should explain why and should state when he will be in a position to provide an estimate. This information should be sent to the Claimant as soon as reasonably possible.

    (f)   where additional documents are relied upon, copies should be provided.

B5.3 The Letter of Response is not intended to have the same formal status as a Defence. If, however, the Letter of Response differs materially from the Defence in subsequent proceedings, the Court may decide, in its discretion, to impose sanctions.

The Letter of Settlement

B5.4 The Letter of Settlement will normally be a without prejudice letter and should be sent if the professional intends to make proposals for settlement. It should:

    (a)   set out the professional's views to date on the claim identifying those issues which the professional believes are likely to remain in dispute and those which are not. (The Letter of Settlement does not need to include this information if the professional has sent a Letter of Response).

    (b)   make a settlement proposal or identify any further information which is required before the professional can formulate its proposals.

    (c)   where additional documents are relied upon, copies should be provided.

Effect of Letter of Response and/or Letter of Settlement

B5.5 If the Letter of Response denies the claim in its entirety and there is no Letter of Settlement, it is open to the Claimant to commence proceedings.

B5.6 In any other circumstance, the professional and the Claimant should commence negotiations with the aim of concluding those negotiations within 6 months of the date of the Letter of Acknowledgment (NOT from the date of the Letter of Response).

B5.7 If the claim cannot be resolved within this period:

    (a)   the parties should agree within 14 days of the end of the period whether the period should be extended and, if so, by how long.

(b)   the parties should seek to identify those issues which are still in dispute and those which can be agreed.

(c)   if an extension of time is not agreed it will then be open to the Claimant to commence proceedings.

B6. Alternative Dispute Resolution

B6.1 The parties should consider whether some form of alternative dispute resolution procedure would be more suitable than litigation, and if so, endeavour to agree which form to adopt. Both the Claimant and professional may be required by the Court to provide evidence that alternative means of resolving their dispute were considered. The Courts take the view that litigation should be a last resort, and that claims should not be issued prematurely when a settlement is still actively being explored. Parties are warned that if the protocol is not followed (including this paragraph) then the Court must have regard to such conduct when determining costs.

B6.2 It is not practicable in this protocol to address in detail how the parties might decide which method to adopt to resolve their particular dispute. However, summarised below are some of the options for resolving disputes without litigation:

•   Discussion and negotiation.

•   Early neutral evaluation by an independent third party (for example, a lawyer experienced in the field of professional negligence or an individual experienced in the subject matter of the claim).

•   Mediation – a form of facilitated negotiation assisted by an independent neutral party.

B6.3 The Legal Services Commission has published a booklet on 'Alternatives to Court', CLS Direct Information Leaflet 23 (www.clsdirect.org.uk/legalhelp/leaflet23.jsp), which lists a number of organisations that provide alternative dispute resolution services.

B6.4 It is expressly recognised that no party can or should be forced to mediate or enter into any form of ADR.

B7. Experts

(The following provisions apply where the claim raises an issue of professional expertise whose resolution requires expert evidence.)

B7.1 If the Claimant has obtained expert evidence prior to sending the Letter of Claim, the professional will have equal right to obtain expert evidence prior to sending the Letter of Response/Letter of Settlement.

B7.2 If the Claimant has not obtained expert evidence prior to sending the Letter of Claim, the parties are encouraged to appoint a joint expert. If they agree to do so, they should seek to agree the identity of the expert and the terms of the expert's appointment.

B7.3 If agreement about a joint expert cannot be reached, all parties are free to appoint their own experts.

(For further details on experts see Guidance Note C6.)

B8. Proceedings

B8.1 Unless it is necessary (for example, to obtain protection against the expiry of a relevant limitation period) the Claimant should not start Court proceedings until:

(a)   the Letter of Response denies the claim in its entirety and there is no Letter of Settlement (see paragraph B5.5 above); or

(b)   the end of the negotiation period (see paragraphs B5.6 and B5.7 above); or

(For further discussion of statutory time limits for the commencement of litigation, please see Guidance Note C7.)

B8.2 Where possible 14 days written notice should be given to the professional before proceedings are started, indicating the court within which the Claimant is intending to commence litigation.

B8.3 Proceedings should be served on the professional, unless the professional's solicitor has notified the Claimant in writing that he is authorised to accept service on behalf of the professional.

C Guidance Notes

C1. Introduction

C1.1 The protocol has been kept simple to promote ease of use and general acceptability. The guidance notes which follow relate particularly to issues on which further guidance may be required.

C1.2 The Woolf reforms envisage that parties will act reasonably in the pre-action period. Accordingly, in the event that the protocol and the guidelines do not specifically address a problem, the parties should comply with the spirit of the protocol by acting reasonably.

C2. Scope of Protocol

C2.1 The protocol is specifically designed for claims of negligence against professionals. This will include claims in which the allegation against a professional is that they have breached a contractual term to take reasonable skill and care. The protocol is also appropriate for claims of breach of fiduciary duty against professionals.

C2.2 The protocol is not intended to apply to claims:

    (a)   against Architects, Engineers and Quantity Surveyors – parties should use the Construction and Engineering Disputes (CED) protocol.

    (b)   against Healthcare providers – parties should use the pre-action protocol for the Resolution of Clinical Disputes.

    (c)   concerning defamation – parties should use the pre-action protocol for defamation claims.

C2.3 'Professional' is deliberately left undefined in the protocol. If it becomes an issue as to whether a defendant is or is not a professional, parties are reminded of the overriding need to act reasonably (see paragraphs A4 and C1.2 above). Rather than argue about the definition of 'professional', therefore, the parties are invited to use this protocol, adapting it where appropriate.

C2.4 The protocol may not be suitable for disputes with professionals concerning intellectual property claims, etc. Until specific protocols are created for those claims, however, parties are invited to use this protocol, adapting it where necessary.

C2.5 Allegations of professional negligence are sometimes made in response to an attempt by the professional to recover outstanding fees. Where possible these allegations should be raised before litigation has commenced, in which case the parties should comply with the protocol before either party commences litigation. If litigation has already commenced it will be a matter for the Court whether sanctions should be imposed against either party. In any event, the parties are encouraged to consider applying to the Court for a stay to allow the protocol to be followed.

C3. Inter-action with other pre-action methods of dispute resolution

C3.1 There are a growing number of methods by which disputes can be resolved without the need for litigation, eg internal complaints procedures, the Surveyors and Valuers Arbitration Scheme, and so on. The Preliminary Notice procedure of the protocol (see paragraph B1) is designed to enable both parties to take stock at an early stage and to decide before work starts on preparing a Letter of Claim whether the grievance should be referred to one of these other dispute resolution procedures. (For the avoidance of doubt, however, there is no obligation on either party under the protocol to take any action at this stage other than giving the acknowledgment provided for in paragraph B1.4).

C3.2 Accordingly, parties are free to use (and are encouraged to use) any of the available pre-action procedures in an attempt to resolve their dispute. If appropriate, the parties can agree to suspend the protocol timetable whilst the other method of dispute resolution is used.

C3.3 If these methods fail to resolve the dispute, however, the protocol should be used before litigation is commenced. Because there has already been an attempt to resolve the dispute, it may be appropriate to adjust the protocol's requirements. In particular, unless the parties agree otherwise, there is unlikely to be any benefit in duplicating a stage which has in effect already been undertaken. However, if the protocol adds anything to the earlier method of dispute resolution, it should be used, adapting it where appropriate. Once again, the parties are expected to act reasonably.

C4. Multi-Party Disputes

C4.1 Paragraph B2.2(a) of the protocol requires a Claimant to identify any other parties involved in the dispute or a related dispute. This is intended to ensure that all relevant parties are identified as soon as possible.

C4.2 If the dispute involves more than two parties, there are a number of potential problems. It is possible that different protocols will apply to different defendants. It is possible that defendants will claim against each other. It is possible that other parties will be drawn into the dispute. It is possible that the protocol timetable against one party will not be synchronised with the protocol timetable against a different party. How will these problems be resolved?

C4.3 As stated in paragraph C1.2 above, the parties are expected to act reasonably. What is 'reasonable' will, of course, depend upon the specific facts of each case. Accordingly, it would be inappropriate for the protocol to set down generalised rules. Whenever a problem arises, the parties are encouraged to discuss how it can be overcome. In doing so, parties are reminded of the protocol's aims which include the aim to resolve the dispute without the need for litigation (paragraph A2 above).

C5. Investigations

C5.1 Paragraph B4.3 is intended to encourage the early exchange of relevant information, so that issues in the dispute can be clarified or resolved. It should not be used as a 'fishing expedition' by either party. No party is obliged under paragraph B4.3 to disclose any document which a Court could not order them to disclose in the pre-action period.

C5.2 This protocol does not alter the parties' duties to disclose documents under any professional regulation or under general law.

C6. Experts

C6.1 Expert evidence is not always needed, although the use and role of experts in professional negligence claims is often crucial. However, the way in which expert evidence is used in, say, an insurance brokers' negligence case, is not necessarily the same as in, say, an accountants' case. Similarly, the approach to be adopted in a £10,000 case does not necessarily compare with the approach in a £10 million case. The protocol therefore is designed to be flexible and does not dictate a standard approach. On the contrary it envisages that the parties will bear the responsibility for agreeing how best to use experts.

C6.2 If a joint expert is used, therefore, the parties are left to decide issues such as: the payment of the expert, whether joint or separate instructions are used, how and to whom the expert is to report, how questions may be addressed to the expert and how the expert should respond, whether an agreed statement of facts is required, and so on.

C6.3 If separate experts are used, the parties are left to decide issues such as: whether the expert's reports should be exchanged, whether there should be an expert's meeting, and so on.

C6.4 Even if a joint expert is appointed, it is possible that parties will still want to instruct their own experts. The protocol does not prohibit this.

C7. Proceedings

C7.1 This protocol does not alter the statutory time limits for starting Court proceedings. A Claimant is required to start proceedings within those time limits.

C7.2 If proceedings are for any reason started before the parties have followed the procedures in this protocol, the parties are encouraged to agree to apply to the court for a stay whilst the protocol is followed.

A(20)   Protocol for the Instruction of Experts to give Evidence in Civil Claims

June 2005

1. Introduction

Expert witnesses perform a vital role in civil litigation. It is essential that both those who instruct experts and experts themselves are given clear guidance as to what they are expected to do in civil proceedings. The purpose of this Protocol is to provide such guidance. It has been drafted by the Civil Justice Council and reflects the rules and practice directions current [in June 2005], replacing the Code of Guidance on Expert Evidence. The authors of the Protocol wish to acknowledge the valuable assistance they obtained by drawing on earlier documents produced by the Academy of Experts and the Expert Witness Institute, as well as suggestions made by the Clinical Dispute Forum. The Protocol has been approved by the Master of the Rolls.

2. Aims of Protocol

2.1 This Protocol offers guidance to experts and to those instructing them in the interpretation of and compliance with Part 35 of the Civil Procedure Rules (CPR 35) and its associated Practice Direction (PD 35) and to further the objectives of the Civil Procedure Rules in general. It is intended to assist in the interpretation of those provisions in the interests of good practice but it does not replace them. It sets out standards for the use of experts and the conduct of experts and those who instruct them. The existence of this Protocol does not remove the need for experts and those who instruct them to be familiar with CPR35 and PD35.

2.2 Experts and those who instruct them should also bear in mind para 1.4 of the Practice Direction on Protocols which contains the following objectives, namely to:

(a)   encourage the exchange of early and full information about the expert issues involved in a prospective legal claim;

(b)   enable the parties to avoid or reduce the scope of litigation by agreeing the whole or part of an expert issue before commencement of proceedings; and

(c)   support the efficient management of proceedings where litigation cannot be avoided.

3. Application

3.1 This Protocol applies to any steps taken for the purpose of civil proceedings by experts or those who instruct them on or after 5th September 2005.

3.2 It applies to all experts who are, or who may be, governed by CPR Part 35 and to those who instruct them. Experts are governed by Part 35 if they are or have been instructed to give or prepare evidence for the purpose of civil proceedings in a court in England and Wales (CPR 35.2).

3.3 Experts, and those instructing them, should be aware that some cases may be 'specialist proceedings' (CPR 49) where there are modifications to the Civil Procedure Rules. Proceedings may also be governed by other Protocols. Further, some courts have published their own Guides which supplement the Civil Procedure Rules for proceedings in those courts. They contain provisions affecting expert evidence. Expert witnesses and those instructing them should be familiar with them when they are relevant.

3.4 Courts may take into account any failure to comply with this Protocol when making orders in relation to costs, interest, time limits, the stay of proceedings and whether to order a party to pay a sum of money into court.

Limitation

3.5 If, as a result of complying with any part of this Protocol, claims would or might be time barred under any provision in the Limitation Act 1980, or any other legislation that imposes a time limit for the bringing an action, claimants may commence proceedings without complying with this Protocol. In such circumstances, claimants who commence proceedings without complying with all, or any part, of this

Protocol must apply, giving notice to all other parties, to the court for directions as to the timetable and form of procedure to be adopted, at the same time as they request the court to issue proceedings. The court may consider whether to order a stay of the whole or part of the proceedings pending compliance with this Protocol and may make orders in relation to costs.

4. Duties of experts

4.1 Experts always owe a duty to exercise reasonable skill and care to those instructing them, and to comply with any relevant professional code of ethics. However when they are instructed to give or prepare evidence for the purpose of civil proceedings in England and Wales they have an overriding duty to help the court on matters within their expertise (CPR 35.3). This duty overrides any obligation to the person instructing or paying them. Experts must not serve the exclusive interest of those who retain them.

4.2 Experts should be aware of the overriding objective that courts deal with cases justly. This includes dealing with cases proportionately, expeditiously and fairly (CPR 1.1). Experts are under an obligation to assist the court so as to enable them to deal with cases in accordance with the overriding objective. However the overriding objective does not impose on experts any duty to act as mediators between the parties or require them to trespass on the role of the court in deciding facts.

4.3 Experts should provide opinions which are independent, regardless of the pressures of litigation. In this context, a useful test of 'independence' is that the expert would express the same opinion if given the same instructions by an opposing party. Experts should not take it upon themselves to promote the point of view of the party instructing them or engage in the role of advocates.

4.4 Experts should confine their opinions to matters which are material to the disputes between the parties and provide opinions only in relation to matters which lie within their expertise. Experts should indicate without delay where particular questions or issues fall outside their expertise.

4.5 Experts should take into account all material facts before them at the time that they give their opinion. Their reports should set out those facts and any literature or any other material on which they have relied in forming their opinions. They should indicate if an opinion is provisional, or qualified, or where they consider that further information is required or if, for any other reason, they are not satisfied that an opinion can be expressed finally and without qualification.

4.6 Experts should inform those instructing them without delay of any change in their opinions on any material matter and the reason for it.

4.7 Experts should be aware that any failure by them to comply with the Civil Procedure Rules or court orders or any excessive delay for which they are responsible may result in the parties who instructed them being penalised in costs and even, in extreme cases, being debarred from placing the experts' evidence before the court. In *Phillips v Symes*[1] Peter Smith J held that courts may also make orders for costs (under section 51 of the Supreme Court Act 1981) directly against expert witnesses who by their evidence cause significant expense to be incurred, and do so in flagrant and reckless disregard of their duties to the Court.

5. Conduct of Experts instructed only to advise

5.1 Part 35 only applies where experts are instructed to give opinions which are relied on for the purposes of court proceedings. Advice which the parties do not intend to adduce in litigation is likely to be confidential; the Protocol does not apply in these circumstances [2, 3].

5.2 The same applies where, after the commencement of proceedings, experts are instructed only to advise (e.g. to comment upon a single joint expert's report) and not to give or prepare evidence for use in the proceedings.

5.3 However this Protocol does apply if experts who were formerly instructed only to advise are later instructed to give or prepare evidence for the purpose of civil proceedings.

---

1.   [2004] EWHC 2330 (Ch)
2.   *Carlson v Townsend* [2001] 1 WLR 2415
3.   *Jackson v Marley Davenport* [2004] 1 WLR 2926

6. The Need for Experts

6.1 Those intending to instruct experts to give or prepare evidence for the purpose of civil proceedings should consider whether expert evidence is appropriate, taking account of the principles set out in CPR Parts 1 and 35, and in particular whether:

(a)   it is relevant to a matter which is in dispute between the parties.

(b)   it is reasonably required to resolve the proceedings (CPR 35.1);

(c)   the expert has expertise relevant to the issue on which an opinion is sought;

(d)   the expert has the experience, expertise and training appropriate to the value, complexity and importance of the case; and whether

(e)   these objects can be achieved by the appointment of a single joint expert (see section 17 below).

6.2 Although the court's permission is not generally required to instruct an expert, the court's permission is required before experts can be called to give evidence or their evidence can be put in (CPR 35.4).

7. The appointment of experts

7.1 Before experts are formally instructed or the court's permission to appoint named experts is sought, the following should be established:

(a)   that they have the appropriate expertise and experience;

(b)   that they are familiar with the general duties of an expert;

(c)   that they can produce a report, deal with questions and have discussions with other experts within a reasonable time and at a cost proportionate to the matters in issue;

(d)   a description of the work required;

(e)   whether they are available to attend the trial, if attendance is required; and

(f)   there is no potential conflict of interest.

7.2 Terms of appointment should be agreed at the outset and should normally include:

(a)   the capacity in which the expert is to be appointed (e.g. party appointed expert, single joint expert or expert advisor);

(b)   the services required of the expert (e.g. provision of expert's report, answering questions in writing, attendance at meetings and attendance at court);

(c)   time for delivery of the report;

(d)   the basis of the expert's charges (either daily or hourly rates and an estimate of the time likely to be required, or a total fee for the services);

(e)   travelling expenses and disbursements;

(f)   cancellation charges;

(g)   any fees for attending court;

(h)   time for making the payment; and

(i)   whether fees are to be paid by a third party.

(j)   if a party is publicly funded, whether or not the expert's charges will be subject to assessment by a costs officer.

7.3 As to the appointment of single joint experts, see section 17 below.

7.4 When necessary, arrangements should be made for dealing with questions to experts and discussions between experts, including any directions given by the court, and provision should be made for the cost of this work.

7.5 Experts should be informed regularly about deadlines for all matters concerning them. Those instructing experts should promptly send them copies of all court orders and directions which may affect the preparation of their reports or any other matters concerning their obligations.

Conditional and Contingency Fees

7.6 Payments contingent upon the nature of the expert evidence given in legal proceedings, or upon the outcome of a case, must not be offered or accepted. To do so would contravene experts' overriding duty to the court and compromise their duty of independence.

7.7 Agreement to delay payment of experts' fees until after the conclusion of cases is permissible as long as the amount of the fee does not depend on the outcome of the case.

8. Instructions

8.1 Those instructing experts should ensure that they give clear instructions, including the following:

(a)   basic information, such as names, addresses, telephone numbers, dates of birth and dates of incidents;

(b)   the nature and extent of the expertise which is called for;

(c)   the purpose of requesting the advice or report, a description of the matter(s) to be investigated, the principal known issues and the identity of all parties;

(d)   the statement(s) of case (if any), those documents which form part of standard disclosure and witness statements which are relevant to the advice or report;

(e)   where proceedings have not been started, whether proceedings are being contemplated and, if so, whether the expert is asked only for advice;

(f)   an outline programme, consistent with good case management and the expert's availability, for the completion and delivery of each stage of the expert's work; and

(g)   where proceedings have been started, the dates of any hearings (including any Case Management Conferences and/or Pre-Trial Reviews), the name of the court, the claim number and the track to which the claim has been allocated.

8.2 Experts who do not receive clear instructions should request clarification and may indicate that they are not prepared to act unless and until such clear instructions are received.

8.3 As to the instruction of single joint experts, see section 17 below.

9. Experts' Acceptance of Instructions

9.1 Experts should confirm without delay whether or not they accept instructions. They should also inform those instructing them (whether on initial instruction or at any later stage) without delay if:

(a)   instructions are not acceptable because, for example, they require work that falls outside their expertise, impose unrealistic deadlines, or are insufficiently clear;

(b)   they consider that instructions are or have become insufficient to complete the work;

(c)   they become aware that they may not be able to fulfil any of the terms of appointment;

(d)   the instructions and/or work have, for any reason, placed them in conflict with their duties as an expert; or

(e) they are not satisfied that they can comply with any orders that have been made.

9.2 Experts must neither express an opinion outside the scope of their field of expertise, nor accept any instructions to do so.

10. Withdrawal

10.1 Where experts' instructions remain incompatible with their duties, whether through incompleteness, a conflict between their duty to the court and their instructions, or for any other substantial and significant reason, they may consider withdrawing from the case. However, experts should not withdraw without first discussing the position fully with those who instruct them and considering carefully whether it would be more appropriate to make a written request for directions from the court. If experts do withdraw, they must give formal written notice to those instructing them.

11. Experts' Right to ask Court for Directions

11.1 Experts may request directions from the court to assist them in carrying out their functions as experts. Experts should normally discuss such matters with those who instruct them before making any such request. Unless the court otherwise orders, any proposed request for directions should be copied to the party instructing the expert at least seven days before filing any request to the court, and to all other parties at least four days before filing it (CPR 35.14).

11.2 Requests to the court for directions should be made by letter, containing.

(a)   the title of the claim;

(b)   the claim number of the case;

(c)   the name of the expert;

(d)   full details of why directions are sought; and

(e)   copies of any relevant documentation.

12. Power of the Court to Direct a Party to Provide Information

12.1 If experts consider that those instructing them have not provided information which they require, they may, after discussion with those instructing them and giving notice, write to the court to seek directions (CPR 35.14).

12.2 Experts and those who instruct them should also be aware of CPR 35.9. This provides that where one party has access to information which is not readily available to the other party, the court may direct the party who has access to the information to prepare, file and copy to the other party a document recording the information. If experts require such information which has not been disclosed, they should discuss the position with those instructing them without delay, so that a request for the information can be made, and, if not forthcoming, an application can be made to the court. Unless a document appears to be essential, experts should assess the cost and time involved in the production of a document and whether its provision would be proportionate in the context of the case.

13. Contents of Experts' Reports

13.1 The content and extent of experts' reports should be governed by the scope of their instructions and general obligations, the contents of CPR 35 and PD35 and their overriding duty to the court.

13.2 In preparing reports, experts should maintain professional objectivity and impartiality at all times.

13.3 PD 35, para 2 provides that experts' reports should be addressed to the court and gives detailed directions about the form and content of such reports. All experts and those who instruct them should ensure that they are familiar with these requirements.

13.4 Model forms of Experts' Reports are available from bodies such as the Academy of Experts or the Expert Witness Institute.

13.5 Experts' reports must contain statements that they understand their duty to the court and have complied and will continue to comply with that duty (PD35 para 2.2(9)). They must also be verified by a statement of truth. The form of the statement of truth is as follows:

> "I confirm that insofar as the facts stated in my report are within my own knowledge I have made clear which they are and I believe them to be true, and that the opinions I have expressed represent my true and complete professional opinion."

This wording is mandatory and must not be modified.

Qualifications

13.6 The details of experts' qualifications to be given in reports should be commensurate with the nature and complexity of the case. It may be sufficient merely to state academic and professional qualifications.

However, where highly specialised expertise is called for, experts should include the detail of particular training and/or experience that qualifies them to provide that highly specialised evidence.

Tests

13.7 Where tests of a scientific or technical nature have been carried out, experts should state:

(a)   the methodology used; and

(b)   by whom the tests were undertaken and under whose supervision, summarising their respective qualifications and experience.

Reliance on the work of others

13.8 Where experts rely in their reports on literature or other material and cite the opinions of others without having verified them, they must give details of those opinions relied on. It is likely to assist the court if the qualifications of the originator(s) are also stated.

Facts

13.9 When addressing questions of fact and opinion, experts should keep the two separate and discrete.

13.10 Experts must state those facts (whether assumed or otherwise) upon which their opinions are based. They must distinguish clearly between those facts which experts know to be true and those facts which they assume.

13.11 Where there are material facts in dispute experts should express separate opinions on each hypothesis put forward. They should not express a view in favour of one or other disputed version of the facts unless, as a result of particular expertise and experience, they consider one set of facts as being improbable or less probable, in which case they may express that view, and should give reasons for holding it.

Range of opinion

13.12 If the mandatory summary of the range of opinion is based on published sources, experts should explain those sources and, where appropriate, state the qualifications of the originator(s) of the opinions from which they differ, particularly if such opinions represent a well-established school of thought.

13.13 Where there is no available source for the range of opinion, experts may need to express opinions on what they believe to be the range which other experts would arrive at if asked. In those circumstances, experts should make it clear that the range that they summarise is based on their own judgement and explain the basis of that judgement.

Conclusions

13.14 A summary of conclusions is mandatory. The summary should be at the end of the report after all the reasoning. There may be cases, however, where the benefit to the court is heightened by placing a short summary at the beginning of the report whilst giving the full conclusions at the end. For example, it can assist with the comprehension of the analysis and with the absorption of the detailed facts if the court is told at the outset of the direction in which the report's logic will flow in cases involving highly complex matters which fall outside the general knowledge of the court.

Basis of report: material instructions

13.15 The mandatory statement of the substance of all material instructions should not be incomplete or otherwise tend to mislead. The imperative is transparency. The term 'instructions' includes all material which solicitors place in front of experts in order to gain advice. The omission from the statement of 'off-the-record' oral instructions is not permitted. Courts may allow cross-examination about the instructions if there are reasonable grounds to consider that the statement may be inaccurate or incomplete.

14. After receipt of experts' reports

14.1 Following the receipt of experts' reports, those instructing them should advise the experts as soon as reasonably practicable whether, and if so when, the report will be disclosed to other parties; and, if so disclosed, the date of actual disclosure.

14.2 If experts' reports are to be relied upon, and if experts are to give oral evidence, those instructing them should give the experts the opportunity to consider and comment upon other reports within their area of expertise and which deal with relevant issues at the earliest opportunity.

14.3 Those instructing experts should keep experts informed of the progress of cases, including amendments to statements of case relevant to experts' opinion.

14.4 If those instructing experts become aware of material changes in circumstances or that relevant information within their control was not previously provided to experts, they should without delay instruct experts to review, and if necessary, update the contents of their reports.

15. Amendment of reports

15.1 It may become necessary for experts to amend their reports:

(a)   as a result of an exchange of questions and answers;

(b)   following agreements reached at meetings between experts; or

(c)   where further evidence or documentation is disclosed.

15.2 Experts should not be asked to, and should not, amend, expand or alter any parts of reports in a manner which distorts their true opinion, but may be invited to amend or expand reports to ensure accuracy, internal consistency, completeness and relevance to the issues and clarity. Although experts should generally follow the recommendations of solicitors with regard to the form of reports, they should form their own independent views as to the opinions and contents expressed in their reports and exclude any suggestions which do not accord with their views.

15.3 Where experts change their opinion following a meeting of experts, a simple signed and dated addendum or memorandum to that effect is generally sufficient. In some cases, however, the benefit to the court of having an amended report may justify the cost of making the amendment.

15.4 Where experts significantly alter their opinion, as a result of new evidence or because evidence on which they relied has become unreliable, or for any other reason, they should amend their reports to reflect that fact. Amended reports should include reasons for amendments. In such circumstances those instructing experts should inform other parties as soon as possible of any change of opinion.

15.5 When experts intend to amend their reports, they should inform those instructing them without delay and give reasons. They should provide the amended version (or an addendum or memorandum) clearly marked as such as quickly as possible.

16. Written Questions to Experts

16.1 The procedure for putting written questions to experts (CPR 35.6) is intended to facilitate the clarification of opinions and issues after experts' reports have been served. Experts have a duty to provide answers to questions properly put. Where they fail to do so, the court may impose sanctions against the party instructing the expert, and, if, there is continued non-compliance, debar a party from relying on the report. Experts should copy their answers to those instructing them.

16.2 Experts' answers to questions automatically become part of their reports. They are covered by the statement of truth and form part of the expert evidence.

16.3 Where experts believe that questions put are not properly directed to the clarification of the report, or are disproportionate, or have been asked out of time, they should discuss the questions with those instructing them and, if appropriate, those asking the questions. Attempts should be made to resolve such problems without the need for an application to the court for directions.

Written requests for directions in relation to questions

16.4 If those instructing experts do not apply to the court in respect of questions, but experts still believe that questions are improper or out of time, experts may file written requests with the court for directions to assist in carrying out their functions as experts (CPR 35.14). See Section 11 above.

17. Single Joint Experts

17.1 CPR 35 and PD35 deal extensively with the instruction and use of joint experts by the parties and the powers of the court to order their use (see CPR 35.7 and 35.8, PD35, para 5).

17.2 The Civil Procedure Rules encourage the use of joint experts. Wherever possible a joint report should be obtained. Consideration should therefore be given by all parties to the appointment of single joint experts in all cases where a court might direct such an appointment. Single joint experts are the norm in cases allocated to the small claims track and the fast track.

17.3 Where, in the early stages of a dispute, examinations, investigations, tests, site inspections, experiments, preparation of photographs, plans or other similar preliminary expert tasks are necessary, consideration should be given to the instruction of a single joint expert, especially where such matters are not, at that stage, expected to be contentious as between the parties. The objective of such an appointment should be to agree or to narrow issues.

17.4 Experts who have previously advised a party (whether in the same case or otherwise) should only be proposed as single joint experts if other parties are given all relevant information about the previous involvement.

17.5 The appointment of a single joint expert does not prevent parties from instructing their own experts to advise (but the costs of such expert advisers may not be recoverable in the case).

Joint instructions

17.6 The parties should try to agree joint instructions to single joint experts, but, in default of agreement, each party may give instructions. In particular, all parties should try to agree what documents should be included with instructions and what assumptions single joint experts should make.

17.7 Where the parties fail to agree joint instructions, they should try to agree where the areas of disagreement lie and their instructions should make this clear. If separate instructions are given, they should be copied at the same time to the other instructing parties.

17.8 Where experts are instructed by two or more parties, the terms of appointment should, unless the court has directed otherwise, or the parties have agreed otherwise, include:

(a)   a statement that all the instructing parties are jointly and severally liable to pay the experts' fees and, accordingly, that experts' invoices should be sent simultaneously to all instructing parties or their solicitors (as appropriate);

and

(b)   a statement as to whether any order has been made limiting the amount of experts' fees and expenses (CPR 35.8(4)(a)).

17.9 Where instructions have not been received by the expert from one or more of the instructing parties the expert should give notice (normally at least 7 days) of a deadline to all instructing parties for the receipt by the expert of such instructions. Unless the instructions are received within the deadline the expert may begin work. In the event that instructions are received after the deadline but before the signing off of the report the expert should consider whether it is practicable to comply with those instructions without adversely affecting the timetable set for delivery of the report and in such a manner as to comply with the proportionality principle. An expert who decides to issue a report without taking into account instructions received after the deadline should inform the parties who may apply to the court for directions. In either event the report must show clearly that the expert did not receive instructions within the deadline, or, as the case may be, at all.

Conduct of the single joint expert

17.10 Single joint experts should keep all instructing parties informed of any material steps that they may be taking by, for example, copying all correspondence to those instructing them.

17.11 Single joint experts are Part 35 experts and so have an overriding duty to the court. They are the parties' appointed experts and therefore owe an equal duty to all parties. They should maintain independence, impartiality and transparency at all times.

17.12 Single joint experts should not attend any meeting or conference which is not a joint one, unless all the parties have agreed in writing or the court has directed that such a meeting may be held[1] and who is to pay the experts' fees for the meeting.

17.13 Single joint experts may request directions from the court – see Section 11 above.

17.14 Single joint experts should serve their reports simultaneously on all instructing parties. They should provide a single report even though they may have received instructions which contain areas of conflicting fact or allegation. If conflicting instructions lead to different opinions (for example, because the instructions require experts to make different assumptions of fact), reports may need to contain more than one set of opinions on any issue. It is for the court to determine the facts.

Cross-examination

17.15 Single joint experts do not normally give oral evidence at trial but if they do, all parties may cross-examine them. In general written questions (CPR 35.6) should be put to single joint experts before requests are made for them to attend court for the purpose of cross-examination[2].

18. Discussions between Experts

18.1 The court has powers to direct discussions between experts for the purposes set out in the Rules (CPR 35.12). Parties may also agree that discussions take place between their experts.

18.2 Where single joint experts have been instructed but parties have, with the permission of the court, instructed their own additional Part 35 experts, there may, if the court so orders or the parties agree, be discussions between the single joint experts and the additional Part 35 experts. Such discussions should be confined to those matters within the remit of the additional Part 35 experts or as ordered by the court.

18.3 The purpose of discussions between experts should be, wherever possible, to:

(a)   identify and discuss the expert issues in the proceedings;

(b)   reach agreed opinions on those issues, and, if that is not possible, to narrow the issues in the case;

(c)   identify those issues on which they agree and disagree and summarise their reasons for disagreement on any issue; and

(d)   identify what action, if any, may be taken to resolve any of the outstanding issues between the parties.

Arrangements for discussions between experts

18.4 Arrangements for discussions between experts should be proportionate to the value of cases. In small claims and fast-track cases there should not normally be meetings between experts. Where discussion is justified in such cases, telephone discussion or an exchange of letters should, in the interests of proportionality, usually suffice. In multi-track cases, discussion may be face to face, but the practicalities or the proportionality principle may require discussions to be by telephone or video conference.

18.5 The parties, their lawyers and experts should co-operate to produce the agenda for any discussion between experts, although primary responsibility for preparation of the agenda should normally lie with the parties' solicitors.

18.6 The agenda should indicate what matters have been agreed and summarise concisely those which are in issue. It is often helpful for it to include questions to be answered by the experts. If agreement cannot be reached promptly or a party is unrepresented, the court may give directions for the drawing up of the agenda. The agenda should be circulated to experts and those instructing them to allow sufficient time for the experts to prepare for the discussion.

18.7 Those instructing experts must not instruct experts to avoid reaching agreement (or to defer doing so) on any matter within the experts' competence. Experts are not permitted to accept such instructions.

---

1.   *Peet v Mid Kent Area Healthcare NHS Trust* [2002] 1 WLR 210
2.   *Daniels v Walker* [2000] 1 WLR 1382

18.8 The parties' lawyers may only be present at discussions between experts if all the parties agree or the court so orders. If lawyers do attend, they should not normally intervene except to answer questions put to them by the experts or to advise about the law[1] .

18.9 The content of discussions between experts should not be referred to at trial unless the parties agree (CPR 35.12(4)). It is good practice for any such agreement to be in writing.

18.10 At the conclusion of any discussion between experts, a statement should be prepared setting out:

(a)   a list of issues that have been agreed, including, in each instance, the basis of agreement;

(b)   a list of issues that have not been agreed, including, in each instance, the basis of disagreement;

(c)   a list of any further issues that have arisen that were not included in the original agenda for discussion;

(d)   a record of further action, if any, to be taken or recommended, including as appropriate the holding of further discussions between experts.

18.11 The statement should be agreed and signed by all the parties to the discussion as soon as may be practicable.

18.12 Agreements between experts during discussions do not bind the parties unless the parties expressly agree to be bound by the agreement (CPR 35.12(5)). However, in view of the overriding objective, parties should give careful consideration before refusing to be bound by such an agreement and be able to explain their refusal should it become relevant to the issue of costs.

19. Attendance of Experts at Court

19.1 Experts instructed in cases have an obligation to attend court if called upon to do so and accordingly should ensure that those instructing them are always aware of their dates to be avoided and take all reasonable steps to be available.

19.2 Those instructing experts should:

(a) ascertain the availability of experts before trial dates are fixed;

(b) keep experts updated with timetables (including the dates and times experts are to attend) and the location of the court;

(c) give consideration, where appropriate, to experts giving evidence via a video-link.

(d) inform experts immediately if trial dates are vacated.

19.3 Experts should normally attend court without the need for the service of witness summonses, but on occasion they may be served to require attendance (CPR 34). The use of witness summonses does not affect the contractual or other obligations of the parties to pay experts' fees.

---

1.   *Hubbard v Lambeth, Southwark and Lewisham HA* [2001] EWCA Civ 1455

A(21)   Guideline figures for the Summary Assessment of Costs

Solicitor's hourly rates

The guideline rates for solicitors provided here are broad approximations only. In any particular area the Designated Civil Judge may supply more exact guidelines for rates in that area. Also the costs estimate provided by the paying party may give further guidance if the solicitors for both parties are based in the same locality.

The following diagram shows guideline figures for each of three bands outside the London area, and a further three bands within the London area with a statement of the localities included in each band. In each band there are four columns specifying figures for different grades of fee earner.

Localities

The guideline figures have been grouped according to locality by way of general guidance only. Although many firms may be comparable with others in the same locality, some of them will not be. For example, a firm located in the City of London which specialises in fast track personal injury claims may not be comparable with other firms in that locality and vice versa.

In any particular case the hourly rate it is reasonable to allow should be determined by reference to the rates charged by comparable firms. For this purpose the costs estimate supplied by the paying party may be of assistance. The rate to allow should not be determined by reference to locality or postcode alone.

Grades of fee earner

The grades of fee earner have been agreed between representatives of the Supreme Court Costs Office, the Association of District Judges and the Law Society. The categories are as follows:

A.   Solicitors with over eight years post qualification experience including at least eight years litigation experience.

B.   Solicitors and legal executives with over four years post qualification experience including at least four years litigation experience.

C.   Other solicitors and legal executives and fee earners of equivalent experience.

D.   Trainee solicitors, para legals and other fee earners.

'Legal Executive' means a Fellow of the Institute of Legal Executives. Those who are not Fellows of the Institute are not entitled to call themselves legal executives and in principle are therefore not entitled to the same hourly rate as a legal executive.

Unqualified clerks who are fee earners of equivalent experience may be entitled to similar rates and in this regard it should be borne in mind that Fellows of the Institute of Legal Executives generally spend two years in a solicitor's office before passing their Part 1 general examinations, spend a further two years before passing the Part 2 specialist examinations and then complete a further two years in practice before being able to become Fellows. Fellows have therefore possess considerable practical experience and academic achievement. Clerks without the equivalent experience of legal executives will be treated as being in the bottom grade of fee earner ie. trainee solicitors and fee earners of equivalent experience. Whether or not a fee earner has equivalent experience is ultimately a matter for the discretion of the court.

Rates to allow for senior fee earners

Many High Court cases justify fee earners at a senior level. However the same may not be true of attendance at pre-trial hearings with counsel. The task of sitting behind counsel should be delegated to a more junior fee earner in all but the most important pre-trial hearings. The fact that the receiving party insisted upon the senior's attendance, or the fact that the fee earner is a sole practitioner who has no juniors to delegate to, should not be the determinative factors. As with hourly rates the costs estimate supplied by the paying party may be of assistance. What grade of fee earner did they use?

An hourly rate in excess of the guideline figures may be appropriate for Grade A fee earners in substantial and complex litigation where other factors, including the value of the litigation, the level of complexity, the urgency or importance of the matter as well as any international element would justify a significantly higher rate to reflect higher average costs

Guideline rates for summary assessment – January 2010

Band One Grade	A**	B	C	D
Guideline Rates	217	192	161	118
Aldershot, Farnham, Bournemouth (including Poole)				
Birmingham Inner				
Bristol				
Cambridge City, Harlow				
Canterbury, Maidstone, Medway & Tunbridge Wells				
Cardiff (Inner)				
Chelmsford South, Essex & East Suffolk				
Fareham, Winchester				
Hampshire, Dorset, Wiltshire, Isle of Wight				
Kingston, Guildford, Reigate, Epsom				
Leeds Inner (within 2 kilometers radius of the City Art Gallery)				
Lewes				
Liverpool, Birkenhead				
Manchester Central				
Newcastle – City Centre (within a 2 mile radius of St Nicholas Cathedral)				
Norwich City				
Nottingham City				
Oxford, Thames Valley				
Southampton, Portsmouth				
Swindon, Basingstoke				
Watford				

Band Two Grade	A**	B	C	D
Guideline Rates	201	177	146	111

Bath, Cheltenham and Gloucester, Taunton, Yeovil

Bury

Chelmsford North, Cambridge County, Peterborough, Bury St E, Norfolk, Lowestoft

Chester & North Wales

Coventry, Rugby, Nuneaton, Stratford & Warwick

Exeter, Plymouth

Hull (City)

Leeds Outer, Wakefield & Pontefract

Leigh

Lincoln

Luton, Bedford, St Albans, Hitchin, Hertford

Manchester Outer, Oldham, Bolton, Tameside

Newcastle (other than City Centre)

Nottingham & Derbyshire

Sheffield, Doncaster and South Yorkshire

Southport

St Helens

Stockport, Altrincham, Salford

Swansea, Newport, Cardiff (Outer)

Wigan

Wolverhampton, Walsall, Dudley & Stourbridge

York, Harrogate

Band Three Grade	A**	B	C	D
Guideline Rates	201	177	146	111

Birmingham Outer

Bradford (Dewsbury, Halifax, Huddersfield, Keighley & Skipton)

Cumbria

Devon, Cornwall

Grimsby, Skegness

Hull Outer

Kidderminster

Northampton & Leicester

Preston, Lancaster, Blackpool, Chorley, Accrington, Burnley, Blackburn, Rawenstall & Nelson

Scarborough & Ripon

Stafford, Stoke, Tamworth

Teesside

Worcester, Hereford, Evesham and Redditch

Shrewsbury, Telford, Ludlow, Oswestry

South & West Wales

London band

Grade	A**	B	C	D
City of London: EC1, EC2, EC3, EC4	409	296	226	138
Central London: W1, WC1, WC2, SW1	317	242	196	126
Outer London: (All other London post codes: W, NW, N, E, SE, SW and Bromley, Croydon, Dartford, Gravesend and Uxbridge)	229–267	172–229	165	121

**An hourly rate in excess of the guideline figures may be appropriate for Grade A fee earners in substantial and complex litigation where other factors, including the value of the litigation, the level of complexity, the urgency or importance of the matter as well as any international element would justify a significantly higher rate to reflect higher average costs.

Counsel's Fees

The following table sets out figures based on Supreme Court Costs Office statistics dealing with run of the mill proceedings in the Queens Bench and Chancery Division and in the Administrative Court. The table gives figures for cases lasting up to an hour and up to half a day, in respect of counsel up to five years call, up to ten years call and over ten years call. It is emphasised that these figures are not recommended rates but it is hoped that they may provide a helpful starting point for judges when assessing counsel's fees. The appropriate fee in any particular case may be more or less than the figures appearing in the table, depending upon the circumstances.

The table does not include any figures in respect of leading counsel's fees since such cases would self evidently be exceptional. Similarly, no figures are included for the Commercial Court or the Technology & Construction Court.

Table of Counsel's Fees

Queens Bench	1 hour hearing	½ day hearing
Junior up to 5 years call	£259	£450
Junior 5–10 years call	£386	£767
Junior 10+ years call	£582	£1,164
Chancery Division		
Junior up to 5 years call	£291	£556
Junior 5–10 years call	£497	£931
Junior 10+ years call	£757	£1,397
Administrative Court		
Junior up to 5 years call	£381	£582
Junior 5–10 years call	£698	£1,164
Junior 10+ years call	£989	£1,746

If the paying parties were represented by counsel, the fee paid to their counsel is an important factor but not a conclusive one on the question of fees payable to the receiving party's counsel.

In deciding upon the appropriate fee for counsel the question is not simply one of counsel's experience and seniority but also of the level of counsel which the particular case merits.

Counsel's fees should not be allowed in cases in which it was not reasonable to have instructed counsel, but it must be borne in mind that, especially in substantial hearings, it may be more economical if the advocacy is conducted by counsel rather than a solicitor. In all cases the court should consider whether or not the decision to instruct counsel has led to an increase in costs and whether that increase is justifiable.

Appendix B
Templates for Drafting Key Documents

B(1) Letter Before Claim under Practice Direction on Pre-action Conduct

B(2) Letter of Claim under Professional Negligence Pre-action Protocol

B(3) Particulars of Claim (Separate from Claim Form)

B(4) Case Summary for Use at a Multi-track Case Management Conference

B(5) Witness Statement

B(6) Hearsay Notice

B(7) Part 36 Offer Letter

B(8) Case Summary for Use at a Fast Track Trial

B(9) Case Summary for Use at a Multi-track Trial ('Skeleton Argument')

B(1)   Letter Before Claim under Practice Direction on Pre-action Conduct

Dear

[Heading]

<u>Letter before Claim</u>

Introduction

['*We act for* [full names] *of* [full address]']

['Our instructions are to recover a debt/damages . . .']

The facts

[Set out the material background facts, eg relevant contract details.]

Legal basis of claim

[State relevant law such as misrepresentation, breach of contractual term(s), negligence, negligent misstatement, and give brief details.]

Factual basis of claim

[Set out material facts in chronological order, establishing the legal claim, eg the breach of contractual terms or tortious duty.]

Liability/Responsibility

['*We have advised our clients that your actions on [date] were in breach of clause 3 of the contract and/or negligent and that they are entitled to be compensated by you.*']

Debt/Damages/Compensation

[Set out details of amount(s) claimed, including any interest due on a debt under a contractual term.]

Documents enclosed

['*The following documents are relied on by our client in support of the claim and copies are enclosed*' (list relevant documents and state what issue each supports, eg receipts in respect of damages claimed).]

Your documents

[Ask for any relevant documents – list the documents required and explain why they are relevant.]

Alternative Dispute Resolution

[Set out any proposal for ADR that your client wishes to make at this stage, including the method(s) of ADR proposed.]

Details of funding arrangement

[Set out relevant details of any CFA and/or AEI policy.]

Practice Direction: Pre-action Protocols

[Enclose copy, if appropriate, and refer to Section II, para 4.]

Acknowledgement deadline

['*Please acknowledge safe receipt of this letter promptly and by no later than* [give a specific date 14 days after posting]'.]

Response deadline

['*Please provide a full response by no later than* [give a specific date 30 days, or longer if appropriate, after posting] *or let us know within that period how much longer you need to provide a full response and why*'.]

Court proceedings

[Threat of court proceedings with associated claim for interest and costs if no acknowledgement or full response within [30] days.]

Copy of this letter

['*A copy of this letter is enclosed and we suggest that you forward it to your insurers/solicitors immediately.*']

Ending

B(2)   Letter of Claim under Professional Negligence Pre-action Protocol

Dear

[Heading]

Letter of Claim

Introduction

[Refer to preliminary notice and any subsequent correspondence.]

[Confirm full name and address of client.]

['*Our instructions are that you negligently . . . and our client is entitled to damages accordingly.*']

The facts

[Set out the material background facts, eg details of the professional services.]

Legal basis of claim

[State the allegations against the professional. As a matter of law, explain what has he done wrong/what has he failed to do.]

Factual basis of claim

[Set out material facts in chronological order, establishing the legal claim.]

[Confirm whether or not an expert has been appointed. If so, provide the identity and discipline of the expert, together with the date on which the expert was appointed.]

Liability/Responsibility

[Explain how the negligence has caused the loss claimed.]

Damages/Compensation

[Give an estimate of the financial loss suffered by the client and state how it is calculated. If details of the financial loss cannot be supplied, explain why and state when you will be in a position to provide the details. If the client is seeking some form of non-financial redress, this should be made clear.]

Documents enclosed

['*The following documents are relied on by our client in support of the claim and copies are enclosed*' (list relevant documents and state what issue each supports, eg receipts in respect of damages claimed).]

Your documents

[Ask for any relevant documents – list the documents required and explain why they are relevant.]

Alternative Dispute Resolution

[Set out any proposal for ADR that your client wishes to make at this stage, including the method(s) of ADR proposed.]

Details of funding arrangement

[Set out relevant details of any CFA and/or AEI policy.]

Acknowledgement deadline

['*Please acknowledge safe receipt of this letter promptly and by no later than* [give a specific date 21 days after posting].']

Response deadline

['*Please provide a full response by no later than* [give a specific date 3 months, or longer if appropriate, after posting] *or let us know within that period how much longer you need to provide a full response and why.*']

Court proceedings

[Threat of court proceedings with associated claim for interest and costs if no acknowledgement (within 21 days) or full response within (3 months or otherwise as stated or agreed).]

Copy of this letter

['*A copy of this letter is enclosed and we suggest that you forward it to your insurers immediately.*']

Ending

B(3)   Particulars of Claim (Separate from Claim Form)

Heading

Name of court, claim number and title of the proceedings

PD 16, para 3.8(1)–(3)

Content

Must include a concise statement of the facts on which the claimant relies: **Rule 16.4(1)(a)**

Should be divided into numbered paragraphs: **PD 5, para 2.2(5)**

So far as possible each paragraph or sub-paragraph should contain no more than one allegation: **QBD Guide, para 5.6.4.3**

The facts and other matters alleged should be set out as far as reasonably possible in chronological order: **QBD Guide, para 5.6.4.4**

Have all numbers, including dates, expressed as figures: **PD 5, para 2.2(6)**

Where a claim is based upon a written agreement, a copy of the contract or documents constituting the agreement should be attached: **PD 16, para 7.3(1)**

Where a claim is based upon an oral agreement, set out the contractual words used and state by whom, to whom, when and where they were spoken: **PD 16, para 7.4**

Where the claimant is seeking interest: **Rule 16.4(2)**

Ending

Statements of case drafted by a legal representative as a member or an employee of a firm should be signed in the name of the firm: **PD 5, para 2.1**

Must be verified by a statement of truth, the form of which is as follows:
'[I believe] [the claimant believes] that the facts stated in these particulars of claim are true.'
PD 16, para 3.4

Failure to verify by a statement of truth: **Rule 22.2**

Must contain the claimant's address for service: **PD 16, para 3.8(4)**

B(4)   Case Summary for Use at a Multi-track Case Management Conference

Heading/title of proceedings

Title of document: <u>Case Summary</u>

<u>Chronology of Proceedings</u>

<u>Agreed Issues of Fact</u>

<u>The Issues in Dispute</u>

Sub-divided into legal and factual issues, if appropriate.

<u>The Evidence Required to Deal with the Disputed Issues</u>

The Claimant

[Legal issues]

Factual

Expert

[Factual issues]

The Defendant

[Legal issues]

Factual

Expert

[Factual issues]

B(5)   Witness Statement

On whose behalf made

Initials and surname of deponent

Number

Exhibit/s " "

Date

PD 32, para 17.2

Title to proceedings
PD 32, para 17.1

Full name, address, occupation/description of deponent and state if a party or an employee of a party. **PD 32, para 18.1(1)–(4)**

Content

The statement must, if practicable, be in the intended witness's own words: **PD 32, para 18.1**

The statement should be expressed in the first person: **PD 32, para 18.1**

A statement is the equivalent of the oral evidence which that witness would, if called, give in evidence: **PD 32, para 20.1**

The statement must indicate which of the statements in it are made from the witness's own knowledge and which are matters of information or belief, and the source for any matters of information or belief: **PD 32, para 18.2**

It is usually convenient for a statement to follow the chronological sequence of the events or matters dealt with; each paragraph of a witness statement should as far as possible be confined to a distinct portion of the subject: **PD 32, para 19.2**

The statement should be divided into numbered paragraphs: **PD 32, para 19.1(5)**

Numbers should be expressed as figures: **PD 32, para 19.1(6)**

Any document should be formally exhibited: **PD 32, para 18.3 (and para 18.4)**

Ending

Statement of truth: I believe that the facts stated in this witness statement are true: **PD 32, para 20.2**

NOTE – Rule 22.3: if the maker of a witness statement fails to verify the witness statement by a statement of truth, the court may direct that it shall not be admissible as evidence.

B(6)   Hearsay Notice

Heading/title of proceedings

Title of document: <u>Hearsay Notice</u>

This notice is given pursuant to the Civil Procedure Rules 1998, Rule 33.2(1)(b) and (2) and s 2(1)(a) of the Civil Evidence Act 1995.

TAKE NOTICE that the [name of party] intends to rely on the following hearsay evidence at trial:

The witness statement of [name of witness]. A copy is served herewith pursuant to the court order of [date].

It is not proposed to call [name of witness] as [state any appropriate reason, eg witness dead].

[Date]

[Signed]

[Address for service]

B(7)   Part 36 Offer Letter

Dear ....

Heading

PART 36 OFFER: WITHOUT PREJUDICE SAVE AS TO COSTS

[Introduction; any relevant background explaining why offer being made/opponent should accept]

For the purposes of CPR, Rule 36.2(2)(b) we confirm that it is our intention that this offer should have the consequences set out in Part 36.

[For the purposes of CPR, Rule 36.2(2)(d) we confirm that this offer relates to the whole of the claim.]

[For the purposes of CPR, Rule 36.2(2)(e) we confirm that this offer takes into account the counterclaim.]

[Set out the proposals clearly and concisely, eg

1.   Your client returns the motor car to our client within seven days of acceptance of this offer.
2.   On receipt of the motor car we will send you £.........................
3.   For the sake of clarity we would confirm that the sum payable under clause 2 is inclusive of interest.]

In accordance with CPR, Rule 36.2(2)(c) this offer is open for acceptance for 21 days from service on you. As we are faxing this letter to you before 4.30pm today, a business day, please acknowledge safe receipt and confirmation of service today.

[Closing]

Yours faithfully,

B(8)   Case Summary for Use at a Fast Track Trial

Heading/title of proceedings

Title of document: <u>Case Summary</u>

<u>The Issues in Dispute</u>

Where appropriate, cross-refer to the statements of case in the trial bundle, including reference to relevant paragraph numbers of the statement of case and page numbers in the trial bundle (eg 'PoC para 3 p 4 & Defence para 2 p 5').

<u>The Evidence Required to Deal with the Disputed Issues</u>

Sub-divided into legal and factual issues, if appropriate.

Where appropriate, cross-refer to the evidence in the trial bundle, including reference to relevant paragraphs in witness statements or experts' reports and page numbers in the trial bundle (eg 'Coulson's statement para 3 p 14').

<u>The Claimant</u>

[Legal issues]

Factual

Expert

[Factual issues]

<u>The Defendant</u>

[Legal issues]

Factual

Expert

[Factual issues]

NOTE: on the fast track the Appendix to PD 28 provides that a case summary (which should not exceed 250 words), outlining the matters still in issue and referring where appropriate to the relevant documents, shall be included in the trial bundle for the assistance of the judge in reading the papers before the trial. See also the case summary for use at a multi-track trial (skeleton argument) on the next page. The guidance for that document should be followed, where appropriate.

B(9)   Case Summary for Use at a Multi-track Trial ('Skeleton Argument')

Heading/title of proceedings

Title of document: Case Summary/Skeleton Argument

The Agreed Issues

Concisely set out the nature of the case generally and the background facts in so far as they are relevant to the matter before the court.

The Issues in Dispute

Sub-divided into legal and factual issues, if appropriate.

Where appropriate, cross-refer to the statements of case in the trial bundle, including reference to relevant paragraph numbers of the statement of case and page numbers in the trial bundle. Avoid formality and may make use of abbreviations, eg C for Claimant, A/100 for bundle A page 100, 1.1.10 for 1 January 2010 etc.

The propositions of law relied on

Cross-references should be made to relevant authorities.

The Evidence Required to Deal with the Disputed Issues

Where appropriate, cross-refer to the evidence in the trial bundle, including reference to relevant paragraphs in witness statements or experts reports and page numbers in the trial bundle (eg 'Report of C's Expert, Jones para 6 p 21').

The Claimant

[Legal issues]

Factual

Expert

[Factual issues]

The Defendant

[Legal issues]

Factual

Expert

[Factual issues]

State the details of the advocate who prepared it.

Appendix C
Flow Diagrams

C(1)   Overview of the Five Stages of Litigation

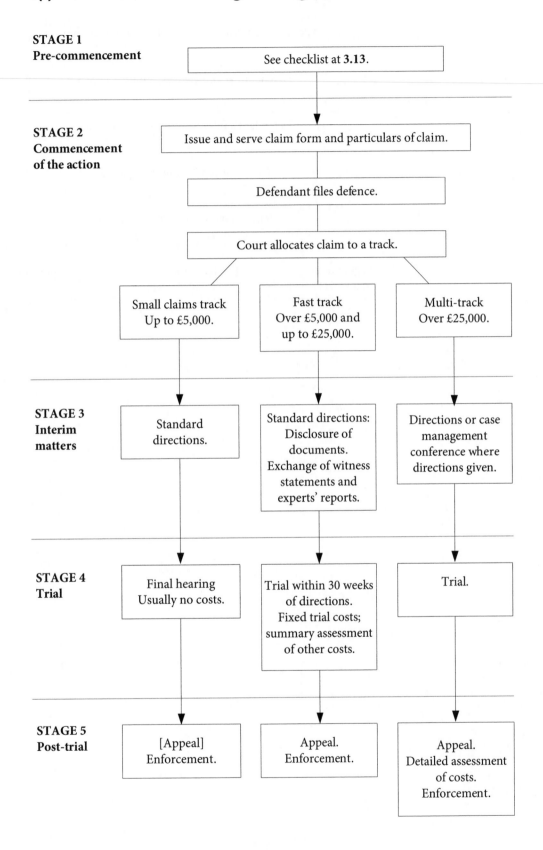

STAGE 1
Pre-commencement

See checklist at **3.13**.

STAGE 2
Commencement
of the action

Issue and serve claim form and particulars of claim.

Defendant files defence.

Court allocates claim to a track.

Small claims track
Up to £5,000.

Fast track
Over £5,000 and
up to £25,000.

Multi-track
Over £25,000.

STAGE 3
Interim
matters

Standard
directions.

Standard directions:
Disclosure of
documents.
Exchange of witness
statements and
experts' reports.

Directions or case
management
conference where
directions given.

STAGE 4
Trial

Final hearing
Usually no costs.

Trial within 30 weeks
of directions.
Fixed trial costs;
summary assessment
of other costs.

Trial.

STAGE 5
Post-trial

[Appeal]
Enforcement.

Appeal.
Enforcement.

Appeal.
Detailed assessment
of costs.
Enforcement.

C(2)   Steps under Practice Direction on Pre-action Conduct

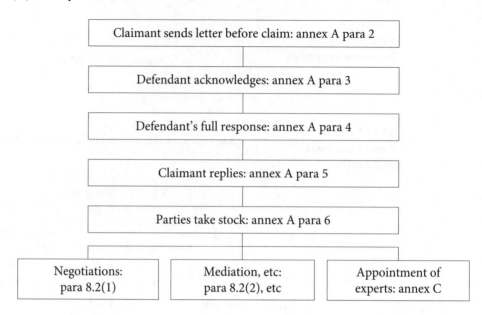

C(3)   Steps under Professional Negligence Pre-action Protocol

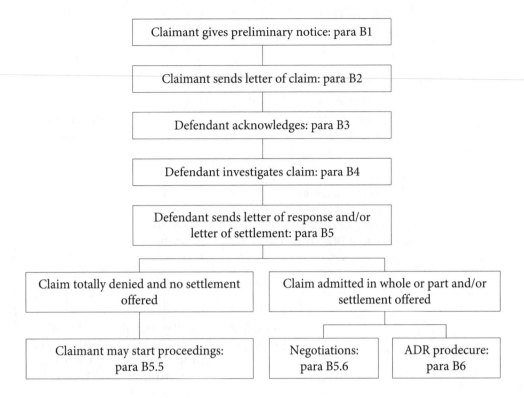

C(4)   Interest

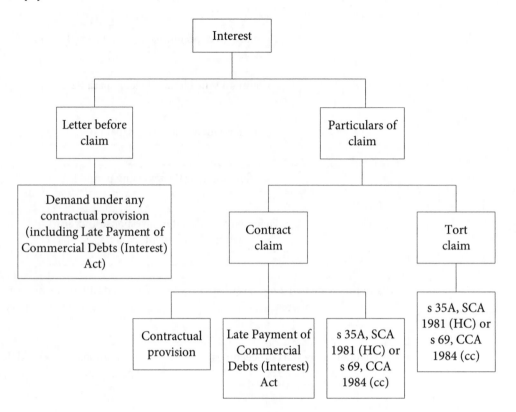

C(5)   Determining Jurisdiction where the Defendant is Domiciled in an EU State (apart from Denmark)

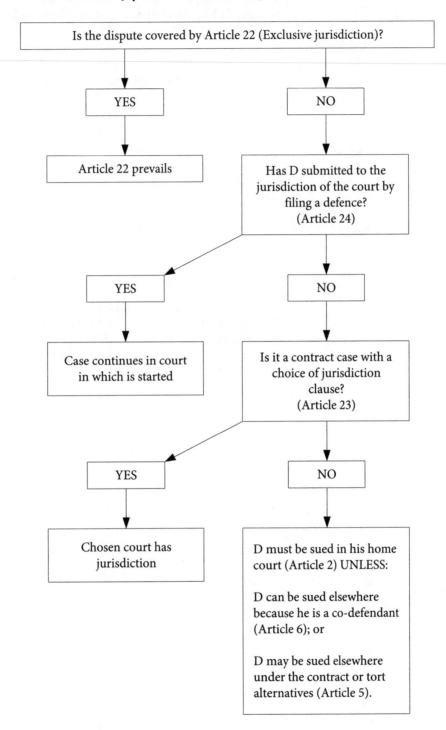

Is the dispute covered by Article 22 (Exclusive jurisdiction)?

YES → Article 22 prevails

NO → Has D submitted to the jurisdiction of the court by filing a defence? (Article 24)

YES → Case continues in court in which is started

NO → Is it a contract case with a choice of jurisdiction clause? (Article 23)

YES → Chosen court has jurisdiction

NO → D must be sued in his home court (Article 2) UNLESS:

D can be sued elsewhere because he is a co-defendant (Article 6); or

D may be sued elsewhere under the contract or tort alternatives (Article 5).

Note: as to the EFTA States and Denmark, see **Chapter 2**.

C(6)   Possible Responses by Defendant to a Claim

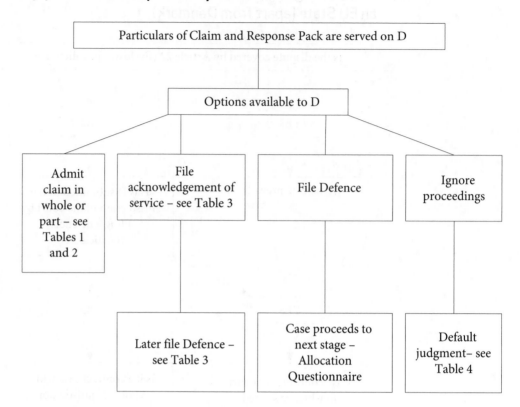

Table 1 – Admission of Claim in Whole but Request Time to Pay   345

C(7)   Table 1 – Admission of Claim in Whole but Request Time to Pay

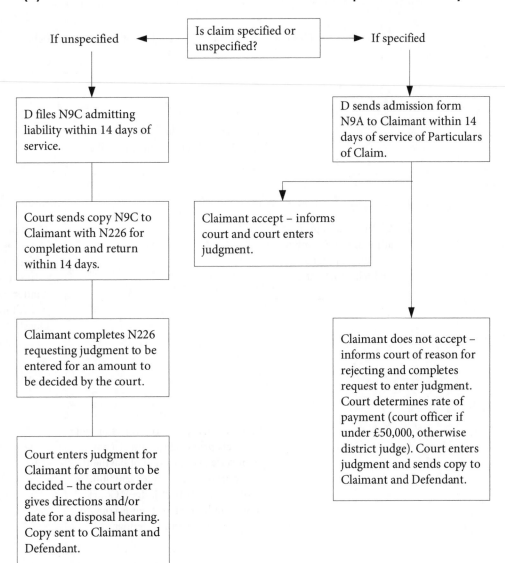

C(8)   Table 2 – Admission of Part of Claim – Specified Amount

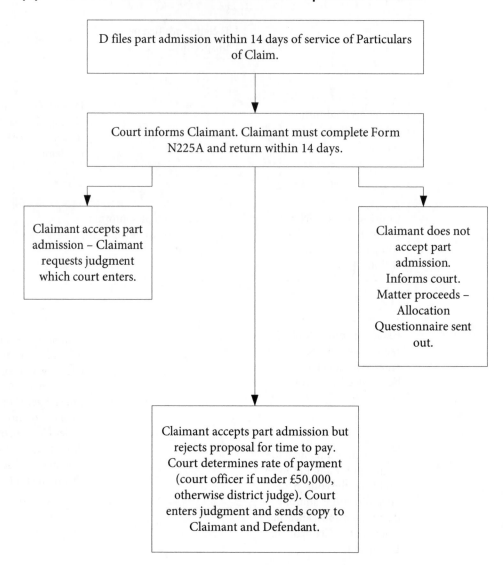

Table 3 – File Acknowledgement of Service   347

C(9)   Table 3 – File Acknowledgement of Service

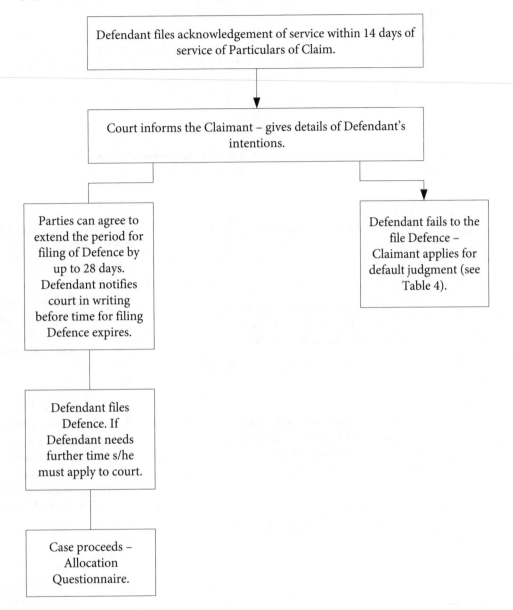

C(10)   Table 4 – Default Judgment

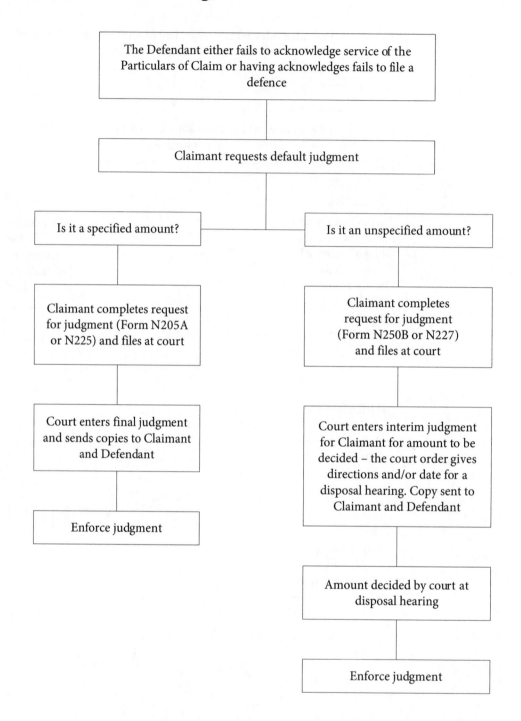

The Defendant either fails to acknowledge service of the Particulars of Claim or having acknowledges fails to file a defence

Claimant requests default judgment

Is it a specified amount?

Is it an unspecified amount?

Claimant completes request for judgment (Form N205A or N225) and files at court

Claimant completes request for judgment (Form N250B or N227) and files at court

Court enters final judgment and sends copies to Claimant and Defendant

Court enters interim judgment for Claimant for amount to be decided – the court order gives directions and/or date for a disposal hearing. Copy sent to Claimant and Defendant

Enforce judgment

Amount decided by court at disposal hearing

Enforce judgment

C(11)   Possible Costs Orders on Setting Aside a Default Judgment

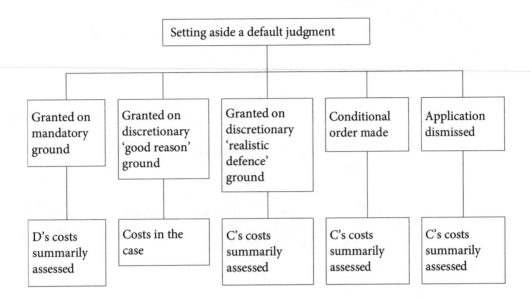

C(12)   Possible Costs Orders on Claimant's Application for Summary Judgment

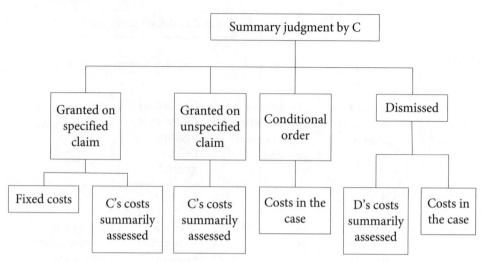

C(13) Consequences of Claimant Accepting Defendant's Part 36 Offer within Relevant Period

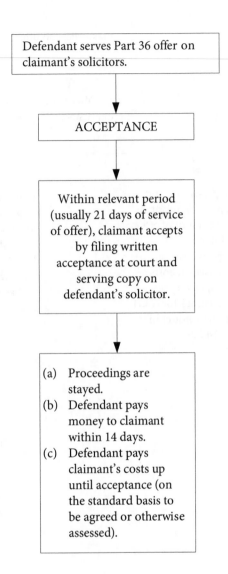

C(14) Consequences of Defendant Accepting Claimant's Part 36 Offer within Relevant Period

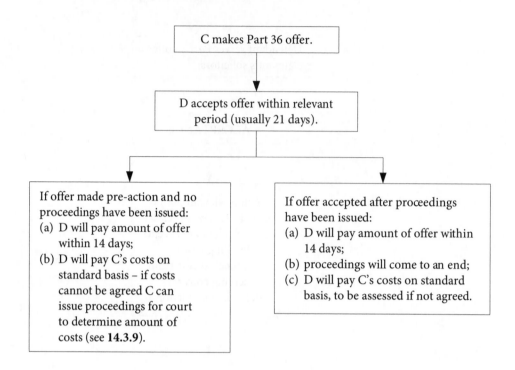

C(15) Consequences of Claimant Accepting Defendant's Part 36 Offer after Relevant Period has Expired

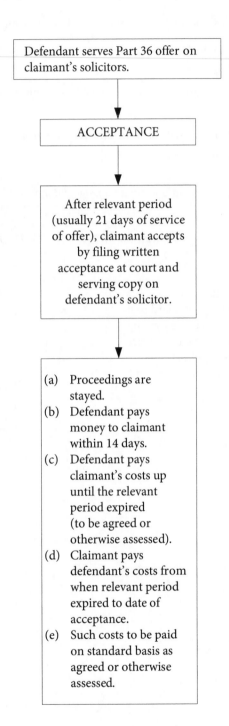

Defendant serves Part 36 offer on claimant's solicitors.

ACCEPTANCE

After relevant period (usually 21 days of service of offer), claimant accepts by filing written acceptance at court and serving copy on defendant's solicitor.

(a) Proceedings are stayed.

(b) Defendant pays money to claimant within 14 days.

(c) Defendant pays claimant's costs up until the relevant period expired (to be agreed or otherwise assessed).

(d) Claimant pays defendant's costs from when relevant period expired to date of acceptance.

(e) Such costs to be paid on standard basis as agreed or otherwise assessed.

C(16)   Consequences of Claimant Failing to Obtain Judgment More Advantageous than Defendant's Part 36 Offer

Rule 36.14(1) This rule applies where upon judgment being entered–

(a)   a claimant fails to obtain a judgment more advantageous than a defendant's Part 36 offer.

Rule 36.14(2) The court will, unless it considers it unjust to do so, order that the defendant is entitled to–

(a)   his costs from the date on which the relevant period expired; and

(b)   interest on those costs.

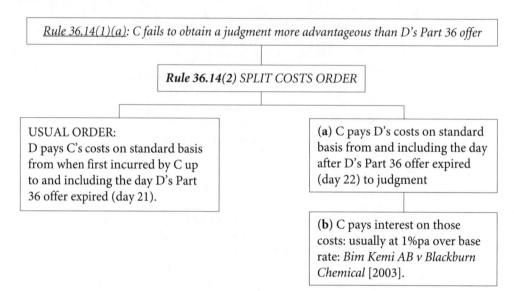

C(17) Consequences of Claimant Failing to Establish Liability at Trial and so not Obtaining Judgment More Advantageous Than Defendant's Part 36 Offer

Order for Interest on Costs under Rule 36.14(2)

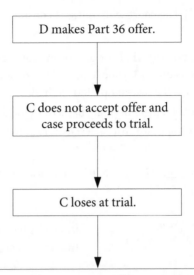

D makes Part 36 offer.

C does not accept offer and case proceeds to trial.

C loses at trial.

C will not receive any damages and will have to pay:
(a) unless it is unjust to do so, D's costs on the standard basis potentially from when first incurred by D up to judgment; and
(b) interest on the costs incurred by D from and including the day after the relevant period expired (day 22) to judgment (see **13.4.5.4**).

C(18) Consequences of Claimant Obtaining Judgment at Least as Advantageous as Own Part 36 Offer

Rule 36.14(1) This rule applies where upon judgment being entered–

(b)   judgment against the defendant is at least as advantageous to the claimant as the proposals contained in a claimant's Part 36 offer.

Rule 36.14(3) The court will, unless it considers it unjust to do so, order that the claimant is entitled to–

(a)   interest on the whole or part of any sum of money (excluding interest) awarded at a rate not exceeding 10% above base rate for some or all of the period starting with the date on which the relevant period expired;

(b)   his costs on the indemnity basis from the date on which the relevant period expired; and

(c)   interest on those costs at a rate not exceeding 10% above base rate.

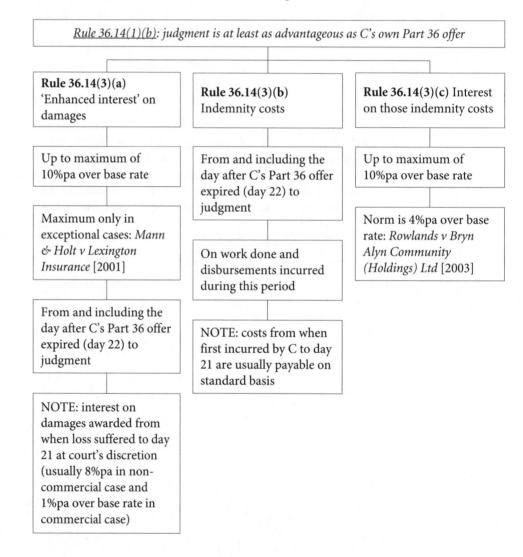

C(19) Consequences of Claimant Obtaining Judgment More Advantageous Than Defendant's Part 36 Offer but not as Advantageous as Own Part 36 Offer

C wins and obtains a judgment more advantageous than D's Part 36 offer but not as advantageous as his own Part 36 offer

C will receive:

(a)   the damages awarded by the court;

(b)   interest at the court's discretion on the damages awarded (see **2.7.2.3**) provided claimed in the particulars of claim;

(c)   costs on the standard basis potentially from when first incurred by C up to judgment.

Part 36 has no effect – C's offer was probably too high and D's offer probably too low.

C(20) The Standard Basis of Assessment of Costs

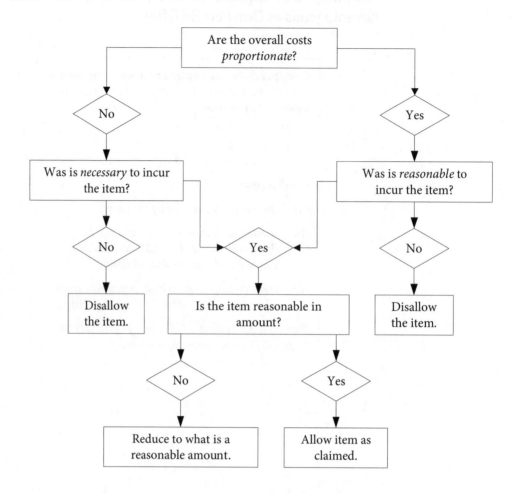

Appendix D
Case Study Documents

D(1)   Case Analysis

D(2)   Letter Before Claim

D(3)   Defendant's Letter of Response

D(4)   Particulars of Claim

D(5)   Defence and Counterclaim

D(6)   Reply and Defence to Counterclaim

D(7)   Defendant's Part 18 Request for Information

D(8)   Case Summary for Use at Case Management Conference

D(9)   Order for Directions

D(10) Claimant's List of Documents

D(11) Witness Statement of Marjorie Trudge

D(12) Experts' Without Prejudice Meeting Statement

D(13) Claimant's Part 36 Offer Letter

D(14) Defendant's Brief to Counsel

D(15) Consent Order

D(1) Case Analysis

When carrying out an initial case analysis (see **2.5**) and periodically reviewing the case thereafter, ensure that you answer the following questions:

1.   Have all possible causes of action and potential defendants been identified?
2.   What as a matter of law must the client establish?
3.   What facts will the client have to establish ('the material facts')?
4.   What evidence is currently available to establish the material facts?
5.   What evidence needs to be obtained in order to establish any particular material fact?
6.   How strong is the client's case? What material facts are favourable and unfavourable?

Consider the case study that follows. Assume that you act for Mr and Mrs Simpson. They own a large house locally and had agreed to let out part of it for a couple of months to a Mr Templar who is moving house. Apparently, when he arrived to take up his tenancy at 11 pm that night, he lost control of his car when driving up the clients' driveway and crashed into their recently completed extension. The clients' garden, the extension, and some of their furnishings and fittings were all damaged.

The first step is to establish whether the clients have any basis for making a claim against Mr Templar. This is known as the cause of action. The most obvious claim is in negligence.

So what, as a matter of law, must the clients prove to make a claim in negligence successfully against Mr Templar?

(a)   That Mr Templar owed them a duty of care.
(b)   The material facts that establish a breach of that duty.
(c)   The material facts that establish that the damage to the client's property was caused by the breach of that duty, ie the link between Mr Templar's car leaving the driveway and crashing into their extension.
(d)   That as a consequence of the crash the clients suffered damage and loss.

This might be presented in a simple case analysis grid chart, as shown below.

Client: Mr and Mrs Simpson.		
Opponent: Mr Templar.		
Cause of action: Negligence.		
Elements to establish	**Facts to establish**	**Available evidence**
Duty of care	That the clients occupy the property and Mr Templar (a road user) entered onto the driveway.	Clients own the property and saw Mr Templar enter the driveway in his car.
Breach of duty	By driving too fast and erratically, Mr Templar lost control, left the drive and did not avoid crashing into the extension.	Clients who saw Mr Templar do this.
Causation	That by crashing into the extension the clients thereby suffered loss.	Clients who saw Mr Templar do this.
Loss and damage	Damage to garden, the extension, some furnishings and fittings.	Clients.

Where does this case analysis take us next?

We need to consider the strengths and weaknesses of the known case, as follows:

(a)   *Duty of care.* This is unlikely to be an issue unless Mr Templar is going to deny that he was the driver. It is well established law that a driver owes a duty to drive to the standard of a reasonable competent driver. By entering the driveway in his car, Mr Templar owed them a duty to drive with reasonable care.

(b)   *Breach of duty.* This will probably be a key disputed issue. Why did the car leave the drive and crash into the house? Any evidence needs to be preserved. It may be appropriate to obtain an expert's opinion at this stage.

(c)   *Causation.* This is unlikely to be an issue unless Mr Templar denies that the crash took place. If breach can be proved, it will not be disputed that his vehicle caused damage to the clients' property.

(d)   *Loss and damage.* However, even if the clients can establish breach of duty (liability), they will still have to prove the amount (quantum) of their claim. Do they have any receipts for repair works already done, or estimates for works that need to be done? These may well be disputed, and the evidence available to prove each item claimed must be considered. At the first interview you will need to itemise each item of loss and analyse the evidence you have or may be able to obtain to prove the amount claimed. This is usually not so problematic where property is damaged as (subject to the duty to mitigate) the cost of replacement/repair is a guide to the amount of the loss. However, where the loss does not have a readily ascertainable financial value, eg loss of profits, more thought must be given to the evidence which can be obtained and relied upon to support the amount claimed.

In the case analysis table above we have some evidence to support each of the legal elements which must be proved. This will not always be the case – you may have no evidence in respect of a particular element, and that column in your case analysis table will be blank.

So what should we do, and how might we develop the chart as the case progresses?

Clearly, we could add a column at this stage, setting out the evidence that should be obtained, for example:

Client: Mr and Mrs Simpson.			
Opponent: Mr Templar.			
Cause of action: Negligence.			
Elements to establish	**Facts to establish**	**Available evidence**	**Evidence to obtain**
Duty of care	That the clients occupy the property and Mr Templar (a road user) entered onto the driveway.	Clients own the property and saw Mr Templar enter the driveway in his car.	
Breach of duty	By driving too fast and erratically, Mr Templar lost control, left the drive and did not avoid crashing into the extension.	Clients who saw Mr Templar do this.	Expert evidence: an examination of the vehicle/driveway may produce evidence which supports the clients evidence as to the speed of the vehicle/loss of control.
Causation	That by crashing into the extension the clients thereby suffered loss.	Clients who saw Mr Templar do this.	

Loss and damage	Damage to garden, the extension, some furnishings and fittings.	Clients.	An expert will need to produce a report detailing the damage to the extension and the cost of repair.

As the litigation progresses you will need to ensure all necessary procedural steps are taken for the evidence to be used at trial. You may find it helpful to classify each piece of evidence as documentary, witness of fact, expert or real.

You must always remember that the process of case analysis is one of evaluation – will the evidence enable the client to succeed on the balance of probabilities. Throughout a case, in order to assess and advise on its merits, we are looking for favourable facts and unfavourable facts (often called 'good' facts and 'bad' facts). For example, it would be a favourable ('good') fact if, say, Mr Templar had previous convictions or points on his driving licence for speeding. That would point towards liability on this occasion. It would not prove liability, but it would be circumstantial evidence implying that he may have been speeding up Mr and Mrs Simpson's drive. Equally it would be an unfavourable ('bad') fact if, say, Mr and Mrs Simpson's builders had left nails or sharp objects on or near the driveway when completing the extension works. If such items caused the tyres on Mr Templar's car to burst and he lost control of the car as a result, he could argue that he was not to blame, in whole or part, for the accident.

At the end of Stage 1 of Civil Litigation, once we know the prospective defendant's response to the claim, we can then record what legal and factual issues are agreed, and those that are disputed. Whilst it will still be necessary for the statements of case to refer to the facts relating to all issues – whether disputed or not – the procedural and evidential focus will be on the issues in dispute between the parties.

D(2)   Letter Before Claim

SOLICITORS LLP
1 Avenue Road
Nowhere
Mythshire
MC1V 2AA

Our reference: 1234/PO

Mr G Templar
1 The Cottage
Grassy Knowle
Nowhere
Mythshire MY76 9T

16 August 2010

Dear Sir,

Incident at Bliss Lodge, Steep Lane, Nowhere on 3 August 2009
Letter Before Claim

We are instructed by Mr W Simpson and Mrs R Simpson of Bliss Lodge, Steep Lane, Nowhere in connection with a claim for damages following an incident which occurred at their home on 2 August 2010.

The facts

Our clients advise us that at approximately 11 pm on 2 August 2010 you drove your motor car, a Land Cruiser 4x4, 4.5 litre turbo model, registration GIT 13 ('the Car'), on their drive. We understand you were about to take up a short-term let in part of the premises. The Car crashed into the recently completed extension of our clients' property causing serious damage to the garden, building, furnishings and fittings.

Legal basis of claim

By entering our clients' premises it became your responsibility to ensure that you drove with the degree of care and skill that would be expected from a competent driver.

Factual basis of claim

We are instructed that you drove up the drive at excessive speed and without properly controlling the Car.

You were seen to swerve repeatedly on and off the driveway. The tyre tracks at the property confirm this. It is clear that you failed to apply your Car's brakes sufficiently or at all and that you failed to steer, manage, control or stop the Car so as to avoid the collision. You thereby breached your obligation to drive on our clients' driveway with the degree of care and skill that would be expected from a competent driver. As a result you drove into our client's extension and this will now have to be demolished, rebuilt and refitted.

Responsibility

We have advised our clients that your actions on 2 August 2010 were negligent and that they are entitled to be compensated by you.

Calculation of damage to the extension at 'Bliss Lodge'

	£
Putting right damage to garden & drive	8,000
Demolishing and rebuilding extension	96,000
Kitchen refit	57,000
Bedroom refit	10,000
TOTAL	**171,000**

Documents relied on

The above figures are based on current available estimates copies of which are enclosed.

In addition to the above losses our clients have been put to considerable expense in making safe the extension.

Calculation of loss in making safe the extension at 'Bliss Lodge'

	£
Weather-proofing the extension	8,000
Installing a temporary alarm system for the parts of 'Bliss Lodge' accessible from the extension	5,000
Making safe the electrical supply to and in the extension	1,000
Sealing off the plumbing supply to the extension	500
TOTAL	**14,500**

Documents relied on

We enclose copies of receipted invoices for the above matters.

Acknowledgment and response

Please acknowledge safe receipt of this letter promptly and by no later than 30 August 2010.

Please also note that unless a full written response is received by 15 September 2010 or such later time as we may subsequently agree with you, we are instructed to start court proceedings for damages, interest and costs without further notice to you.

Practice Direction on Pre-Action Conduct

We advise you to notify your insurers of this claim, if you have not already done so and take independent legal advice. Should you choose not to instruct solicitors, we enclose a copy of a Practice Direction issued by the courts and we draw your attention to the power of the courts to impose sanctions under paragraph 4.

Alternative Dispute Resolution

At this stage we are not aware that you have any grounds to dispute this claim. If we receive a full written response as requested then our clients will then be in a better position to consider if any alternative dispute resolution method is appropriate to any issue you raise.

Raven Lunar Insurance Plc

Following the incident you informed our clients that you were insured with this company. We enclose a copy of a letter that we have sent to that company giving formal notification of the possible commencement of court proceedings.

Yours faithfully,

D(3)   Defendant's Letter of Response

Advocates & Co
30 Cheapway
Nowhere
Mythshire
MB2X 5PP
DX Never2020
Telephone: 0307 637-2222
Fax: 0307 637-7321

20 September 2010

Our Ref: CF/GIT/12
Your Ref: 1234/PO

Solicitors LLP
1 Avenue Road
Nowhere
Mythshire
MC1V 2AA

Dear Sirs

Incident at Bliss Lodge, Steep Lane, Nowhere

Your clients: Mr and Mrs Simpson

Our client: Mr G Templar

We acknowledged your letter before claim on 19 August and you subsequently agreed that we had until 24 September to make this full response. We have had an opportunity to investigate this claim on behalf of our client and his insurers. Please note that we are instructed as follows.

Denial of liability

Our client denies liability for the damage to your clients' property.

He did not lose control of his car through any fault of his own but because broken shards of glass were present on your clients' driveway. This glass caused two of the tyres on our client's car to burst. For that reason alone he lost control of the car.

In these circumstances our client did not drive negligently.

Counterclaim

Further, your clients' failure to clear away the glass amounts to a breach of their duty of care to our client as a visitor to their property under the Occupiers' Liability Act 1957.

Contributory negligence

Please note that should your clients pursue their claim our client will allege contributory negligence in the alternative on these facts.

Calculation of loss

As a result of your clients' breach of duty our client has suffered the following losses.

1. His car, a 4x4 Land Cruiser, has been damaged beyond economic repair. It has been confirmed as a write-off due to a twisted chassis and other damage. We enclose a letter from We-Haul Recovery & Repair Service confirming this to be the case. Our client's loss on this item is equivalent to the value of the vehicle which was purchased new for £58,995 only the week before this incident.

2. His Diasan PC notebook was also irreparably damaged. This machine's specification is 450mhz, 200Gb hard disk with 128 Mb RAM 32 speed CD Rom notebook with ISDN card and built-in printer. This was only 1 month old and a replacement is valued at £6,500.

3. His Mercuriam satellite mobile phone was also irreparably damaged. Again this was relatively new and a replacement would cost about £2,000.

4. As his vehicle could not be driven away after this incident, your clients arranged for a local towing service, We-Haul, to tow this away at our client's expense. He has paid their invoice of £440.63 which loss he now seeks from your clients.

5. Our client has had to hire a car while he awaits delivery of the vehicle to replace his Land Cruiser. He has been quite modest in the car he has hired (a Ford Focus). Car hire is £150 per week excluding insurance. He is not due to take delivery of his replacement Land Cruiser until the end of October and our client intends to continue with the hire contract for the Ford Focus.

6. As your clients know, our client had 2 months in which he required accommodation in between selling his London property and completing the purchase of his new home. He has therefore had to obtain alternative accommodation. He spent the first week at The Cherub Inn in Wye-on-Wey at a cost of £175 per night excluding meals, totalling £1,225. Thereafter he has found rooms to rent at £600 a week. Our client claims the difference between this amount spent and what he would have paid to your clients in rental of the stable block, namely £450 a week.

7. Our client has also had to pay for the storage of the Land Cruiser at We-Haul's premises. This costs £50 per week and will continue until the parties can agree that the car is no longer required.

Documents relied on

We enclose:

1. A letter from We-Haul Recovery & Repair Service about the car and a copy of the purchase note.

2. A copy receipt for the Diasan PC notebook.

3. A copy receipt for the Mercuriam satellite mobile phone.

4. A copy receipted invoice from We-Haul for the towing charge.

5. A copy of the hire agreement for the Ford Focus.

6. A copy receipted invoice from The Cherub Inn and for the rooms our client rented.

7. A copy of the storage agreement with We-Haul.

ADR

It is clear that on the issue of liability we have differing expert views. In these circumstances we consider that ADR is inappropriate. However, it may well be that certain items of quantum can be agreed between us subject to the issue of liability. Perhaps you would telephone the writer to discuss? Thereafter we can better consider the question of expert evidence and ADR as to quantum.

<u>Acknowledgement and response</u>

Please acknowledge receipt of this letter by 4 October or in the alternative please telephone the writer by then. Subject to any telephone conversation we may have, please let us have a full response by 20 October 2010.

Please note that we do have instructions to issue proceedings against your client for damages, interest and costs should we not hear from you as requested.

Yours faithfully,

D(4)   Particulars of Claim

IN THE HIGH COURT OF JUSTICE   WF-11-1234
QUEEN'S BENCH DIVISION
WEYFORD DISTRICT REGISTRY

BETWEEN   MR WILLIAM ULYSSES SIMPSON (1)   Claimants
                        MRS RUPINDER SIMPSON (2)

                                    and

                        MR GEOFFREY IAN TEMPLAR   Defendant

PARTICULARS OF CLAIM

1.   At all material times the Claimants owned the property known as 'Bliss Lodge', Steep
     Lane, Nowhere, Mythshire, GU15 6AB ('the Property').

2.   On 2 August 2010 at about 11.00 pm, the Defendant drove a Land Cruiser 4x4, 4.5 litre
     turbo model registration number GIT 13 ('the Car') down the driveway leading to the
     Property. In the circumstances, the Defendant was under a duty of care that he would
     exercise reasonable care and skill when using the driveway.

3.   In breach of that duty and owing to the negligent driving of the Defendant, the Car left
     the driveway and collided with the Property, partially destroying a recently-constructed
     two-storey extension.

PARTICULARS OF NEGLIGENCE

The Defendant drove negligently in that he:

   (a)   drove at excessive speed;

   (b)   lost control of the Car;

   (c)   swerved repeatedly on and off the driveway;

   (d)   failed to apply the Car's brakes sufficiently or at all;

   (e)   failed to steer, manage, control or stop the Car so as to avoid the collision.

4.   Owing to the Defendant's negligence, the Claimants have suffered loss and damage.

PARTICULARS OF LOSS AND DAMAGE

	£
Costs incurred rendering the extension safe following the collision:	
– Weather-proofing the extension	8,000.00
– Installation of temporary alarm system for parts of Bliss Lodge accessible from the extension	5,000.00
– Making safe electrical supply to and in the extension	1,000.00
– Sealing off plumbing supply to the extension	500.00
	14,500.00

Particulars of the estimated costs that follow are given in the attached Schedule.

Estimated costs to be incurred repairing damage to the extension:–

– demolishing and rebuilding the extension	96,000.00
– refitting custom-made kitchen	57,000.00
– refitting bedroom	10,000.00
– remedial and reinstatement works to garden and driveway	8,000.00
	171,000.00
TOTAL	185,500.00

5.   In respect of damages awarded to them the Claimants claim interest under s.35A of the Senior Courts Act 1981 at such rate and for such period as the court thinks fit.

AND THE CLAIMANTS CLAIM:

(1)   Damages as stated in paragraph 4 above;

(2)   Interest as stated in paragraph 5 above.

Dated 4 March 2011   Signed: *Solicitors LLP*

STATEMENT OF TRUTH

I believe that the facts stated in these Particulars of Claim are true.

Signed: *William Ulysses Simpson*
....
WILLIAM ULYSSES SIMPSON
FIRST CLAIMANT

Signed: *Rupinder Simpson*
....
RUPINDER SIMPSON
SECOND CLAIMANT

The Claimants' solicitors are Solicitors LLP, 1 Avenue Road, Nowhere, Mythshire, MC1V 2AA where they will accept service of proceedings on behalf of the Claimants.

To: the Defendant and the Court Manager

D(5)   Defence and Counterclaim

IN THE HIGH COURT OF JUSTICE   WF-11-1234
QUEEN'S BENCH DIVISION
WEYFORD DISTRICT REGISTRY

BETWEEN   MR WILLIAM ULYSSES SIMPSON (1)   Claimants
                      MRS RUPINDER SIMPSON (2)

and

MR GEOFFREY IAN TEMPLAR   Defendant

DEFENCE AND COUNTERCLAIM

DEFENCE

1. The Defendant admits paragraph 1 of the Particulars of Claim. The Claimants were the occupiers of the Property and the Defendant was a visitor within the meaning of the Occupiers' Liability Act 1957 ('the Act'). The Defendant visited the Property at the Claimants' invitation on 2 August 2010 to use accommodation in a converted stable block there.

2. The Defendant admits paragraph 2.

3. Save that the Defendant admits that he lost control of the Car and that it collided with the Property, the Defendant denies for the reasons that follow that he drove negligently as alleged in paragraph 3 or at all or that the matters complained of were caused as alleged or at all.

4. Further or alternatively, the collision was caused or contributed to by the breach of statutory duty of the Claimants.

PARTICULARS OF BREACH OF STATUTORY DUTY

The Claimants acted in breach of statutory duty in that they:

(a) unknown to the Defendant caused or allowed shards of broken glass to be present on the driveway of the Property which caused the front and rear offside tyres of the Car to suddenly burst, thus resulting in him losing control of the Car;

(b) failed by means of notices or otherwise to warn the Defendant of the presence and position of the glass referred to in (a);

(c) required or allowed the Defendant to use the driveway when it was unsafe;

(d) exposed the Defendant to danger and a foreseeable risk of damage to his property;

(e) failed to take proper care for the Defendant's safety.

5. As to paragraph 4, the Defendant admits that the Property was damaged by the collision but denies for the reasons set out above that he caused any damage. The Defendant otherwise makes no admissions as to the loss or damage alleged by the Claimants in paragraph 4 of the Particulars of Claim as he has no knowledge of such.

6. In the circumstances, the Defendant denies that the Claimants are entitled to the relief claimed in paragraph 4 or any relief.

COUNTERCLAIM

7. The Defendant repeats paragraphs 1 to 5 of the Defence.

8. Owing to the above matters, the Defendant has suffered loss and damage.

PARTICULARS OF LOSS AND DAMAGE

	£
Value of Defendant's Car irreparably damaged	58,995.00
Value of other items in the Car irreparably damaged:	
– Diasan PC notebook computer	6,500.00
– Mercuriam satellite mobile phone	2,000.00
Towing charges paid to We-Haul in removing the Car	440.63
Cost of storing the Car at We-Haul's premises for nine weeks at £50.00 per week	450.00
Alternative car hire charges for thirteen weeks at £150.00 per week	1,950.00
Additional cost of alternative accommodation in Nowhere	1,825.00
TOTAL	**72,160.63**

9.   The Defendant therefore counterclaims from the Claimants damages in respect of the above.

10.   The Defendant claims interest under s.35A of the Senior Courts Act 1981 on damages awarded to him at such rate and for such period as the court thinks fit.

AND THE DEFENDANT COUNTERCLAIMS:

(1)   Damages as stated in paragraph 9 above;

(2)   Interest as stated in paragraph 10 above.

Dated 23 March 2011

Signed: *Advocates & Co*
....

STATEMENT OF TRUTH

I believe that the facts stated in this Defence and Counterclaim are true.

Signed: *G I Templar*
....
GEOFFREY IAN TEMPLAR
DEFENDANT

The Defendant's solicitors are Advocates & Co, 30 Cheapway, Nowhere, Mythshire, MB2X 5PP where they accept service of proceedings in behalf of the Defendant.

To: the Claimants

To: the Court Manager

D(6)   Reply and Defence to Counterclaim

IN THE HIGH COURT OF JUSTICE   WF-11-1234
QUEEN'S BENCH DIVISION
WEYFORD DISTRICT REGISTRY

| BETWEEN | MR WILLIAM ULYSSES SIMPSON (1) | Claimants |
| | MRS RUPINDER SIMPSON (2) | |

and

MR GEOFFREY IAN TEMPLAR   Defendant

REPLY AND DEFENCE AND COUNTERCLAIM

REPLY

1. The Claimants admit paragraph 1 of the Defence.

2. The Claimants deny that they were in breach of statutory duty as alleged in paragraph 4 of the Defence or at all. The Claimants also deny that the collision was caused or contributed to by their breach of statutory duty. The Claimants contend that:

    (a) There was no broken glass and/or debris on the driveway. Alternatively, if there was broken glass and/or debris on the driveway, it was placed there by the actions of the Defendant, referred to in paragraph (b) below, whereby the Defendant swerved onto broken glass and/or debris on the grass and thereby caused it to scatter;

    (b) There was a small amount of builders' debris on the grass bordering the right hand side of the driveway. The debris was well away from the normal passage of any vehicle and did not constitute a hazard. It was solely due to the Defendant's excessive speed that he lost control of the Car, veered off the driveway onto the grass and drove onto the debris;

    (c) If the Defendant had been driving at an appropriate speed, he should have been able to control the Car, after the front and rear offside tyres burst, so as to avoid colliding with the Property.

3. Except where the Defendant has made admissions and except as appears in this statement of case, the Claimants join issue with the Defendant upon his Defence.

DEFENCE TO COUNTERCLAIM

4. The Claimants repeat paragraphs 1, 2 and 3 above.

5. As to paragraph 8 of the Counterclaim, the Claimants admit that the Defendant's Car suffered damage but deny for the reasons given above that they caused such loss and damage. The Claimants otherwise do not admit the loss and damage alleged in paragraph 8 of the Counterclaim as they have no knowledge of such.

6. In the circumstances the Claimants deny that the Defendant is entitled to any damages whatsoever.

Dated: 1 April 2011.

Signed: *Solicitors LLP*

STATEMENT OF TRUTH

I believe that the facts stated in this Reply and Defence to Counterclaim are true.

Signed: *William Ulysses Simpson*
....
WILLIAM ULYSSES SIMPSON
FIRST CLAIMANT

Signed: *Rupinder Simpson*
....
RUPINDER SIMPSON
SECOND CLAIMANT

The Claimants' solicitors are Solicitors LLP, 1 Avenue Road, Nowhere, Mythshire, MC1V 2AA where they will accept service of proceedings on behalf of the Claimants.

To: the Defendant and the Court Manager

D(7)   Defendant's Part 18 Request for Information

IN THE HIGH COURT OF JUSTICE   WF-11-1234
QUEEN'S BENCH DIVISION
WEYFORD DISTRICT REGISTRY

BETWEEN   MR WILLIAM ULYSSES SIMPSON (1)   Claimants
                      MRS RUPINDER SIMPSON (2)

and

MR GEOFFREY IAN TEMPLAR   Defendant

DEFENDANT'S PART 18 REQUEST FOR FURTHER INFORMATION

This Request is made on 8 April 2011 and the Defendant expects a response to it no later than 22 April 2011

1.   Under paragraph 4 of the Particulars of Claim, please provide a detailed description and financial breakdown of all work undertaken and each and every item of cost incurred in respect of:

   (a)   weather-proofing the extension;

   (b)   installing a temporary alarm system at Bliss Lodge;

   (c)   making safe the electrical supply to and in the extension;

   (d)   sealing off plumbing supply to the extension.

2.   Under the same paragraph, please provide a detailed description and financial breakdown of all work which it is proposed be undertaken and each and every item of cost it is proposed to incur in respect of:

   (a)   demolishing and rebuilding the extension;

   (b)   refitting custom-made kitchen;

   (c)   refitting bedroom;

   (d)   remedial and reinstatement works to garden and driveway.

Advocates & Co

30 Cheapway, Nowhere, Mythshire, MB2X 5PP
Solicitors for the Defendant

To the Claimants

D(8)   Case Summary for Use at Case Management Conference

IN THE HIGH COURT OF JUSTICE   WF-11-1234
QUEEN'S BENCH DIVISION
WEYFORD DISTRICT REGISTRY

BETWEEN   MR WILLIAM ULYSSES SIMPSON (1)   Claimants
                          MRS RUPINDER SIMPSON (2)

                                   and

                          MR GEOFFREY IAN TEMPLAR   Defendant

**Case Summary agreed by the parties for the purpose of the case
management conference to be held on 22 June 2011**

Chronology of Proceedings

Claim form	4 March 2011
Particulars of claim	4 March 2011
Acknowledgment of service	11 March 2011
Defence and Counterclaim	22 March 2011
Reply and defence to Counterclaim	1 April 2011
Allocation questionnaires	13 April 2011

Agreed Issues of Fact

1. On 19 July 2010 the Defendant agreed with the Claimants to rent the stable block of Bliss Lodge, Steep Lane, Nowhere, Mythshire, the Claimants' property and home known as 'Bliss Lodge' for the period of two months commencing on 2 August 2010.

2. The Defendant drove onto the driveway leading to 'Bliss Lodge' on 2 August 2010 at about 11.00 pm.

3. The Defendant's car crashed into Bliss Lodge.

4. The car was a Land Cruiser registration no. GIT 13. The car is a write-off.

5. There was substantial damage done to Bliss Lodge.

6. The quantum of the Defendant's Counterclaim is agreed, subject to liability, as follows:

	£
Land Cruiser	58,995.00
Diasan Notebook	6,500.00
Mercuriam mobile telephone	2,000.00
We-Haul Ltd towage charges	440.63
We-Haul Ltd storage charges	450.00
Excess accommodation costs for 2 months	1,825.00
Car hire 13 weeks	1,950.00
	72,160.63

Issues in Dispute – Claim

1. Was the Defendant driving negligently by going too fast and/or without due care and attention down the Claimants' drive?

2. Was there glass on or near the drive?

3. If so, should the Defendant have been in a position to take appropriate avoiding action?

4. Did the Defendant's negligence cause the damage to the Claimants' property?

5. Were the Claimants contributorily negligent in leaving glass on or near the drive?

6. What are the Claimants' losses and can these be recovered in full from the Defendant?

Issues in Dispute – Counterclaim

1. Were the Claimants in breach of their duties under the Occupiers' Liability Act 1957 in leaving or allowing their builders to leave glass on the drive?

2. Did the Claimants' breach of statutory duties cause the damage to the Defendant's car and possessions?

3. Was the Defendant contributorily negligent in any way?

4. Can the Defendant's losses be recovered in full from the Claimants?

The Evidence Required to Deal with the Disputed Issues

The Claimants

The First Claimant will give evidence as to the Defendant's driving, the accident and consequent damage.

The Second Claimant will give evidence about the location of the glass, the accident and consequent damage.

As to expert evidence, the Claimant wishes to rely on:

(a) Anthony Bacon: accident reconstruction expert: as to the cause of the accident

(b) Fiona McFadden: structural engineer: in respect of structural damage to the Claimant's property

(c) John Eaves: quantity surveyor: as to quantum of the Claimants' claim in respect of structural damage to their property.

The Defendant

The Defendant will give evidence as to his driving, the accident and consequent damage.

Colonel Trudge, the Claimants' neighbour, will give evidence as to the Defendant's driving and consequent damage.

Mrs Marjory Trudge will give evidence as to the location of the glass.

As to expert evidence, the Defendant wishes to rely on:

(a) Raymond Crow: an accident reconstruction expert: as to the cause of the accident

(b) Kieran O'Donnell: building surveyor: in respect of structural damage to the Claimant's property and its quantum.

The Defendant does not agree with the Claimants that evidence from a structural engineer is required.

Signed:

Solicitors LLP	Advocates & Co
Solicitors LLP	*Advocates & Co*
--------------------------------	--------------------------------
Dated 14 June 2011	Dated 14 June 2011

D(9)   Order for Directions

IN THE HIGH COURT OF JUSTICE   WF-11-1234
QUEEN'S BENCH DIVISION
WEYFORD DISTRICT REGISTRY
DISTRICT JUDGE HARDCASTLE

BETWEEN   MR WILLIAM SIMPSON (1)   Claimants
                          MRS RUPINDER SIMPSON (2)

                                and

                          MR GEOFFREY IAN TEMPLAR   Defendant

                          <u>ORDER FOR DIRECTIONS</u>

Upon hearing the solicitors for the parties and upon reading the agreed Case Summary dated 14 June 2011

IT IS ORDERED as follows:

DISCLOSURE OF DOCUMENTS

1.   Disclosure will take place as follows:–
      (a)   each party will give standard disclosure by list no later than 1 July 2011;
      (b)   inspection will be completed and/or copies served no later than 15 July 2011.

WITNESSES OF FACT

2.   Each party will serve on every other party the witness statements of all witnesses of fact on whom he wants to rely by simultaneous exchange no later than 2 August 2011.

3.   Only the evidence of those witnesses whose evidence is exchanged may be called at trial.

EXPERT EVIDENCE

4.   The parties have permission to use the following expert witnesses:
      (a)   One expert on accident reconstruction each.
      (b)   One building surveyor each.

5.   The parties will simultaneously exchange expert reports setting out the substance of any expert evidence on which they intend to rely no later than 30 August 2011.

6.   Questions to the expert witnesses must be served by 13 September 2011 and replies must be provided by 27 September 2011.

7.   Reports must be agreed, if possible, no later than 11 October 2011.

8.   If the reports are not agreed within that time there will be a without prejudice discussion between the relevant experts no later than 25 October 2011 to identify whether there are any issues that can be agreed between them and to agree those issues.

9.   The experts will prepare for and file with the court a statement of the issues on which they agree and on which they disagree with a summary of their reasons and that statement will be filed with the court with the pre-trial checklist, listing questionnaire.

10.   The experts have permission to give oral evidence at the trial provided that the substance of the evidence to be given has been disclosed as above and has not been agreed.

REQUESTS FOR INFORMATION ETC.

11.   Each party will serve any requests for information or clarification based on any document disclosed or statement served by another party no later than 14 days after disclosure or service.

12.   Any such request will be dealt with within 21 days of service.

DOCUMENTS TO BE FILED WITH PRE-TRIAL CHECKLISTS

13.   The parties must file with their pre-trial checklists copies of their experts' reports, witness statements and any replies to requests for further information.

DATES FOR FILING PRE-TRIAL CHECKLISTS AND THE TRIAL

14.   Each party must file a completed pre-trial checklist no later than 24 January 2012.

15.   The trial of this case will take place on a date to be fixed between 6 April and 5 May 2012.

COSTS

16.   The costs of the case management conference be costs in the case.

Dated 22 June 2011.

D(10)   Claimant's List of Documents

List of documents:
standard disclosure

Notes

- The rules relating to standard disclosure are contained in Part 31 of the Civil Procedure Rules.

- Documents to be included under standard disclosure are contained in Rule 31.6

- A document has or will have been in your control if you have or have had possession, or a right of possession, of it **or** a right to inspect or take copies of it.

In the	
High Court of Justice Queens Bench Division Weyford District Registry	
Claim No.	WF-11-1234
Claimant (including ref)	SIMPSON (Ref: A1)
Defendant (including ref)	TEMPLAR (Ref: 6/9/A)
Date	29/06/11

Disclosure Statement

I, the above named

☑ Claimant   ☐ Defendant

☐ Party (if party making disclosure is a company, firm or other organisation identify here who the person making the disclosure statement is and why he is the appropriate person to make it)

state that I have carried out a reasonable and proportionate search to locate all the documents which I am

required to disclose under the order made by the court on (date of order) | 22/06/11 |

☑ I did not search for documents:-

   ☑ pre-dating | 01/01/09 |

   ☐ located elsewhere than
   | N/A |

   ☐ in categories other than
   | N/A |

   ☐ for electronic documents

☑ I carried out a search for electronic documents contained on or created by the following:
(list what was searched and extent of search)

Our home PC files and e-mails.
Our mobile phones.
The files on the first claimant's laptop.

☐ I did not search for the following:-

☐ documents created before [   ]

documents contained on or created by the ☐ Claimant   ☐ Defendant

☐ PCs   ☐ portable data storage media
☐ databases   ☐ servers
☐ back-up tapes   ☐ off-site storage
☐ mobile phones   ☐ laptops
☐ notebooks   ☐ handheld devices
☐ PDA devices

documents contained on or created by the ☐ Claimant   ☐ Defendant

☐ mail files   ☐ document files
☐ calendar files   ☐ web-based applications
☐ spreadsheet files   ☐ graphic and presentation files

documents other than by reference to the following keyword(s)/concepts
(delete if your search was not confined to specific keywords or concepts)

[   ]

I certify that I understand the duty of disclosure and to the best of my knowledge I have carried out that duty. I further certify that the list of documents set out in or attached to this form, is a complete list of all documents which are or have been in my control and which I am obliged under the order to disclose.

I understand that I must inform the court and the other parties immediately if any further document required to be disclosed by Rule 31.6 comes into my control at any time before the conclusion of the case.

☐ I have not permitted inspection of documents within the category or class of documents (as set out below) required to be disclosed under Rule 31(6) (b) or (c) on the grounds that to do so would be disproportionate to the issues in the case.

[   ]

Signed | *W. Simpson   R. Simpson* | **Date** | *29 June 2011*

(Claimant)(~~Defendant~~)(~~'s litigation friend~~)

List and number here, in a convenient order, the documents (or bundles of documents if of the same nature, e.g. invoices) in your control, which you do not object to being inspected. Give a short description of each document or bundle so that it can be identified, and say if it is kept elsewhere i.e. with a bank or solicitor

I have control of the documents numbered and listed here. I do not object to you inspecting them/producing copies.

1. Correspondence between the Claimants' solicitors and the Defendant or the Defendant's solicitors from 16/08/10 to date.
2. Copy letter from Claimants' solicitors to Defendant's insurers dated 16 August 2010.
3. Bundle of plans, estimates and receipts for the construction of the Claimants' extension - various dates in 2009 and 2010.
4. Bundle of receipts and estimates in respect of the costs referred to in paragraph 4 of the Claimants' particulars of claim - various dates in 2010.
5. Statements of case in these proceedings - various dates in 2011.

List and number here, as above, the documents in your control which you object to being inspected. (Rule 31.19)

I have control of the documents numbered and listed here, but I object to you inspecting them:

1. Correspondence, attendance notes, memoranda, instructions to counsel and counsel's advice and similar documentation between the Claimants' solicitor and the Claimants.
2. An expert's report.
3. Correspondence between the Claimants' solicitor and witnesses, both expert and factual, including proofs, statements, reports, drafts and similar documentation.

Say what your objections are

I object to you inspecting these documents because:

As to the documents referred to in section 1 above, these were created for the sole purpose of giving or receiving legal advice and so are covered by legal professional, advice privilege.
As to the document referred to in section 2 above, this was obtained by the Claimants when this litigation was reasonably contemplated for the sole purpose of taking legal advice in regard to this litigation and so is covered by legal professional, litigation privilege.
As to the documents referred to in section 3 above, these were created from when this litigation was reasonably contemplated to date for the sole purpose of obtaining or collecting evidence to be used in this litigation and so are covered by legal professional, litigation privilege.

List and number here, the documents you once had in your control, but which you no longer have. For each document listed, say when it was last in your control and where it is now.

I have had the documents numbered and listed below, but they are no longer in my control.

The original of the copy letters referred to in the first list above. These were last in the Claimants' control on the day that the originals were posted or othwerwise sent.

D(11) Witness Statement of Marjorie Trudge

On behalf of the Defendant
M Trudge
1st
Exhibit: MT 1
8 July 2011

WF-11-1234

IN THE HIGH COURT OF JUSTICE
QUEEN'S BENCH DIVISION
WEYFORD DISTRICT REGISTRY

BETWEEN   MR WILLIAM ULYSSES SIMPSON (1)   Claimants
MRS RUPINDER SIMPSON (2)

and

MR GEOFFREY IAN TEMPLAR   Defendant

WITNESS STATEMENT OF MARJORIE TRUDGE

Marjorie Trudge, retired pharmacist of Paradise Manor, Steep Lane, Nowhere, Mythshire, MB22 7TB will say as follows.

1. I have lived at Paradise Manor with my husband, Harold for the past 35 years. Paradise Manor is next door to Bliss Lodge and I have known the Simpson family since they moved there in 1990.

2. During the early evening of 2 August 2010 whilst I was dusting in a bedroom which overlooks Bliss Lodge, I saw a builders' van stop approximately half way down the driveway. A couple of men got out and ran back to the house. Within a minute I saw them come out holding a pane of glass. I thought they must have forgotten it. They were walking rather fast but I was rather surprised when I saw them drop it just before they reached the van. They had started to clear it up and had swept it into a pile at the side of the drive when Mr Simpson came out. He looked at his watch and seemed to indicate that he was happy for them to go, which they did. He then went back into the house. I did not see him come back out again during the next 30 or so minutes which I spent cleaning the room.

3. I refer to the sketch plan marked "**MT1**". I was asked by Mr Templar's solicitors to prepare this. I have indicated with a cross as best as I can where the plane of glass was dropped. As far as I can recall it was very close to the third light away from the house on the right-hand side of the drive as you go up it towards the house.

4. Unfortunately, I am unlikely to be able to give evidence in this case. I am about to go to Australia to care for my sister who is very ill. I don't expect to return during the next 12 months.

I believe that the facts stated in this witness statement are true.

Signed: *Marjorie Trudge*

Dated   8 July 2011

'MT1'

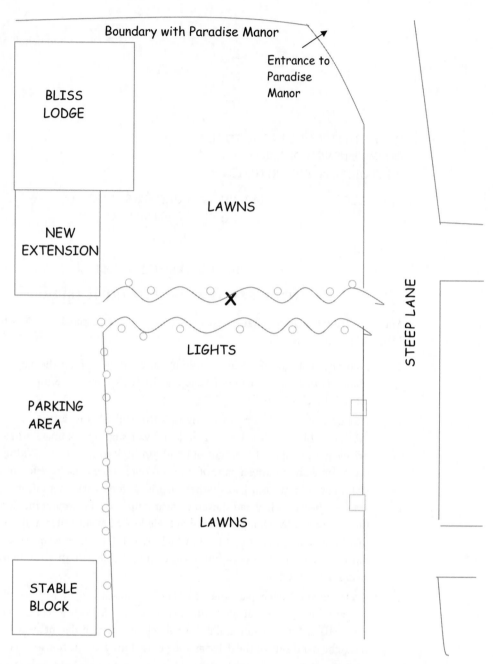

I verify that this is the exhibit "MT1" referred to in my witness statement dated 8 July 2011

Signed: *Marjorie Trudge*

D(12)   Experts' Without Prejudice Meeting Statement

<u>SIMPSON AND SIMPSON -v- TEMPLAR</u>

<u>CASE No. WF-11-1234</u>

<u>NOTE OF 'WITHOUT PREJUDICE' MEETING BETWEEN MR JOHN EAVES AND MR KIERAN O'DONNELL ON 19 OCTOBER 2011 IN ACCORDANCE WITH THE ORDER FOR DIRECTIONS DATED 22 JUNE 2011</u>

To: the court

Date: 19 October 2011

The meeting took place at the offices of O'Donnell & Co, at 64 High Street, Nowhere at 9.30 am. It was followed by a short site visit to the Claimants' property at Bliss Lodge, Steep Lane, Nowhere.

Agreed Issues

We agreed that:

1.   The sum of £8,000 claimed in respect of emergency weatherproofing work following the accident was reasonable in all the circumstances given the inclement weather in August 2009.

2.   A sum of £2,275 is agreed in respect of the installation of a temporary security system at the property pending full repairs.

3.   £1,500 is reasonable for the associated electrical and plumbing work.

4.   There was no structural damage to the main fabric of Bliss Lodge arising from the accident. We agreed that the evidence of slight subsidence in the back of the playroom where the extension abuts the house pre-dates the accident and is in any event not a cause for concern.

5.   There is structural damage to the extension's joists. These will need to be stripped out and re-fixed. As a result the extension's roof will need to be removed and rebuilt.

6.   The extension's foundations are only marginally damaged and can be made good with minor repairs.

7.   The cost of refitting the kitchen is agreed at £38,775. It is agreed that the majority of the units will need to be replaced because of water damage.

Disputed Issues

1.   Mr Eaves for the Claimants maintains that the load-bearing walls of the extension are fundamentally damaged and need to be demolished and rebuilt. This effectively means that the whole extension has to be demolished.

   Mr O'Donnell for the Defendant maintains that only part of one load-bearing wall must be rebuilt. There is no requirement to demolish the whole extension and the extent of any rebuilding work can be limited to the removal and repair of the roof and joists referred to in paragraph 5 above and the repair *in situ* of the one damaged wall.

In terms of cost (all figures exclude VAT), the figures are as follows:

	Mr Eaves	Mr O'Donnell
Demolition work	£25,600	Nil
Clear site	£8,645	Nil
Rebuild walls	£36,600	£12,460
Make good interior plastering and tiling	£6,700	£5,000

2.   The cost of removing the roof, repairing the joists and replacing the roof is disputed:–

Mr Eaves   £18,550

Mr O'Donnell   £14,750

3.   The extent of repairs required to the bedroom and the associated costs are not agreed:–

Mr Eaves	Strip out, replaster and rewallpaper and make good windows and paintwork	£6,560
	Make good floor joists and boards and re-carpet	£4,200
Mr O'Donnell	Minor repairs to lower half of walls in bedroom including re-wallpaper where necessary	£1,300
	Make good floor joists, boards and re-carpet	£2,300

John Eaves
....
John Eaves
(for the Claimants)

Kieran O'Donnell
....
Kieran O'Donnell
(for the Defendant)

D(13)   Claimant's Part 36 Offer Letter

SOLICITORS LLP
1 Avenue Road
Nowhere
Mythshire
MC1V 2AA

Our reference: 1234/PO
Your Ref: CF/GIT/12

Advocates & Co
30 Cheapway
Nowhere
Mythshire,
MB2X 5PP

1 November 2011

Dear Sirs,

Simpson v Templar

PART 36 OFFER: WITHOUT PREJUDICE SAVE AS TO COSTS

We refer to previous correspondence in this matter.

Our clients are confident that should this matter proceed to trial they will be successful in establishing liability and recovering the full amount claimed from your client. However, in a final attempt to settle the matter we have our clients' instruction to make your client an offer of settlement. For the purposes of CPR, Rule 36.2(2)(b) we confirm that it is our intention that this offer should have the consequences set out in Part 36.

In accordance with CPR, Rule 36.2(2)(d) and (e), the offer on the part of our clients is to accept the sum of £175,000 in relation to the whole of their claim for damages, after taking into account your client's counterclaim. For clarity we would confirm that the offer is inclusive of interest.

In accordance with CPR, Rule 36.2(2)(c) this offer is open for acceptance for 21 days from the date of service. As we are sending this to you today by first-class post we calculate that the offer will be deemed to be served on 3 November 2011. Please acknowledge and confirm.

Yours faithfully,

D(14)   Defendant's Brief to Counsel

IN THE HIGH COURT OF JUSTICE   WF-11-1234
QUEEN'S BENCH DIVISION
WEYFORD DISTRICT REGISTRY

BETWEEN   MR WILLIAM ULYSSES SIMPSON (1)   Claimants
MRS RUPINDER SIMPSON (2)

and

MR GEOFFREY IAN TEMPLAR   Defendant

**BRIEF TO COUNSEL TO APPEAR ON BEHALF OF THE DEFENDANT AT
THE TRIAL OF THE ACTION ON 18 APRIL 2012**

Counsel has the following copy documents:

(1)   Bundle of correspondence between the parties and solicitors;

(2)   Statements of case;

(3)   Allocation questionnaires and pre-trial checklists;

(4)   Orders made during the action;

(5)   Claimants' Part 36 offer letter;

(6)   Case summary from case management conference;

(7)   Documents obtained from the Claimant on inspection;

(8)   The Defendant's documents in Part 1 of his list;

(9)   Exchanged witness statements;

(10)   Civil Evidence Act Hearsay Notice;

(11)   Exchanged expert reports;

(12)   Replies from experts to parties' questions;

(13)   Experts' 'without prejudice' statement filed at court;

(14)   Case summary from pre-trial review hearing;

(15)   Directions for trial;

(16)   Proposed index for trial bundle;

(17)   Proposed index for core bundle;

(18)   Previous instructions to counsel and advice.

BACKGROUND

1.   We act for the Defendant in this action. Counsel will be familiar with the main issues having advised on evidence after disclosure. The action is fixed for trial on 18 April 2012 at 10 am at Weyford District Registry.

FACTS

2.   Counsel is referred to the case summaries prepared in advance of the case management conference and pre-trial review. The facts are briefly as follows.

3.   On 2 August 2010 the Defendant drove his brand new car, a 4x4 Land Cruiser to the Claimants' property Bliss Lodge, where he was due to take up a two month tenancy in that property's converted stable block. The Claimants had given him directions. He arrived at about 11 pm. This was observed by the Claimants' neighbour, Colonel Trudge. According to his wife, Mrs Marjory Trudge, the Claimants' builders had earlier that day dropped a pane of glass on the Claimants' driveway. It is the Defendant's case

that some broken glass was left on the drive. The Defendant drove over the glass which caused his two offside tyres to burst. The car went out of his control. The drive was relatively steep and the Defendant's car careered into Bliss Lodge itself, severely damaging the Claimants' newly built extension.

Issues – liability

4. The issues in the action turn mainly on whether:
   (a) the Defendant can be shown to have driven negligently; and
   (b) the Claimants breached their duty, as occupiers, to the Defendant under the Occupiers' Liability Act 1957, in failing to clear away the broken glass and debris and/or warn the Defendant adequately of its presence. It is clear from Mrs Trudge's statement for the Defendant that the Claimants were aware of the glass on and around the drive and there are no issues arising about the liability of the builders.

5. There is a dispute on the facts about the precise location of the pile of glass and debris. The Claimants maintain that it was to the side of the drive and that the Defendant, in driving too fast down the drive, drove slightly off the drive and over the glass. Their position is that if he had not been driving negligently he would not have strayed off the drive and would not have hit the glass. This is supported by their expert, Mr Bacon.

6. Clearly if the Claimants succeed on these points, the counterclaim on the Occupiers' Liability Act is likely to fail at least in part. The Defendant will then face at least partial liability for the damage to Bliss Lodge. The evidence on these points is dealt with in more detail below.

Evidence on liability

7. Counsel is referred to the reports of the accident reconstruction experts, Mr Bacon for the Claimants and Mr Crow for the Defendant and to the witness statements of Mr Simpson, Colonel and Mrs Trudge. The witness statements are self-explanatory.

8. Neither expert's report is favourable to the Defendant in terms of the speed at which he was allegedly driving before the accident.

9. The experts' reports are inconclusive on the question of whether the broken glass was originally on or beside the drive. Therefore, this remains a disputed fact and will have to be resolved by non-expert evidence only (see above). Mr Bacon says that there is evidence of tyre tracks on the grass and he thinks it likely that they were made before the car hit the glass. This opinion is based on the car's subsequent erratic route. However, Mr Crow says he is unable to tell whether the car went over the grass or glass first. He may well be vulnerable in cross-examination. Both experts are of the view that the car hit the house at something approaching 35 to 40 mph. It appears from the reports that there was glass both on and next to the drive at the time of the inspections, possibly as a result of the accident.

10. Subject to the above comments we have advised the Defendant that there is a risk that the Judge may find in favour of the Claimants. We have discussed settlement and the possibility of a Part 36 offer in order to try to protect his position as to costs. Nevertheless, he is determined to defend the action and pursue his counterclaim. Please would Counsel telephone upon receipt of these instructions to discuss. A pre-trial conference can be arranged should counsel consider it necessary.

Claimant's Part 36 Offer

11. Counsel will note that the Claimants made a Part 36 offer that expired on 24 November 2011 to settle the claim for £175,000 inclusive of interest and taking the Defendant's counterclaim into account. We have advised the Defendant of the potential additional interest and costs payable under CPR Rule 36.14(3) should the Claimants obtain a judgment at least as favourable as that at trial.

Issues – quantum

12.   The quantum of the counterclaim is agreed, subject to liability, at £72,160.63 (see the case summary).

13.   The Claimants' quantum is not agreed. Full details of the issues which are still disputed appear in the without prejudice meeting statement filed by the parties' respective experts on 19 October 2011.

14.   There are no issues of remoteness of damage arising and the dispute on quantum relates almost wholly to the scope of demolition and repair work required to the Claimants' extension. The difference amounts to approximately £72,000.

Trial

15.   Duncan Murray of Instructing Solicitors will be attending the trial. We will make the necessary arrangements to ensure that Colonel Trudge attends. Mrs Trudge will not be attending trial. Mrs Trudge is in Australia caring for her ailing sister. A Civil Evidence Act Hearsay Notice was served when her witness statement was exchanged and the Claimants' solicitors have not objected to her absence.

16.   Counsel is asked to liaise with Duncan Murray as to the final content of the Trial and Core Bundles.

17.   Please let us know if Counsel requires any further information.

Counsel is briefed to appear at the trial of the action on 18 April 2012 at Weyford District Registry at 10 am.

Advocates & Co
9 April 2012

D(15)   Consent Order

IN THE HIGH COURT OF JUSTICE   WF-11-1234
QUEEN'S BENCH DIVISION
WEYFORD DISTRICT REGISTRY

BETWEEN   MR WILLIAM ULYSSES SIMPSON (1)   Claimants
                       MRS RUPINDER SIMPSON (2)

                                and

                    MR GEOFFREY IAN TEMPLAR   Defendant

CONSENT ORDER

Upon the parties agreeing to settle this matter

AND BY CONSENT

IT IS ORDERED THAT

1.   The Defendant pay the Claimants the sum of £150,000 by 2.30 p.m. on Friday, 20
      April 2012;

2.   Upon payment, claim WF-11-1234 and its associated counterclaim be stayed;

3.   There be no order as to costs.

We consent to the terms of   We consent to the terms of
this order.   this order.

Solicitors LLP   Advocates & Co

Solicitors LLP   *Advocates & Co*
-------------------------------   ---------------------------------------
Dated 4 April 2012   Dated 4 April 2012

Index